Exhortation and Controls

Exhortation and Controls

The Search for a Wage-Price Policy 1945–1971

CRAUFURD D. GOODWIN
Editor

CRAUFURD D. GOODWIN *and* R. STANLEY HERREN

H. SCOTT GORDON

WILLIAM J. BARBER

JAMES L. COCHRANE

NEIL DE MARCHI

ARNOLD R. WEBER

THE BROOKINGS INSTITUTION
Washington, D.C.

Copyright © 1975 by
THE BROOKINGS INSTITUTION
1775 Massachusetts Avenue, N.W., Washington, D.C. 20036

Library of Congress Cataloging in Publication Data:

Main entry under title:

Exhortation and controls.

  (Studies in wage-price policy)
  Bibliography: p.
  1. Wage-price policy—United States—History—
Congresses. I. Goodwin, Craufurd D. W. II. Series.
HC110.W24E94   331.2'1'01   75-23483
ISBN 0-8157-3208-2
ISBN 0-8157-3207-4 pbk.

9 8 7 6 5 4 3 2 1

THE BROOKINGS INSTITUTION is an independent organization devoted to nonpartisan research, education, and publication in economics, government, foreign policy, and the social sciences generally. Its principal purposes are to aid in the development of sound public policies and to promote public understanding of issues of national importance.

The Institution was founded on December 8, 1927, to merge the activities of the Institute for Government Research, founded in 1916, the Institute of Economics, founded in 1922, and the Robert Brookings Graduate School of Economics and Government, founded in 1924.

The Board of Trustees is responsible for the general administration of the Institution, while the immediate direction of the policies, program, and staff is vested in the President, assisted by an advisory committee of the officers and staff. The by-laws of the Institution state: "It is the function of the Trustees to make possible the conduct of scientific research, and publication, under the most favorable conditions, and to safeguard the independence of the research staff in the pursuit of their studies and in the publication of the results of such studies. It is not a part of their function to determine, control, or influence the conduct of particular investigations or the conclusions reached."

The President bears final responsibility for the decision to publish a manuscript as a Brookings book. In reaching his judgment on the competence, accuracy, and objectivity of each study, the President is advised by the director of the appropriate research program and weighs the views of a panel of expert outside readers who report to him in confidence on the quality of the work. Publication of a work signifies that it is deemed a competent treatment worthy of public consideration but does not imply endorsement of conclusions or recommendations.

The Institution maintains its position of neutrality on issues of public policy in order to safeguard the intellectual freedom of the staff. Hence interpretations or conclusions in Brookings publications should be understood to be solely those of the authors and should not be attributed to the Institution, to its trustees, officers, or other staff members, or to the organizations that support its research.

Foreword

THE SEARCH for a way to reconcile full employment, reasonable price stability, and free economic institutions has preoccupied economists and policymakers of nearly all advanced industrial countries for more than three decades. In attempts to solve the problem of inflation, chronic since the end of the Second World War, most industrial nations have experimented with various forms of governmental wage-price intervention.

For the first time in its history, the United States in 1971 accepted the imposition of wage and price controls in an economic climate not significantly distorted by war. The controls, which began as a ninety-day freeze and were later made mandatory throughout most of the private economy, remained in effect in one form or another until the end of April 1974. These developments occurred in a country that places great faith in competitive markets as a regulator of business activity and during an administration that had earlier opposed any governmental intervention in private wage and price decisions.

The purpose of this book is to trace and explain the evolution of decision making on wage-price policy over the thirty-year period that started with the Truman administration. Every president, beginning with Truman, has in one way or another contributed to the development of this policy. Although this history is well known, the internal discussions, analysis, and planning have never been fully exposed to public view.

This study was undertaken at the suggestion of the National Archives and Records Service and the Eisenhower, Kennedy, and Johnson presidential libraries. While the project was being planned, it became evident that the end of the Second World War was a logical benchmark; thus the Truman Library was enlisted in the project. Each of these presidential libraries contains thousands of records concerned with the day-to-day formulation and execution of economic policy, most of which had never been examined in a systematic, scholarly way and some of which had not previously been publicly available. The libraries, desiring to call attention to the new body of material as well as to that already available, proposed that Brookings organize a symposium on the development of wage-price policies based on their files.

In response to this proposal, Brookings organized a team of economic analysts to prepare papers for a two-day conference of experts, which was held at Boston University in November 1974 under the auspices of the John F. Kennedy Library. The conferees included major officials in all five administrations who participated in the development and execution of wage-price policies, as well as business leaders and academic specialists. Five of the papers examine in depth the origins, nature, and consequences of the wage-price policies pursued in each administration. These are by Craufurd D. Goodwin of Duke University and R. Stanley Herren of Vanderbilt University on the Truman administration, H. Scott Gordon of the University of Indiana and Queen's University (Ontario) on the Eisenhower administration, William J. Barber of Wesleyan University on the Kennedy administration, James L. Cochrane of the University of South Carolina on the Johnson administration, and Neil de Marchi of Duke University on the first Nixon administration. A sixth paper, prepared by Arnold R. Weber of Carnegie-Mellon University, draws lessons from the historical record for the guidance of future administrations in this country and other countries which are grappling with these problems. The original papers were revised by the authors in response to comments and suggestions of the conference participants and became six chapters of this book to which Craufurd Goodwin added an introduction and summary of the conference discussion.

For their cooperation in making their records and other facilities available for the preparation of the papers, the Brookings Institution and the authors are grateful to James B. Rhoads, Archivist of the United States, and his associate, Daniel J. Reed, Assistant Archivist for Presidential Libraries; Benedict K. Zobrist, director of the Harry S. Truman Library; John E. Wickman, director of the Dwight D. Eisenhower Library; Dan H. Fenn, Jr., director of the John F. Kennedy Library; and Harry J. Middleton, director of the Lyndon B. Johnson Library. The Institution and the authors are also indebted to Lawrence J. Hackman, director of special programs of the Kennedy Library, for his assistance in organizing the Boston conference.

The work on this volume, which is the fourth in the Brookings series of Studies in Wage-Price Policy, was financed in large part by a grant from the National Science Foundation. The manuscript was edited by Elizabeth H. Cross; the data were verified by Evelyn P. Fisher; and the index was prepared by Annette H. Braver.

The views expressed here are those of the contributors and should not be ascribed to the staff members, officers, or trustees of the Brookings Institution or to the National Science Foundation.

KERMIT GORDON
President

August 1975
Washington, D.C.

Contents

Text Table

Appendix Tables

Introduction

CRAUFURD D. GOODWIN

EVERY PRESIDENT from Truman on has faced inflation as a major problem of his administration and has had to construct a policy for its solution. Truman was compelled initially to administer and then to dismantle a complex system of controls during the first few months after World War II. He returned to controls at the time of the Korean outbreak. In between, he and his advisers wrestled with threats of both recession and secular inflation, conditions that they saw as lingering clouds on the American horizon. Of the five presidents only Truman faced a full three-pronged inflation caused by excess demand, cost-push, and worldwide shortages of food and raw materials, although Nixon in 1973 saw the deadly trilogy reappear. Eisenhower enjoyed a term of office during which prices were relatively stable and no specific tools of wage and price control were required. In this period, however, economists inside and outside government perceived what they took to be a new phenomenon, inflation and unemployment occurring together—the worst fears of the Truman years borne out. Even without excess demand, prices had a tendency to inch upward. The abbreviated Kennedy administration brought a new level of involvement of professional economists to the top ranks of the executive branch of government, as well as the reappearance of an inflationary threat and the formulation of a new "guidepost" strategy to deal with it. Under Johnson, guideposts and the vigorous presidential "jawboning" that accompanied them were put fully to the test, as provided by the Vietnam War. The Nixon administration in its early years responded to the policies of its predecessors by rejecting direct wage-price intervention and returning to exclusive dependence on fiscal and monetary policy and improvements in market efficiency. This approach ended abruptly with the unexpected announcement on August 15, 1971, of a mandatory system of controls.

This collection of essays sets out to trace and explain in detail the development of executive decision making in the United States about wage-price policy during the three decades since the end of World War II.

The authors of the essays were trained as economists rather than as historians, but they have written extensively on the history of economic

1

thought and economic policy. A unique feature of the undertaking, which gives it both strength and weakness, is that, with the exception of the chapter on the Nixon administration, the account is based mainly on the collections of the presidential libraries, the contents of which record the day-to-day evolution of policy. The directors of these libraries were partly responsible for initiating the project. For the authors, who are accustomed to using printed source material, immersion in these archives was a rich and rewarding experience, but it also revealed to them certain limitations in their end product. First of all, while focusing on presidential decision making has the advantage of affording one an intimate look at a main center of power, it fails to reveal much that took place in Congress, the business community, the economics profession, and elsewhere in the executive branch. These essays therefore do not pretend to tell the whole story of the development of wage-price policy in the United States but only one important facet of it. Second, there are gaps in the presidential library collections that may give a selective and potentially unrepresentative character to parts of the story. In particular, access to the records of the various Councils of Economic Advisers depends to a substantial degree on the generosity of individual Council members and staff, who have been free to take their records with them upon departure from government. Material from the CEA staff and from many important White House aides is especially sparse. Nor are the records of other departments and agencies fully accessible because they are often still part of current files, and relevant primary materials from the private sector are particularly hard to obtain. Finally, the authors became ever more aware of the difficulty of telling this intriguing but complex story in limited space and without giving extensive background on the political events and other aspects of economic policy that shaped wage-price policy. Wherever possible references are provided to additional sources on such closely related topics as the evolution of monetary, fiscal, and foreign policy.

A number of generalizations about the development of wage-price policy during the entire period under review are suggested by these essays and, in fact, make the collection more than the sum of its parts. It may be helpful to the reader to have some of these in mind as he examines the individual contributions.

First, it is clear that as early as 1945 and intermittently thereafter economists in and out of government were persuaded that inflation more than the prewar bogeys of unemployment and maldistribution of income could become the Achilles' heel of a free-price economy. Price stability, they concluded, simply might not be consistent with the economic and social institutions that characterize a modern democracy, especially strong trade unions, oligopolistic industries, and a public commitment to full employment. Predictably, concern about the dangers of secular inflation fluctuated directly with changes in the price level, but after extended periods of price increases such as the late 1940s or late 1960s attention turned seriously to systemic explanations. That moderate inflation might be permanently consistent with substantial levels of unemployment was clearly perceived by the late 1950s. Because of America's self-image throughout the period as the economic as well as the political leader of the noncommunist world, secular inflation was seen to be perilous not only for the domestic economy but for the entire international economic order as well.

The weight given to various ill effects of inflation varied over the three decades. Truman perceived the main danger as being the depression that had always before followed inflation, and could be expected to do so again. He and members of his administration did discuss and worry about the hardships imposed on segments of society by inflation, but his chief worry continued to be that what goes up too rapidly must come down with a crash. During the next three presidents' administrations the effects of inflation on international competitiveness and the balance of payments joined its other costs at center stage. During the latter part of the Nixon administration, when inflation at near-record peacetime rates had been sustained for some time, concern about massive citizen unrest occasioned by real or imagined hardships was uppermost.

Matching the perception of the profound dangers of inflation was abiding faith in the capacity of reasonable men to do something about it. This faith found expression in three directions. First, from the beginning of the thirty-year period until the end presidents were advised to bring together leaders of those segments of the economy that allegedly contributed to the inflation problem—above all, big business and big labor—so that in some sort of cooperative fashion they could solve this public problem. The repeated failure of labor-management conferences and committees under both Democratic and Republican administrations did not dampen the enthusiasm for this device (the most recent example being the conference on inflation of September 1974). Second, the power of public opinion was widely believed to be an effective restraint on "irresponsible" agents of inflation. If only the people were aware of the potentially inflationary impact of key decisions, this argument ran, they would rise in righteous wrath and smite the transgressor. The frequent proposals for advance notification of price increases was predicated mainly on this belief in the power of public opinion. Third, though in different degrees under different presidents, presidential advisers had firm faith in the capacity of economic science to find answers to this as to other economic problems. Confidence was probably greatest during the administrations of Kennedy and Johnson, but in general a striking finding of these studies is the persistent optimism of both economists and consumers of economics despite the seeming intractability of the problems with which the science dealt.

A wide range of explanations and solutions for inflation were advanced within the government. To some extent the weight attached to each depended on the doctrinal convictions and political persuasions of the proponents. Keynesian, or "liberal," economists tended to lean toward cost-push explanations and advocated various techniques of threat and persuasion to restrain noncompetitive industrial sectors from raising their prices. They roundly rejected an increase in unemployment as a cure for inflation, but they did favor tax increases and see controls as a last-choice alternative. "Neoclassical," or conservative, economists, on the other hand, were more inclined to blame labor than business, and they tended to favor monetary and fiscal policy, especially a reduction of government expenditures, as a means of reducing effective demand; except during the aberration of the first Nixon administration they vigorously opposed all controls. This distinction among "types" of economists according to their views on wage-price policy is by no means neat and clear. As time went on and all devices and explanations were found to have their weaknesses, the distinction became more a matter of emphasis than of firm conviction.

During periods when monetary and fiscal policy seemed incapable of halting inflation, not only were controls seriously contemplated but earnest discussions took place about whether systemic changes had occurred in the American and world economies that made inflation inevitable. It was feared that changes of at least four types might have taken place: a growth of monopolistic elements' power so great that prices were flexible only upward; a commitment of governments to full employment (and the related "fine tuning") so strong that resistance to price and wage restraints in key markets had been weakened; a shift in production toward services in which improvements in efficiency were few; and a new ethos among workers that demanded rising money wages and declining effort regardless of changes in productivity. To the extent that analysts accepted systemic explanations for inflation they tended to turn toward such long-run alternatives as antitrust action, labor market reform, and education or reinvigoration of the work force.

Unexpected developments in foreign affairs repeatedly had a marked effect on the evolution of wage-price policy. In most cases international conflicts or fear of involvement therein brought sharp increases in military expenses. These developments led repeatedly to use or serious contemplation of direct controls in the face of inadequate monetary and fiscal policies, such as prevailed during the Korean War and in the aftermath of Vietnam. The sudden end of World War II, of course, was the reverse of the other situations. Then public relief at the conclusion of hostilities led to premature abandonment of controls. In at least one case—the Berlin crisis of 1961—President Kennedy was able to take advantage of the public sense of emergency to turn away from direct controls and make informal restraints more effective.

Perhaps the single most controversial element of wage-price policy in the postwar period has been the practice of direct intervention by the executive in pricing decisions. Arguments against this practice were proffered early and were often repeated. Above all, critics noted, such arbitrary actions by the government were inconsistent with a competitive economic system; if competition was inadequate the correct approach was antitrust action or regulation, not hectoring of the monopolies.

Moreover, presidential intervention, or "jawboning" as it came to be called, seemed manifestly inequitable on several counts. Usually a few very visible "key" industries of high concentration were singled out for special attention. Labor complained that collective bargaining was especially vulnerable while the pricing of many goods on which workers depended remained inviolate. Moreover, pressure was almost always against the price-raiser, seldom against those who failed to lower prices. Above all, the critics said, it was paradoxical that "public-spirited" price-makers in the economy who responded cooperatively to executive intervention should suffer by receiving lower prices for their goods while "unpatriotic" price-makers gained from their lack of cooperation.

Despite the obvious weaknesses of and objections to jawboning, it was used in varying degrees by every administration examined here. Certain sectors of the economy were selected for special attention either because they were the focus of consumer interest (e.g., automobiles and meat), because they seemed to be a determinant of national growth (e.g., steel or petroleum), or because they exhibited low elasticity of supply (e.g., housing). In labor markets, to preserve equity, the concept of average productivity gains as a basis for awards was developed under Truman and grew into the celebrated wage "guideposts" of the Kennedy and Johnson years.

The place of economic growth in the fight against inflation presented yet more uncertainties for presidential advisers. It seemed that upward pressures on prices increased at near full capacity and this provided one argument against excessive stimulation of the economy. On the other hand, average costs could be expected to decline in the long run with economies of scale and growth in output. Moreover, in the short run there was danger that too much restraint, as well as too little, would be inflationary by forcing producers into uneconomic small runs. All administrations reached the conclusion that, other things being equal, a level of economic activity near to full capacity but not quite at it was most conducive to price stability. Some Council members, such as Leon Keyserling under Truman, became known especially for their emphasis on full employment and growth as the best conditions for fighting inflation.

A subtheme of these essays is the increasing use of professional economists in government, not only in the Council of Economic Advisers but as presidential aides, specialists throughout the executive branch, and even as cabinet officers. At times, the evolving role of the CEA was closely tied to the development of wage-price policy. In offering advice about the control of inflation the Council often found itself at a great disadvantage because of limited or false information about defense or foreign policy. Moreover, in the implementation of guidepost restraints and jawboning the Council was drawn away from its staff advisory function toward the tasks of an administrative agency or, as suggested by one Council chairman, an economic "general staff." The hope of some members was that the Council would deal with strategy rather than with tactics, but this distinction was never clearly drawn. The varying styles of the several councils must be noted, the result in part of differences in presidential preference and in part of the differences of the Council members themselves. Relations with leaders of the economics profession were one indication of Council style; these varied from distant during the Truman years to remarkably close under Kennedy. As the years went on it became increasingly difficult for any president to contemplate economic policy formation seriously without professional advice. But whether he took it from a single source or many, direct or in digested form through a nonprofessional filter, had a marked influence on the result. The Councils' relations with the public also varied. In general it appears that the Councils that enjoyed the greatest intimacy with their presidents found it most difficult to serve other constituencies. Candor with the public became impossible when policy adviser became policy determiner.

A striking feature of the whole story recorded here is the short institutional memory of the economic advisory arms of government. Repeatedly, circumstances and policy measures, whether labor-management conferences or productivity rules, were discussed as if they had never occurred or been proposed before. The phenomenon is largely the result of the presidential form of government wherein each new chief executive brings in his own advisers and sweeps out the old. Nevertheless the observer cannot help wondering if more provision for the accumulation of wisdom and experience might not be valuable. To an important degree this function was performed in an informal way by a dozen or so prominent persons who appeared to deal with wage-price problems in several administrations: for example, Gardner Ackley, Arthur F. Burns, Gerhard Colm, John T. Dunlop, Kermit Gordon, Walter W. Heller, John P. Lewis, Paul W. McCracken, Arthur M. Okun, Walter S. Salant, Charles L. Schultze, Herbert Stein, Robert C. Turner, and Henry C. Wallich. But should an important social system have to depend on such accidents of fate?

It is common for historians to experience acute feelings of *déjà vu* when working through an extended period of years. This collection of essays is no exception. It is not an account of human reason progressively discerning more clearly, understanding more completely, and conquering more effectively the complex problems of wage-price policy that face society. Rather, a repetitive cyclical development seems more accurately to characterize the story. Problems were discovered and then rediscovered. Solutions were tried and tried again, with varying degrees of success. "Guideposts" accompanied by jawboning are one example: they had roots in the Truman era, flowered under Kennedy and Johnson, and seem fated now for rebirth under President Ford. It would be hard for anyone to argue that wage-price policy at the end of the fifth administration was demonstrably more enlightened than at the end of the first, or that the executive's understanding of the problems was a great deal more profound.

Humility may be an unfamiliar mask for economic advisers to wear. But an optimist may hope that the sobering experience of the past three decades will lay the basis for far greater progress in the next.

I

The Truman Administration: Problems and Policies Unfold

CRAUFURD D. GOODWIN *and* R. STANLEY HERREN

A MERICA emerged from World War II with deep foreboding about postwar recession. An Elmo Roper poll for *Fortune* magazine in 1945 showed that only 41.0 percent of respondents believed that the United States would be "able to avoid . . . a widespread depression." In the words of the magazine's editors, "unemployment continues to be the No. 1 bogey on the public mind" and "runaway prices are far below unemployment on the list of problems that the public established in this Survey."[1]

The serious recession that followed World War I was recalled by most people, yet in retrospect it can be seen that at least three conditions were markedly different from 1920. First, the United States had experimented bravely in the 1930s with a variety of economic measures to cure recession, and the memory of this experience was still fresh a decade later. Second, the economic performance of 1942–45 had been especially impressive; at least during the emergency of war and with a regime of tight controls the American economy had proved that it could be bountifully productive. Third, and by no means of least significance, a body of doctrine associated with the writings of John Maynard Keynes had become widely known among economists and some policymakers in government, universities, business, and the labor movement. The main policy implication of "Keynesian economics" was that nations could be masters of their own economic destinies, even when faced with the enigma of the business cycle. Governments had the power and the responsibility to affect private consumption, savings, and investment as well as levels of public expendi-

Note. Much of the research for this paper was carried out in the Harry S. Truman Library, Independence, Missouri. We express appreciation to the staff of the library, and especially to archivist Dennis E. Bilger, for every courtesy and full cooperation. Several participants in the events under examination kindly read early drafts of the manuscript and preserved us from some error; we absolve them from what remains and thank especially David E. Bell and Walter S. Salant.

1. *Fortune*, vol. 32 (August 1945), pp. 257–58.

ture through monetary and fiscal devices. Consequently they could influence employment, prices, growth rates, and other variables with which their citizens were vitally concerned.[2]

By the summer of 1944 serious thinking had already begun within the federal government about reconversion problems. A series of meetings of economists in major departments during August, initiated by Alvin H. Hansen, produced a statement of "goals and guiding principles" of postwar employment that effectively summarized professional conclusions and was submitted to President Roosevelt on October 9, 1944.[3] The first condition for achieving the goals of worldwide full employment and growth, they said, was continuity in "the flow of total expenditures." But second came the "stable value of money," both for the maintenance of employment and for distributive justice. "Stability in the cost of living is essential to full employment. It is clearly a responsibility of the Government to safeguard the savings of the people by stabilizing the purchasing power of money and by preventing development of conditions that lead to inflation or deflation."[4] In a competitive peacetime economy, the economists thought, price stability should be maintained by increasing wages and

2. For discussion of the evolving relationship between economic theory and policy during this period, see especially Donald N. Winch, *Economics and Policy* (Walker, 1970). For accounts of the Keynesians' struggle for influence, see Herbert Stein, *The Fiscal Revolution in America* (University of Chicago Press, 1969), chaps. 5–8, and Alan Sweezy, "The Keynesians and Government Policy, 1933–1939," in American Economic Association, *Papers and Proceedings of the Eighty-fourth Annual Meeting, 1971* (*American Economic Review*, vol. 62, May 1972), pp. 116–24, with discussions by Leon H. Keyserling, Robert R. Nathan, and Lauchlin B. Currie, ibid., pp. 134–41; see also Byrd L. Jones, "The Role of Keynesians in Wartime Policy and Postwar Planning, 1940–1946," ibid., pp. 125–33.

3. Economists involved in the discussion included Walter S. Salant, Jacob L. Mosak, and James S. Earley (Office of Price Administration—OPA); Marriner S. Eccles, Alvin H. Hansen, Richard A. Musgrave, Kenneth B. Williams (Federal Reserve Board); Emile Despres (Office of Strategic Services and Department of State); Gerhard Colm and Arthur Smithies (Bureau of the Budget). Comments on the meetings by Colm, together with the report, are in Employment Act Symposium folder, Colm Papers, Truman Library. The statement was jokingly referred to as the "pink paper" after the British "White Paper on Employment" (1944), by which the American report was much influenced. The statement is reprinted in *History of Employment and Manpower Policy in the United States: Twenty Years of Experience Under the Employment Act of 1946*, Subcommittee on Employment and Manpower of the Senate Committee on Labor and Public Welfare, 89 Cong. 2 sess. (1966), vol. 7, pt. 1, pp. 1–27.

4. Memorandum, "Postwar Employment: Goals and Guiding Principles," October 9, 1944, Employment Act Symposium folder, Colm Papers, Truman Library (or see reprint in *History of Employment*).

salaries in proportion to productivity gains in the economy. As a pioneer enunciation of the correct principles on which to base a government "incomes policy" this statement is worth citing at length. It said:

Increases in productivity should be passed on to the public as a whole. This can be accomplished by an orderly upward adjustment of wages and salaries more or less in proportion to the general increase in productivity per man employed. Industries with low wage levels should pass on their increases in productivity in higher wages. Industries which enjoy a greater than average increase in productivity should reduce prices so as to give the widest possible benefits to consumers. The automobile industry and the radio industry, which experienced exceptionally rapid progress, lowered their prices to consumers and succeeded in stimulating mass consumption of their products. In general, however, gains from raising productivity, when passed on to the public through orderly upward adjustment of wages, salaries, and other money incomes, contribute to maintaining stability of the cost of living.[5]

Immediate postwar inflation would be a danger, the economists thought, but "this will not require the adoption of new measures or the maintenance of all wartime controls. It will be necessary to retain, until the danger is past, some of the machinery that has assured economic stabilization during the war." In the long run they relied on "enlightened business practices" to produce high volume, low prices, and mass private consumption.[6] An important government responsibility would be to prevent monopolies from reaping the rewards of advancing productivity.

The economists saw stagnation as the main problem facing America, but they counted on government to stimulate business and agriculture, to undertake public works, and to "open new frontiers."[7] Yet alongside this new confidence about the capacity of government to deal with the economic problems of a postwar world grew a nagging doubt about the *will* of society to act sensibly.

Initial Optimism

In one of his first pronouncements after becoming President in April 1945, Harry Truman praised the effectiveness of wartime price and wage

5. Ibid., pp. 4–5 in both sources.
6. Ibid., pp. 7, 4.
7. Ibid., pp. 6, 10–12.

regulation and appealed for its continuation for some reasonable period into peacetime. In this statement Truman voiced one of the first of many warnings that inflation, if unchecked, could bring about a breakdown of the entire democratic order. He said:

I think that our price control and stabilization program has been one of the most remarkable achievements of this war. Had it not been for OPA and the stabilization program we should have had run-away inflation. In other countries, run-away inflation has sown the seeds of tyranny and disorder. In this country, we have kept inflation under control. . . . Congress has given us a good law and I hope Congress will extend that law for at least another year.[8]

Economic planners in Washington during the first four months of Truman's presidency could act on the assumption that the end of the war was at least a year away. VE-day on May 8 seemed to clear only the first of two unconnected hurdles in Europe and Japan, and consequently a *gradual* transition from wartime controls to a free economy seemed likely. George W. Taylor of the National War Labor Board produced a four-point plan that would have brought real hourly earnings up to prewar levels, increased minimum wages, and permitted increases through collective bargaining that would not affect prices.[9] The Taylor plan prompted Fred M. Vinson, director of the Office of War Mobilization and Reconversion (OWMR), to instruct William H. Davis, director of the Office of Economic Stabilization (OES), to work out a full wage-price program. The resulting staff memorandum continued to picture stagnation as the main problem; it saw "a mixture of temporary inflationary influences upon prices, resulting from continuing shortages of inventories and finished goods, and an underlying softening of pressures upon basic resources, especially manpower." The authors of the memorandum predicted that "labor costs per unit of output associated with any given volume of production" would tend to decrease after the war because of a reduction in overtime pay and shift premiums, improvement in the quality of the labor

8. "Statement by the President Commending the Office of Price Administration. May 1, 1945," in *Public Papers of the Presidents of the United States: Harry S. Truman, 1945,* p. 28. The *Public Papers* of Truman's presidency are in eight volumes covering the years 1945 to 1952–53 (Government Printing Office, 1961–66); hereafter *Public Papers.* Mary Hinchey discusses events during Truman's first two years in "The Frustration of the New Deal Revival, 1945–1946" (Ph.D. dissertation, University of Missouri, 1965).

9. Memorandum, Robert R. Nathan to Fred Vinson, June 18, 1945, Folder "Wage Policy," Record Group 250, Box 234, Entry 38, National Archives.

force combined with downgrading of positions, better equipment, and technological improvement,[10] and that these deflationary factors would be offset less and less over time by inflationary low-volume production. These considerations, together with the need to preserve industrial peace and maintain long-run consumer demand, pointed toward the desirability of authorizing higher wages and a sharing among capital and labor of business profits, which were already beginning to mount. The memorandum concluded as had the "statement" of 1944: "It is not desirable to increase hourly earnings in each industry in accordance with the rise of productivity in that industry. . . . The proper goal of policy is to increase hourly earnings generally in proportion to the average increase of productivity in the economy *as a whole.*" No estimate of average productivity gains was put forward, but it is clear that the "productivity rule" was proposed on this occasion not to restrain avaricious unions, but to guarantee that wage increases would be sufficient to maintain aggregate effective demand.[11]

In a memorandum of August 12, with the situation dramatically changed by the destruction of Hiroshima on August 6, Davis took a more nervous, short-term view of the labor situation. He saw the reconversion period in its initial stages, which seemed now to be much closer, as likely to be "characterized by substantial unemployment" as well as "inflationary price rises" and "deflationary restriction of incomes." He recommended that "the President immediately convene a conference of labor and management, under government auspices, to work out a plan for the peaceful settlement of labor disputes that substantially affect the reconversion program" and "that the President call on labor and management for a continuation of the no-strike, no-lockout pledge in the interim period, before the conference meets and during its deliberations until some new plan is worked out and made effective." For the longer run he was somewhat more optimistic: "With the ending of war production and resultant unemployment there is no longer any threat of an inflationary bidding up of wage rates by competition in a short labor market."[12]

All the planning of early summer for gradual reconversion came to naught when on August 14 Japan surrendered. Over a long weekend policies were shaped which the planners had hoped could evolve over many

10. Memorandum, "Wage-Price Policy," July 30, 1945, Walter S. Salant Papers, Truman Library, pp. 1–3.
11. Ibid., pp. 11–12.
12. Memorandum, Davis to the President, August 12, 1945, Official File 407 (1945), Truman Library.

months. It has been argued that Truman's announcement on August 16 of a six-point program for rapid decontrol was influenced, in an important way, by the prevailing views of labor and business.[13] Certainly most segments of society yearned for an end to restrictions. Union leaders were anxious to return to conditions of normal collective bargaining and were confident they could make substantial gains thereby. Businessmen, on the other hand, believed that they deserved higher profits and knew that firms which returned to producing consumer goods first would do best. Everyone was optimistic about how he would come out in the scramble. In essence, then, the VJ-day decision was to implement immediately many of the reconversion plans that planners had intended to unfold gradually, in particular removal of controls on wage increases that seemed unlikely to affect prices. The Taylor plan for modifying wage standards was put into effect by Executive Order 9599 of August 18, 1945, removing controls on wage increases that did not affect prices and effectively crippling the wartime machinery of price control.[14]

At least in announcing the changes and for a short time thereafter Truman professed continued optimism on the price front. He said, using almost the exact words of Davis four days earlier, "With the ending of war production, however, there is no longer any threat of an inflationary bidding up of wage rates by competition in a short labor market."[15] In his 21-point program for reconversion sent to Congress on September 6, Truman again made it clear that in his view inflation was a wartime problem and it should be necessary now only to "hold the line on prices and rents until fair competition can operate to prevent inflation and undue hardship on consumers."[16] A special short-run cause of postwar inflation, Truman admitted, might be pressure from businessmen during reconversion while they were temporarily operating with few economies of scale. Then they would try "to secure prices high enough to provide immediate profits over and above their temporarily high costs of production

13. John T. Dunlop, "The Decontrol of Wages and Prices," in Colston E. Warne and others, eds., Labor in Postwar America (Remsen Press, 1949), pp. 3–24.
14. For an account of events during this period, see Barton J. Bernstein, "The Truman Administration and the Politics of Inflation" (Ph.D. dissertation, Harvard University, 1963), and articles by Bernstein cited in Richard S. Kirkendall, ed., The Truman Period as a Research Field (University of Missouri Press, 1967), p. 143.
15. "Statement by the President Proposing Measures to Insure Industrial Peace in the Reconversion Period. August 16, 1945," Public Papers, 1945, p. 221.
16. "Special Message to the Congress Presenting a 21-Point Program for the Reconversion Period. September 6, 1945," ibid., p. 264.

due to their initial low volume." But even this aberration could not be tolerated, Truman insisted, because American consumers were "entitled to buy washing machines, vacuum cleaners, automobiles and other products at prices based on our traditional system of high output and low unit costs."[17]

Prices and Jobs

The main point at issue among government advisers in the fall of 1945 was how rapidly the economy should be decontrolled. The senior officials of OPA, led by Chester Bowles, feared rapid inflation and urged caution, but arrayed against them were many others, liberals and conservatives, who saw unemployment as the menace and urged rapid decontrol. The employment pessimists won out and the War Production Board (WPB) soon lifted most of its restraints; with the end of allocation instructions in industries such as textiles and apparel, materials flowed into high-priced lines, placing an intolerable burden on price control. Restraints on construction were also removed as were controls over the distribution, slaughtering, and allocation of meat. Newly appointed Secretary of the Treasury Vinson, who was uncertain about the danger of inflation, designed his tax policy mainly to stimulate the economy, rather than constrain it, through tax reduction.[18]

The state of informed public concern by mid-1945 about both inflation and unemployment in the longer run is manifested in the hearings before a subcommittee of the Senate Committee on Banking and Currency on S. 380, the bill that in different form became the Employment Act of 1946.[19] The original bill provided for the preparation of a "national

17. Ibid., p. 272.
18. See A. E. Holmans, *United States Fiscal Policy, 1945–1959: Its Contribution to Economic Stability* (Oxford University Press, 1961), chap. 4. Additional discussion of economic events during this period can be found in Hinchey, "The Frustration of the New Deal Revival"; Darrel Cady, "The Truman Administration's Reconversion Policies, 1945–47" (Ph.D. dissertation, University of Kansas, 1974); Bert G. Hickman, *Growth and Stability of the Postwar Economy* (Brookings Institution, 1960); and Conrad A. Blyth, *American Business Cycles, 1945–50* (Praeger, 1969).
19. For a survey of the professional economic literature of the time on the problem of maintaining price stability with full employment, see John T. Dunlop, "Wage-Price Relations at High Level Employment," in American Economic Association, *Papers and Proceedings of the Fifty-ninth Annual Meeting, 1947* (*American Economic Review*, vol. 37, May 1947), pp. 243–53.

budget" in which, among other things, "the President shall set forth . . . a general program for preventing inflationary economic dislocations."[20] Accordingly the committee and witnesses before it examined this prescription as well as the wider (and more central) issue of how to maintain full employment.[21] Senator James E. Murray, the bill's sponsor, expressed the principal worry underlying the 1945 hearings—that unless remedial action were taken the years after World War II would be similar to those after World War I, with a short inflationary boom followed by a prolonged collapse. He said, "Again in this period, all the conditions are developing which may create a dangerous inflation, to be followed by a dangerous deflation in the years which will follow the ending of the war."[22] In response to the fear that the proposed Full Employment Act might itself be inflationary, that the remedy would worsen the disease, its defenders prepared the following answer: "The best guaranty against inflation is an expanding production of goods and services. It is the aim of the Bill to stimulate the highest possible production by private enterprise."[23]

Senator Joseph C. O'Mahoney, thought to be one of the most competent economists in Congress, and a powerful advocate of the bill, described how prices had oscillated wildly not only after World War I but after the Civil War as well. He said, "It happened before; it can happen again, unless we are to undertake to provide against it by an intelligent application of our minds to the establishment of preventive measures."[24] Representative Wright Patman testified: "If we do not prevent inflation here at home we will lose the war on the home front."[25] The extent to

20. *Full Employment Act of 1945*, Hearings before a Subcommittee of the Senate Committee on Banking and Currency, 79 Cong. 1 sess. (1945), p. 7. The hearings ran from July 30 to September 1, 1945. On the Employment Act, see Stephen K. Bailey, *Congress Makes a Law: The Story Behind the Employment Act of 1946* (Columbia University Press, 1950); Gerhard Colm, ed., *The Employment Act: Past and Future* (National Planning Association, 1956).
21. The centrality of the employment theme was emphasized by Kermit Gordon, "Price-Cost Behavior and Employment Act Objectives," in *Twentieth Anniversary of the Employment Act of 1946: An Economic Symposium*, Hearing before the Joint Economic Committee, 89 Cong. 2 sess. (1966), pp. 59–66.
22. *Full Employment Act of 1945*, Hearings, p. 16. The same argument was made by Secretary of Commerce Henry Wallace, ibid., p. 984. See also Henry A. Wallace, *Sixty Million Jobs* (Simon and Schuster, 1945).
23. "Questions and Answers on the Full Employment Bill," n.d., Full Employment Bill folder, Samuel I. Rosenman Papers, Truman Library, p. 3.
24. *Full Employment Act of 1945*, Hearings, p. 36. Similar testimony from the National Lawyers Guild is on p. 801.
25. Ibid., p. 57.

which inflation at this time was visualized as a prelude to collapse rather than as a secular phenomenon was revealed by Senator Robert A. Taft, who said, "My definition of inflation has always been an activity which is artificially built up to an extent that we cannot permanently maintain."[26]

Relatively few witnesses at the employment bill hearings visualized the postwar world as facing inflationary dangers different from those of earlier years. But a few did conclude that a commitment to full employment might be inconsistent with price stability. Senator Taft said, "I think it would produce an inflationary condition which cannot be maintained without constantly increasing inflationary measures."[27] Several academic economists who submitted briefs to the committee elaborated on the nature of this danger, that secular price increases would result from changes in social philosophy and public policy implicit in the bill. Harry Gunnison Brown of the University of Missouri argued that so long as there were monopolies the proposed commitment to full employment would guarantee inflation.

Several sentences in S. 380 are indicative of a praiseworthy desire to restrain monopolies and any and all monopolistic devices and practices. Such a policy should accompany any attempt to promote full employment. For monopolistic price increases decrease the ability of the public to buy— unless there is a corresponding increase of money to buy with and so a constant rise of prices, inflation—and so they decrease the possibilities for the fullest employment. However, there is a similar tendency from Government attempts to limit the output and hold up the price of agricultural products. And, too, there is a like tendency from the forcing up of wages either by control of the labor supply in various lines or by Government enactment. The higher the wages which are required, the more circulating medium must be issued—with, soon, correspondingly higher prices—in order that there may be full employment.[28]

Michael Kalecki, from the International Labour Office in Montreal, wrote privately to Senator Murray that there were only three ways through which the federal government could make good a guarantee of full employment: by "1) stimulating private investment; 2) redistribution of income from profits and high salaries to wages; 3) public expenditure

26. Ibid., p. 45.
27. Ibid., p. 624.
28. Ibid., pp. 1017–18. See also the testimony of Walter A. Morton of the University of Wisconsin, p. 1154.

financed by taxation. The possible contribution of method 1) is limited," and "to cover the gap by methods 2) and 3) will be extremely difficult because they will involve a drastic 'squeezing' of profit margins (which must be accompanied by rigid price control) or a very heavy taxation of profits."[29]

J. M. Clark was more optimistic about the sense of responsibility and self-restraint of trade unions required for price stability. "It's not so clear that they would refrain from taking an inflationary ride on the program, but this danger may not be great. I believe the mandates of Government officials charged with spending should include discretion enough to give them more bargaining power than at present, as a protection against inflationary demands or extortionate ones."[30] Gottfried Haberler of Harvard University worried about the inflationary effects of attempting to eliminate pockets of unemployment.

This kind of situation which requires much more complicated policies than stimulation of aggregate expenditure will be very important during the years after the war. It will be essential to prevent partial, localized unemployment from spreading depression to other fields. This can be done by supporting aggregate expenditure if it is necessary; but it does not follow that unemployment can be eradicated by simply spending more until full employment is reached. Long before that point is reached, inflationary price rises would be produced. If it were possible to shift labor and other resources easily and quickly from excess areas to the points where scarcities exist, we would not need to worry. But experience teaches that such shifts cannot always be made sufficiently fast.[31]

Henry C. Simons from the University of Chicago concluded: "Once internal monetary stabilization is initiated at a suitable price level, we should set ourselves resolutely against using inflation as a means for enlarging employment."[32]

Oscar Lange, representing a very different tradition at Chicago, urged Congress not to heed the Cassandra cries of the economists about inflation. He was optimistic about a restrained response from all parties.

Some economists are likely to criticize the bill on the ground that it may have inflationary consequences. This may occur in either of two ways.

29. Letter, Michael Kalecki to Senator James E. Murray, May 5, 1945, Folder 251, "Full Employment, Misc.," Colm Papers, Truman Library.
30. Full Employment Act of 1945, Hearings, p. 1032.
31. Ibid., pp. 1092–93.
32. Ibid., p. 1211.

First, serious bottlenecks may exist in certain parts of the economy, preventing expansion of output. If it should happen that the increase of expenditure resulting from the provisions of the bill is directed to products of the bottleneck industries, a price inflation may result without alleviation of unemployment in other parts of the economy. Proper planning of expenditures-increasing measures, and if necessary, special facilities for retraining labor and increasing the supply of labor in the bottleneck industry, will avoid such consequences. Second, full employment conditions may induce trade unions to raise money wages beyond what is warranted by the increase in the productivity of labor. If such a policy would be pursued generally by organized labor, a price inflation would result. This point seems to worry many economists. I believe that the experience of the war has shown that the American labor movement is imbued with a sufficient sense of public responsibility to avoid policies which would lead to price inflation.[33]

The Role of Labor

As early as midsummer 1945 public attention shifted to the process of collective bargaining as a likely cause of inflation. The issue was joined firmly on September 15, when after the failure of Chester Bowles's plan to get all parties to agree to an across-the-board, no-strike "non-inflationary" wage increase of 10 percent, Walter Reuther of the United Automobile Workers announced an all-out campaign for a 30 percent increase, which, he insisted, could come out of corporate profits and need not cause inflation in product prices.[34] Reuther's appeal was for a fundamental shift in income-distribution patterns in the United States toward what he believed these patterns had been before the war. If such a shift failed to occur, his critics pointed out, the effect of his tactic would be inflation. For a time, however, it is fair to say, some government officials doubted that Reuther's income transfer could be achieved without harmful side effects.[35]

33. Ibid., pp. 1111–12.
34. See Chester Bowles, *Promises to Keep: My Years in Public Life, 1941–1969* (Harper and Row, 1971), pp. 130–31. Bowles claimed subsequently that Secretary of Labor Lewis B. Schwellenbach, who could not see the danger of inflation, resisted and blocked the continuation of controls by the War Labor Board implicit in the 10 percent plan. Ibid.
35. Director William Davis of the OES, Robert Nathan of the OWMR, and Secretary of Commerce Wallace all issued reports supporting in varying degrees

By mid-autumn, however, after the automobile industry had rejected Reuther's demand, a combination of inflation and labor-management strife seemed about to threaten the smooth conversion to peacetime and the "fair competition" for which President Truman had confidently hoped. The dangers were perceived to be loss of production, social upheaval, and the generation of income inequities. In a memorandum of October 22, 1945, Bowles set forth three alternative "proposals" to deal with the situation, with "advantages" and "disadvantages" listed after each one. The first was for a "stated percentage" increase to be permitted in all prices with wage gains not covered thereby to be treated as a "voluntary" income transfer by management from other factor shares. Bowles expected that this alternative would lead to inflation of 8 or 12 percent rather than the target of 3 percent. The other two proposals were for government approval of all wage increases not judged to be inflationary and for uncontrolled collective bargaining within the limits of controlled prices on goods. The first of these latter two alternatives he found to be administratively impractical and the second inequitable. Bowles's own fourth recommendation was for a "vigorous and specific program" with a directive "to me as Price Administrator which will clearly state that any wage increases, with certain exceptions to cover maladjustments and inequities, should be disregarded in setting prices."[36] He still argued that "management, in most industries, is in excellent shape to pay higher wage rates under the present price ceilings, and still provide an excellent return

---

Reuther's contention that substantially higher wages could easily come out of profits. See Barton J. Bernstein, "Walter Reuther and the General Motors Strike of 1945–1946," *Michigan History*, vol. 49 (September 1965), pp. 260–77. In a review of the situation for the acting stabilization administrator on September 28, Walter Salant noted, "To the extent that improved quality of labor and incorporation in peacetime production of wartime technological improvements increase the production obtained from an hour's labor, an increase in hourly earnings is compatible with the maintenance of existing costs and prices." Memorandum, Salant to Thomas I. Emerson, "Background for Determination of Wage Policy," September 28, 1945, Memoranda-1945 folder, Salant Papers, Truman Library. Robert Nathan reported the OPA judgment that "a 10% to 15% wage rate increase will result in a rise in the cost of living of from 2% to 5%." And he also stressed the importance of high wages to maintain employment. "A high wage policy is a pre-requisite to overcoming this basic weakness of our system." Robert R. Nathan to John W. Snyder, "The Labor and Wage-Price Problem," September 28, 1945, Folder "Economics 8," General Classified file of the Office of the Director of Records of the Office of War Mobilization and Reconversion, Record Group 250, Box 151, Entry 16, National Archives, pp. 3–4.

36. Memorandum, Bowles to Samuel I. Rosenman, October 22, 1945, Wages and Prices Speech file 1, Rosenman Papers, Truman Library, p. 7.

to its stockholders."[37] In the longer run Bowles was less clear about how procedures could be developed to ensure a noninflationary peacetime economy. Like Davis two months before, he urged that the government turn this problem over to leaders of the private sector at a labor-management conference and insist that any fundamental systemic reform become a responsibility of the citizenry broadly conceived rather than of the government. "The Labor Management Conference should develop and agree upon democratic procedures which will assure the success of collective bargaining. You are counting on them to meet in a spirit of cooperation, and with a full understanding of the legitimate needs of our workers on the one hand and the right of management to a fair profit on the other."[38] Bowles thought that the proposed conference might well end up recommending an arbitration procedure, but he could not state explicitly on what basis such a mechanism would proceed. He concluded: "The success of the wage price policy which I have recommended depends on our ability to make collective bargaining work. If we fail to accomplish that, I have grave fears indeed, for the future of our free enterprise system."[39]

It should be emphasized that during the autumn of 1945 the advice President Truman received from his economic advisers warned at least as much of intolerable unemployment as of serious inflation. Because of bitter memories of his own personal losses and humiliation in the depression of 1921, Truman was especially receptive to such warnings. The OWMR predicted on September 8 that *"even under the optimistic estimate of the speed of reconversion and the rise in non-war output, unemployment of 6–8 million is indicated as a problem throughout 1946."*[40] An informal survey carried out by Louis Bean at a meeting of the Committee for Economic Development (CED) on October 17 yielded the estimates shown in table 1. On September 28 Robert Nathan, economist with the OWMR, wrote to Director John W. Snyder about what he saw as America's main economic challenge in the months ahead. "The reason that full

37. Ibid., p. 9.
38. Ibid., p. 9.
39. Ibid., p. 10.
40. "Economic Projections: Prepared within the technical staff of the Office of War Mobilization and Reconversion, Memorandum No. 1, September 8, 1945," Official Files of the Committee, Folder "Reconversion Working Committee Post VJ-Day Plans," Record Group 250, Box 389, Entry 16, National Archives. Everett E. Hagen was the chief economist of OWMR. He recalled this period in "The Reconversion Period: Reflections of a Forecaster," *Review of Economic Statistics*, vol. 29 (May 1947), pp. 95–101.

Table 1. *Responses to Questions Asked in Survey, Committee for Economic Development, 1945*

Respondent	Price increase (percent)		Unemployed (millions)		Peak of unemployment	Should OPA policy be as tough as at present?
	By July 1946	By July 1947	By July 1946	By July 1947		
Ted Yntema (CED)	10	15	5	4	3/46	Yes
Howard Myers (CED)	5	10	3.5	2	2/46	Yes
Gardiner Means (CED)	3	5	8	5	6/46	No
Melvin de Chazeau (CED)	5	12	7	4	7/46	No
Albert Hart (CED)	5	−5	5	4	4/46	No
Robert Lenhart (CED)	5	0	6.5	5.5	3/46	Yes
Herbert Stein (CED)	. . .	. . .	7	5.5	2/46	No
Louis Bean (Budget)	2	7	8	6	7/47	Yes
Roy Blough (Treasury)	6	8	4.5	2.3	1/46	No
Gerhard Colm (Budget)	0	5	6	4	3/46	No
Bertrand Fox (WPB)	3	1	7	5	4/46	No
Raymond Goldsmith (WPB)	10	25	5	4	3/46	No
Lincoln Gordon (WPB)	3	12	5	4	4/46	No
Richard Heflebower (OPA)	4	10	5	3	5/46	No
Hugh Killough (BLS)	5	10	5	3	3/46	No
Leon Henderson	10	15	5	4	3/46	Yes
M. Joseph Meehan (Commerce)	10	0	5	8	. . .	Yes
Walter Salant (OPA)	7	−5	6	8	3/47	Yes
Arthur Smithies (Budget)	3	5	4	6	7/47	Yes
Frank Garfield (Federal Reserve)	2	5	6	8	7/47	Yes
Don Wallace (OPA)	10	20	6	3	4/46	Yes

Source: Adapted from an informal survey by Louis Bean at a meeting of the Committee for Economic Development, October 17, 1945; Folder 251, "Full Employment, Misc.," Colm Papers, Truman Library.

employment is going to be very elusive and probably unattainable without basic changes in policy, is the deficiency in mass buying power and the excess of saving during periods of prosperity. Our income distribution tends to result, in periods of prosperity, in a huge volume of savings which require such large investments that capacity soon tends to outrun consumption and depressions result."[41]

In a radio address delivered on October 30 (and "received by 98.4 percent of all the radios that were in use") Truman reflected the ambivalent advice of his economists in setting forth the mounting problem of the economy as he saw it. First of all he now gave equal weight to dangers of "wide unemployment" and "runaway inflation." In discussing the second danger he stressed the distributional ill effects of price increases:

White-collar workers would find that their fixed salaries buy less food and clothing than before. Farmers' incomes would shrink because they would have to pay so much more for what they buy. Increased earnings would mean nothing to business itself. War bonds, insurance policies, pensions, annuities, bonds of all kinds would shrink in value, and their incomes would dwindle in buying power.[42]

As a restraint on inflationary pressures the President appealed for reason and moderation on all sides. Following the advice of his economists, he argued that because of reductions in overtime costs, job reclassification, increases in productivity, rising profits, and an end to the excess profits tax, industry could afford to increase wages moderately without price inflation. Following Bowles's recommendation, he conceded that in exceptional cases the OPA should now allow modest price increases justified by rising wage costs. Truman did not himself recommend any new machinery to deal with the current situation, and clearly, like his advisers, he was puzzled about how to deal with it. With a statement of almost naive optimism about the capacity of reason and responsible citizenship to prevail, he summoned the Labor-Management Conference in November to explore the situation and, he hoped, to demonstrate that the contending parties in collective bargaining could "come to understanding and agreement without political or Government pressure." In his charge to this gathering he pointed out that "if bargaining produces no results, then there must be a willingness to use some impartial machinery for reaching decisions on the basis of proven facts and realities." Clearly the President

41. Memorandum, Nathan to Snyder, "The Labor and Wage-Price Problem," p. 4.

42. "Radio Address to the American People on Wages and Prices in the Reconversion Period. October 30, 1945," *Public Papers*, 1945, p. 443.

was attempting to convey a high sense of urgency. "If the people do not find the answers here, they will find them some place else. For these answers must and will be found. The whole system of private enterprise and individual opportunity depends upon finding them."[43]

Regardless of the darkening clouds of inflation on the horizon, throughout 1945 President Truman comforted himself that these dangers would be simply short-term by-products of reconversion from wartime and were not likely to be features of the real peacetime which was just around the corner. His public optimism, of course, may have been designed partly to dampen expectations.[44] After the failure of the Labor-Management Conference to reach any agreement on new means to control inflationary wage increases, Truman's most radical proposal was still only for legislation to extend the principles of the Railway Labor Act, such as fact-finding boards and cooling-off periods, to other nationwide industries.[45] Nevertheless, the failure of the Labor-Management Conference was one indication to the President and to the nation that any sort of "socio-economic contract" among segments of the economy was not to be, and that therefore inflation might not be merely a transitory phenomenon but could become an intractable problem of the postwar world.

Shifting the Blame for Inflation

Concern with "continuing inflationary pressures" pervaded President Truman's public statements during the last months of 1945 and the early

43. "Address at the Opening Session of the Labor-Management Conference. November 5, 1945," *Public Papers*, 1945, pp. 460, 461, 462. In December President Truman described the threat of inflation in housing as "the most menacing in our economy." "The President's News Conference of December 12, 1945," ibid., p. 534. As an emergency measure he reinstated controls over the construction industry.

44. An example of this is "The President's News Conference of November 29, 1945," ibid., p. 507. In a memorandum to Stabilization Administrator John C. Collet, Walter Salant warned of "the current development of inflationary psychology." The apparent effect of the collapse of controls, he said, had been to stimulate demand at a time when supplies had been reduced in anticipation of higher prices. Memorandum, Salant to Collet, November 13, 1945, Memoranda-1945 Folder, Salant Papers, Truman Library. Everett Hagen reached similar conclusions in a report for the director of the OWMR. He feared "a terrific short-lived inflationary boom followed by collapse." Memorandum, Hagen to John W. Snyder, Hans A. Klagsbrunn, and Robert R. Nathan, "Implications of Present Trends in Output and Employment," November 22, 1945, Folder "Labor and Wages (5002)," Classified File of the Deputy Director for Reconversion 4006–6002, Record Group 250, Box 246, Entry 45, National Archives, p. 2.

45. "Special Message to the Congress on Labor-Management Relations. December 3, 1945," *Public Papers*, 1945, p. 516.

part of 1946.[46] It was clear, however, that the danger was still viewed mainly as stemming from a business cycle exacerbated by conversion to peacetime. Doubt about which was the greater immediate threat, inflation or
unemployment, seems to explain the vacillation on new policy formulation. John Dunlop says of this period: "The most significant aspect of the
three months after V-J Day was the uncertainty that was allowed to develop with respect to the new stabilization program and to the future of
industrial relations. . . . The occasion for establishing an immediate postwar political balance of labor, management and farmer was lost. The lost
opportunity produced the subsequent deluge."[47]

Notes kept by Budget Director Harold D. Smith of a White House
Conference on the Budget Message, January 15, 1946, suggest that the
concept of controlling inflation through fiscal policy was far from being
universally accepted by this date and was subservient to interagency rivalries, the political significance of taxes in an election year, and the notion
that a balanced budget at all times was responsible finance.[48] Truman's
own instincts were all for balanced budgets or, at most, for occasional
surpluses to retire debt when feasible. As late as 1956 he wrote in his
memoirs, "There is nothing sacred about the pay-as-you-go idea so far as
I am concerned, except that it represents the soundest principles of financing that I know."[49] Truman had welcomed the coincidence of his own
judgment with advisers' recommendations for fiscal restraint when, by
late 1945, they had recognized that inflation was a major problem.[50] The
difficulty came in carrying out the policy; expenditures were already reduced from wartime levels, but Congress had lowered taxes as well and
was in no mood to reverse field.

Monetary policy was crippled even more than fiscal policy, also by

46. See "The President's News Conference on the Budget. January 19, 1946,"
Public Papers, 1946, p. 25, and "Message to the Congress on the State of the Union
and on the Budget for 1947. January 21, 1946," ibid., p. 48.

47. Dunlop, "The Decontrol of Wages and Prices," pp. 16–17.

48. Diary, January 15, 1946, Harold D. Smith Papers, Truman Library.

49. *Memoirs by Harry S. Truman*, vol. 2: *Years of Trial and Hope* (Doubleday,
1956), p. 41. On this general question, see Holmans, *United States Fiscal Policy*,
chaps. 1–10; Stein, *The Fiscal Revolution in America*, chap. 9; Marriner S. Eccles,
Beckoning Frontiers: Public and Personal Recollections (Knopf, 1951); Ralph E.
Freeman, ed., *Postwar Economic Trends in the United States* (Harper, 1960).

50. Treasury Secretary Vinson discussed higher taxes to fight inflation as early as
January 14. See Vinson, Memorandum for the President, January 14, 1946, Official
File 419-F, Truman Library.

instinctive and political constraints. Just as Truman found it morally correct to operate with a balanced budget he felt it morally repugnant to manipulate interest rates upward and thereby reduce the capital of millions of citizens who had patriotically purchased government bonds during the war. Moreover, there was considerable doubt among Truman's advisers about whether higher interest rates would effectively restrain inflation even if it were politically and ethically correct to implement them. Hence the Federal Reserve cooperated with the Treasury to "peg" rates at the relatively low levels prevailing on government securities.

The extent to which inflation was perceived as a symptom of a postwar boom that might lead to depression was demonstrated in a radio broadcast on January 3, when Truman said: "Whether we fall into a period of great deflation because of unemployment and reduced wages and purchasing power, or whether we embark upon a period of great inflation with reduced production and spiraling prices—the result will be equally disastrous."[51] On this occasion, the President reviewed his efforts to cope with the problem and for the first time introduced a political strategy which he was to employ for the next two years. His wage-price policies had been largely unsuccessful, he said, because of a lack of cooperation from others: "many obstacles have been thrown in our path as we have tried to avert the dangers of inflation and deflation."[52] Some parts of labor, management, and even Congress had refused either to accept his proposals or to suggest sensible alternatives of their own. In the case of the General Motors strike that had been running since November, management, the United Automobile Workers (UAW), and Congress had all been unwilling to endorse his idea for a fact-finding board with statutory powers. In consequence, he implied, the prospect before the nation was that cost-push inflation would create circumstances where effective demand would be inadequate to support production. "We cannot keep purchasing power high or business prosperous if prices get out of hand. There is no use talking about the expanded production upon which steady jobs depend, unless we keep prices at levels which the vast majority of the people can afford to pay."[53] Truman argued that strikes caused inflation not only because they raised wages in labor markets but also because they limited production in goods markets. He repeated his optimistic pronouncements of 1945

51. "Radio Report to the American People on the Status of the Reconversion Program. January 3, 1946," *Public Papers*, 1946, p. 3.
52. Ibid.
53. Ibid., p. 5.

that as soon as normal peacetime production was resumed price stability might follow. But until that happy time some form of temporary price control would continue to be crucial.

The inflationary pressures now at work can bring an inflation and a crash that will be much more serious than 1920. That is why it is so important to get a high volume of production and a large supply of marketable goods right away. Production is the greatest weapon against inflation.

Until enough goods can be made to supply the demand, the power of the Government must be used to keep prices down—or inflation will soon be upon us.[54]

In his State of the Union Message later in January Truman addressed the problem of inflationary psychology, exacerbated currently by expectations of a further reduction of controls by midyear. Manufacturers who, reportedly, "continue[d] to hold back goods and decline[d] to submit bids when invited" made inflation a self-fulfilling prophecy. On this occasion Truman's assessment of immediate inflationary dangers had for the first time a mildly hysterical tone. "The inflationary pressures on prices and rents, with relatively few exceptions, are now at an all-time peak. Unless the Price Control Act is renewed there will be no limit to which our price levels would soar. Our country would face a national disaster."[55] In an important policy proposal he recommended that agricultural subsidies be continued as one means of guaranteeing low food prices; this might at least lessen worker unrest.[56]

In February 1946 President Truman announced that he was compelled to substantially reduce the residue of wartime wage and price controls, not because the transition to peacetime had yet been achieved in an orderly way but because partial controls under intense pressure had produced severe inequities. Unexpected pressures from world demand for food and labor-management conflict in steel and automobiles had overwhelmed the fragile structure. In the case of steel, he believed, the alternatives were to authorize wage and price increases or seize the plants to

54. Ibid.
55. "Message to the Congress on the State of the Union," *Public Papers*, 1946, p. 54.
56. At the end of the war farmers urged a speedy end to subsidies and controls so that consumers could become accustomed to higher agricultural prices and a firm base could be established for the coming recession. See Allen J. Matusow, *Farm Policies and Politics in the Truman Years* (Harvard University Press, 1967), pp. 38–46.

maintain production, as suggested by Chester Bowles. He chose the former (he would make the opposite choice on the same issue at the end of his presidency in 1952). In agriculture, with a voluntary program of grain conservation yielding few results, the question was whether to introduce incentive pricing.[57] His main worry, Truman said, was that the reduction in incentives caused by the remaining inequities in the price system would limit the increase in production upon which he depended for the ultimate elimination of inflationary pressures. He cautioned:

While many groups of wage and salary earners may qualify for increases under this policy, in order to bring their pay into line with the increased cost of living, or with the existing wage levels of the industry or area, the program is not to be interpreted as permitting indiscriminate wage increases. . . . Production is our salvation. Production is the basis of high wages and profits and high standards of living for us all. Production will do away with the necessity for Government controls.[58]

It was clear to the most innocent of observers that government restraints were fast becoming a paper tiger.

A brief article in the New York Times Magazine of January 6 by Alvin H. Hansen, which caught the attention of the White House during this period, gives some clue to the intellectual search that was in progress. Hansen described the course of wages and prices for the previous century and observed that while the long-run trend of prices had been stable wages had more than doubled. He concluded: "This development was, I think, a wholesome one. And now that we are compelled to adopt a conscious policy, through collective bargaining and Government mediation, with respect to wages and prices, I believe we can do no better than to strive for a result broadly similar to that reached in the nineteenth century."[59]

Hansen found the prospect of falling average prices with rising productivity dangerous to the maintenance of full employment. He saw equal danger in wages rising less rapidly and more rapidly than average

57. See ibid., chap. 3. Under Secretary of State Dean Acheson recommended, as an alternative, requisitioning grain from the producers; see Barton J. Bernstein, "The Postwar Famine and Price Control, 1946," Agricultural History, vol. 38 (October 1964), p. 240. Concerning the steel strike, see Bowles, Promises to Keep, pp. 138–47, and Barton J. Bernstein, "The Truman Administration and the Steel Strike of 1946," Journal of American History, vol. 52 (March 1966), pp. 791–803.

58. "Statement by the President Upon Issuing Order Modifying the Wage-Price Policy. February 14, 1946," Public Papers, 1946, pp. 118, 119.

59. "Wages and Prices: The Basic Issue," New York Times Magazine, January 6, 1946, Rollins College Speech file, Rosenman Papers, Truman Library, p. 1.

productivity. In the former a "disastrous profits inflation" as in the 1920s could result; in the latter, of course, there would be an inflation in the prices of goods and services. He declared emphatically that "wages in general should rise in accordance with *average* over-all gains in productivity."[60] He offered only a general plan for how this objective might be achieved, calling for healthy collective bargaining and improvement in government statistics on productivity for individual industries as well as for the entire economy. Some means should then be found for these data to be taken into account in the collective bargaining process.

It is evident that under modern conditions we are compelled to take an over-all view of wages and prices. The facts laid on the collective bargaining table, industry by industry, must include the over-all picture of the economy as a whole, in addition to the facts relating to the industry in question. . . . The public interest must be recognized in each agreement or the general welfare will suffer. Hence the need for comprehensive statistics bearing on the economy as a whole. These, no less than the specialized statistics of each industry, must become a part of the data controlling each piecemeal wage agreement.[61]

Judge Samuel Rosenman, an aide to President Truman, sent the Hansen article to Acting Commissioner of Labor Statistics A. F. Hinrichs for comment. Hinrichs replied that "Hansen's general conclusions are sound" but "his detailed treatment of the facts must be used with care." He also provided more detailed data about price and wage changes plus a "summary" of Hansen's argument for President Truman's use.[62] This exchange is important because it can be seen that the notion of productivity "guideposts" was certainly in the air by early 1946, even if not exactly so designated. One can see repeated expressions of faith by the President in fact-finding machinery, based in part on this idea that open information on costs and revenues would reveal productivity and therefore the wage that would be "fair" to labor and management.[63] Mounting appreciation of the "power of statistics" in labor negotiations was exhibited outside government as well as in. For example, officials of the Office of War

60. Ibid., p. 3.
61. Ibid., p. 4.
62. Two letters from Hinrichs to Rosenman, both dated January 30, 1946, concerning Hansen's article. Rollins College Speech file, Rosenman Papers, Truman Library.
63. See "Background Material on Fact Finding," memorandum prepared for President Truman's speech to the nation of January 3, 1946, Rosenman Papers, Truman Library.

Mobilization and Reconversion reported in December 1946 that the Bureau of Labor Statistics (BLS) was receiving pressure from CIO representatives because of a proposed change in the method of calculating the consumer price index.[64]

Housing construction and several basic materials such as steel and coal continued to be primary targets for pronouncements about inflation in 1946.[65] Because of the great need for new accommodations and a high degree of inelasticity in both demand and supply, there was reluctance to allow a free housing market to bring about equilibrium. To control price increases in this sector and to limit "speculation" Truman recommended that the next sale price of a home become the effective ceiling price for that property for the duration of the emergency. "Under this plan, any home-owner could sell his property in a free and open market. However, such property could not then be resold by a speculator for a higher price resulting in a quick and unearned profit."[66]

Truman's repeated public support for the principle if not the fact of direct controls plus his appeals for an increase of production and public-spirited behavior from business, labor, and consumers rang increasingly hollow as cures for the rapid inflation of 1946. Even in his own administration there were occasional signs of near panic. For example, the deputy administrator of the Price Department of the OPA, Geoffrey Baker, worried in May about "inflation of disastrous proportions" of up to 50 percent within a year or so, fed by speculative psychology and "followed by a severe collapse."[67] Everett Hagen of the OWMR noted that it was quite possible for inflation and unemployment to rise together in the less competitive industries where lower production led to higher unit costs. "Since the production difficulties leading to low output may also reduce the demand for labor, it is paradoxically true that during the period, the higher unemployment is, the greater will inflationary pressure be."[68] Charges were made with increasing vehemence by business groups such as the CED that

64. Memorandum, J. Donald Kingsley to John R. Steelman, December 23, 1946, Official File 15-C, Truman Library.

65. For example, "Statement by the President Upon Releasing Report of the Director of War Mobilization and Reconversion. April 3, 1946," *Public Papers*, 1946, p. 180.

66. "Address at the Jackson Day Dinner. March 23, 1946," ibid., p. 167.

67. Memorandum, Baker to Price Department Staff, May 1, 1946, OPA Folder–Misc. clippings, Clark Clifford Papers, Truman Library.

68. "Economic Prospects During 1946," May 6, 1946, General Classified file of the Office of War Mobilization and Reconversion, Folder "Economics," Record Group 250, Box 28, Entry 5, National Archives.

government monetary and fiscal policies were in fact fueling the fires of inflation. The President, they said, need look no further than his own backyard to discover the cause of his problems. Marriner Eccles, chairman of the Federal Reserve Board, asserted that "a fiscal policy which brings about a substantial budget surplus is by far the most effective means left at our disposal to meet inflation pressures," and he argued for reduced government expenditures coupled with an excess profits tax. He said, "It is the responsibility of the Administration to recommend what is needed."[69] Truman categorically denied that he could do more.[70] However, the fundamental difference in approach between the selected market restraints he recommended and the aggregate expenditure and credit policies proposed by his critics became a major topic of controversy during the remainder of the first term.

Passage of a weak price control bill by Congress in mid-1946 provided Truman with the best opportunity to date to expound his evolving position on the issue of inflation. In the message accompanying his veto of this bill on June 29 he said that the proposed machinery was wholly inadequate to the task. "It is a choice between inflation with a statute and inflation without one." One objection was to an amendment from Senator Taft, which would have allowed industrial price rises in response to labor cost increases; this, Truman said, would be like setting a match to "a fire about to sweep a city." Again, as so often before, he expressed his faith in greater production and economies of scale to reduce inflation: "at the very time when we should be getting the benefit of high volume in the form of lower prices, the Taft Amendment would inflate prices."[71] The fear of inflation, he said, became its own cause: "The simple fact is that the average business man or farmer who knows that his price will soon be higher will not sell any more goods this week than he has to—be they suits or sewing machines or cattle."[72]

On this occasion President Truman set forth his wage-price policy succinctly and explained for the first time that he considered price stability

69. Undated memorandum from Eccles, OPA Folder–Misc. clippings, Clifford Papers, Truman Library.

70. "The President's News Conference of April 3, 1946," Public Papers, 1946, p. 177.

71. "Veto of the Price Control Bill. June 29, 1946," ibid., p. 324. The veto message was drafted by Clark Clifford and Paul A. Porter, OPA administrator. See Cabell Phillips, The Truman Presidency: The History of a Triumphant Succession (Macmillan, 1966), pp. 109–10.

72. "Veto of the Price Control Bill," p. 325.

to be crucial not only to the future of the American economy but to the creation of an effective world economic order as well. Presumably in response to his critics, he emphasized that microeconomic market controls, which he defended as necessary short-term expedients, must be linked with responsible long-term macroeconomic fiscal policy, with which, he was confident, an unrestricted and stable free market system could ultimately operate alone.

If the stabilization laws are renewed in effective form, it is expected that the Federal budget will be balanced during the coming year, thus eliminating the deficit which was a basic source of inflationary difficulties.

As the inflationary pressures lessen, commodity after commodity can be removed from controls and we can emerge with a stable economy in which the traditional American free enterprise competitive system can take command. Not until then will the law of supply and demand keep prices at reasonable levels. So long as demand far exceeds supply, the law of supply and demand will drive prices up.

Let us remember further that inflation and collapse in the United States would gravely jeopardize our efforts to build the kind of international economic relations that will provide a solid basis for world peace.[73]

In a radio address to the nation on the same day as the veto message, President Truman explained his action to the people: "I gave the subject long days and nights of consideration. I consulted with practically every top official in the Government. Either personally or through representatives I obtained the views of people in agriculture, industry, and labor, as well as many others."[74] In somewhat more colorful language he repeated the arguments he had made earlier to Congress.

Veto of the price control bill in June led to a brief but dramatic inflationary episode in July that paved the way for enactment of a tougher law at the end of that month. In signing the second price control bill on July 25 President Truman reported: "The Bureau of Labor Statistics index of 28 basic commodities in the primary markets has shown an increase of 24.8 percent in the 26 days since June 28, 1946 as against an increase of only 13.1 percent in the three years and 42 days between the signing of the

73. Ibid., p. 327. A similar promise of fiscal restraint was contained in "Statement by the President Summarizing Reconversion Progress. July 11, 1946," *Public Papers*, 1946, p. 343.

74. "Radio Address to the Nation on Price Controls. June 29, 1946," *Public Papers*, 1946, pp. 329–30.

hold-the-line order on May 17, 1943 and June 28, 1946."[75] Truman found this second bill too little and too late, but still an improvement over its predecessor. He pledged a continuing, multifaceted attack on inflation, including "sterner fiscal and monetary measures than would otherwise be called for."[76] His good faith was displayed in tough communications to executive departments. On August 1 he wrote: "The present inflationary situation and the need for reducing the public debt make it imperative that expenditures be held at the lowest possible level. . . . We must do everything within our power to reduce inflationary pressures. One of the most effective means of doing this is to reduce Federal expenditures."[77] Two days later, on August 3, he ordered that "all postponable public works be deferred until private demands for goods and services slacken off."[78] Despite pressure for price increases from particular sectors such as food, Truman insisted for a while on holding the line. For example, he said in September, "An increase in prices or abandonment of price control on meat now would, in the long run, add to rather than solve our difficulties."[79]

The law passed on July 25 left grains, livestock, meat, dairy products, and cottonseed, soybeans, and their products without price controls until August 20. Then a three-member Price Decontrol Board put livestock and meat back under control, an action designed to guarantee a proper diet to low-income workers and thereby speed up industrial production. The law gave control over agricultural prices to Secretary of Agriculture Clinton P. Anderson, who, after battling with OPA Director Paul Porter, raised

75. "Special Message to the Congress Upon Signing the Second Price Control Bill. July 25, 1946," ibid., p. 360. The OPA kept the White House apprised of the probable results of decontrol. A memorandum of July 10 predicted increases in livestock and meat prices of 40–50 percent, in dairy products of 25–45 percent, "even larger increases in grain prices," and "substantial increase in the cost of living and a wage-price spiral." Memorandum, "Full Effects of the Amendments Decontrolling Livestock, Meat, Poultry, Eggs, and Dairy Products," July 10, 1946, OPA Folder, Clifford Papers, Truman Library.

76. "Special Message to the Congress Upon Signing the Second Price Control Bill," p. 362. Subsequently Truman referred to this period as "when the price control situation was all 'balled up.' " "The President's News Conference on the Review of the Budget. August 20, 1947," *Public Papers*, 1947, p. 387.

77. "Memorandum on the Need for Reducing Expenditures. August 1, 1946," *Public Papers*, 1946, p. 369.

78. "Letters Calling for Reductions in Expenditures for Construction. August 3, 1946," ibid., p. 404.

79. "The President's News Conference of September 26, 1946," ibid., p. 435.

prices 15 percent above the June levels. Livestock farmers, however, were not satisfied and declared a producers' strike to end controls once and for all. By late September meat had disappeared from many markets. Consumers demanded meat immediately, and congressional elections were only one month away. The OPA had now unquestionably become a political liability.[80]

On October 14 Truman made a dramatic announcement by radio to the nation. The problem of meat had, he said, made it necessary virtually to terminate controls on this and a wide range of other products. The hiatus in price controls in July and August had led to an intensely speculative slaughter of animals with the result that two months later, after the reimposition of controls, a severe shortage existed. Many possible solutions to the problem had been considered, including even government seizure of packing houses and livestock on the farms, but these had been rejected. Accordingly, "there is only one remedy left—that is to lift controls on meat." Moreover, Truman continued, the presence of this one major uncontrolled item, meat, tolled the death knell for controls generally: "The action which will be taken tomorrow in freeing meat from controls means that their [Porter and Anderson] programs of lifting controls will have to be accelerated under existing legal standards."[81] He now called on the American people "to exercise restraint and common sense if inflation is to be avoided and adequate production is to be achieved."[82] In November he announced formally the general termination of price and wage controls with the exception of those on sugar, rice, and rent. The reason, he said, was not that smooth reconversion had been accomplished but that, in anticipation of an end to price ceilings, speculative withholding of goods and loss of public faith had gotten out of hand. He concluded on a rather hesitant note of optimism about a return to a "free economy."

The lifting of price controls and wage controls results in the return to a free market with free collective bargaining. Industry has sought removal of price controls while labor has pressed for removal of control of wages.

80. Matusow, *Farm Policies,* pp. 56–61.
81. "Radio Report to the Nation Announcing the Lifting of Major Price Controls. October 14, 1946," *Public Papers,* 1946, pp. 453, 454. See also memorandum, Justice Department to Clark Clifford, October 3, 1946, Clifford Papers, Truman Library.
82. "Radio Report," p. 455. This incident angered many liberal Democrats and provided them with "yet another example of the president's weak and erratic leadership." Alonzo L. Hamby, *Beyond the New Deal: Harry S. Truman and American Liberalism* (Columbia University Press, 1973), p. 136.

Both have insisted that removal of these controls would lead to increased production and fewer work stoppages.

High production removes the hazard of inflation and brings prices within the reach of the mass market. Wage rates not justified by labor productivity and prices not justified by manufacturers' costs may bring the illusion of prosperity. In the long run, however, good wages, full employment and sound business profits must depend upon management and workers cooperating to produce the maximum volume of goods at the lowest possible price.

Today's action places squarely upon management and labor the responsibility for working out agreements for the adjustment of their differences without interruption of production.[83]

The withholding of supplies and general revulsion against controls help to explain the resounding triumph of the Republicans in the congressional elections. The prospect that they would act soon if he did not was an extra stimulus to this final act of decontrol.

Enter the Economists

The first half of Truman's first term not only produced the challenge of severe peacetime inflation, it also witnessed the formal entry of professional economists into the Executive Office of the President. American economists had, of course, been making pronouncements on current economic problems for more than a century, but in most cases well outside the government system, especially the executive branch. There had been notable exceptions even in the executive, such as F. W. Taussig, who served as chairman of the U.S. Tariff Commission from 1917 to 1919. Franklin Roosevelt also had brought economists, such as Rexford Tugwell, Lauchlin Currie, and Gardiner Means, into his "brain trust" and other posts in his administration in the 1930s. However, outside the Treasury and the Budget Bureau, these early economists in government were primarily general advisers who happened to have special economic competence. Formal recognition of the need for professional economic advice at the highest levels of government came in the Employment Act of 1946, which provided for a Council of Economic Advisers and a congressional Joint Committee on the Economic Report (subsequently the

83. "Statement by the President Upon Terminating Price and Wage Controls. November 9, 1946," *Public Papers*, 1946, p. 477.

Joint Economic Committee) with appropriate staff.[84] The immediate stimulus for these innovations was undoubtedly fear of postwar depression coupled with the evident confidence of "Keynesian" economists that they had at last discovered the means to achieve economic stability. Liberal legislators and the economists themselves wished through the Employment Act to institutionalize the American "will" on the question of employment to go with the Keynesian "way." Widespread use of economists in government during the war, particularly in such regulatory agencies as the OPA and the OWMR, and in such analytical bodies as the OSS, had built on the foundations of the 1930s and reduced still further the novelty of economists-specialists taking important peacetime roles. However, it was ironic that in severe and continuous peacetime inflation the new advisers faced a problem with which neither they nor their advocates had expected to have to cope.

Although the Employment Act was signed in February 1946, it was not until August that the Council of Economic Advisers was formed and autumn before it was in operation. The members were Edwin G. Nourse, chairman, an agricultural economist and vice-president of the Brookings Institution, Leon H. Keyserling, vice chairman, a lawyer-economist with wide experience in both the executive and legislative branches of government, and John D. Clark, a former businessman, lawyer, and dean of the School of Business at the University of Nebraska. Keyserling had won second prize in 1944 in the Pabst Postwar Planning Awards, and he had worked closely with the staff of the Senate Committee on Banking and Currency for passage of the Employment Act.[85] Keyserling had the most finely developed political sense of the three, and this fact among others tended to generate tension from the start.[86]

One of President Truman's goals in his selection of the first Council members was to achieve "balance" in experience and viewpoint. In a sense this objective acknowledged his perception of economic advice as only partly "scientific" and at least partly political. To this balance Key-

84. See Bailey, *Congress Makes a Law.* See also the third section of this chapter, "Prices and Jobs."
85. For information on the formation and development of the Council, see especially Edward S. Flash, Jr., *Economic Advice and Presidential Leadership: The Council of Economic Advisers* (Columbia University Press, 1965).
86. Charles Murphy, one of Truman's closest aides, commented years later: "Our views tended to coincide more with Leon's than with Nourse's. . . . We never had any substantial policy differences with him." Transcript, Charles S. Murphy Oral History Interview, Truman Library, p. 43.

THE TRUMAN YEARS   37

serling brought the heritage of the New Deal and sponsorship by Senator Robert F. Wagner, Sr.; Clark brought experience in business and a long friendship with Senator O'Mahoney; Nourse, suggested by Charles G. Ross, Truman's press secretary, came with the detachment of the independent public policy analyst who could be counted upon to present options rather than a single recommendation. In his statement of July 29, 1946, announcing the appointment of Nourse the President noted that the Employment Act had charged the Council "to formulate and recommend national economic policies to promote employment, production, and purchasing power under free competitive enterprise."[87]

Nourse's concept of the Council was of a detached panel of nonpolitical near-equals, coordinated by a chairman, delivering their wisdom to be taken or left by political leaders. For a President untrained even in the rudiments of economics this approach of presenting different explanations of events and policy occasionally created more confusion than light. The story has been told that Truman, faced with a report from Nourse which said this "on the one hand" and that "on the other," appealed with an anguished cry for a one-armed economist.

At least for the first few months of its existence the Council appears to have had little influence on policy. Nourse was instructed to work principally through John R. Steelman, formerly director of the OWMR and from December 1946 the Assistant to the President. Nourse certainly had the impression in November and December of 1946 that by this time his work still was of little consequence. He wrote in his personal diary after one meeting with the President,

There was nothing in this half-hour interview which in any way suggested that the President was interested in the content of the work our staff had been doing or in the conclusions toward which we were moving in diagnosing the country's economic situation or the recommendations that we might be offering him on December 16. . . . I left with the feeling that his decisions were already pretty well taken, and this on the basis of information that comes to him casually from a variety of sources, with the final determinant his own political judgment.[88]

87. Ibid.; "Statement by the President Upon Nominating Edwin G. Nourse as a Member of the Council of Economic Advisers. July 29, 1946," *Public Papers, 1946*, p. 365.
88. Edwin G. Nourse, *Economics in the Public Service: Administrative Aspects of the Employment Act* (Harcourt, Brace, 1953), p. 137. Other agencies that had coveted the Council's functions and responsibilities were reluctant to accept the new

The question of how best to deal with the control of meat prices was one on which Nourse believed he should have been consulted more. Certainly Nourse thought he had received the clear signal from Truman that the first Economic Report of the President should be brought into line with the policy recommendations of the State of the Union Message to appear soon thereafter, rather than vice versa.

Some of the earliest recommendations from the Council to the President on inflation were contained in a letter of December 17, 1946, and were sufficiently broad and tentative to raise few questions. The letter said: "The policy which the Council recommends is to adopt all available policies to restrain further price advances and, where possible, to bring about lowering of prices. Success in this effort would forestall a business recession caused by a collapse in market demand for goods, and it would strike at the very root of the problem responsible for labor unrest and for work stoppages which would seriously interfere with production and employment."[89] In this letter, as in earlier Truman pronouncements, inflation was perceived much less as an evil in itself than as a probable cause of depression. On specific issues the Council's advice about anti-inflation policy was less confident. Their recommendations included "intensification of the antitrust drive," "the establishment of a sound process of collective bargaining," "expansion of house building," "a budget surplus . . . of at least $3 to $5 billion," and "low interest rates."[90] Clearly the Council was unwilling to sacrifice long-range objectives such as improvements in housing or support of government bond prices for what was thought might

---

boy on the block. See Richard E. Neustadt, "Presidency and Legislation: The Growth of Central Clearance," *American Political Science Review*, vol. 48 (September 1954), pp. 658–59.

89. Nourse, *Economics in the Public Service*, p. 139. Other economists in government at this time, with whom the Council were in contact, were growing increasingly pessimistic about inflation. Donald Kingsley of the OWMR estimated that half of the liquid assets then in the hands of consumers were in households with incomes under $4,000 and were thus "potentially available" to be converted into excessive "effective demand." "Curbs on Inflation: Fiscal and Monetary Policies," Records Relating to Manpower and Veterans Affairs, Folder "Economics 8," Record Group 250, Box 150, Entry 16, National Archives, p. 2. See also Richard B. Heflebower to John Steelman and Harold Stein, "Status of the Stabilization Program," September 11, 1946, General Classified Files of the Office of the Director of Records of the Office of War Mobilization and Reconversion, Folder "Economics 8," Record Group 250, Box 150, Entry 16, National Archives, p. 19.

90. Nourse, *Economics in the Public Service*, pp. 139–40.

be a transitional problem. Moreover, an imminent recession seemed still to be the greater danger.

By the time the President submitted his first Economic Report to the Congress on January 8, 1947, the Council's views had been fully incorporated by or at least reconciled with those of the White House staff. Nourse recounts that the President passed the first draft of the report that he submitted immediately to Steelman, who shortened it and modified its style. The final draft was more optimistic in tone than the Council version. A working group of secretaries, including John W. Snyder (Treasury), W. Averell Harriman (Commerce), and Lewis B. Schwellenbach (Labor), plus the Council, Steelman, and various assistants reached agreement on a compromise draft.[91] Policy recommendations for dealing with inflation contained in both the State of the Union Message for 1947 and the Economic Report were very similar to those in Nourse's letter of December 17. Yet it must be emphasized that these recommendations were not markedly different from what was already accepted government policy.[92] The long-run danger was still recession; and with respect to inflation high hopes were held for appeals to management, labor, and farmers to show restraint and understanding until a bad situation had passed.

As the Council began to acquire staff and to organize itself in 1947, inflation was placed well up on its list of priorities. When fields were apportioned, Chairman Nourse took as one of his four, "price relations and policies."[93] Paul T. Homan, newly arrived from Cornell, had special responsibility for "bringing together the various phases of the price and distributive analysis," while a "research or analytical group was designated as the Wage-Price Committee . . . to examine the state of professional economic thinking and actual business practice in such fields as wage

91. See ibid., pp. 141–42. Clark Clifford objected to the technique in the first Council draft "of asking so many questions and then not answering them." See 1947 President's Economic Report Folder, George M. Elsey Papers, Truman Library.

92. "Annual Message to the Congress on the State of the Union. January 6, 1947," *Public Papers*, 1947, p. 3, and "Special Message to the Congress: The President's First Economic Report. January 8, 1947," ibid., pp. 15–16. Nourse wrote in his diary on January 14, 1947, that he had mentioned at a White House meeting that the State of the Union Message accorded with the Council's thinking. "To this [Clark] Clifford rejoined, 'it should, since it was largely taken from that source.' " Nourse, *Economics in the Public Service*, p. 175.

93. Nourse, *Economics in the Public Service*, p. 470.

policy, price policy, collective bargaining, profit margins."[94] Nourse communicated his mounting concern about inflation to the President on March 7 and received an appreciative reply on March 10.[95] When asked about inflation at a news conference in March, President Truman could observe, "The Economic Council is making a complete survey of the situation on which they will make a report to me very shortly."[96] The reports he received became increasingly gloomy. The Council said that inflation currently posed a serious "threat to continued prosperity," and efforts should be made (1) to "persuade business executives to reduce prices promptly," (2) to maintain tax rates and run a budget surplus, (3) to restrict installment credit, and (4) to increase the "amount of statistical fact-finding" on the subject.[97] Nourse has recorded that at this time his concern about inflation was increased by uncertainty about the economic effects of the Truman Doctrine of foreign military aid, which had been announced on March 12 but the details of which Truman had failed to divulge to the Council. This would not be the last time that unexpected foreign policy developments would upset the calculations of economists about inflation.

In public pronouncements at this time Truman stressed repeatedly that with the current rate of inflation the American business system and its leaders were on trial. "They want free enterprise. They have got it. Now let's see if they will make it work." And again, "If we get a fair deal for everybody, why the country will be all right. . . . I don't think it is practicable to reinstitute price controls. . . . We want free enterprise in this country, but everybody has got to work at it, if we are going to have it."[98]

94. Ibid., pp. 156–58. A memorandum of February 20, 1947, from Gerhard Colm to Messrs. Wallace, Waugh, Salant, Shoup, Wright, and Warren described the functions of a proposed Council "committee on stabilization devices," which included "building up a tool chest of stabilization devices" and "planning for various contingencies," either a "boom" or a "slump." Inflation was pictured as a symptom of the former. Personal diary entry 1947-8, Nourse Papers, Truman Library.

95. Memorandums from Nourse to the President and the President to Nourse, March 7 and 10, 1947, 1947-12 and 1947-13, Nourse Papers, Truman Library. Truman asked Nourse to "keep your finger on the situation and keep me fully informed on the program."

96. "The President's News Conference of March 26, 1947," *Public Papers*, 1947, p. 186; Nourse, *Economics in the Public Service*, pp. 177–78.

97. Letter, CEA to the President, April 7, 1947, personal diary entry 1947-19, Nourse Papers, Truman Library.

98. "The President's News Conference of April 10, 1947," *Public Papers*, 1947, pp. 201, 202.

On April 21 Truman spoke on the subject of inflation to a group of newspaper editors in New York. The speech, drafted by members of the White House staff, showed the effects of comments from many of those responsible for economic policy in government, including, in addition to the CEA, secretaries Snyder, Harriman, and Anderson, and Marriner Eccles and Samuel Rosenman, and it gave official notice by the executive that inflation was now the paramount economic problem facing the nation. On this occasion Truman dealt less with remedies than with the magnitude of the problem and its costs.[99] He used metaphors that the CEA thought would be most persuasive. For example:

It is a dangerous economic fallacy to say that prices are not too high, simply because people are still buying. A bridge designed to carry 10 tons is not safe with 15 tons on it even though it has not yet begun to cave in. The excess weight must be taken off the bridge in time. When it begins to crack, it is too late.

There is one sure formula for bringing on a recession or a depression: that is to maintain excessively high prices. Buying stops, production drops, unemployment sets in, prices collapse, profits vanish, businessmen fail. . . . Our private enterprise system now has the responsibility for prices. . . . Private enterprise must display the leadership to make our free economy work by arresting this trend.[100]

Although at this time he wished to stress the danger of inflation, Truman revealed that he was still uncertain about how to handle it politically. When asked at a news conference in May 1947, "Do you think that we might be over the peak of inflation?" he replied, "I never have thought that we were in inflation. What we have been trying to do is to prevent inflation."[101]

To complicate matters even further Truman and his aides were receiving at this time conflicting views of the economic situation, with some saying that inflation would be a problem for years to come and others arguing that the dread depression was at last at hand, masked in its early

---

99. The George Elsey file on this speech shows the extent to which the growing number of newspaper stories on inflation during the period were taken into account. April 21, 1947, speech folder, Elsey Papers, Truman Library. The original draft of the speech came from the CEA with a characteristic emphasis on growth as the way to work out of inflation.

100. "Address in New York City at the Annual Luncheon of the Associated Press. April 21, 1947," *Public Papers, 1947*, pp. 213, 214.

101. "The President's News Conference of May 8, 1947," ibid., p. 237.

stages by an unprecedented worldwide shortage of food and raw materials.[102]

At a news conference in June 1947, in response to some reported remarks by Senator Taft about the need to cut government programs as a cure for inflation, Truman read a prepared statement that indicated the evolving official position on the subject. Prices, he said, were determined by aggregate demand for and supply of goods. America simply could not afford to limit demand, either domestically for the products and services its citizens needed or abroad, where world reconstruction and defense were crucial. "To say that we should abandon our efforts directed toward enduring world peace and freedom because these efforts create economic problems is like saying that we should have abandoned our war effort because it created economic problems."[103] The only sensible policy was for industry to increase supply rapidly and thereby achieve stability with fair profits. At the same time, on the advice of the CEA and the Federal Reserve Board, he now vetoed a bill to reduce income taxes in the same month, saying that while strong demand was important there was no need to increase it just then. "The time for tax reduction will come when general inflationary pressures have ceased and the structure of prices is on a more stable basis than now prevails."[104] Surplus finance and antitrust

102. Truman received a strong memorandum from Marriner Eccles on April 24 urging him to maintain restrictive monetary and fiscal policies so long as inflation persisted but warning him also that tax reductions, relaxation of credit, and public works should be kept in the wings ready to deal with the "deflationary spiral" that might begin at any time. Letter, Eccles to the President, April 24, 1947, Official File 327 (January–July 1947), Truman Library. Robert Warren, a consultant to the CEA, said the onset of recession was "obscured by the insensitivity of our statistical data." Rising food prices "activated wage demands" and pointed up the need for reimposition of rationing "for the same reason that Captain Bligh rationed food to his boat crew." Letter, Robert Warren to Fred Waugh, April 9, 1947, personal diary entry 1947-19, Nourse Papers, Truman Library, p. 3. Charles Hardy, chief of staff of the congressional Joint Economic Committee, feared a sustained inflation because of an entrenched psychology. See memorandum, J. D. Clark to Nourse, April 11, 1947, personal diary entry 1947-19, Nourse Papers, Truman Library.

103. "The President's News Conference of June 5, 1947," *Public Papers*, 1947, p. 263. The statement had been prepared jointly by Clifford and Keyserling.

104. "Veto of Bill to Reduce Income Taxes. June 16, 1947," ibid., p. 280. The veto message was markedly similar in language and argument to a letter from the Council on the subject dated June 5, 1947; Letters and Memoranda (1946–47) folder, Clark Papers, Truman Library. See also letter, Eccles to the President, undated, Bill file, H.R. 1, Truman Library. Also in June Truman vetoed the Taft-Hartley labor bill, but concern about inflation was not a major consideration in that case. See R. Alton Lee, *Truman and Taft-Hartley: A Question of Mandate* (University of Kentucky Press, 1966).

policy were the main tools against inflation available to the government. The same arguments were repeated a month later when a second tax-reduction bill was vetoed. "There is no justification for tax reduction so long as price stability at sound levels has not been secured and business, employment, and national income continue at peak levels."[105]

The President's midyear Economic Report to the Congress in 1947 dealt specifically with problems requiring immediate attention, and consequently prices and wages received detailed treatment. The report concluded that in labor markets some inflationary pressures had appeared because unions and management had not observed the productivity golden rule.

In some cases wage increases are still needed to attain workable relations in the wage and salary structure, and to alleviate hardship due to wages which are substandard or which have risen substantially less than the increase in the cost of living.

Except for such special circumstances, wage increases should be related to general trends in productivity and not made on a basis which forces price increases or prevents price reductions needed to assure sale of increasing supplies.[106]

A spectacular wage settlement in the coal industry a week before added drama and urgency to this statement.[107]

In the goods markets, the report admitted, an export surplus related to foreign aid had "created some strain," but the most important consideration was that producers had failed to increase supplies as much as had been hoped and even expected.

Claims made by the advocates of early decontrol, that OPA prices had retarded production and that it would promptly catch up with demand

105. "Veto of Second Bill to Reduce Income Taxes. July 18, 1947," *Public Papers, 1947*, p. 343.

106. "Excerpts from Special Message: The President's Midyear Economic Report to the Congress. July 21, 1947," ibid., p. 349. Nourse had expressed similar concern in May in a rare appearance before organized labor. He feared "an inflationary spiral of annual wage increases followed by annual price increases which promptly extinguish the gains for the consumer." If the problem could not be solved under responsible collective bargaining he could see no alternative to government arbitration. "Organized Labor and Economic Stabilization," speech to the Brotherhood of Railway and Steamship Clerks, May 14, 1947, Nourse Papers, Truman Library.

107. In one of its first ventures into the practice of moral suasion of price-makers, the Council on this occasion prepared a stern statement for presidential delivery. "Statement by the President on the Wage Increase of the Coal Miners. July 14, 1947," *Public Papers, 1947*, pp. 332–33.

after the removal of the controls, were not fully borne out by developments. Production, with important exceptions, did not increase as rapidly in the first few months after decontrol as in the last few months before decontrol.[108] There were again hints that producer recalcitrance might constitute conspiracy in restraint of trade, whereas in the case of raw materials "a tremendous amount of gambling on those commodity exchanges . . . causes high prices principally in the food products."[109] Reflecting continuing faith in the capacity of right-thinking and patriotic citizens to limit inflation through their individual actions, the Council applauded its own efforts at public education: "There can be little doubt that the Nationwide focus of attention on this matter acted as an important anti-inflationary force."[110]

Truman's mounting concern about inflation was shared now by many segments of the economy, which believed they were beginning to suffer grievous loss.[111] Truman's strategy on inflation, which grew in seriousness over the late summer and autumn, was not to minimize the problem. Rather, he regularly read to various audiences increases in the price indexes and appealed for personal sacrifice and reduction of waste.[112] He deplored the hardships inflation brought to those on fixed incomes, but he still saw the depression that high prices would induce as the greatest danger. He continued to direct attention to key industries, and in September the Council undertook a controversial "discussion" with the steel industry of proposed price increases.[113]

108. "Excerpts from Special Message," pp. 350, 352.
109. "The President's News Conference of August 14, 1947," *Public Papers, 1947*, p. 381, and "The President's News Conference of October 16, 1947," ibid., p. 467.
110. *The Midyear Economic Report of the President*, 1947, p. 32.
111. For example, testimony of Leon Henderson, spokesman for Americans for Democratic Action, at a congressional hearing in July; *Current Price Developments and the Problem of Economic Stabilization*, Hearings before the Joint Committee on the Economic Report, 80 Cong. 1 sess. (1947), pp. 481–84. For a very dramatic expression that unrestrained inflation would lead to a serious depression, see "Report of the Committee on Economic Stability," Sponsored by Americans for Democratic Action (May 1947). On the committee, which was chaired by Chester Bowles, were many prominent economists such as Lauchlin Currie, John Kenneth Galbraith, Robert Nathan, and Seymour E. Harris.
112. For example, "Remarks to Members of the Citizens Food Committee. October 1, 1947," *Public Papers, 1947*, pp. 452–53; and "Radio and Television Address Concluding a Program by the Citizens Food Committee. October 5, 1947," ibid., pp. 456–57.
113. Nourse was especially sensitive to the charge that the Council was taking on

On October 23 President Truman called a special session of Congress to consider the two related problems of inflation and European aid. This action followed a series of communications from the CEA which said that the "immediate emergency" required examination of the "full armory of control measures" with a view to supplementing the current policies of education and voluntary cooperation with a "program of positive action."[114] In a radio address on October 24 Truman explained the gravity of the domestic situation. Consumer prices, he said, were rising at an annual rate of 16 percent. If this spiral of inflation continued, depression would surely follow, with worldwide consequences. "We could choose the course of inaction. We could wait until depression caught up with us, until our living standards sank, and our people tramped the streets looking for jobs. Other democratic nations would lose hope, and become easy victims of totalitarian aggression. That would be the course of defeatism and cowardice."[115]

The debate that went on within the administration over what proposals to make to the special session was probably the most important discussion of inflation policy during Truman's presidency. It was characterized above all by major participation from the CEA and ultimate triumph for this group's recommendations. The main issue was how strong to make the proposals. Over the summer the Council had come more and more to believe that America's foreign commitments for economic aid and for military expenditures would concentrate pressure on a few commodities such as steel, staple foods, and fertilizer. By October 31 the Council staff had put together a firm ten-point program emphasizing fiscal

a manipulative role, and he replied publicly to a September 5 column by Stewart Alsop as follows: "It is not true that the Council virtually went down on its knees . . . in an attempt to persuade United States Steel not to raise its prices. The Council's role is fact-finding and economic interpretation for the President's use, not putting pressure on members of industry or labor for any specific course of action." Personal diary entry 1947-27, Nourse Papers, Truman Library.

114. Memorandum, Nourse and Keyserling to the President, "Third Quarter Review," October 1, 1947, personal diary entry 1947-28, Nourse Papers, Truman Library. Clark reported to Steelman after his return from a trip through the West that despite the emergency public opinion would not support price controls. Letter, October 13, 1947, Clark to Steelman, Clark Papers, Truman Library.

115. "Radio Address to the American People on the Special Session of Congress, October 24, 1947," Public Papers, 1947, p. 479. An early draft of this address by Leon Keyserling, dated October 19, is in Presidential Call for Special Session folder, Elsey Papers, Truman Library. Political features of the 1947 special session are discussed in Susan M. Hartmann, Truman and the 80th Congress (University of Missouri Press, 1971), chap. 5.

and monetary policy and wide-ranging standby controls.[116] The full Council endorsed the plan on November 5. Alternative proposals came from Harriman of the Commerce Department, who stressed voluntary restraint, and Webb of the Budget Bureau, who favored very selective controls over only a few items, in particular housing, food, and grains.[117] The decision to accept the CEA's recommendation was based on a mixture of economic and political reasoning, though mainly the latter. With the presidential elections only a year away the dominance of political considerations was understandable. Happily, on this occasion political and economic logic coincided. A White House staff memorandum dated November 19 argued most effectively that on the one hand the people wanted firm action against inflation, but on the other the President was not likely to receive authority for such action from the Republican Congress. The memorandum explained:

If the President recommends a bold program and the Congress refuses to go along with him, then we will be storing up valuable ammunition to use at a later time. . . . Our record on prices must be crystal clear because there is the ever present danger that if prices continue to go up, the people may be so irritable and irrational about the problem that they will vote the "ins" out and the "outs" in. . . . Because of the probability of increasingly high prices in 1948, it is possible that this issue will reach a climax in the summer of 1948. This would come at a highly propitious time for the President and the Democratic Administration.[118]

The proposals that Truman put to the special session, and that stood as the basis of wage-price policy for the next several years, were as follows:

116. Memorandum, Staff to CEA, November 1, 1947, and memorandum, CEA to the President, November 5, 1947, both in personal diary entry 1947-32, Nourse Papers, Truman Library.

117. The alternatives were spelled out in a memorandum from James E. Webb to the President, "Suggestions for the Anti-Inflation Section of the President's Message to the Congress," November 13, 1947, Webb Papers, Truman Library.

118. "Confidential Memo for the President," November 19, 1947, Clifford Papers, Truman Library. The same arguments were contained in Clark Clifford's notes for the Message to the Special Session, n.d., Message for Special Session folder, Clifford Papers, Truman Library. Chester Bowles strongly endorsed Clifford's reasoning in a letter to the President, saying, "If we can load the blame for all that has happened and all that is likely to happen squarely on their shoulders, I believe we will be richer by five or six million votes in 1948." Letter, Chester Bowles to the President, November 5, 1947, Official File 327 (July–December 1947), Truman Library. Clifford, Keyserling, and Murphy were all members at this time of an informal group, later called the "progressive caucus," which sought to influence the President on domestic affairs. See Hamby, Beyond the New Deal, pp. 182–83.

1. *To restore consumer credit controls and to restrain the creation of inflationary bank credit.*

2. *To authorize the regulation of speculative trading on the commodity exchanges.*

3. *To extend and strengthen export controls.*

4. *To extend authority to allocate transportation facilities and equipment.*

5. *To authorize measures which will induce the marketing of livestock and poultry at weights and grades that represent the most efficient utilization of grain.*

6. *To enable the Department of Agriculture to expand its program of encouraging conservation practices in this country, and to authorize measures designed to increase the production of foods in foreign countries.*

7. *To authorize allocation and inventory control of scarce commodities which basically affect the cost of living or industrial production.*

8. *To extend and strengthen rent control.*

9. *To authorize consumer rationing on products in short supply which basically affect the cost of living.*

10. *To authorize price ceilings on products in short supply which basically affect the cost of living or industrial production, and to authorize such wage ceilings as are essential to maintain the necessary price ceilings.*[119]

When the administration position had been announced the cabinet endorsed it more or less wholeheartedly. Harriman told the House Committee on Banking and Currency that the rapid inflation was destroying the basic allocative role of the price system and that standby controls might be needed as an alternative. Production was threatened by a misallocation of such essential items as steel, while "the form of rationing of the necessities of life that results from price increases gives a disproportionate share to those with higher incomes at the expense of those with lower incomes." Secretary of Labor Schwellenbach said, "If we are successful in checking the upward movement of prices and in lowering the costs of common foods, we shall have a basis for calling on labor voluntarily to withhold demands for further wage increases."[120] When Secre-

---

119. "Special Message to the Congress on the First Day of the Special Session. November 17, 1947," *Public Papers*, 1947, p. 498. Leon Keyserling's suggested draft for the address, dated November 11, 1947, is in Address to Congress, Domestic Economics folder, Elsey Papers, Truman Library.

120. *Economic Stabilization Aids*, Hearings before the House Committee on Banking and Currency, 80 Cong. 1 sess. (1947), pp. 136, 179.

tary of the Treasury Snyder took issue publicly with Marriner Eccles of the Federal Reserve Board over the recommendation for tight monetary policy, and especially increased reserve requirements, the Council complained directly and vociferously to the President.[121]

In a second message to the special session in December, Truman argued that despite inflationary pressures foreign aid was still possible and desirable. Behind this announcement lay another one of the early successes of the Council. Shortly after Secretary of State George C. Marshall's outline of what would become the European Recovery Program, or "Marshall Plan," at the Harvard Commencement in June 1947, the President requested that studies of the broad significance of the proposed program be made by three separate committees. The Council was asked "to study the impact of foreign aid upon the domestic economy." A working group of Paul Homan, Gerhard Colm, and Walter Salant prepared the report, which was presented to the President on October 28, the first such special study to date. In his message the President paid special tribute to the Council's work. "During recent months the Council of Economic Advisers made an intensive study of the impact of foreign aid on our domestic economy. The Council concluded that a program of the size now contemplated is well within our productive capacity and need not produce a dangerous strain on our economy."[122]

President Truman was probably not surprised that the special session took action on only three of his ten recommendations, and these three "of minor importance compared with the others." (In fact, he had let several weeks pass before he even submitted draft legislation for congressional consideration.) Regulation of credit, rationing, and price control had been denied. He expressed his "deep disappointment" at "such feeble steps toward the control of inflation" in a message dated December 28.[123] Effective steps might not have been taken against inflation by the special session, but a firm political foundation had been laid for the campaign of 1948.

121. Memorandum, CEA to the President, Official File 151 (April–December 1947), Truman Library.
122. "Special Message to the Congress on the Marshall Plan. December 19, 1947," Public Papers, 1947, p. 524. The study was released as "The Impact of Foreign Aid Upon the Domestic Economy," A Report to the President by the Council of Economic Advisers (1947; processed).
123. "Statement on the Resolution Enacted in Response to the President's Message of November 17," Public Papers, 1947, pp. 532–34.

Groping for Policy

Truman began 1948 with a ringing declaration that inflation was the "one major problem which affects all our goals." In his State of the Union Message he reported that wholesale prices were increasing at an annual rate of 18 percent and retail prices at 10 percent. In the budget message and in his Economic Report that followed soon after he gave as much weight to the social dislocations caused by inflation to millions of families, schools, and hospitals as to the threat it posed of another depression.[124] To the old argument that inflation ultimately destroyed the demand on which it fed, Truman added the new charge that it caused uncertainty and thereby led to recession. "When a price-wage spiral breeds business uncertainty and impairs confidence, employment and production go down instead of up."[125] He appealed for the remaining seven of the ten anti-inflationary weapons requested in November and he pledged for his own part to continue to seek a government budget surplus.[126] To reduce the burden of inflation on low-income families he recommended a "cost of living tax credit" of $40 for each taxpayer and dependent; the lost revenue would be made up by an increase in corporate taxes.[127] At his news conference on January 10, in response to a question from a reporter about how the amount of the tax credit had been determined, Truman replied, "The suggestion came from the Economic Advisers that this was a proper approach

124. "Annual Message to the Congress on the State of the Union. January 7, 1948," *Public Papers*, 1948, p. 9. In the Economic Report to the Congress one week later, these rates were revised upward to 20 percent and 12 percent. "Excerpts from Annual Message: The President's Economic Report to the Congress. January 14, 1948," ibid., p. 64; "Annual Budget Message to the Congress, Fiscal Year 1949. January 12, 1948," ibid., pp. 19–59.
125. "Economic Report," ibid., p. 70.
126. In vetoing an income tax reduction bill on April 2, 1948, Truman said, "The most important force restraining inflation has been the Government surplus and the use of this surplus to reduce the public debt. This bill would reduce or eliminate this important weapon against inflation." "Veto of the Income Tax Reduction Bill. April 2, 1948," ibid., p. 202.
127. See "Annual Message on the State of the Union," ibid., pp. 9–10, and "Budget Message, Fiscal Year 1949," ibid., pp. 21–22. Keyserling added to the defense of this proposal the arguments that it would dampen wage demands and afford relief to the most disadvantaged. Memorandum, "General Economic Merits of the President's Tax Plan," n.d., State of the Union (1948)–Taxation folder, Clifford Papers, Truman Library.

to the situation."[128] On the advice of the Council he refused also to look on the light side of any news, and when confronted with a decline of some commodity prices in February he still could see no reason for optimism.[129]

On monetary policy as a weapon against inflation Truman was doubtful and vague. Moreover, after three years in office he still retained the belief, rooted in a broad populism as well as in his own personal experience, that the value of war bonds purchased in good faith by many patriotic citizens must be preserved at all costs. Secretary of the Treasury Snyder held similar views. He told a congressional committee that interest-rate policy was not an effective anti-inflation device: "If a man is going in to borrow money for inflationary purposes, the interest rate he pays is not going to be a deterring part of his consideration. . . . The trouble is that the legitimate business operators would be penalized and this might affect production adversely."[130] The CEA also supported this position because it believed that a rise in the interest rates could unsettle the financial markets and that the bluntness of the tool might bring on a depression.[131]

In his Economic Report of January 14, 1948, a document that had been drafted largely by the Council of Economic Advisers, Truman said: "Among the strategic points at which to curb the inflation movement, none is potentially more powerful than the restriction of bank credit."[132] Yet when asked at a news conference four days earlier whether he was

128. "The President's News Conference on the Budget. January 10, 1948," *Public Papers*, 1948, p. 17. The CEA urged the President to maintain taxes during this period, especially on corporate profits, on anti-inflation grounds. Memorandum, CEA to the President, December 13, 1947, personal diary entry 1947-42, Nourse Papers, Truman Library.

129. "Special Message to the Congress on Housing. February 23, 1948," *Public Papers*, 1948, p. 158. Truman's pessimism was consistent with the conclusions of the Committee on Periodic Reports of the CEA, which in March 1948 stated, "The break in the commodity markets does not portend an early downturn in prices and business activity." Memorandum, Committee on Periodic Reports to CEA, March 1, 1948, Periodic Reports folder, Clark Papers, Truman Library.

130. *Economic Stabilization Aids*, Hearings, p. 40.

131. The first clear discussion of this came in the 1949 *Economic Report of the President*, pp. 40–43. Clark and Keyserling stated their views explicitly in a letter to Chairman O'Mahoney of the Joint Economic Committee on November 20, 1950; Charles S. Murphy Files, Truman Library. They argued then that interest rates should be kept low to encourage investment. Selective credit controls could limit loans to nonessential users. A rise in the general level of interest rates would increase the cost of new capital in an indiscriminate way and thus discourage worthwhile growth.

132. "Economic Report," *Public Papers*, 1948, p. 72.

trying to "contract bank credit in order to fight inflation," he had replied, "I don't think so. We are not trying to contract bank credit where it will increase production. We are only trying to contract bank credit where it does not increase production, or for speculative purposes—particularly speculative."[133] He did not specify how bank credit to increase production could be distinguished from that which would merely increase prices. Apparently the housing industry, with its low short-run elasticity of supply, was one sector where additional credit caused inflation, and consequently emergency and wartime housing aids were to be specifically "limited to the types of construction most urgently needed, particularly rental housing and lower-cost housing."[134]

The Economic Report repeated the analysis first stated publicly by the CEA in its report on the impact of foreign aid. The Council thought that selective price controls could be very effective in a situation of demand-pull exacerbated by inflexibilities in a few particular markets. "The nature of the inflation from which we are suffering arises in part from the total excess of buying power over the available supply of goods and in part from relative scarcities at strategic points in the economy which give impetus to particular price-wage spirals." Truman still called for "voluntary restraint" from both "those who price goods and those who buy goods." And he still asserted confidently that "the removal of impediments to maximum production will provide the surest long-run remedy for scarcity prices and the exploitation of monopolistic situations."[135]

Clearly there was still considerable disagreement within the executive branch about just what did determine pricing policies. In the Economic Report, which represented CEA views, it was suggested rather tentatively that in the corporate sector the problem of inflation lay with the behavior of large oligopolistic firms, which would seldom reduce prices, even in booms, because they feared retaliation from competitors (the kinked demand curve) and because they accumulated large profits at times of high and efficient production to carry them through periods cf inefficient low-level production. In the labor market, the report said, wages were fixed with an inadequate "understanding of the long-range interests of management and labor in the context of the interests of the whole economy." The President announced that he had instructed the Council "to deter-

133. "News Conference on the Budget," ibid., p. 18.
134. "Budget Message, Fiscal Year 1949," ibid., p. 38.
135. "Economic Report," ibid., pp. 65, 70.

mine what price and wage policies and practices are appropriate . . . to do away with business fluctuations of the violence known in the past."[136]

Concern about inflation was not confined to the executive branch during this period. The Senate Committee on Banking and Currency in January heard from a variety of official witnesses on the subject, as well as from professional economists such as Seymour Harris, who testified that "unless we stop the inflation this year we are going to have a galloping inflation, a real inflation." Significantly, during these hearings when quizzed about the data upon which noninflationary wage increases might be based, the commissioner of the Bureau of Labor Statistics was forced to reply, "During and since the war our information on productivity is limited."[137]

Interest in the causes of inflation and its cure was growing throughout the economics profession at this time. As in earlier years there was no unanimity of view, although there was nearly a consensus on serious excess demand in the economy being the primary cause of inflation. Most economists favored more strenuous fiscal and monetary policies to restrain demand; few favored a return to price controls and rationing.[138] Sumner Slichter and Gottfried Haberler were in a minority when they recommended the development of a national wage policy to deal with the powerful trade unions that insisted on raising wages more rapidly than productivity.[139] Jacob Viner complained of the new presidential practice of "exhortation," which he attributed directly to persuasion from the Council.[140]

In February several present and former government economists took part in a second anniversary symposium on the Employment Act, and in their comments indicated the point to which government thinking had moved on how to restrain inflation in times of relative normality. There was considerable gloom about prospects for achieving price stability with full employment, but Gerhard Colm, a senior economist on the CEA staff, returned to a variant of the conference device that had been tried in 1945. Colm's comments were important both for the ideas they con-

---

136. Ibid., p. 90.

137. *National Stabilization*, Hearings before the Senate Committee on Banking and Currency, 80 Cong. 2 sess. (1948), pt. 2, p. 559, and pt. 1, p. 195.

138. "Ten Economists on the Inflation," *Review of Economics and Statistics*, vol. 30 (February 1948), pp. 1–29.

139. Ibid., pp. 5, 14; Sumner H. Slichter, *The American Economy: Its Problems and Prospects* (Knopf, 1948), p. 43.

140. "Can We Check Inflation?" *Yale Review*, vol. 37 (Winter 1948), p. 198.

tained and because they made one of the first uses of a new piece of terminology, the "guidepost." He said:

I am thinking of proposals such as collective bargaining on the national level where at least once a year labor and management sit together and discuss the relationship of prices and wages for the economy as a whole and agree on certain general principles which then become guideposts for specific negotiations and agreements for particular industries. Here is a field for investigation and exploration. I do believe that we need some new patterns of price and wage negotiations if we are to have a constant high level of employment and want to avoid constant inflationary pressures.[141]

While Truman was loudly proclaiming the dangers of inflation in the early spring of 1948 his assistants in the White House were receiving at least some reassurance that the worst might be nearly over. Robert C. Turner, on Steelman's staff, wrote on March 5 that many of the circumstances that had fed inflation in 1947 seemed now to be changing: withdrawals from savings and business investments were both slowing down; net exports were declining and, contrary to popular belief, would be reduced still more by the Marshall Plan; there was even a fair chance for a recession in the second half of 1948. Turner drew the following "policy implications" from these facts:

The recent change in the economic situation means that proposals for price control, wage control, and rationing can now be justified only on a standby basis. No controls enacted now could have much influence on wage or price increases this spring, and after that there is no indication that either will be needed. . . . In general, we should soft-pedal statements about "rising prices," and "inflation," and should allow our previous demands for anti-inflation controls to lie in storage for a while, and probably ultimately die a natural death.[142]

But then for the second time since World War II unexpected developments in foreign policy again altered the outlook for inflation. The communist coup in Czechoslovakia in February marked a new step in the cold war and drastically changed the underlying assumptions of economic

---

141. *The Employment Act of 1946* (George Washington University, 1948). See also Gerhard Colm, "On the Road to Economic Stabilization," *Social Research*, vol. 15 (September 1948), pp. 265–76.

142. Memorandum, Robert C. Turner to Steelman, March 5, 1948, Miscellaneous file, Turner Papers, Truman Library, p. 2.

policy as well as of external affairs. Now there would be greatly increased defense expenditures.

Economists in the Bureau of the Budget warned immediately that if national defense expenditures were greatly increased, as proposed, the economic situation could change seriously. A memorandum from W. F. Schaub and Arthur Smithies said:

If it proves impossible to keep taxes high enough, the alternatives seem to be either inflation or price control over a wide area.

Whether or not taxes are increased, allocation controls seem necessary and the sooner they are granted the better. Even before the program gets under way, the expectation of it could give rise to widespread hoarding of materials.[143]

The Council wrote to the President at the same time: "We feel we must face the question whether, at the very outset of this new spending program, we would not need to set aside the free market practices that we have been trying to guide toward stabilized peacetime operation and substitute a rather comprehensive set of controls of materials, plant operation, prices, wages, and business credit."[144]

Throughout the spring of 1948 the attitude of most government economists toward prices remained worried for the short run, cautiously optimistic for the medium term, and tempered by the belief that a slight change in conditions would move inflation once again out of control. Nourse's fears of inflation were closely tied to his dislike of military spending in general, which he regarded as both unproductive and "potentially destructive."[145] At this time Truman took the unusual step of releasing to the public two Council reports to him on inflation, the first critical of

143. Memorandum, W. F. Schaub and Arthur Smithies to the Director, March 23, 1948, Webb Papers, Truman Library. A memorandum from Wilbert Fritz to Arthur Smithies, dated March 24, made similar recommendations. Subsequent memorandums from Smithies and J. Weldon Jones said that the President should push hard for point seven of his ten points, authorization for allocation and inventory control of scarce commodities, in the interest of national defense. Memorandums, Arthur Smithies to Messrs. Jones, Homan, and Watkins, April 12, 1948; J. Weldon Jones to Webb, April 19, 1948; Paul T. Homan, J. Weldon Jones, Ralph Watkins, and Arthur Smithies to Nourse et al., April 16, 1948; all in Mobilization file 1, Webb Papers, Truman Library.
144. Memorandum, CEA to the President, March 24, 1948, personal diary entry 1948-6, Nourse Papers, Truman Library.
145. See, for example, Edwin Nourse, "Economic Stabilization in a Troubled World," speech at Illinois Institute of Technology, May 19, 1948, personal diary entry 1948-21, Nourse Papers, Truman Library.

recent steel price increases and the second critical of a coal work stoppage and a tax reduction passed by Congress over Truman's veto.[146]

The President's continuing concern was expressed in an address on April 17 which was broadcast nationwide by radio. On the advice of the CEA he revealed no lessening of his sense of urgency, and for this occasion he tied control of inflation not only to continued American prosperity but to the welfare of the free world.

Thus, a strong American economy is the bedrock upon which rest the hopes for establishing a peace of free men in the world. Without it we can provide neither aid, nor leadership, nor example.

The strength and vitality of our economy are being undermined by inflation.[147]

The Politics of Inflation

During the summer and autumn of 1948 a sharp contrast of styles developed in the approach taken toward the problem of inflation by men in government. Economic advisers speculated in private councils about whether the worst was over and argued about the most appropriate countermeasures to be employed. However, no such doubt or uncertainty could be discerned in the President. In a stream of public addresses, after-dinner speeches, and rear-platform remarks, he carried a relatively simple message: from the beginning of his presidency he had urged that price controls be retained until "production caught up with demand." This a Republican Congress, controlled by special interests, had been unwilling to do.

They have decided that the National Association of Manufacturers and the National Chamber of Commerce of the United States know all about prices and price controls.

Well now, we have price controls and rationing now, just as we have under Government controls, only those price controls are controls so that only the man who has the money is able to get the necessities of life.[148]

146. Memorandums, CEA to the President, March 10 and April 1, 1948 (released March 13 and April 9), personal diary entries 1948-5 and 1948-9, Nourse Papers, Truman Library.
147. "Address Before the American Society of Newspaper Editors. April 17, 1948," *Public Papers*, 1948, p. 222. See also memorandum, CEA to the President, March 24, 1948, personal diary entry 1948-6, Nourse Papers, Truman Library.
148. "Rear Platform Remarks in Ohio and Indiana. June 4, 1948," *Public Papers*,

The only solution, he said, was government control of prices. "This is the method of democracy. These are the goals of abundance. A nation which reaches these goals will never succumb to the evils of communism."[149] Repeatedly, Truman accused the Republicans of fueling inflation for their own selfish interests, and even of denying appropriations for the Bureau of Labor Statistics so that the country would not appreciate the extent of the robbery in progress. "They don't want to hold the brake on prices. They don't want us to know by the speedometer what the prices are and how they affect the country."[150]

To make his points abundantly clear to the voters Truman called another special session of Congress to deal with inflation and other matters for July 26, which he observed was "Turnip Day" in Missouri. An unsigned memorandum of June 29 had explained the political value of such a session: "This Congress is so closely controlled by reactionaries and lobbyists that it cannot pass satisfactory bills to stop the disastrous inflation which is frightening the people.... On the issue of price control, which will be the hottest issue of this campaign, the Congress cannot possibly act.... This Congress is run by men who cannot pass price-control legislation without losing their financial backers and incurring the wrath of the N.A.M., the U.S. Chamber of Commerce, and other such groups."[151] In preparation for this session and at the request of Clark Clifford the CEA submitted on July 19 a detailed memorandum on "The Government's Anti-Inflation Program."[152] The Council reaffirmed the seriousness of the situation: "The promised expansion of production which was to follow the end of wartime price control" was not taking place, and "we are forced to the realization that the problem of inflation will not be solved merely by voluntary action."

The Council's program, which was similar to that of 1947, fell under

---

1948, p. 286. See also "Remarks at the Young Democrats Dinner. May 14, 1948," ibid., p. 260.

149. "Address in Chicago Before the Swedish Pioneer Centennial Association. June 4, 1948," ibid., p. 290. See also "Address at the Stadium in Butte, Montana. June 8, 1948," ibid., p. 305.

150. "Address at the Stadium in Butte," p. 306. See also various addresses and speeches in *Public Papers*, 1948, pp. 314, 316, 351, 376, 407.

151. "Should the President Call Congress Back?" June 29, 1948, Clifford Papers, Truman Library. The politics of the 1948 special session are discussed in R. Alton Lee, "The Turnip Session of the Do-Nothing Congress: Presidential Campaign Strategy," *Southwestern Social Science Quarterly*, vol. 44 (December 1963), pp. 256–67; and Hartmann, *Truman and the 80th Congress*, pp. 189–95.

152. Memorandum, CEA to the President, July 19, 1948, Letters and Memoranda (1948–49) folder, Clark Papers, Truman Library.

three general heads. First, it recommended a federal budget surplus to "mop up" loose purchasing power through taxation, if necessary through an excess profits tax.[153] To supplement fiscal policy Congress should authorize the Federal Reserve System to regulate both commercial bank reserves and consumer credit. Monetary policy, however, should continue to support the government bond market, and "every occasion should be taken to reassure the American people that it [the peg] will not be abandoned." The memorandum acknowledged that monetary restraint might cause some "disemployment," meaning unemployment of workers who would "promptly be reabsorbed."

The second Council recommendation was for "some control on the distribution and use of industrial critical materials," especially steel, lead, tin, copper, zinc, and several other minor commodities. Such a policy should be carried out by a "coordinated control-of-materials office," whose aims would be to protect the defense program and "make civilian production more orderly."

The third Council recommendation, over which there was some internal disagreement, was for reestablishment of "authority for price and wage control and rationing." But it was emphasized that the pressure for such controls was lessening and "a request for sweeping and unreserved authority to control any and all prices would be economically unwise" for both psychological and administrative reasons. The memorandum noted that Chairman Nourse doubted the practicability of selective controls.[154] It was suggested that large corporations might be required to

153. An excess profits tax was viewed as an effective anti-inflation device because it reduced "excess demand by reducing the means available for financing business expansion," and contributed to wage stability by responding to "the belief that business is earning extraordinary profits." Memorandum, Walter Salant to Frederick J. Lawton, "Purpose of Proposed Excess Profits Tax," July 29, 1948, Special Session: Excess Profits Tax folder, Lawton Papers, Truman Library.

154. Clark described himself as "on the reluctant side of this proposal." He acknowledged the political strategy involved, but insisted, "There is much more involved than the contest between the President and the Congress." Memorandum, Clark to Nourse and Keyserling, July 17, 1948, personal diary entry 1948-28, Nourse Papers, Truman Library. Keyserling, the main advocate, argued that because the CEA had discerned peacetime inflation to be especially the result of "specific pressures at discernible points" the "selective use of price and wage powers and rationing" was clearly called for. Moreover, "selective controls in Canada are working effectively, and afford a demonstration that selective controls can serve the more limited dangers of peacetime inflation just as war controls demonstrably serve the more extreme and all inclusive dangers of a war economy." Memorandum, Keyserling to Nourse and Clark, "Comments on Anti-Inflationary Program," July 18, 1948. This and Nourse's memorandum on the subject are in personal diary entry 1948-28, Nourse Papers, Truman Library.

issue notification of price changes so that "the force of publicity and public opinion may be brought more effectively to bear." Modification of agricultural price supports might also bring down food prices. The Council memorandum concluded, as it said, with "a word of caution." No serious thought should be given to "the re-establishment of another OPA." Moreover, "any claim that these controls would provide a quick and easy solution for the whole problem of inflation would be an overstatement of dubious help in meeting the real economic dangers confronting the country."[155]

Truman's message to the July special session followed the Council's recommendations very closely as did his midyear Economic Report three days later. He explained that the problem was caused by consumer and government demands for goods and services greater than supplies and was accentuated by large defense and foreign aid programs. It was exacerbated by high wage claims and excessive credit creation. He appointed Paul Porter, former administrator of the OPA, as special assistant to present the case to Congress. Porter stressed the seriousness of the situation and argued that inflation typically moved in a three-phase sequence: "First . . . excess of total demand. . . . The effects of this initial phase are then intensified by the price-wage spiral. Finally, an increasing credit and money supply is essential to support the operations of the economy at the higher income and price levels; and the increased money supply, in turn, tends to reinforce the excess demand." It was the duty of the government to restrict this excess demand in all phases.[156]

155. Memorandum, CEA to the President, July 19, 1948, p. 11. It was clear at this time as well as at others that for Keyserling, at least, controls were expected to do more than merely restrain inflation. They could also rectify more fundamental faults in the price system. For example, on this occasion he looked to substantial reform of the housing market. He wrote: "It is highly urgent to bring about a drastic change in the *composition* of the houses being built, in terms of the distribution between sale and rental housing, between luxury housing and necessity housing." Memorandum, Keyserling to Nourse and Clark, "Comments on Anti-Inflationary Program," July 18, 1948, personal diary entry 1948-28, Nourse Papers, Truman Library. This complexity of purpose for controls remained a bone of contention within the Council.

156. *Inflation Control*, Hearing on S.J. Res. 157 before the House Committee on Banking and Currency, 80 Cong. 2 sess. (1948), p. 7. Porter, like Keyserling, had been favorably impressed by the Canadian experience with selective controls. See his article, "It Could Have Happened Here: How Canada Licked Inflation," *Democratic Digest* (Women's Division, Democratic National Committee), vol. 25 (July 1948), pp. 15ff. At this time Marriner Eccles, recently demoted from the chairmanship of the Federal Reserve Board, called for tighter monetary and fiscal restraints. He

Truman received from the special session only some additions to consumer credit and bank controls. Full hearings were not even held on several of his proposals, and neither the advocates nor the critics of these measures had an opportunity to wrestle with all their implications. In particular, the White House did not have to explain more fully how the expected partial controls, and especially selective wage controls, would operate. The President announced on August 16, after the end of the session: "The failure to take adequate measures in this critical situation is final proof of the determination of the men who controlled the 80th Congress to follow a course which serves the ends of special privilege rather than the welfare of the whole Nation."[157]

Inflation became one of the main planks in Truman's campaign platform in the fall of 1948 despite reports from the Council that "inflationary pressures" were moderating.[158] His message was simple. The most appropriate measures to restrain prices were clear for anyone to see and he had proposed them. Only the selfishness of his opponents had stood in the way of success. Now he required a decisive mandate and a sympathetic Congress to bring prices in hand once and for all. As he said in Denver on September 20, "I know you are troubled by high prices. Well,

---

angered the administration by asserting, in contradiction of Porter, that some of Truman's own programs, such as that for housing, were inflationary. *Inflation Control*, Hearing on S.J. Res. 157, p. 173. Keyserling, in reply to Eccles and Republicans who took the same line, insisted that some positive programs such as government support for low-cost housing should not be sacrificed because paradoxically they were deflationary; they shifted resources from high- to low-priced goods. "The truth is that our immediately soluble problem is less one of total production than of the composition of production and the distribution of the product. . . . While the problem is partly to relieve inflation by more production as fast as we can, the bigger problem is that inflation is impairing production in detail and in the long run will impair it in general." *Inflation Control*, Hearings on Control of Inflation before the Senate Committee on Banking and Currency, 80 Cong. 2 sess. (1948), p. 345. Keyserling's argument was subsequently described by Howard S. Ellis as "either befuddlement or dissimulation," in *Review of Economics and Statistics*, vol. 31 (August 1949), p. 175. Keyserling replied angrily, qualifying his assertion somewhat in "Housing and Inflation: Reply to Professor Ellis," *American Economic Review*, vol. 40 (March 1950), pp. 170-73. Housing policy during this period is discussed in Richard O. Davies, *Housing Reform During the Truman Administration* (University of Missouri Press, 1966).

157. "Statement by the President Upon Signing Resolution 'To Aid in Protecting the Nation's Economy Against Inflationary Pressures.' August 16, 1948," *Public Papers*, 1948, p. 450.

158. For example, memorandum, Periodic Reports Committee, October 29, 1948, Periodic Reports folder, Clark Papers, Truman Library. See also Benjamin Caplan,

put the blame where it belongs—on the leaders of the Republican Party."[159] As the campaign moved along Truman departed noticeably from the cautious path laid down by his advisers and called specifically for broad price control; he even harkened back to the "halcyon days" of wartime and the OPA. Repeatedly he told the story of how the NAM in 1946 allegedly spent $3 million to kill the OPA.[160] For example, he said in Los Angeles on September 23, "There is no great mystery about how to stop the cost of living from going higher and higher. The best way to stop it is with price control. Everybody knows that when we had price control the average family was not gouged by inflated prices."[161] And in Philadelphia on October 6, "There was no good reason why prices could not have been held down after the war ended—until supply caught up with demand. . . . But the unholy alliance of big business and the Republican Party did not want it that way."[162] Truman was no longer making an appeal for legislation. This was a try for reelection. It is noteworthy, all the same, that the exigencies of politics had ultimately led to the abandonment of the subtleties of economics and the facts of history. For whatever reasons, Truman was unexpectedly successful in obtaining both the mandate he requested and the Democratic Congress he sought.

The Eye of the Storm

It seemed possible to some government economists that the worst inflationary pressures were over before the election of November 1948. It seemed probable soon after. Nevertheless, President Truman, having directed much of his campaign toward the ills of inflation and the need for its control, was not about to take chances. Less than two weeks after winning the election he asked Nourse to head a cabinet committee on an anti-inflation program with representatives from the Departments of the

---

"A Case Study: The 1948–1949 Recession," in *Policies to Combat Depression*, A Conference of the Universities–National Bureau of Economic Research (Princeton University Press for the National Bureau of Economic Research, 1956).

159. "Address at the State Capitol in Denver. September 20, 1948," *Public Papers*, 1948, p. 519.

160. "Address in Louisville, Kentucky. September 30, 1948," ibid., p. 654, and "Address at Convention Hall in Philadelphia. October 6, 1948," ibid., pp. 680–82.

161. "Address at the Gilmore Stadium in Los Angeles. September 23, 1948," ibid., p. 558.

162. "Address at Convention Hall in Philadelphia. October 6, 1948," ibid., p. 680.

Treasury, Commerce, Labor, Agriculture, and the Interior, and the Board of Governors of the Federal Reserve System. This group drafted relevant portions of the Economic Report presented to Congress on January 7. The Council, through its Stabilization Devices Committee, provided staff assistance.[163]

Drawing upon the work on an anti-inflation program of an interagency committee, which operated at a lower level than the cabinet committee, Truman made legislative proposals to deal with "inflationary pressures" in his State of the Union Message on January 5 as well as in the Economic Report.[164] In most respects these recommendations were similar to those presented to the special sessions of Congress of November 1947 and July 1948: to strengthen some credit controls, continue export controls, grant authority to regulate commodity speculation and fix priorities and allocations in transportation and scarce materials, extend and strengthen rent control, increase some taxes, and provide standby authority to impose price ceilings for certain scarce commodities. A novel proposal was "to authorize an immediate study of the adequacy of production facilities for materials in critically short supply, such as steel; and, if found necessary, to authorize Government loans for the expansion of production facilities to relieve such shortages, and to authorize the construction of such facilities directly, if action by private industry fails to meet our needs."[165] The Economic Report took account of "the recent appearance of wider areas in the economy where supply conditions have improved, where the pressure of demand has been reduced, and where price inflation has been halted or reversed," but, it continued, "these adjustments have not proceeded far enough to justify a cessation of concern about inflation." Truman assured Congress that "this situation calls for a vigorous anti-inflation

163. Memorandum from Walter S. Salant, "Comments on Latest Draft of 'Survey of Stabilization Devices,'" November 9, 1948, Stabilization Devices (1948) folder, Salant Papers, Truman Library. Nourse joined Clark and Keyserling in December in telling Truman that inflation was still the most important economic problem facing the nation, but he refused to endorse wage and price controls for the current situation. Memorandum, CEA to the President, "Anti-Inflation Program," December 7, 1948, personal diary entry 1948-34, Nourse Papers, Truman Library.
164. Nourse, *Economics in the Public Service*, pp. 228–30.
165. "Annual Message to the Congress on the State of the Union. January 5, 1949," *Public Papers, 1949*, pp. 3–4. Notes found in the Elsey papers (State of the Union Drafts folder 2) indicate that Walter Reuther may have influenced the specific mention of steel. The general notion of supply targets to be established by the government had been discussed within the administration for some time, and was a special favorite of Keyserling. For example, Leon H. Keyserling, "For 'A National Prosperity Budget,'" *New York Times Magazine*, January 9, 1949.

program now, while at the same time we must pursue those policies of adjustment and expansion which will be needed to promote balanced economic growth over the years."[166]

Behind the tentative proposal in the State of the Union Message for study of expanded production facilities in certain industries lay a concern that had affected administration approaches to inflation from the beginning—that restricted production in a few key industries could generate a cost-push increase in prices that would have ramifications throughout the economy. Attention was now focused squarely on steel. Several administration economists argued that the steel industry because of its oligopolistic character failed to respond to the stimuli that governed a competitive market. In particular, during periods of relatively full employment steel firms did not increase capacity in response to buoyant demand because of the potential oligopolistic gains from restraint or because they expected recession; as a result prices rose, the high prices cut off demand and reduced economic activity, and this bottleneck made recession inevitable. A memorandum of February 15 from Louis Bean of the Department of Agriculture discussed a draft statement on steel by Bertram Gross of the CEA staff. Bean claimed that "the shortage in steel and steel products in 1948 is in large measure responsible for a subnormal level of national productivity." He estimated the "cost" of steel shortages in terms of aggregate production forgone in 1948 at 10 percent of gross national product, or about $25 billion, and suggested that a "normally balanced economy" in 1949 would produce 100 million tons, although only 86 million tons were actually being produced. Bean saw steel as a cause of business fluctuation and inflation "well into the future" and called for "such cooperation between industry and Government as will lead to a stepped up expansion . . . thereafter, in line with the future growth in demand."[167] Bean observed that the historical record "nicely illustrates the effect of retarded expansion in one depression period on inflation in the subsequent full employment period, and the undermining of that full employment period by continued shortages."[168]

166. "Special Message to the Congress: The President's Economic Report. January 7, 1949," *Public Papers*, 1949, pp. 14, 18.

167. Bean, "Notes on the Relation of Steel to the Economy as a Whole," attachment to memorandum, Louis H. Bean to Bertram M. Gross, "Statement on Steel and Steel-Making Materials," February 15, 1949, Steel folder 1, David D. Lloyd Papers, Truman Library.

168. Bean to Gross, "Statement on Steel and Steel-Making Materials," p. 2. An advocate outside the CEA of the proposal in the State of the Union Message was

These strong anti-inflation proposals generated two types of questions both inside and outside government. The first type concerned principle: should the government take actions to fight inflation that might damage the entire economic system—that might create more ills than they would cure? From the rather vague proposal in the Economic Report (page 22) for "promotion of supply and production" the Council specifically dissociated itself. John D. Clark argued that such action would inject "so many uncertainties into the business world" that it could be justified only in a far greater emergency than currently existed. Clark feared "a process whereby some agency designated by the President may rush around the economy introducing government action of a kind no one can predict at any number of places no one can foretell."[169] Nourse said the scheme "would do as much as almost anything would to prejudice a cooperative spirit between business and government." Keyserling was fearful that responsibility for full employment and production might be lifted from the shoulders of business.[170] In their collective recommendation to the President the Council said, "We do not yet have sufficient information to advocate the enactment of these proposals at this time."[171]

But the most pointed questions about Truman's latest anti-inflation program concerned its timing. Increasingly and with more and more plausibility, commentators suggested that the government was fighting the last war. The Periodic Reports Committee of the Council observed as early as February 2 that "elements of weakness in prices and employment . . . require close watching."[172] In fact, at the beginning of 1949 America was just entering the postwar recession that had been widely predicted and feared for four years. The consumer price index for all items fell from 72.4 in the last quarter of 1948 to 71.7 in the first quarter of 1949, to 71.6 in the second quarter, and to 71.0 in the third. Wholesale prices ex-

C. Girard Davidson, an assistant secretary of the interior. See William O. Wagnon, Jr., "The Politics of Economic Growth: The Truman Administration and the 1949 Recession" (Ph.D. dissertation, University of Missouri, 1970), p. 59.

169. Memorandum, Clark to Nourse and Keyserling, January 14, 1949, CEA folder, Murphy Files, Truman Library.

170. Letter, Nourse to Clifford, January 3, 1949, and memorandum, Keyserling to Clifford, December 20, 1948, Elsey Papers, Truman Library.

171. Memorandum, CEA to the President, "Legislation to Effectuate Stabilization Policies," January 14, 1949. Letters and Memoranda (1948–49) folder, Clark Papers, Truman Library.

172. "Monthly Staff Report to the Council," February 2, 1949, Periodic Reports folder, Clark Papers, Truman Library.

perienced a steeper decline, from 82.7 in the fourth quarter of 1948 to 77.8 in the third quarter of 1949 (seasonally adjusted). Over the same period nonagricultural employment fell from 50.8 million to 49.8 million.[173]

For several months into 1949 the administration continued to warn of inflation; Nourse, who was the first Council member to change, later recalled that the CEA at this time received comment that was "often disparaging—but sometimes amused."[174] Only in March, after the Federal Reserve Board had already relaxed some credit controls, did Truman, on the advice of the Council, modify his position.[175] The following exchange occurred at his press conference of March 3:

Q. *Does this mean that the spiral is going down?*

THE PRESIDENT. *Not necessarily.*

Q. *Is it going up?*

THE PRESIDENT. *It's going both ways. (Laughter)*[176]

In his usual homely way Truman was giving a brief foretaste in 1949 of what would be known more than twenty years later as "stagflation."

As the spring went on there were continuing differences among government economists about proper policies. In mid-March Nourse spoke to the Executives' Club of Chicago on "The Gentle Art of Disinflation."[177] Yet at about the same time Clark argued that the present situation "affords a springboard from which renewed inflation might easily start," and he warned against "premature action in releasing controls and thereby freeing the forces of business expansion from all restraint."[178] The Periodic Re-

---

173. 1967 = 100 for the consumer and wholesale price indexes reported in this chapter; all are seasonally adjusted. See the appendix, tables A-7 to A-10.

174. *Economics in the Public Service*, p. 236. Nourse dissented from the majority position on the continuing danger of inflation in a memorandum, CEA to the President, "February Report," February 4, 1949, personal diary entry 1949-5, Nourse Papers, Truman Library. Especially embarrassing to Nourse was testimony of Keyserling and Clark about the dangers of inflation before the Joint Committee on the Economic Report in February. See also Truman's affirmation of the inflation danger; "The President's News Conference of February 10, 1949," *Public Papers*, 1949, p. 130.

175. The Council met with Truman on March 2 and confirmed to him by letter on March 8 that the situation was ambiguous, with some "remaining inflationary forces." Keyserling and Clark to the President, March 8, 1949, Monthly Reports folder, Clark Papers, Truman Library.

176. "The President's News Conference of March 3, 1949," *Public Papers*, 1949, p. 156.

177. *Economics in the Public Service*, p. 235.

178. John D. Clark, "Draft of Quarterly Report to the President," March 31, 1949, Quarterly and Monthly Reports folder, Clark Papers, Truman Library.

ports Committee of the Council, however, argued in April that now "the need for 'stand-by' control authority is certainly less urgent than the need for measures that provide support and stimulus to the economy."[179] Others in the administration were also continuing to fight inflation at this time. Without consulting the CEA, the secretary of agriculture proposed direct payments to farmers as a means of sustaining farm incomes while keeping food prices low.[180]

It was paradoxical, but also perhaps indicative of the problems encountered in long-range planning for economic policy, that some of the most serious discussions of secular inflation were completed in 1949, just as the danger was generally thought to be over. One of the best of these was "An Approach to Wage and Price Policies" by Paul Homan, the CEA staff member assigned to the problem.[181] Using a study by John C. Davis and Thomas K. Hitch,[182] Homan explored the feasibility of applying the cherished rule, which went back to the early days of the Council, that wage increases should be limited to the average increase in productivity at the community level. First, the government would have "to spell out the principle in quantitative terms, providing a statistical basis of productivity increase as a guide to particular negotiations." The second step "would be to intervene with advice and influence in order to affect the outcome of particular negotiations. . . . Probably public intervention would best be reserved for special cases of great importance." But Homan was clearly not optimistic, and he examined various well-known obstacles to price stability such as "bottleneck" industries and the proclivity of governments to use higher wages as a means of increasing the proportion of consumption in the gross national product. Almost by default he turned to a variant of the labor-management conference held in 1945, this time to be made "tripartite" by the addition of the federal government. There

179. "Staff Report—First Quarter, 1949," April 4, 1949, Periodic Reports folder, Clark Papers, Truman Library.
180. See Matusow, *Farm Policies*, chap. 9. In "Presidency and Legislation," p. 661, Richard Neustadt reported: "The so-called 'Brannan Plan' was first set forth informally in the shape of 'suggestions for study' put to congressional committees in testimony by the then Secretary of Agriculture."
181. An earlier CEA staff paper dealing with the problem was a memorandum, Donald Wallace to the Committee on Wage-Price Relations and Policies, "Some Explorations in Problems of Price-Wage-Profit Relations and Policies," August 9, 1948, CEA staff file, Nourse Papers, Truman Library.
182. Later published as "Wages and Productivity," in *Review of Economics and Statistics*, vol. 31 (November 1949), pp. 292–98.

"the public members would press upon the private members the dictates of public policy."[183] The novelty of Homan's concern should be stressed, as long-term continuing inflation was a new phenomenon.

In May the Council led by Keyserling told the President that "April developments remove still farther the possibility of a new spurt of inflation," and "there is not the need that there was previously for an all-out anti-inflation program." Instead attention should be paid primarily to relief of recession. Among the proposals put forth in January, the Council noted, the request for a study of ways to promote production and supply as a means of sustaining employment might still be supported; this would be in line with Title II of the administration's "Spence bill" then before Congress.[184] About American public and private activities abroad the Council was glad to note, "With a lessening of inflationary pressures it becomes more feasible to consider these programs in terms of the general requirements of national and world policy without the competing consideration of inflationary impact."[185]

By June even Clark was able to discern "strong indications that the inflationary forces have definitely subsided," and he feared that such events as major strikes, which earlier would have been inflationary, "under present circumstances would be depressing upon the economy."[186] Clark claimed that Truman's "many appeals for business moderation" and "similar admonitions within the business world itself" had helped restrain the inflation.

Official recognition of the change from inflation to recession came in

183. Paul Homan, "An Approach to Wage and Price Policies," April 27, 1949, CEA staff file, Nourse Papers, Truman Library.

184. This bill, H.R. 2756, introduced by Congressman Brent Spence of Kentucky, was designed to promote maximum employment, production, and purchasing power.

For a detailed account of the response of the Truman administration to this first postwar recession, see Wagnon, "The Politics of Economic Growth." He argues that Keyserling's emphasis on the need to stimulate growth became the economic rationale for the "Fair Deal." For additional comment on Keyserling's views, see Hamby, *Beyond the New Deal*, pp. 297–303. Walter Salant has described the Truman Council's emphasis on an expanding economy during this period in "Some Intellectual Contributions of the Truman Council of Economic Advisers to Policy-Making," *History of Political Economy*, vol. 5 (Spring 1973), pp. 36–49 (Brookings Reprint 269).

185. CEA to the President, "Appraisal of April Economic Developments and Issues of Current Policy and Action," May 5, 1949, Quarterly and Monthly Reports folder, Clark Papers, Truman Library, pp. 6–7.

186. Clark, "Proposed Draft of Council Report to President," June 3, 1949, ibid.

the President's midyear Economic Report and was explained by the President in a radio and television broadcast on July 13. Truman pointed out that he had long warned that if firm steps were not taken prices "would topple over and bring about a decline in production and employment."[187] Now that against which he had warned had come to pass.

The need for standby controls over prices and wages continued to receive some attention during the remainder of 1949 and even into the first half of 1950, especially in connection with the Spence "economic stability" bill and the economic expansion act (S. 281) of 1949 proposed by Senator James E. Murray. But the focus of these two bills was on the need for planning in the broadest sense, and in any event they both died in Congress. The CEA, which was torn by dissension during much of this period (culminating in Nourse's departure on November 1, 1949), turned to problems of growth and unemployment and to the immediate need for moderate deficit financing.[188] In the Economic Report for 1950 Truman could say for the first time that "prices now seem at or near a stable level consistent with continued expansion of business activity," and he even noted that "technological progress should in part be reflected in price reductions from time to time" while "wage adjustments" should follow increasing productivity.[189]

In January Keyserling, now acting chairman of the Council, told the Joint Committee on the Economic Report, "I say again, as I have said before, that the long-range and chronic problem of the American economy

187. "Special Message to the Congress: The President's Midyear Economic Report. July 11, 1949," *Public Papers*, 1949, p. 356; "Radio and Television Report to the American People on the State of the National Economy. July 13, 1949," ibid., p. 371.

188. See, for example, the defense of the federal deficit in a memorandum from Clark and Keyserling to the President, August 26, 1949, Letters and Memoranda (1948–49) folder, Clark Papers, Truman Library. Nourse disagreed with his Council colleagues about the desirability of deficit finance in other than serious depressions, because he believed it would generate secular inflation. Apparently this difference was one reason for his resignation. See his personal diary entries 1949-72 and 1949-75 for August 9 and 13, Nourse Papers, Truman Library. His skepticism of deficit financing is expressed in a memorandum, Nourse to the President, August 26, 1949, personal diary entry 1949-79, Nourse Papers, Truman Library. After leaving the Council Nourse developed his fear that dependence on deficit finance in minor recessions would lead first to accelerating inflation and in the end to a controlled economy; Edwin G. Nourse, *The 1950's Come First* (Holt, 1951).

189. "Annual Message to the Congress: The President's Economic Report. January 6, 1950," *Public Papers*, 1950, p. 25.

has been to prevent ultimate demand from falling behind productive capacity."[190] By April the Council was explaining more definitively to the President that "the insufficient expansion of consumer expenditures to maintain maximum production and employment is now a central problem of our economy." It was the first time that the Council had had to urge that "advancing productivity" be "translated more largely than it recently has been into wage and salary increases and other income gains." The Council saw stable prices with "rising levels of wages and other incomes" as the best of all worlds, and they stressed the power of moral suasion to make this possible: "The pronouncements by the President and by the Council with respect to sound price and wage and profit policies have had an observable effect upon the economy. They have influenced the course of business action."[191]

An important report by a group of experts appointed by the secretary-general of the United Nations (*National and International Measures for Full Employment*, published in 1949 by the UN) provided an occasion for the CEA to restate its position on macroeconomic issues in May 1950. The need for "wage-price-profit" policy, the Council said, was present in boom as in recession, to restrain demand as well as to stimulate it. However, general price control was appropriate only in conditions of "severe inflationary pressure" or "monopoly." "Voluntary" devices, such as labor-management conferences to supplement collective bargaining, were far preferable to controls when they could be made to work. Such devices were especially important in the United States, where the main long-run danger from inflation lay in "an upward pressure on money wage and price increases which may result from a sellers' market for labor."[192] By the

190. *January 1950 Economic Report of the President*, Hearings before the Joint Committee on the Economic Report, 81 Cong. 2 sess. (1950), p. 15.

191. Memorandum, CEA to the President, "Quarterly Report on the Economic Situation," April 17, 1950, Quarterly and Monthly Reports folder, Clark Papers, Truman Library, pp. 9, 11.

192. CEA, "Comments on U.N. Experts' Report: Recommendations Concerning Domestic Measures, May 1, 1950, Draft," Official File 396 (February 1950–December 1950), Truman Library, pp. 26–27. Optimism within the Truman administration about the effectiveness of "conferences" to settle distributive disputes went back, of course, to 1945. The device was discussed also by Paul Homan in his April 1949 report, "Approach to Wage and Price Policies," and in the 1950 *Economic Report of the President* (p. 9) as well as in the CEA's Annual Economic Review attached thereto (p. 101). For comments by professional economists, see Henry C. Wallich, "United Nations Report on Full Employment," *American Economic Review*, vol. 40 (December 1950), pp. 876–83; and Jacob Viner, "Full Employment at Whatever Cost," *Quarterly Journal of Economics*, vol. 64 (August 1950), pp. 385–407.

summer of 1950 some observers thought that serious inflation would soon become a danger again. But the Council assured government officials that "the unused human and industrial resources are still so large that we do not believe any inflation will develop which will be serious enough to forbid Government spending at a steady rate."[193] What threw this optimistic judgment far wide of the mark, as it had before and would again, was an unexpected development in foreign affairs.

Wartime Inflation Again: The Korean Emergency

The invasion of South Korea by North Korea on June 25, 1950, was as much of a surprise to government economists as it was to military planners. The first problem for everyone was to decide how serious the situation was and what the significance of the American commitment would be for the United States. Initially, President Truman steadfastly minimized the situation to the public. America, he said, was engaged only in a "police action," and severe shortages or inflation need not be expected.[194] But among Truman's advisers there was uncertainty and disagreement. How many troops would be required and for how long? How much money? Would the immediate agitation of Congress subside? Would the public accept a massive wartime program? The main policy dispute was over the degree of mobilization to be requested. Stuart Symington of the National Security Resources Board (NSRB) argued for a tough twenty-title "Emergency Powers Act." Averell Harriman, special assistant to the President, and Keyserling, now chairman of the Council, believed neither the Congress nor the country was prepared for full mobilization and recommended a more limited approach. The President accepted the latter position on July 15, and for the next four days a drafting team led by David Bell and George Elsey of the White House staff and Marshall Shulman from the State Department prepared a special message which went to Congress on July 19.[195]

The economic segment of the special message stressed the inherent

193. Letter, Keyserling and Clark to Frederick J. Lawton, director, Bureau of the Budget, April 28, 1950; and memorandum, CEA to the President, "June 1950 Report on the Economic Situation," June 14, 1950, Clark Papers, Truman Library.

194. "The President's News Conference of July 13, 1950," Public Papers, 1950, pp. 522–23.

195. George Elsey, memorandum for the file, "Preparation of President's Message to Congress on Korea, July 19, 1950," Message to Congress (July 19, 1950) folder, Elsey Papers, Truman Library.

strength of the American economy and recommended only modest policy changes, which were strongly reminiscent of those presented to Congress a few years before—in particular, authority for the allocation of materials, limits on nonessential government expenditure, higher taxes, credit restraint, and production loans. The Council's advice to the President on monetary policy was unchanged. Selective credit controls would be helpful, but no disturbance should be created in the market for government securities. Truman concluded: "If a sharp rise in prices should make it necessary, I shall not hesitate to recommend the more drastic measures of price control and rationing."[196] The President's midyear Economic Report on July 26 simply elaborated this moderate position.

But as the summer wore on and the news from Korea did not improve, pressure for more vigorous controls increased, especially from Congress, where Representative John C. Kunkel introduced a bill for a broad price freeze. Testimony from Bernard M. Baruch before the Senate Committee on Banking and Currency on July 26 calling for all-out mobilization, including price control and rationing, had a great impact. On August 1 Truman did write to the two committee chairmen considering the defense production bill, saying that he would be agreeable to "standby" wage, price, and rationing authority so long as he was allowed "wide discretion and flexibility" in its implementation.[197] Truman vigorously opposed any control program that would be general or automatic as recommended by Senators J. William Fulbright, Paul H. Douglas, and Ralph E. Flanders.[198] Unlike advice given in 1947 and 1948, Truman heard from economists in and out of government at this time that partial controls would not work; it must be all or nothing.[199]

Both Truman and leaders in Congress were determined that fiscal policy in this emergency should both learn from and be more enlightened than that of World War II. Above all, inflation should be prevented

196. "Special Message to the Congress Reporting on the Situation in Korea. July 19, 1950," *Public Papers*, 1950, pp. 534–36.

197. "Letter to Committee Chairmen on the Defense Production Bill. August 1, 1950," ibid., pp. 566–67.

198. See discussion of this point in "The President's News Conference of August 3, 1950," ibid., pp. 568–69; and an unsigned memorandum, "Major Difficulties with the Fulbright Amendment," August 4, 1950, Stephen J. Spingarn Files, Truman Library.

199. Examples are a letter, Richard Lester to the President, August 17, 1950, Official File DPA (1950), Truman Library, and a memorandum, Harold L. Enarson to David H. Stowe, "Summary of Conversation with George Taylor and W. Willard Wirtz," August 31, 1950, Spingarn Files, Truman Library.

through the limitation of effective demand by higher taxes. Senator O'Mahoney warned other members of the Joint Economic Committee on July 18 that "Russia is counting on us to bring about our own fiscal collapse by our failure to support necessary military outlays by increased taxes."[200] The sharply higher income and corporate taxes embodied in the Revenue Act of 1950, signed in September 1950, and the excess profits tax of January 1951 signaled a victory over budget deficits and monetary expansion as a means of financing the war. As it happened, this piece of fiscal policy lessened the need for the direct controls that were to follow.

Nevertheless, during August the attention of the White House was directed toward getting the defense production bill through Congress. Undoubtedly the relatively short time that had elapsed since World War II conditioned the responses of lobbyists and bureaucrats—as it did those of consumers, who rushed out to buy sugar, and businessmen, who built up inventories. Special interests representing business, agriculture, and labor exerted pressure for relief, to the point where Truman found it necessary to write a letter to the president of the Senate deploring the weakening of the bill.[201] Truman's economic advisers were particularly interested in whether there would be a single new agency, a coordinator of programs, or a distribution of powers among existing agencies.[202]

Truman signed the Defense Production Act on September 8 and authorized various agencies to exercise the new powers, coordinated by Stuart Symington, chairman of the NSRB. In a radio and television broadcast after signing the act Truman emphasized that he still saw inflation as one of the main dangers ahead, and he appealed for voluntary restraints on buying by consumers and businessmen and wage restraints in collective bargaining. He also announced proposals for additional taxes, for gathering information about prices and costs, and for establishing an Economic Stabilization Agency (ESA) headed by a stabilization administrator, an Office of Price Stabilization (OPS) with a director of price stabilization,

200. Letter, O'Mahoney to Joint Economic Committee members, July 18, 1950, Official File 396 (February 1950–December 1950), Truman Library. Senator Douglas also favored higher taxes.

201. "Letter to the President of the Senate on the Defense Production Bill. August 18, 1950," Public Papers, 1950, pp. 589–90.

202. Memorandum, Keyserling to Charles Murphy, "Your Check List on Economic Controls as discussed among us on Friday, August 18," August 21, 1950, DPA speech folder, Elsey Papers, Truman Library, and memorandum, CEA to the President, "Weekly Report on the Economic Situation," August 29, 1950, Quarterly and Monthly Reports folder, Clark Papers, Truman Library.

and a Wage Stabilization Board (WSB). The ESA would "go to work first on present danger spots," but "if these efforts fail, price ceilings and wage restrictions will have to follow." Truman expressed continuing concern that the standby controls given him by the act were not selective enough, too general in form.[203] He and others were particularly concerned that wage and price controls might be tied together and create problems of timing and inequities.

The NSRB set out to assemble a staff during September; this would include veterans of the World War II OPA. One of these was James F. Brownlee, who later became chief of staff for Alan Valentine of the ESA. He advised the White House to proceed very slowly with controls: "We are not now faced by an acute emergency in which drastic controls are essential to survival. . . . We must recognize that to try to freeze all wages and all prices now would be to perpetuate distortions and unfairness. In time, they might destroy the dynamic forces that have made the American economy great."[204] Alan Valentine, who became administrator of the ESA on October 7, held views even stronger than these. Although he was given responsibility for administering a program of "direct" controls, he put most of his faith in the indirect tools of monetary and fiscal policy. He wrote in a private memorandum in November: "Price and wages controls do not prevent but only postpone (and possibly direct a little) inflation and conceal it. No use to tie on lid unless you are also turning down the fire under the pot."[205]

Despite the optimism of the President's statement on September 9, the Budget Bureau was estimating inflation of 8 to 10 percent for the year, and the CEA less than a week later expressed mounting concern that, unless the moderate program it favored of still higher taxes, credit restraint, and compulsory allocation of some commodities was pursued with greater vigor, the government could be in serious trouble. Keyserling and Clark issued the following somber warning: "If the avoidable inflation comes because our effort is half-hearted, the cost of the expanding defense program will be incalculably higher, the damage to the economy will be

203. "Radio and Television Address to the American People Following the Signing of the Defense Production Act. September 9, 1950," *Public Papers, 1950*, pp. 626–31.
204. Memorandum from Brownlee, September 5, 1950, DPA speech folder, Elsey Papers, Truman Library.
205. Cited in Gardner Ackley, "Selected Problems of Price Control Strategy, 1950–1952" (Defense History Program, manuscript, 1953; copies in White House Office Library and on microfilm, Record Group 295, National Archives), p. 106.

great, and the public reaction against all those in authority will be severe. Moreover, if the tax, credit, and allocation powers which should be adequate if used in time are delayed or dissipated, the need for extensive price and wage controls will become imperative. We will then find ourselves in the unfortunate position, without a general war, of trying to administer a type and variety of direct controls which it will be terribly difficult to administer effectively without the degree of popular support and cooperation which was accorded during the actual course of World War II."[206]

Keyserling, in particular, found the situation especially complicated because of the danger that controls might be either too weak or too strong: "Controls in excess of necessity would discourage maximum production for the long pull." He saw the Korean conflict as in all probability only the beginning of a long cold war struggle with communism in which America would ultimately triumph because of its strong economy. To achieve this end the government should establish "overall targets or goals," "fire the American people with a resolution," and provide the necessary minimal regulations. "But preoccupation with controls should not further divert public attention from the truth that production, and still more production, is the greatest of all the nonsecret weapons in the arsenal of American democracy."[207] Keyserling counted on Title III of the Defense Production Act to get the "right" goods produced by funneling "scarce" materials to "essential" uses.[208]

During the early autumn of 1950, as far as economic advisers in government could see, two contrary trends were in operation. In Korea the "police action" was proceeding well and did not appear to need any new legislation. The United Nations forces, after initial setbacks, recovered lost ground and by October appeared near victory. On the home front, on the other hand, inflation mounted at a disturbing rate. The CEA kept the President apprised of the danger. The problem, the Council pointed out, was that normal recovery from a recession with a modest increase of prices had been greatly accentuated by defense expenditures and anticipation of a war economy. Expectations of high returns had caused "a surprisingly

206. Memorandum, CEA to the President, September 12, 1950, Clark Papers, Truman Library.
207. Leon H. Keyserling, "Production: America's Great Non-Secret Weapon," speech delivered to the Herald Tribune Forum, New York, October 23, 1950, Official File 985 (1949–50), Truman Library.
208. Memorandum, Keyserling to Lawton, August 23, 1950, Murphy Files, Truman Library; and memorandum, CEA to the President, October 19, 1950, Clark Papers, Truman Library, pp. 7–8, 11–12.

large number . . . of corporations" to offer wage increases "although no negotiations for new contracts had been under way." On September 26 the Council reported that "the price-wage spiral is already under way, and it will accelerate."[209]

The development of wage-price policy during the early months of the Korean War soon became very much like a reverse, or mirror, image of events during the previous five years. In 1945 President Truman and his advisers had concluded that America at peace would not tolerate a system of tight controls. But they had quickly found that the alternative restraints on inflation open to them were of limited effectiveness. Fiscal policy was hampered by pressures for normal peacetime expenditures and Congress was reluctant to maintain high taxes. Monetary policy was crippled by the widely accepted need to stabilize the bond market. Hortatory statements to labor, management, and consumers seemed of little use and doubtful morality. Partial controls were unwieldy and unpopular. By 1948, when secular inflation gave promise of becoming permanent, Truman's advisers were thinking more and more of some long-term systemic adjustments to bring pressure to bear on major noncompetitive segments of the economy, especially labor markets and oligopolistic industries—only to have the problem temporarily submerged by recession. In policy, the early months of the Korean emergency put the economists back to 1945–48. The circumstances of the conflict, like the immediate postwar years, were not sufficiently critical to justify full mobilization and controls, and yet the government in this interim situation did not have the capacity (or perhaps the will) to constrain the pressures generated by a mounting defense budget and attendant expectations. After the initial success of the September tax increase, passed in the first flush of emergency, Congress was reluctant to raise rates further and strenuously resisted proposals from Truman for an excess profits tax in November. The tax was enacted only after stormy debate.[210]

Discussions of the anti-inflationary weapons open to government and the constraints upon them from July to November 1950, like the economic conditions, were remarkably like those of 1945–48. And the results were similar as well: the consumer price index rose from 71.2 in the second

209. Memorandum, CEA to the President, "Special Report on Economic Trends and Policies," September 26, 1950, Letters and Memoranda (1950) folder, Clark Papers, Truman Library.
210. See Holmans, United States Fiscal Policy, chaps. 8 and 9.

quarter of 1950 to 74.0 in the fourth quarter, the wholesale price index from 79.3 to 86.9. Even familiar "bottlenecks" in steel and construction returned, together with venerable Republican critics like Senator Taft, who said the problem lay with unreasonable unions and government extravagance at home.[211] The CEA, as it had before, continued to urge higher taxes, tightened priorities, and limitations on consumer credit.

The entrance of the People's Republic of China into the Korean War in November 1950 simplified the problems facing government economists. It removed them from a situation analogous to that of 1945-48, with which they had not yet learned to deal, to one of real national emergency in which, it seemed, wartime controls and full mobilization were not only unquestionably needed but would in all probability be widely tolerated.

The Council as well as other economic advisers in the government lost no time in telling the President their views about what should be done at this new critical time. The only major difference among them was over the most desirable speed at which to move to full controls. John D. Clark, Stuart Symington, and Senator O'Mahoney, chairman of the Joint Economic Committee, favored an immediate freeze, while Keyserling, Roy Blough (who had joined the Council in June), Alan Valentine of ESA, Steelman, and others favored a series of steps during which the administrative machinery could be set up and appropriate consultations could be held with political and social groups to preserve national unity.[212] Both Symington and Valentine, although differing on the best rate of implementation, agreed on the desirability of the President's appealing to businessmen—"on their honor"—to restrain prices. The criticism Clark made of this device, which was termed "jawboning" by some observers at the time, is worth recounting, because it would be repeated so often by critics in later years. He said: "The businessman who does not increase his price as he will have the lawful right to do will gain nothing but a right to a medal. The scalawag who does increase his prices gets immediate profit....

211. At a news conference in November Truman replied to a charge by Taft that higher taxes would, in fact, be inflationary. "The President's News Conference of November 16, 1950," *Public Papers, 1950*, p. 715.

212. Memorandum, CEA to the President, "Further Action on Price and Wage Controls," December 7, 1950, Official File 985 (1949–50); George M. Elsey, memorandum for the file, "Meeting of the President on the Economic Situation . . . December 11, 1950," Economic Mobilization Meeting folder, Elsey Papers; memorandum, O'Mahoney to Valentine, December 6, 1950, Charles S. Murphy Papers; all in the Truman Library.

If businessmen are to be denied the lawful right to make their own prices, the President should not bring this about by the coercion of threats; he should act under the law to fix the lawful price."[213]

Truman accepted the gradualist approach and announced this policy to the nation on December 15, when he declared a national emergency.[214] The difficulties that the ESA quickly ran into with its initial concentration on industrial materials and manufactured articles were pointed out to the President at a press conference by a reporter who said he had the "impression that we are holding the line on Cadillacs but not on food."[215]

A principle underlying wage-price policy in wartime is that the control of inflation ceases to be an end and becomes instead a means to obtaining the real goal of victory. Robert Turner of the White House staff expressed this well when he wrote to Keyserling on December 28: "If inflation control were the only objective, it would theoretically be possible to achieve it . . . by fiscal and monetary policy alone. But inflation control is, after all, only a subsidiary objective. The main objective is ultimate victory. Direct price control can help to achieve this objective."[216] A theme of the advice given the President by the CEA during this period was that the country must be made to appreciate the impossibility of having a full measure of guns and butter at the same time. Keyserling explained that some of the Fair Deal objectives would have to be held in abeyance. "We cannot put so much more of our resources into national defense and yet do all of these other things, and it will not take a Harvard economist to detect the gross discrepancy."[217]

An Era of Tight Controls

During the first half of 1951 the economic mobilization with broad controls decided upon in December 1950 was gradually put into effect. Many of the problems encountered in the process were of administrative

213. Comment by John D. Clark on seventh draft of December 12, 1950, National Emergency Speech folder, Murphy Files, Truman Library.

214. "Radio and Television Report to the American People on the National Emergency. December 15, 1950," *Public Papers*, 1950, pp. 741–46.

215. "The President's News Conference of December 28, 1950," ibid., p. 761. Truman's reply was "No comment." The ESA had issued its first and only mandatory freeze order—on automobiles—on December 17.

216. Memorandum, Turner to Keyserling, December 28, 1950, Official File 396 (February 1950–December 1950), Truman Library.

217. Memorandum, Keyserling to Murphy, January 5, 1951, Murphy Files, Truman Library.

strategy and need receive only brief attention here.[218] The magnitude of the challenge was spelled out on January 12 in the President's Economic Report. During 1951, Truman said, using Defense Department estimates, the proportion of national output directed to defense had to rise from 7 to nearly 18 percent. Consequently, the potential for inflation was very great, which would "undermine production, destroy confidence, generate friction and economic strife, impair the value of the dollar, dissipate the value of savings, and impose an intolerable burden upon fixed income groups. . . . This is why we must have a stringent stabilization program."[219] He requested economic stabilization powers consisting of higher taxes, more stringent credit limitations, and price and wage controls.[220] During January Truman announced a "National Manpower Mobilization Policy" and a "Materials Policy Commission" (headed by William S. Paley) to study ways of preventing shortages of materials from jeopardizing national security and creating bottlenecks to future "economic expansion."[221] The sense of urgency and concern that prevailed in America at this time about shortages of materials and rising commodity prices determined on world markets was not equaled again until the oil crisis of 1973. The prospect of inflation generated abroad was part of the reason for the worry, but an additional element was the sense that somehow foreigners had gained a role in determining the nation's destiny.

A full freeze was delayed until the end of January, at least partly by controversy among senior advisers, especially ESA Administrator Valentine, who wanted to go slowly, and OPS Director Michael V. DiSalle,

218. Economic aspects of the Korean mobilization have been dealt with in Flash, *Economic Advice and Presidential Leadership*; Hamby, *Beyond the New Deal*, chap. 20; Bert G. Hickman, *The Korean War and United States Economic Activity, 1950–1952*, Occasional Paper 49 (National Bureau of Economic Research, 1955); and Ackley, "Selected Problems." Ackley was economic adviser to the OPS.

219. "Annual Message to the Congress: The President's Economic Report. January 12, 1951," *Public Papers*, 1951, p. 32. In his study of this period Ackley wrote: "On the matter of national security expenditures, the record continues to be one of gross overestimate of the future level and rate of increase of such expenditures. . . . Actually, the *staff* of the Council of Economic Advisers was much more cautious in its appraisal of defense spending prospects than it was possible for the Council to be in its published statements. Staff of the Council and the Bureau of the Budget were constantly working to get more realism into estimates originating with the Department of Defense." "Selected Problems," p. 509.

220. "Economic Report," *Public Papers*, 1951, pp. 41–44.

221. "Memorandum Establishing a National Manpower Mobilization Policy. January 17, 1951," ibid., pp. 108–10, and "Letter to William S. Paley on the Creation of the President's Materials Policy Commission. January 22, 1951," ibid., p. 118.

who urged speed. Growing evidence of the difficulty in implementing partial controls was also a determinant. For example, Harold Enarson, in the White House, explained that the Wage Stabilization Board believed: "Selective wage control is impossible; it simply won't work."[222] On January 26, by which time Valentine had resigned and such authorities as Chairman Burnet R. Maybank of the Senate Banking and Currency Committee were claiming that the country was on the brink of disaster, the Office of Price Stabilization "issued a General Ceiling Price Regulation (16 F.R. 808), freezing prices on most commodities and services at the highest levels charged between December 19, 1950, and January 25, 1951." At the same time, by order of the WSB (16 F.R. 816), wages and other compensation were frozen at the rates paid on January 25.[223] On February 2 Truman recommended to Congress a "pay as we go" tax program for reasons of fiscal responsibility, equity, and "to help prevent inflation."[224]

In a memorandum of February 26 Truman asked for a study of how best, in the current emergency, to reconcile the conflicting goals of credit restraint and debt refinance. He received his response in part through a joint statement on March 3 from the Treasury Department and the Federal Reserve System, which said they were now in full "accord" on common goals,[225] and in a report from the director of defense mobilization on May 17, which said the two goals were not inconsistent if appropriate techniques for credit restraint were employed. What the accord meant, of course, was that the Federal Reserve had at last gained its freedom from Treasury hegemony. This was a new policy road and hard for Truman to accept. In effect it meant that his long-cherished goal of preserving the money value of government bonds must now be sacrificed to what others argued was the greater good of protecting the value of the currency by

222. Memorandum, Enarson to Murphy, December 15, 1950, Murphy Files, Truman Library.

223. "The President's News Conference of January 25, 1951," *Public Papers*, 1951, pp. 124–25; "Memorandum Urging Agency Cooperation in Enforcing Price and Wage Stabilization Orders. January 27, 1951," ibid., p. 127, note.

224. "Special Message to the Congress Recommending a 'Pay as We Go' Tax Program. February 2, 1951," ibid., pp. 134–35.

225. "Memorandum Requesting a Study of the Problems of Debt Management and Credit Controls. February 26, 1951," ibid., pp. 163–66, and "Statement by the President in Response to a Joint Announcement by the Treasury Department and the Federal Reserve System. March 3, 1951," ibid., pp. 179–80. For a more detailed description of the accord, see Stein, *Fiscal Revolution in America*, chap. 10, especially pp. 271–77; G. L. Bach, *Making Monetary and Fiscal Policy* (Brookings Institution, 1971), pp. 78–85; and Eccles, *Beckoning Frontiers*, pp. 479–99.

restrictive monetary policy. John D. Clark of the CEA agreed with the President's decision but continued to express doubt about the merit of monetary policy.

As any economist knows from his first course in principles, a price freeze in a complex free economy is bound to generate innumerable problems, and 1951 was no exception. One of the first appeared in the labor field, where in February representatives of labor withdrew from mobilization agencies, charging that workers were being asked to absorb the lion's share of the costs of a tough stabilization program in which the machinery was dominated by big business, in particular by Charles E. Wilson, director of the recently created Office of Defense Mobilization (ODM) and former president of General Electric.[226] The CEA, which as a staff agency was outside the stabilization process, tried to enter this issue by suggesting that flexibility lay in fringe benefits.[227] It took the creation of yet another body, the National Advisory Board on Mobilization Policy, to bring labor and management representatives back together again.

Another problem was in agriculture where the sacred principles of parity (a primitive form of what is now called "indexing") came into conflict with stabilization.[228] Moreover, the subsidies of World War II, which might have been one solution, were remembered bitterly by farmers. A most controversial action was taken by OPS Director DiSalle in late April to control the price of meat: he called for price cuts of 20 percent, to take place in three steps. This action highlighted a third broad problem—the correction of the so-called inequities that existed when the freeze was imposed; either "roll-forwards" or rollbacks were bound to disturb a fragile equilibrium, and of course an increase in one man's equity was another's exploitation.

226. Memorandum, Richard Neustadt to Charles Murphy, "The Current Crisis on Wage Stabilization," February 16, 1951, David H. Stowe Papers, Truman Library. The main issue was the justice of "Regulation 6," which prohibited wage increases more than 10 percent above levels of January 15, 1950, without prior WSB approval.

227. Memorandum, Keyserling to Murphy, February 27, 1951, CEA folder, Murphy Files, Truman Library.

228. See Matusow, *Farm Policies*, chap. 10; Ackley, "Selected Problems," pp. 253–54. On beef, see Ackley, pp. 422ff. Ackley states: "The fact is, that so long as 100% of parity is required, product by product, as the minimum level for agricultural ceilings, any price control will inevitably contain a serious hole" (p. 254). He notes from the experience of this time that meat's "importance seems far to transcend its share in national output or consumer expenditure. The cost of living is high when hamburger, or T-bone steak, is expensive. Price control works well if beef is available, of good quality, and low in price" (p. 423).

With the ESA at the center of the action in 1951 the CEA clearly felt neglected. It took as its role provision of general commentary on the performance of government programs and their implications for the future. It repeatedly brought to the President's attention such conclusions as: (1) inflationary forces were likely to increase over time as defense expenditures took effect; (2) the Federal Reserve action in raising interest rates was liable to cause considerable harm; selective controls should have been used instead; (3) a new planning effort should be undertaken for "rigorous programming of competing requirements," preferably using the Council as "a general economic staff"; (4) farm prices should be controlled as thoroughly as others; (5) firmer action on the entire price front would lead to "more effective stabilization on the labor or farm front" as well; in particular, price increases should not be granted where profits were more than 85 percent of those in the three best years, 1946–49; (6) every effort should be made to get Congress to raise taxes; (7) wage increases should be made only if price control was ineffective; anti-inflationary fringe benefits should be explored; and (8) the importance of increased capacity and supply should not be overlooked when implementing controls.[229]

Understandably the stabilization administrators were not overjoyed by this critical commentary from CEA. A major bone of contention was whether questions of "equity" among businesses should be submerged and a much tougher stand taken with all profitable firms, as Keyserling recommended; such a policy was defended as a basis for a firm line toward other segments of the economy. At a meeting on April 11, where tempers ran high, one participant's memory of the reply made by Gardner Ackley of the ESA to Keyserling on this point was, "Your proposal (CEA) is illegal, unsound, and, beyond that, utterly impractical."[230] It is noteworthy that during this period the CEA under Keyserling often found itself presenting the political dimensions of issues to supplement the mainly economic interpretation offered by economists in other parts of the government. Keyserling's characteristic reply to the stabilization administrators was, "Your policy is impossible in terms of labor's reaction to it."[231]

229. These and other points were developed in a memorandum, CEA to the President, "Quarterly Report on the Economic Situation," April 6, 1951, Official File 985 (1951–53), Truman Library.

230. Memorandum, Harold L. Enarson to David H. Stowe, "Conference on Price Policy, April 11, 1951," Price Stabilization Issues folder, Enarson Papers, Truman Library, p. 7. Also see Ackley, "Selected Problems," pp. 326–30.

231. "Conference on Price Policy," p. 9.

The OPS issued *interim* pricing standards for manufactured goods in late April and for machinery in early May which allowed for a pass-through, by price increases, of higher direct costs from certain base periods, regardless of profit rates. This "self-administering" feature was described as necessary until "tailored regulations" for particular industries could be prepared.[232]

The attention of government economists during the late spring and summer of 1951 was taken up primarily with preparing a case for the renewal of the Defense Production Act in a satisfactory form. For this purpose the relatively hawkish position of the CEA on inflation was used both internally and externally. For example, a special "up-to-the-minute appraisal of the economic situation and outlook" prepared for the President by the Council on June 5 was released to the press three days later. This report predicted that "inflationary pressures" would soon "be stronger than any yet confronted since the initial Korean outbreak," and it called for higher taxes, credit restraint, and "firm stabilization of prices" through controls for "two years or so."[233] In public pronouncements Truman repeatedly used the language of economics mixed with that of politics to appeal for the means to close the "inflationary gap" which he expected to persist for two to three years.[234] In a "Radio and Television Report to the American People on the Need for Extending Inflation Controls" on June 14, Truman added pathos to the debate by reading letters from average citizens who were suffering from rising prices. Again his message was that despite some illusory signs of relief "the full force of inflationary pressure is still to come," and he appealed for members of Congress not to let the National Association of Manufacturers and other lobbyists fool them again into believing, as they had in 1946, that direct controls were unnecessary.[235] Truman knew that he was facing bitter criticism not only

232. See testimony of Michael V. DiSalle in *Defense Production Act Amendments of 1951*, Hearings before the Senate Committee on Banking and Currency, 82 Cong. 1 sess. (1951), p. 2893.

233. CEA to the President, June 5, 1951, Press Conference Statement folder, Elsey Papers, Truman Library. Charles Murphy had suggested to the President in April that the Council's tough quarterly report be used "as a teeing off point" with the Office of Price Stabilization, whose policy "seems to most of us to be too liberal." Memorandum, Murphy to the President, "Stabilization Problems," April 8, 1951, Charles E. Wilson–ODM folder, Murphy Files, Truman Library.

234. For example, "Remarks at a Conference of the Industry Advisory Councils of the Department of the Interior. May 9, 1951," *Public Papers*, 1951, pp. 272–73, and "The President's News Conference of June 7, 1951," ibid., pp. 320–21.

235. *Public Papers*, 1951, pp. 333–38. An extensive letter on inflation from Tru-

from the NAM but from many segments of the economy which believed they had been excessively injured, especially the meat producers and individual firms such as Westinghouse Electric.

In fact, the act, which was finally passed at the end of July, was declared by the President to be gravely deficient. In particular it prohibited all price rollbacks, established ceilings based on percentage markups over costs instead of dollar prices, and wiped out quotas on slaughtering beef, opening the way to black markets supplied by unregulated packinghouses. The ESA report to the President on the act described it in the harshest of terms, using a wealth of hyperbole. The "Capehart formula" for flexible ceilings "crashes aimlessly through present pricing formulas like a bulldozer." The act itself "will cause prices to rise like a gas-filled balloon on a windy day."[236] Truman signed the act on the ground that there was no realistic alternative, but once again he could announce to the American people that special interests and an uncooperative Congress had guaranteed a damaging rate of inflation upon which he could have only limited influence.[237]

Despite the dark predictions of July, inflation moved relatively slowly during the rest of 1951. The consumer price index rose from 77.7 in the third quarter to only 78.8 in the fourth, and wholesale prices remained almost stable. This pleasant turn of events precipitated some predictable division within the CEA between Clark, who thought he detected a "softening," and Keyserling, who still believed that the worst had only been delayed and was around the corner.[238] These differing views were evident in Council advice on the 1953 budget and undoubtedly weakened the CEA's effect. The Council's contribution to a series of studies called

man to a "fairly representative middle class housewife" was released on July 19. "Letter to Mrs. C. Irving Guyer on the Need for Controlling Inflation. July 19, 1951," ibid., pp. 400–01. The "Special Message to the Congress: The President's Midyear Economic Report. July 23, 1951," ibid., pp. 411–17, dealt extensively with the need for tough controls.

236. Memorandum from the General Counsel, ESA, "Defense Production Act Amendments of 1951," July 30, 1951, Official File DPA (1951), Truman Library.

237. "Statement by the President upon Signing the Defense Production Act Amendments. July 31, 1951," Public Papers, 1951, pp. 435–37, and "Special Message to the Congress After Further Review of the Defense Production Act Amendments. August 23, 1951," ibid., pp. 478–83.

238. See memorandum, Keyserling to Clark and Roy Blough, "Comment on draft of Monthly Report," September 7, 1951, and Clark, "Draft of Monthly Report," September 7, 1951, Clark Papers, Truman Library.

NSC 114 (still classified in 1974) seemed to one reader to have a strange "split personality." The Keyserling portion (supported subsequently by a letter from Keyserling to the President) spoke of the U.S. capacity to stand a much larger military effort if there were "vigorous enough government direction of the economy." The Clark-Blough portion, on the other hand, warned of "the economic and political infeasibilities of getting and keeping the kind of fiscal policy and inflation controls needed to sustain a higher level and longer continued military buildup."[239]

By the fall of 1951 both wage and price regulation under the new Defense Production Act had been worked out. The OPS on November 9 began to issue regulations implementing Senator Homer E. Capehart's amendment providing for the pass-through of costs. "Tailored regulations" for specific industries were found to be so time-consuming that they were limited to highly "speculative" markets (e.g., used machine tools, feathers and down, brass and bronze ingots).[240] The Wage Stabilization Board for its part attempted "to 'unscramble the mess' which the country's wage structure had gotten into during the turbulent year of 1950,"[241] while at the same time attempting to reconcile the potentially conflicting goals of industrial peace, free collective bargaining, and maximum defense production. Escalator clauses related to the cost of living were introduced into agreements at the insistence of labor.[242] Wage increases to reflect improvements in productivity remained in dispute.

The old and troublesome problem of wages and prices in the steel industry emerged prominently toward the end of 1951. In a sense this industry symbolized the difficulties of limiting inflation in any oligopolistic industry that was dominated by a powerful union and produced goods critical to the war effort. The objectives of maintaining a willing and efficient labor force, maximum production, and price stability seemed impossible to attain simultaneously. When strikes threatened, as they did in steel, the question became which goal or goals should be sacrificed so

239. Richard Neustadt, who described the Council study, added, "I can't get over the impression that Leon really thinks war is inevitable." Memorandum, Neustadt to Murphy, "NSC 114 and Leon Keyserling's letter to the President," November 17, 1951, National Security Council folder, Murphy Files, Truman Library.

240. Ackley, "Selected Problems," pp. 444–82.

241. George Taylor to Eric Johnston, "A Report on Wage Stabilization," August 31, 1951, Taylor Papers, Truman Library.

242. See Benjamin C. Roberts, *National Wages Policy in War and Peace* (London: Allen and Unwin, 1958), p. 71.

that the others could be achieved, or what fundamental changes in the economic system should be introduced to make all the goals attainable at once.

The Council advised the President to take a tough line with the steel companies and the union, both because the product was crucial and because whatever was done would become a pattern throughout the economy. It recommended that the President "announce a firm policy of holding the general price line" and at the same time announce permission for modest wage increases to cover increases in the cost of living and other small increases in proportion to productivity gains throughout the whole economy (estimated by the Council at about 2 percent). The Council predicted confidently that "quantitative analysis can establish guides to allowable wage increases under this principle." Unless such firm announcements were made, it insisted, the government was likely to be faced with an inflationary package of wage and price increases from the union and firms that could not be resisted. The recommended policy could either lay the basis for arbitration or set the limits for collective bargaining. But in either event the government must not back down.[243]

The playing out of the steel industry drama has been described adequately elsewhere.[244] Briefly it went as follows. Bargaining got nowhere because the companies insisted on settling the price issue first. The OPS "leaked" the information that neither the industry earnings standard nor the Capehart amendment would allow the increases demanded by the industry. But the government, after talking tough, had backed down in 1946. On December 22 the President referred the dispute between the United Steelworkers of America and the steel companies, which was at an impasse, to the Wage Stabilization Board.[245] On March 20, 1952, independent of the OPS and the White House, the Board recommended a substantial wage increase and a modified union shop. The CEA told the

243. Memorandum, CEA to the President, "Prices and Wages in the Steel Industry," November 28, 1951, Letters and Memoranda (1951–52) folder, Clark Papers, Truman Library.

244. See especially Grant McConnell, *The Steel Seizure of 1952*, Inter-University Case Program, no. 52 (University of Alabama Press for ICP, 1960; Bobbs-Merrill, 1970); Charles Sawyer, *Concerns of a Conservative Democrat* (Southern Illinois University Press, 1968), pp. 255–77; Richard E. Neustadt, *Presidential Power: The Politics of Leadership* (Wiley, 1960), pp. 13–16, 21–25.

245. "Statement by the President on the Labor Dispute in the Steel Industry. December 22, 1951," *Public Papers*, 1951, pp. 651–52.

President that the Board's recommendations "in their long-range impact
... may be somewhat out of line, but they are not very seriously out of
line, with the broad principles of wage policy that have been set forth in
various Economic Reports of the President." The Council suggested that
the President not "tamper with these recommendations now" and that he
allow only modest price increases in accordance with the Capehart amendment to the Defense Production Act while requiring the remaining additions to wages to come from profits. It is mildly amusing to find the
Council on this occasion reminding the President that "more than pure
economics is involved in the current situation." The Council blamed the
"current crisis" on disorganization within the government itself, which
had not provided for a "unified policy on wages and prices."[246]

Within the administration there was fundamental disagreement over
the proposed settlement and the extent to which the steel companies
should be required to absorb the cost of wage increases. Director of Defense Mobilization Wilson stated publicly that the settlement threatened
the entire stabilization program. This culminated on March 30 in Truman's acceptance of Wilson's resignation. John Steelman, ever ready to
fill a breach, was appointed his successor on an interim basis.[247] On April
8, after the steel firms had rejected the proposed terms, to avert a strike
that seemed imminent Truman ordered federal seizure of the steel plants.
In a radio and television address to the nation explaining his action Truman gave as his short-run goal uninterrupted war production.[248] But the
ultimate objective was "to prevent a wage-price spiral that would send
prices through the roof, and wreck our economy and our defense program." Truman said the proposed settlement was "fair and reasonable"
and for the government to make further price concessions "would be a
terrible blow to the stability of the economy of the United States of
America." "If we knuckled under to the steel industry, the lid would be

---

246. Memorandums, CEA to the President, "Need for a Unified Government
Policy in the Steel Matter," and "Current Issues in the Steel Industry," March 28,
1952, Letters and Memoranda (1950–52) folder, Clark Papers, Truman Library.
247. See "Letter Accepting Resignation of Charles E. Wilson as Director of
Defense Mobilization. March 30, 1952," *Public Papers, 1952–53*, pp. 226–27; and
Harold L. Enarson, memorandum for the file, "Events Relating to Charlie Wilson's
Resignation," April 1, 1952, Memos (September 1951–July 1952) folder, Enarson
Papers, Truman Library.
248. This was on the advice of Secretary of Defense Robert A. Lovett, who insisted there could be no interruption of steel production.

off."[249] Only ten days after announcing that he would not be a candidate for reelection Truman had, in fact, taken the toughest anti-inflation stand of his administration. Radical and dramatic though the action appeared to most observers, it was in fact perfectly consistent with the policy on steel recommended by the CEA in 1949. Truman's critics argued that he should have invoked the provisions of the Taft-Hartley Act instead, but that action, Truman said, would simply have avoided the fundamental issues in the conflict.

Seizure of the steel plants aroused heated controversy throughout the country, and Truman was charged with, among other things, ignoring the importance of the union shop provision of the proposed settlement and of opening the way for socialism or totalitarian controls.[250] The issue of seizure was settled on June 2, when the Supreme Court ruled it unconstitutional, but the deeper question came to the surface again later in the month when the long-awaited strike took place. A settlement was finally reached at the White House on July 24. Because of the complex psychological impact of the strike, government economists were uncertain whether its effects were inflationary or deflationary.[251]

As early as the end of 1951 some government economists had begun to worry that the Korean conflict had simply camouflaged conditions that in peacetime would have created a recession. For example, in December William McChesney Martin, Jr., of the Federal Reserve could see powerful deflationary forces which "but for the pressures of the defense program might have plunged us into depression." He "stayed awake nights wondering what we would do to sustain our prosperity if we did not have the defense program."[252] But administration statements, on the advice of the Council, remained cautious. The 1952 State of the Union Message announced that a "critical part of our defense job this year is to keep down inflation," and the Economic Report warned that there was still need for higher taxes, more savings, and continued credit, price, and wage controls

249. "Radio and Television Address to the American People on the Need for Government Operation of the Steel Mills. April 8, 1952," *Public Papers*, 1952–53, pp. 246–50.

250. For instance, "Letter to C. S. Jones in Response to Questions on the Steel Situation. April 27, 1952," ibid., pp. 299–301; and questions at "The President's News Conference of May 1, 1952," ibid., p. 308.

251. Memorandum, Robert C. Turner to John Steelman, "Is the Steel Strike Inflationary or Deflationary?" July 23, 1952, Turner Papers, Truman Library.

252. Memorandum, Enarson to Steelman, "December 17–18 Meeting of the President's Mobilization Advisory Board," January 2, 1952, Memos (September 1951–July 1952) folder, Enarson Papers, Truman Library.

to curb "an inflationary outburst."[253] The perennial campaign for the maintenance of the Defense Production Act, in 1952 as before, was based on the claim that "the potential pressures toward inflation are now greater than they were when the price upsurge took place a little more than a year ago."[254] In its report to the President for the first quarter of 1952 the Council conceded that prices and wages were indeed remaining relatively stable, and "there are deflationary as well as inflationary possibilities which require close study." But, undoubtedly with the experience of 1945–46 in mind, the Council concluded cautiously: "It is essential to resist premature decontrol, both of materials and of prices and wages." A range of very uncertain macroeconomic variables could be discerned by the Council; this included defense needs, consumer spending patterns, and a "strengthening of opinion in business circles that, barring new international crises, our present stability is more likely to issue into a deflationary rather than an inflationary problem."[255]

By June of 1952, with prices almost stable during the first two quarters and peace in Korea clearly not far off, decontrol had to be in the air. The economists in the administration were divided about how to proceed; their advice varied according to their perceptions of events as well as of self-interest. The Council joined with the Treasury and the Commerce departments in arguing that it was unfair and unwise to relax some indirect controls such as those over credit, as the Federal Reserve had done, while direct controls remained in effect.[256] Despite the difference in views the President's midyear Economic Report in July was remarkable for its continued emphasis on the danger of inflation and for its concession that mild secular inflation might not after all be the worst of all worlds: "It is

253. "Annual Message to the Congress on the State of the Union. January 9, 1952," *Public Papers*, 1952–53, p. 14, and "Annual Message to the Congress: The President's Economic Report. January 16, 1952," ibid., p. 47.

254. "Special Message to the Congress Urging Extension and Strengthening of the Defense Production Act. February 11, 1952," ibid., p. 147; also "Letter to the President of the Senate on Proposed Amendments to the Defense Production Act. May 29, 1952," ibid., pp. 385–88.

255. Memorandum, CEA to the President, "Quarterly Report on the Economic Situation," April 21, 1952, Quarterly and Monthly Reports folder, Clark Papers, Truman Library.

256. See Harold L. Enarson, memorandum for the file, "Mobilization Advisory Board Meeting, June 16," Memos (September 1951–July 1952) folder, Enarson Papers, Truman Library. At this meeting William Davis remarked that "price officials will never decontrol of their own will." See also memorandum, Turner to Steelman, "Report on Today's Meeting on Regulation X," June 5, 1952, Turner Papers, Truman Library.

wrong to assert that the economy in the long run has moved down-hill, simply because prices have moved up-hill. . . . The time when a single dollar could buy the most, during the whole period from World War I until now, was in 1932—at the very bottom of the great depression."[257]

Paradoxically some of the earliest pressures for decontrol came from the OPS where Director DiSalle appointed a decontrol (later suspension) committee to study the question. Gardner Ackley, economic adviser to the director, argued for early termination of current measures while they still had some popularity so as to preserve controls as a "social instrument" for use at a later time. He said: "A long cold war period, coupled with certain institutional features of our economy, suggest that our times may very well become an 'age of inflation,' as many have maintained."[258] Ackley was not successful in fully persuading Ellis Arnall and Tighe E. Woods, successive directors of the OPS after DiSalle, of the virtue in his plan, but his assumption about the unpopularity of controls was borne out by the action of Congress in substantially reducing appropriations for the stabilization agencies.

By August 1952, even though Truman had by this time indisputably become a lame-duck President, "electionitis," as he himself called it, took over discussion of wage-price policy as well as almost everything else in government. With prices obviously subject to far less pressure than in 1948 it was much harder to make inflation a campaign issue. All the same, with the memory of the success of this issue four years before still relatively fresh, Truman referred to it often in his speeches on behalf of the Democratic candidates, Adlai E. Stevenson and John J. Sparkman. He even

257. "Special Message to the Congress: The President's Midyear Economic Report. July 19, 1952," *Public Papers*, 1952–53, p. 491; see also p. 494. Various departments were asked to make suggestions for this report. See Official File 396 (July 1952–January 1953), Truman Library. Robert C. Turner of the ESA complained that the Council review "underestimated considerably the possible impact of recessionary forces." Memorandum, Turner to J. P. Lewis, June 26, 1952, Chronological file, June–September 1952, Turner Papers, Truman Library. The notion that a slow rate of inflation might not be an unmixed evil was gaining credence in the academic community at this time. Sumner Slichter, whose views were highly respected in Washington, wrote in August: "The net advantage to the country of a slowly-rising price level over a stable one is the greater amount of employment, and hence the greater amount of production and the higher standard of consumption, that are made possible by a slowly advancing price level." Sumner H. Slichter, "How Bad Is Inflation?" *Harper's Magazine*, vol. 205 (August 1952), p. 57.

258. Memorandum, Ackley to Governor Ellis Arnall, "Basic Price Control Strategy and Planning," June 20, 1952, reproduced in Ackley, "Selected Problems," p. 573.

announced that he was contemplating another special session of Congress to consider price control, just as in 1948.[259] Truman's statements on the relationship between the Republicans and inflation were most reminiscent of his earlier ringing declarations, which had everywhere been greeted with "Give 'em hell, Harry." The Republicans, he said, had "ganged up" to kill or "cripple" anti-inflation policies and controls in every year since the end of World War II. They did this because of pressure from special interests that benefited from the higher prices.[260] Now, "the first thing they would do, if they were elected, would be to remove all price controls and let everything that the common, everyday man has to buy go sky high." This alleged class difference in dealing with inflation was stressed by Truman again and again; only the broad-based Democratic party, he insisted, had an instinct to control it. General Eisenhower's pledge to end controls and lower taxes "sounds like sensible economics to a man whose life has been spent on Army posts. But the American people know more about the economic facts of life than he apparently has ever learned. They can't afford this kind of ignorance or confusion—or sheer hypocrisy—in the President of the United States."[261] Despite this, Dwight Eisenhower was elected President of the United States on November 4, 1952.

The price and wage control system of Truman's administration began to come to pieces even before the end of his term as a result of pressures such as new wage disputes and the recognition that under the Republicans it would all end anyway.[262] The coup de grace for the WSB came in December after Truman intervened in a coal strike and overruled a board decision by increasing the size of the award to the miners; Chairman Archibald Cox and all industry members resigned. As no wage increases could legally be implemented without WSB approval, the effect was a paralysis of wage control.[263]

The valedictory for Truman's wage-price policy came in his final Economic Report submitted to the Congress on January 14. As so often be-

259. "The President's News Conference of August 7, 1952," *Public Papers*, 1952–53, p. 511, and "The President's News Conference of August 14, 1952," ibid., p. 519.
260. "Address in Tacoma at a Rally in the Armory. October 2, 1952," ibid., p. 688. See also remarks in various addresses and rear platform appearances on pp. 546, 558, 672, 767–68.
261. "Rear Platform and Other Informal Remarks in Minnesota. October 28, 1952," ibid., p. 968. See also pp. 819, 913, and 1014.
262. "Letter to the Administrator, Economic Stabilization Agency, on the New Wage Agreement in the Coal Industry. December 4, 1952," ibid., pp. 1066–68, and "Letter . . . on the Wage Stabilization Board. December 13, 1952," ibid., p. 1076.
263. See Roberts, *National Wages Policy*, pp. 76–77.

fore, he claimed success in coping with the two major "spurts" of inflation at the end of World War II and the beginning of the Korean emergency, within the limits imposed by an uncooperative Congress, of course. But concerning "the more general and enduring problem of maintaining full employment without inflation" he was admirably tentative. He said:

Much more work needs to be done in this direction, in the field of fiscal policy, monetary and credit policy, and other public policies which are not limited to use in emergency periods. Even more important, we must learn more about the value of individual and group self-restraints, about the general economy and its interrelationships, and about those private price and wage policies which may contribute most to a stable and growing economy.[264]

This was certainly a suitably sound and sober word of advice to pass on to the next and subsequent administrations.

Multiple Challenge and Varied Response

At the end of World War II President Truman and his economic advisers, considerably to their surprise, found inflation rather than unemployment, stagnation, or cries for the redistribution of income and wealth the main economic challenge facing them. Moreover, the inflation turned out to be exceptionally complex, containing elements of all three types recognized today: cost-push, demand-pull, and that caused by increases in world commodity markets. In general, the economists in government took a major hand in shaping anti-inflation policy, or at least in spelling out the options; at first they were spread loosely throughout different agencies of government, but after 1946 they were strengthened by the new Council of Economic Advisers.

Early in Truman's first term, under pressure of public demand arising from fears of unemployment and a crisis in such areas as meat, the apparatus of wartime controls was quickly dismantled or nullified, and the problem of rapid inflation had to be attacked almost with a clean slate. Moreover, it was quickly found that what could be written on this slate was disturbingly little. Monetary policy was severely constrained by the decision to maintain the value of government bonds. Requests to Congress for increased power to restrain credit were slow to be made and

264. "Annual Message to the Congress: The President's Economic Report. January 14, 1953," *Public Papers*, 1952–53, p. 1184.

even slower to be granted. Fiscal policy as an anti-inflation device was readily comprehended and approved by Truman and recommended by his advisers. But it too was inhibited by a Congress anxious to lift the burden of wartime taxes and faced with inflexible expenditures for domestic programs and unexpected charges for foreign aid and cold war defense.

Hope within the Truman administration for relief from inflation in the long run centered largely on increasing production. The argument had a micro as well as a macro dimension. For the individual firm or industry, expanding production would lower costs and prices; in markets generally, increased supplies would take the pressure off prices so long as they outran aggregate demand. The effects of interruption to growth from any cause, including strikes and monopoly restraint, whether in boom or recession, were thought to be potentially disastrous; price changes would be magnified either upward or downward. The notion of growth as an antidote for inflation was generally shared by Truman's advisers, but it was a particular favorite of Leon Keyserling, who was first vice-chairman and then chairman of the CEA.

Truman's economists recommended three major anti-inflation policies that would have involved systemic change in the economy. In part because of the force of events, none of these took hold permanently. The first was for a voluntary citizen-operated mechanism for amicable settlement of wage disputes on the basis of reason applied to facts, especially those describing the productivity of industry. This idea died in the shambles of the Labor-Management Conference of 1945; it reappeared again and again in slightly different form, especially in 1949 and 1952, but always to no effect. It was from this proposal that the idea of productivity guideposts emerged. This device, it should be noted, was designed as much to support wages during recessions as to control them at other times. The second recommendation, for a system of standby price and wage controls for use in peacetime inflation emergencies, was rejected by a Republican Congress in 1947 and 1948. Controls during the Korean emergency were essentially a reversion to the system of World War II. The third recommendation, for some form of government intervention on the supply side of critical markets characterized by oligopolistic industries and industry-wide bargaining, notably steel, was just beginning to receive serious study when the recession of 1949 shifted attention to other matters. Intervention of a drastic sort to restore steel production as well as to control prices was undertaken in 1952. But this action has to be interpreted more as an exigency of wartime than as an innovation in the fight against secular inflation.

It is worth noting that the one factor which, more than any other, destroyed the plans and projections of Truman's economists about inflation was an unpredictable series of foreign events. The first surprise was the unexpected end of World War II, but there followed soon after a succession of developments in the cold war, and finally the Korean War. It is tempting to speculate how wage-price policy might have evolved after World War II if unhampered by subsequent wars, hot and cold.

What tentative generalizations can be made about the nearly eight years of Truman's struggle with inflation? First, virtually all of the causes of inflation as we understand them today were discussed within the administration at one time or another—cost-push, demand-pull, monopoly, bottlenecks, monetary expansion, budget deficits, and transmission from other countries—although the expression of these ideas was usually less sophisticated than it has been in recent years. For example, while no one spoke about the "validation" of inflation, it was commonly held that rapid price increases in certain sectors such as housing, steel, or meat compelled the government to increase purchasing power and thereby spread the inflation throughout the economy. Moreover, although no one drew Phillips curves, the concept of a trade-off between employment and inflation was used regularly in discussion as early as 1945. Almost the whole armory of weapons against inflation was also reviewed and tried: monetary restraint, budget surpluses, "jawboning" of businessmen, unions, and consumers, partial controls, full controls, guideposts, freezes, shifts to cheaper goods, and direct intervention in the operation of key industries. Naturally, there were wide differences of opinion, comprehension, and degrees of sophistication among government officials about these devices. But many of the fundamental difficulties that limited the policies' effectiveness, such as insupportable social and political pressures against partial controls, were well understood by the end of the period. Moreover, the debate and inquiry that were encouraged inside and outside government over these years laid a strong foundation for the development of policy in later presidencies.

Advances were made in the politics as well as in the economics of inflation under Truman. For example, he discovered quickly that there were fundamental political barriers to obtaining and carrying out an effective anti-inflationary program in peacetime. Politicians and the people simply seemed to lack the will. The problem was solved for him by the recession of 1949, but it remained to plague his successors in later years. Moreover, both Truman and his advisers found that the danger of inflation became an obstacle to effecting various positive "Fair Deal" programs that they held dear. From advisers such as Keyserling, Truman received recommendations that anti-inflation controls be used in part to obtain these objectives indirectly. At a more personal level Truman came to recognize that inflation could be an excellent political issue. Very early in his first term he began to build a case that would enable him to charge that responsibility for the problem lay with his political opponents.

One point at least should emerge clearly from these pages. Any attempt to portray the Truman years as a dark age in the attack on inflation, after which came blinding light in the 1950s, 1960s, or even 1970s, is surely wrong. In fact, what may be the most depressing message is that since 1952 so little has changed.

II

The Eisenhower Administration:
The Doctrine of Shared Responsibility

H. SCOTT GORDON

NO SPECIFIC POLICIES of wage and price control were introduced during President Eisenhower's term of office. The Korean War control system of the Truman administration was quickly dismantled in the spring of 1953 and the legislative authority provided by the Defense Production Act of 1950 was allowed to lapse. Thereafter, the administration consistently opposed suggestions, which were made from time to time, that controls be reintroduced, and it even discouraged the idea, which also surfaced occasionally, that Congress should at least reenact authorization powers that would permit the executive to impose controls quickly in an "emergency." Thus, if one were to interpret the topic of this book literally, the Eisenhower period might be recorded as a blank page, and the reader could skip to the next chapter.

There are, however, good reasons (other than Parkinson's Law) for this paper's inclusion. The Eisenhower period was one of considerable importance in the history of wage-price policy in the United States, not because of specific policies, but because it was an era of change in the stability of the American economy and, equally important, an era of corresponding change in professional economic opinion about the inherent stability characteristics of a market economy. Before the mid-1950s, economists had good empirical grounds for attributing the phenomenon of inflation to the force of aggregate monetary demand pressing against the real productive capacities of the economy, and American economists had almost as good reasons to associate inflation with the special pressures of a war economy. The emergence during President Eisenhower's second term of simultaneous inflation and unemployment in a peacetime economy oc-

Note. Much of the material on which this paper is based is in the Dwight D. Eisenhower Library, Abilene, Kansas. I am grateful to the officers and staff of the library, especially David Haight and Don Wilson, for their generous and skillful assistance.

casioned a significant change in economic thinking. The simple Keynesian textbook model, in which the macroeconomy is characterized by a virtual corner, along one axis of which there is a state of unemployment with price stability and along the other a state of full employment with inflation, gave way to the Phillips curve, which raised much more complex issues of stabilization policy.[1] What emerged was a widespread view, to which the only vigorous intellectual opposition was the "monetarist school," that to be stable a market economy requires government control of its structure as well as its aggregates. This general view, which has a longer history in Britain and Western Europe than in the United States, has had considerable influence on the theory of stabilization policy, one of the most important aspects of which is the growth of the opinion that some form of wage-price, or "incomes," policy is a necessary item in the array of stabilization instruments.

Viewed this way, the history of "wage-price policy" in the 1950s becomes a history of stabilization policy in general; the "blank page" quickly becomes filled and could easily expand well beyond the length that has been allotted to this chapter. I have thus severely limited the scope of this inquiry. I will discuss the emergence of concern about inflation in the United States in the 1950s and the responses of the administration to it, but not the broader evolution of economic opinion during this period. I will discuss wage-price policy and its close substitutes, but not stabilization policy. I will discuss the institutions of government that had immediate relevance to the issue of wage-price policy, but I will not describe the general framework of economic policy formation in Washington.

The Emergence of Concern about Inflation

The attitude of the Eisenhower administration toward inflation was in part determined by its general stance as a conservative administration

1. Goodwin and Herren point out in chapter 1 that the "trade-off" concept is evident in the official thinking of the Truman era. Although this is undoubtedly correct, the theory was not specifically stated until the emergence of simultaneous inflation and unemployment in the mid-1950s.

The corner concept was revived, a decade after Phillips, by the Phelps-Friedman model, which involves a "natural" rate of unemployment that is linked, in the long run, to the general equilibrium conditions of price stability. Milton Friedman, "The Role of Monetary Policy," *American Economic Review*, vol. 58 (March 1968), pp. 1–17; and Edmund S. Phelps, "Money-Wage Dynamics and Labor-Market Equilibrium," *Journal of Political Economy*, vol. 76 (July–August 1968), pp. 678–711.

pledged to "sound" economic policy, which, in the image of the time, included an uncompromising position on the necessity of maintaining the purchasing power of the dollar. At the time of the election campaign of 1952 the price increases associated with the Korean War were tapering off, but General Eisenhower was strongly urged by his political advisers to smite the Democrats on the inflation issue, which he repeatedly did in his campaign speeches. The Republican party position on this point was clearly stated by Governor Sherman Adams of New Hampshire, who was a senior campaign adviser to the general (and became assistant to the President when the new administration took office):

A great deal of attention is being given to having General Eisenhower make more and more speeches concerning inflation and the high cost of living as the importance of this issue is fully recognized by all of us. He continually belabors this point in rear platform addresses and often uses illustrations to make the point. The Cleveland speech was a full dress approach to the menace of inflation. As you know, this speech was not used and is now being re-done for the purpose of striking the same note again and still more vigorously.[2]

Republican candidates during the campaign severely criticized the Truman administration's policy of wage-price controls as a gross interference with the operations of a free economy. Thus the Eisenhower administration took office in 1953 with a commitment to halt inflation and to do so without controls.

The consumer price index remained stable during the last quarter of 1952 and some observers advised the new administration to look in other directions for the major focus of its economic policy,[3] but its initial macroeconomic policy was squarely aimed at inflation. Monetary policy was already restrictive when the administration took office and was further tightened by the Federal Reserve System early in 1953. The adoption of a contractionary fiscal policy presented more difficulty because not only was the budget already in deficit but the special Korean War taxes authorized by the Revenue Act of 1951 were due to expire shortly. Some members of the Republican party (including the new chairman of the House Ways and Means Committee, Daniel A. Reed of New York) felt that the party was politically committed to reducing taxes and that the

2. Adams to Robert Wood Johnson, September 28, 1952, Official Files 115-E, Box 568, Eisenhower Library.
3. See, for instance, Dexter M. Keezer to Gabriel Hauge, March 10, 1953, Neil H. Jacoby Papers, Box 2, Eisenhower Library.

Korean levies should be allowed to lapse. The first bill introduced in the Eighty-third Congress was one by Reed calling for a reduction of income tax rates six months earlier than required by the existing statute. This led to some sharp disagreement over what should be the administration's first budgetary and fiscal policy.[4] The President decided that the problem of inflation took precedence, and he sent a special message to Congress in May urging that the legislative branch recognize the unsoundness of reducing taxes when the budget was already in deficit and the pace of economic activity high.[5]

The administration's initial view of the macroeconomic balance, however, was speedily overtaken by events. The economy began to turn soft in mid-1953 and unemployment became the main target of public attention. Prices were stable for the next two years, and again it seemed reasonable for observers to interpret the American economy as subject to inflationary pressure only in time of war. Secretary of the Treasury George M. Humphrey continued to emphasize inflation as a danger and opposed the use of deficit budgeting under any conditions, but he was strongly opposed by the Council of Economic Advisers.[6] Despite his personal influence with the President, there is no evidence that his views on these matters prevailed, and the tax cut of 1954, however it might be interpreted as an act of policy, is evidence to the contrary.

The Council of Economic Advisers was in serious difficulty, both internally and in its relations with Congress, when President Eisenhower took office, and there was some talk early in 1953 that it should be dismantled. Its reorganization by Arthur Burns, however, quickly transformed it into an agency more powerful in the formation of economic policy than it had been since its original establishment by the Employment Act of 1946. As part of Burns's suggested reorganization the President also created the Advisory Board on Economic Growth and Stability

4. Oral History Interview with Gabriel Hauge, Columbia Oral History Project, Eisenhower Library, pp. 58–59. Reed later led congressional opposition to the administration's proposal to postpone the expiry date of the excess profits tax.

5. "Special Message to the Congress Recommending Tax Legislation. May 20, 1953," *Public Papers of the Presidents of the United States: Dwight D. Eisenhower, 1953* (1960), pp. 318–26. The *Public Papers* of Eisenhower's presidency are in eight volumes covering the years 1953–60 (Government Printing Office, 1958–61). Hereafter *Public Papers.*

6. Oral History Interview with Neil H. Jacoby, Columbia Oral History Project, Eisenhower Library. For a different interpretation of Humphrey's views, see A. E. Holmans, "The Eisenhower Administration and the Recession, 1953–5," *Oxford Economic Papers*, vol. 10 n.s. (February 1958), p. 48.

(ABEGS), composed of high-level officers from the most important departments and agencies of the government, which acted as a central economic policy planning and coordinating agency for the administration under the chairmanship of the chairman of the CEA.[7]

The work of the CEA and ABEGS shows quite clearly that, with the arrival of price stability in 1953 and its persistence for the following two years, inflation ceased to be a major concern of the administration's senior economic advisers. In the spring of 1954, for example, the CEA carried out an extensive study of the factors affecting economic growth, assigning staff responsibilities under twenty-three topics to be examined; none of these dealt directly or indirectly with inflation.[8] ABEGS placed inflation on its weekly discussion agenda for the first time on June 27, 1956.[9] The first three of President Eisenhower's Economic Reports, delivered to Congress early in 1954, 1955, and 1956, gave little attention to inflation as an immediate or even latent problem. In brief, the public and internal papers of the first Eisenhower administration lend little support to the contention advanced by some observers that the administration was myopic about the inflation problem in these years.

Although the Economic Reports of this period show little interest in inflation, there are some brief remarks in the reports of 1955 and 1956 that are worth noting as harbingers of the administration's thinking on inflation when it reemerged as an important issue in 1957. The report of 1955, written against the background of a recession economy, expressed the view that "the apparent stability of prices in the face of falling manufacturing activity was one of the striking features of the recent contraction."[10] Why this was "striking" was perhaps not immediately apparent, but it later became clear that what Burns and others had in mind was that if prices do not fall during recessions and rise even moderately during expansions, there will be a sizable erosion in the value of money in the long run. Viewed in these terms, the price stability of 1954 was not a matter for unrestrained satisfaction; the CEA would have preferred to see the price index decline.

The Economic Report of 1956 contains the following passages: "We

---

7. On the CEA's reorganization and the role of ABEGS, see Edward S. Flash, Jr., *Economic Advice and Presidential Leadership: The Council of Economic Advisers* (Columbia University Press, 1965), chaps. 4, 5.

8. Jacoby Papers, Box 1, Eisenhower Library.

9. Arthur F. Burns Papers, Box 9, Eisenhower Library.

10. *Economic Report of the President*, 1955, p. 95.

do not wish to realize this objective [economic growth] at the price of inflation, which not only creates inequities, but is likely, sooner or later, to be followed by depression." And further on: "Success in preventing depression depends in large part upon a willingness to avoid the excesses that can so easily develop during prosperity."[11] Without, I hope, overworking the capacities of hindsight, this can be seen as a preview of the council's (and the government's) later antipathy to the concept of a trade-off between inflation and unemployment and their insistence that the achievement of price stability must be regarded as a necessary precondition to the attainment of the other major objectives of economic policy.

The interest of politicians and the general public in the problem of inflation is, like that of economists, some function of how much inflation is currently taking place. So much is hardly surprising, but this interest does not seem to drop to zero when the rate of change of prices does. Even during periods of effective price stability, some degree of public concern about inflation persists and receives periodic reinforcement from the publication of the consumer price index, a negligible increase in which is featured by the mass media as an "all-time high." Clearly there is such political potential in the inflation issue that it is difficult to resist any opportunity to make yardage on the point. Thus, for example, after a negligibly small rise in the consumer price index in the fall of 1953, Lyndon B. Johnson, then Democratic leader in the Senate, wrote in the following strong terms to the secretary of labor:

The facts cited in the last report of the Bureau of Labor Statistics on the consumer price index are shocking. It seems incredible that the cost of living is the one rising factor in an economy that is declining in so many other respects.

I can understand an increase in some items due to seasonal trends and temporary dislocations. But the knowledge that the over-all index has reached an all-time high is deeply disturbing.[12]

Secretary Mitchell's reply was lengthy, and cautious.

Americans have no direct experience of major inflation, yet seem to be as sensitive to it as other people who do. In the United States the time that elapses between a rise in prices and strong expression of public disapproval of it is very short. This, at any rate, was the case when prices began to rise during Eisenhower's second term. The consumer price index

11. *Economic Report of the President*, 1956, pp. 28, 43.
12. Johnson to James P. Mitchell, November 10, 1953, Official Files 6-A, Box 139, Eisenhower Library.

spurted upward by about 5 percent in 1957–58, and continued to rise irregularly and slowly throughout the remainder of his presidency. It was by no means a major inflation, and most other industrial countries would have been very pleased with a similar performance, but nevertheless it touched a cord of public concern that was taut and ready to vibrate. Early in 1957 the White House requested that ABEGS give some special attention to inflation, which, it noted, "looms as an important discussion point this year,"[13] and in September it asked the CEA to give it assistance on the inflation problem because "this one is really stopping our speakers."[14] The administration had ample reason, quite early, for thinking that inflation was a problem with dangerous political potential.

In professional circles, concern about inflation was equally great, but its source was not so much the price increases themselves as the coincidence of inflation with recession. This concern persisted in the face of a general level of unemployment that remained relatively high for an extended period. It seemed to predict a world in which the price level would move in only one direction.[15] The tendency at this time for pension funds and other financial institutions with long-term liabilities, which traditionally had invested only in fixed-interest securities, to begin placing funds in equities was a further indication that this prediction was being generally accepted.[16]

The economic literature began to discuss what J. M. Clark called "a new kind of inflation."[17] Alvin Hansen, who in 1954 decried the fear of inflation in peacetime as "grossly exaggerated"[18] and in 1957 counseled the acceptance of moderate inflation as a condition of full employment

13. Gabriel Hauge to Raymond J. Saulnier, February 4, 1957, Official Files 115-E, Box 568, Eisenhower Library.

14. Howard Pyle to Saulnier, September 20, 1957, Official Files 115-E, Box 568, Eisenhower Library.

15. The variety of views held by professional economists in 1958 is indicated by the papers of the panelists who spoke on the subject of inflation before the Joint Economic Committee. See *January 1958 Economic Report of the President*, Hearings before the Joint Economic Committee, 85 Cong. 2 sess. (1958).

16. See William Fellner and others, *The Problem of Rising Prices* (Paris: OEEC [Organisation for European Economic Co-operation], 1961), p. 10.

17. John M. Clark, *The Wage-Price Problem* (American Bankers Association, 1960), p. 1. For an early statement of this theme see Roy L. Reierson, "Is Inflation Avoidable?" in American Economic Association, *Papers and Proceedings of the Sixty-ninth Annual Meeting, 1956* (*American Economic Review*, vol. 47, May 1957), pp. 145–60.

18. *January 1954 Economic Report of the President*, Hearings before the Joint Committee on the Economic Report, 83 Cong. 2 sess. (1954), p. 857.

and growth, was by 1959 expressing concern over the upward trend of prices as "a brand-new fact in our economic life."[19] G. L. Bach argued that the United States was in the grip of a long-run inflationary drift that would, for reasons varying from the commitment to full employment to the ending of the gold standard, continue to be "a persistent force over the decades ahead."[20] The economic analysis of inflation was given a powerful impetus and a new orientation by the publication of A. W. Phillips' paper on the relation between unemployment and wage rates in the United Kingdom,[21] which generalized the phenomenon in both time and space and provided it with a new technical focus in the "Phillips curve." For the next decade or more, economic research on inflation was dominated (except for the monetarist approach of Milton Friedman and his associates) by econometric investigation of the Phillips-curve relationship and examination of the institutional and structural features of the economy that tended to make inflation a ubiquitous and nonreversing phenomenon.

In other countries the problem of domestic inflation had long been connected with the problem of equilibrium in the balance of international payments under the regime of fixed exchange rates that had prevailed since the Bretton Woods agreements of 1944. During the second Eisenhower administration this became an American problem too, as the dollar in 1958 lost its longstanding status as a scarce currency. The CEA and other agencies began to examine the international competitiveness of the American economy.[22]

One of the responses to the continuing rise of prices and the newly perceived Phillips curve relationship was simply to alter the aims of economic policy. The level of unemployment considered by economists to be acceptable crept upward during the late 1950s from 2.5 or 3 percent to 4.5 or 5 percent, and the level of acceptable inflation from zero to 1.5 or 2 percent a year. This numbers game, however, only revealed the basic weakness of the trade-off concept—the lack of any means by which the

19. Alvin H. Hansen, *The American Economy* (McGraw-Hill, 1957), p. 45, and *Economic Issues of the 1960s* (McGraw-Hill, 1960), p. 22.

20. *Inflation: A Study in Economics, Ethics, and Politics* (Brown University Press, 1958), pp. 38–45.

21. "The Relation Between Unemployment and the Rate of Change of Money Wage Rates in the United Kingdom, 1861–1957," *Economica*, vol. 25 n.s. (November 1958), pp. 283–99.

22. See R. J. Myers to the Under Secretary of Labor, October 2, 1959, and a CEA-commissioned paper by Henry C. Wallich on "Prices, Materials Costs and Labor Costs in the United States and other Industrial Countries," Mitchell Papers, Box 139, Eisenhower Library.

welfare costs of inflation and unemployment could be assessed in order to calculate the optimal combination of the two. Most economists of the Keynesian and liberal persuasions adopted the view that unemployment was the greater evil because of its income distribution and growth-hampering effects, and that full employment should therefore be the primary aim of policy, inflation being accepted, if need be, as the price that had to be paid for vigorous economic activity. The opposite conclusion, which generally identified economists of more conservative political persuasion, was based mainly on two (related) propositions: the impossibility of constraining an indefinite inflation to a moderate rate; and the necessity of long-run price stability to the maintenance of economic growth, full employment, and balance-of-payments equilibrium.[23]

The response of the Eisenhower administration to the appearance of peacetime inflation was the firm adoption of these "conservative" propositions. It is impossible to predict what the administration's position would have been if Arthur Burns had remained chairman of the CEA, but, in my opinion, its hard anti-inflation line was in part due to Burns's replacement, Raymond J. Saulnier. From the beginning of his chairmanship late in 1956 Saulnier saw inflation as the main economic problem facing the country.[24] He was strongly opposed to the idea of a trade-off between unemployment and inflation as a foundation for policy, and he too advanced the view that price stability was necessary to the achievement of other economic and social objectives.[25]

Burns was unhappy at the trend of administration thinking. Though he had earlier called attention to the danger of long-run inflation, he did not believe that short-run policy should be dominated by it. He apparently felt that the view that budget deficits are always wrong was gaining ground inside the administration, and he wrote confidentially to the President, saying, in part:

The onerous and punitive taxes of the 1930's did more to impair con-

23. The latter conclusion was shared, though, by the normally "liberal" Committee for Economic Development in its *Defense Against Inflation: Policies for Price Stability in a Growing Economy* (CED, 1958), which was drafted mainly by Herbert Stein and Joseph A. Pechman. See also statement by Frazar B. Wilde, chairman of the CED's Research and Policy Committee, to the Joint Economic Committee, February 6, 1957, CEA Papers, Box 16, Eisenhower Library.

24. Oral History Interview with Raymond J. Saulnier, Columbia University Oral History Project, Eisenhower Library, p. 26.

25. See Saulnier, *The Strategy of Economic Policy* (Fordham University Press, 1962), pp. 21–28, and Saulnier, "Anti-inflation Policies in President Eisenhower's Second Term," paper delivered before the American Historical Association, December 30, 1973 (processed).

fidence, in my judgment, than the increase in spending. There were, of course, plenty of other factors that added to the anxiety of the business world—the labor legislation of the time, Rooseveltian talk about a maximum income of 25 thousand, governmental tolerance of sit-down strikes, the threat to property represented by the court-packing proposal, etc.

Turn, next, to the fiscal years 1954 and 1955. We had sizable deficits then, but confidence (except for a very brief spell in early 1954) was never higher. Why? Because people knew that the government was concerned about the integrity of the dollar, because they saw that the deficits arose from tax cuts rather than increases in spending, because they had evidence that the encroachments of government on private enterprise were being stopped, and because they had renewed faith in the integrity of government itself.

Go back to World War I, when we ran even larger deficits. Again, they did nothing to impair confidence. Why? Because people felt that the first necessity was to win the war, that sharp temporary increases in expenditure were essential, and that it was impractical to raise taxes as much as spending.

Without going further, I want to nail down my conclusion: namely, that although people prefer to have a balanced budget, their confidence will not be impaired by a temporary budget deficit if they see an essential purpose (such as defense) or a conservative objective (such as tax cuts as a preliminary to closer control over expenditure) served by the deficit. Or to put the same thing in another way, what people react to is the broad direction and accent of governmental policy. A deficit that arises from one set of circumstances may destroy confidence, while a deficit under another set of circumstances may actually strengthen confidence.

And what is true of deficits is true of surpluses. . . .

If these historical remarks are not too wide of the mark, then it is an oversimplification to assert, as some fine and thoughtful citizens do, that a balanced budget or surplus is necessary to build confidence. The very opposite can be true and in fact has been true at times.

He went on to recommend that the budget for fiscal 1959 be modeled on an increase of $5 billion or $6 billion in expenditures on defense, science, and education; a reduction of $3 billion in other expenditures; and an increase in revenues of $2 billion.[26]

In a public lecture series he gave in the fall of 1957, Burns pointedly

26. Burns to President Eisenhower, November 27, 1957, James P. Mitchell Files, Box 95, Eisenhower Library.

remarked, "The nation needs assurance that the government or one of its central organs [the CEA or the Fed?] will not become so engrossed in the long-run problem of creeping inflation that any immediate problem of recession is neglected."[27] The following year, in a speech to the Joint Council on Economic Education on November 20, a copy of which he had sent directly to the President, he noted that there is "a suggestion which keeps recurring, that the way to control inflation is to be less zealous about checking recessions," calling this "a council of despair."[28]

Burns's views were very disturbing to the White House staff, which not only played a role in the formation of policy, but carried the main responsibility for advising the President on its political implications. Despite Burns's strong concern about inflation, the staff felt that his views tended to undercut the administration's position, which came under heavy public criticism as the economy went into recession in 1958. Gabriel Hauge, the President's administrative assistant for economic affairs, asked John H. Hamlin to prepare a detailed response to Burns's speech of November 20. Hamlin sent his comments to Hauge, who added his own comments. Following is an excerpt from the memorandum:

Dr. Hauge's comments	*[Hamlin's] comments on Arthur F. Burns talk of 11/20/58*
	5. He says the "gravest lesson of the recession" is that prices no longer fall in recession. Further inflation is increasingly expected and this "poses a serious threat to our Nation's economic health and progress."
We want real wages to rise, not money wages in recession.	*Certainly we do not want wages and personal income to fall? So perhaps we could live with the price rise.*
	My personal opinion is that we should take the position that:
NO! Once this is accepted I think we are in trouble.	*1. Inflation, while not desirable, is not a very serious matter, probably less serious than severe deflation, greatly overrated by those who view with alarm, and unavoidable in a free economy.*

27. Arthur F. Burns, *Prosperity Without Inflation* (Fordham University Press, 1957), pp. 87–88.

28. Burns to President Eisenhower, November 17, 1958, enclosing his speech "Some Lessons of the Recent Recession," Official Files 114, Box 560, Eisenhower Library.

2. The present outlook is against substantial
further inflation.

I don't go for an
analysis supporting
acquiescence in
inflation.

1. a. The number of people for whom fixed
dollar value sources of income are important is
small, probably less than 2%.

b. Incomes of nearly every type have consistently gone up faster than prices, increasing
real income.

c. A study I did on some 60 foreign countries of the relation of economic growth and
price trends suggests no relation, unless possibly
in extreme cases where prices are rising more
than 20% per year.

d. It would be unfair and undesirable if
prices were not free to adjust, as the service costs
are now doing.[29]

Hauge's reaction was by this date the firm official line. As early as the
fall of 1957, the President had expressed the view that inflation is inconsistent with sound economic growth,[30] a point that he reiterated on
numerous occasions.[31] In January 1959 he established a Cabinet Committee on Price Stability for Economic Growth, the title of which in itself
bespoke the administration's view of the nature of the inflation problem.

From the standpoint of wage-price policy, the most significant aspect
of the discussion of inflation in the late 1950s was not the Phillips-curve
relationship or the issue of the compatibility of inflation with other economic objectives, but a striking shift in etiology, a search for the causes
of this "new kind" of inflation not in general macroeconomic conditions
but in the institutional structure of the economy. This trend of thinking
coalesced around two themes: the role of labor unions in creating "wage
inflation" and the role of large firms' market power in establishing "administered prices."

The concept of "wage inflation" appeared with increasing frequency
in the economic literature of the late 1950s as the chief element in the
theory that the "new kind" of inflation which had taken hold of the
economy was a "cost-push" rather than a "demand-pull" type. One of

29. Hamlin and Hauge, n.d., Hamlin Papers, Box 3, Eisenhower Library.
30. *Public Papers*, 1957, p. 195.
31. See, for instance, *Public Papers*, 1958, p. 115; *Public Papers*, 1959, p. 125.

the many themes of the OEEC study, for example, was that the process of wage setting by collective bargaining, especially in "key industries," had emerged as an *independent* factor in inflation. The majority of this international group of experts came to the conclusion that "the essential element, to be stressed first of all, is that the stabilization authorities must have a wages policy for dealing with the problem of wages—just as they must have monetary and fiscal policies for dealing with the problem of demand."[32] The other point focused on in this debate—the power of large businesses to "set" prices—was the main theme of the *Staff Report on Employment, Growth, and Price Levels* of the Joint Economic Committee in 1959, which was unwilling to recommend direct government intervention in wage- and price-making processes and doubted the desirability of attacking union power, but strongly urged a reinvigoration of antitrust activity and tariff reduction to restore competitiveness in product markets (page xxxvii). The two themes of the debate tended (perhaps inevitably) to develop political implications, the Republican party becoming identified with the "wage inflation" theme and the Democratic party with "administered prices." The latter was brought forcefully to public attention in mid-1957 by the Kefauver Committee's hearings on administered prices in key industries.[33] Within the CEA, Charles L. Schultze had argued as early as mid-1957 that inflation could occur without overall excess demand if price increases in a few key sectors of the economy had the effect of producing waves of cost increases throughout the rest of the economy.[34] The Council, however, found the wage-push thesis more persuasive. E. H. Chamberlin published a strong attack on labor union power in January 1958[35] and was

32. Fellner and others, *The Problem of Rising Prices*, p. 56. Fellner and another member of the group of authors, Friedrich Lutz, dissociated themselves from this conclusion (pp. 63–64). On the question of the importance of "the key group" of heavy industries in the determination of general wage levels, see Otto Eckstein and Thomas A. Wilson, "The Determination of Money Wages in American Industry," *Quarterly Journal of Economics*, vol. 76 (August 1962), pp. 379–414.

33. *Administered Prices*, Hearings before the Subcommittee on Antitrust and Monopoly of the Senate Committee on the Judiciary, 85 Cong. 1 sess., 2 sess. (1958, 1959), pts. 1–5. The hearings continued into 1961 and were published in twenty-seven parts.

34. Schultze, "Wholesale and Consumer Prices, 1955–1957," June 24, 1957, CEA Papers, Box 22, Eisenhower Library.

35. Edward H. Chamberlin, "The Economic Analysis of Labor Union Power" (American Enterprise Institute for Public Policy Research, 1958; processed).

commissioned by the CEA during the following summer to prepare a study on "Approaches to Dealing with Wage-Push Inflation."[36] Chamberlin suggested a large number of measures that would have entailed legislative and administrative intervention in the processes of wage determination. Though privately sympathetic to ideas of this sort, the administration was acutely conscious of the political dangers of labor market intervention. When major wage negotiations were under way, particularly in the automobile and steel industries, the administration was repeatedly urged to enter the arena in the interests of price stability. On only one occasion, however—the steel strike of 1959—did the administration involve itself in this fashion.

The Policy on Controls

The wage and price control system that was in force at the time of President Eisenhower's inauguration was initiated by executive order on September 9, 1950, under Title IV of the Defense Production Act of 1950, which provided limited-term authority for the executive to act in such matters and created the Economic Stabilization Agency to discover where and when controls were needed. The agency issued general wage and price freeze regulations on January 26, 1951. Under the agency's general supervision various boards operated, dealing with prices, wages, salaries, rents, and so on. It was an elaborate and sizable enterprise, with a budget of $101 million for fiscal 1952 and a staff as of December 31, 1952, of almost ten thousand.[37] In its preliminary preparation of the 1954 budget in the fall of 1952, the Truman administration made provision for the continuation of the agency, and one of the last acts of the Eighty-second Congress was to pass a ten-month extension of the control authority.[38]

The operation of the control system was fraught with severe difficulties from the beginning, especially on the wage front. A climacteric was reached on the eve of the change of administration when John L. Lewis of the United Mine Workers called a strike over the refusal of the Wage

36. CEA Papers, Box 6, Eisenhower Library. Joseph Aschheim was also commissioned at the same time to make an "Appraisal of Suggested Measures for Non-Monetary Control of Wage-Induced Inflationary Pressure," CEA Papers, Box 4, Eisenhower Library.

37. Memorandum, "Highlights of the Economic Stabilization Agency," January 14, 1953, Official Files 13, Box 188, Eisenhower Library.

38. Public Law 429, 82 Cong. 2 sess., June 30, 1952 (66 Stat. 300).

Stabilization Board to authorize a wage increase in the soft coal industry as high as that negotiated between the union and the mine owners. President Truman intervened, overruling the WSB's decision, whereupon Chairman Archibald Cox resigned, followed on December 6, 1952, by the mass resignation of the industry members of the board. Thus the Eisenhower administration inherited an elaborate bureaucracy of control, but one in disarray at the top. A decision on the issue had to be made speedily for, under the existing law, no new wage increases could be implemented without the authority of the board. In effect, the resignation of Cox and the industry members produced an absolute freeze on wages, and a large number of petitions to the WSB were held in abeyance.

The Republican party platform for the elections of 1952 advocated removal of "injurious price and wage controls." Numerous Republican candidates for the House and Senate expressed their strong support of this during the campaign, but the presidential candidate stopped short of making an explicit commitment to end the control system.[39]

Following his election victory, Eisenhower was strongly urged by leading Republicans to make the immediate ending of controls a substantive and symbolic act of his forthcoming administration. Senator Robert A. Taft, after the President the most influential Republican, wrote to him in early January as follows:

At our recent meeting, I suggested that after your inauguration you might by Executive Order remove all wage and price controls. After thinking over the matter further I would like to make this in the form of a definite recommendation, because I consider it advisable, both from the point of view of government principle and also from the political standpoint.

Wage and price controls are absolutely contrary to the whole theory of free enterprise, which rests on freedom of competition and the fixing of prices through the basic laws of supply and demand. Furthermore, price controls in time of peace have never been effective against a real economic pressure. Higher prices and black markets have inevitably resulted. I believe that price control can only be justified when a condition of war or a tremendous emergency makes it impossible substantially to balance the

39. F. E. McCaffree to Allen Wallis, August 7, 1959, and memorandum on "Republican and Democratic Stands on Price Control in 1952 Presidential Election Campaign," prepared by the Research Division of the Republican National Committee, Wallis Papers, Box 2, Eisenhower Library. McCaffree was surprised to discover that he could find no explicit commitment in Eisenhower's campaign speeches.

budget. Then such controls can have some temporary effect in delaying inflation or reducing its speed. Otherwise, the control of credit and the prevention of increased borrowing by the government, business, and consumers, are far more effective. In recent years the people have come to feel that price control is part of the ordinary operation of a free economy, and that belief is very dangerous to continued liberty.[40]

The President-elect replied the following day, expressing general agreement with Taft's position but stopping short of any firm commitment.[41] He clearly felt that this was a matter that warranted caution and perhaps resistance to the overzealous members of his party. He sought further opinions, especially from those whom he had selected to become senior officials of his administration. The flow of advice that came back to him from these sources favored the ending of controls. There were some differences of opinion, however, on whether this should be done immediately upon taking office. Sinclair Weeks, who was to become the new secretary of commerce, favored immediate removal,[42] as did George Humphrey (Treasury) and Charles E. Wilson (Defense).[43] Joseph M. Dodge (Bureau of the Budget) and Gabriel Hauge favored a go-slow policy.[44] The die, however, had already been cast by the resignation of Cox and the industry members of the Wage Stabilization Board. The President had either to reconstitute the board immediately or end controls. He chose the latter course, ending all wage and salary controls and a large number of price controls on February 6, 1953.[45] Michael V. DiSalle, administrator of the Economic Stabilization Agency under President Truman, prepared, as his final act in office, a paper called "There Are also Problems with Indirect Controls," which argued for the continuation of direct controls on a selective basis and the establishment of an Economic

40. Taft to Eisenhower, January 8, 1953, Official Files 114-E, Box 564, Eisenhower Library.

41. Eisenhower to Taft, January 9, 1953, same file.

42. Weeks to Eisenhower, "Recommendations Concerning Direct Price, Wage and other Controls asked for in General Eisenhower's Memorandum to the Undersigned dated 9 December, 1952," n.d., Official Files 114-E, Box 564, Eisenhower Library. See also M. S. Pitzele to Gabriel Hauge, "Wage Controls," December 22, 1952, same file.

43. Oral History Interview with Sherman Adams, Columbia University Oral History Project, Eisenhower Library, p. 253. These names were not proffered by Adams but suggested by the interviewer, Ed Edwin.

44. See Charles F. Willis, Jr., to Sherman Adams, January 29, 1953, Official Files 114-E, Box 564, Eisenhower Library.

45. Public Papers, 1953, p. 46, note.

Stabilization Commission.[46] Gabriel Hauge, evaluating DiSalle's paper at the request of Sherman Adams, said that, in his opinion, "the thesis is right . . . about the limitations of indirect controls" but felt that any long-term needs in this area could be met by the planned reconstruction of the Office of Defense Mobilization and the Council of Economic Advisers "or its successor."[47] The remainder of the Truman control system was speedily dismantled in the ensuing few months.

Having decided to do away with the inherited system of controls, the Eisenhower administration had next to decide what its policy should be toward the authorization contained in the Defense Production Act. The 1952 amendment to this act extended authority to control wages and prices until April 30, 1953. Should this be extended further as a standby provision or should some other authorization for emergency powers be sought? The administration's decision to take no initiative on the matter with Congress indicated that it was willing, or preferred, to allow the control authority to lapse. The issue was sharpened by the introduction of a bill on February 2, 1953, by Senator Homer E. Capehart, chairman of the Senate Committee on Banking and Currency, which would have replaced the standby powers of the Defense Production Act with a new Emergency Stabilization Act. The bill provided control authorization and would establish a National Advisory Council composed of business, labor, agriculture, military, and consumer representatives whose advice to the President would be a statutory precondition to the institution of controls. The President would also be authorized to keep a control bureaucracy in continuous existence even though no controls were in force.

The administration's first view on standby authority was indicated by the President in his first State of the Union Message to Congress, issued on the same day that Senator Capehart introduced his bill in the Senate. He came out clearly against controls on principle and indicated that he would not ask Congress to extend Title IV of the Defense Production Act before its expiration date of April 30, 1953, although he did recommend that authority to control rents in communities with serious housing shortages, chiefly "defense areas," should be continued for a while. He went on to say that the price situation would be closely watched and he would not

46. January 31, 1953, Official Files 114-E, Box 564, Eisenhower Library. See also memorandum of November 25, 1952, by Edward L. Phelps, Jr., assistant director of the Office of Price Stabilization, Official Files 9-O, Box 188, Eisenhower Library.

47. Hauge to Adams, February 10, 1953, Official Files 114-E, Box 564, Eisenhower Library.

hesitate to ask Congress for powers if conditions warranted.[48] The following day, Arthur Burns appeared before the Senate Committee on Banking and Currency in hearings on his nomination to the CEA and was asked his opinion of controls by Senator John W. Bricker. He indicated strong opposition to them but acknowledged that he "would not exclude direct controls under all circumstances. In a time of grave national emergency, direct controls might be desirable."[49] The White House asked the Defense Mobilization Board to study the issue of standby authority, and on March 10 Gabriel Hauge reported to the President the DMB recommendation that the administration should not ask for the authority but that it should not object if Congress wished to enact such powers.[50] This was the position adopted subsequently by the President in his public comments on the question.[51] The Capehart bill, however, was not to the administration's liking and after an initially passive attitude toward it the White House actively opposed it and it did not become law.

It is interesting to note that the original control authorization was part of an act dealing with national defense; the Capehart bill was construed in terms of an "emergency" arising from war or threat of war; and the entire discussion of the necessity for wage-price control authority at this time centered around the special problems created by threats to national security. Despite its general rejection of controls and its opposition to the Capehart bill, the administration continued internal discussion of the possible need for standby control authority in the event of war.[52] It was not until the late 1950s that the issue of controls was discussed in the context of a peacetime economy. When prices began to rise in 1957, the administration found itself repeatedly being pressed to consider the introduction of controls.[53] The public opinion polls during this period showed that the administration was politically vulnerable on the inflation issue and that the public favored controls, but the President's economic advisers were con-

48. "Annual Message to the Congress on the State of the Union. February 2, 1953," *Public Papers*, 1953, pp. 22–23.

49. *Nomination of Arthur F. Burns*, Hearing before the Senate Committee on Banking and Currency, 83 Cong. 1 sess. (1953), p. 5.

50. Hauge to President Eisenhower, March 10, 1953, Official Files 114-E, Box 564, Eisenhower Library.

51. See, for example, *Public Papers*, 1953, p. 48.

52. Charles F. Willis, Jr., to L. A. Warren (president of Safeway Stores, Inc.), June 6, 1955, Official Files 114-E, Box 564, Eisenhower Library.

53. For example, the President's news conferences of July 3 and September 3, 1957. *Public Papers*, 1957, pp. 516, 643.

sistently and unanimously opposed to controls.[54] Early in 1957 the President began to speak of the necessity for "restraint" on the part of labor and business as a necessary supplement to the traditional stabilization weapons of fiscal and monetary policy. This became a major item in the administration's anti-inflation policy.

The Policy of Exhortation

The administration decided to mount a full-scale battle against inflation in the late 1950s by means of public appeals for voluntary restraint. The first major shots fired on this front were contained in the President's Economic Report and State of the Union Message of January 1957.

As usual, the Economic Report was prepared by the Council of Economic Advisers. In the fall of 1956 the senior staff members of the Council were asked to submit suggestions for the forthcoming report. Of the ten responses,[55] only those by Charles L. Schultze and Frank E. Norton suggested that inflation be made a topic of special consideration. Schultze had earlier prepared some memorandums on cost-price relations as background material for a possible treatment of the subject in the report.[56] In other memorandums Clarence D. Long suggested that the report should have a section on "recent wage increases" to examine their impact on costs and prices.[57] Norton called attention to the need for an examination of "recent developments in price-cost relations, especially unit labor costs in key industries, with their implication for control of inflation via monetary policy." Schultze felt that "it would be particularly appropriate to examine briefly some of the prerequisites for the compatibility of price stability with full employment" and suggested that "a public restatement of some of the requirements for price stability might be quite useful, particularly for business and labor leaders." Norton and Schultze repeated

54. Oral History Interview with Raymond J. Saulnier, Columbia University Oral History Project, pp. 34–35, and drafts of memorandums by Don Paarlberg, May 13, 1959, and Allen Wallis, August 6, 1959, Wallis Papers, Box 2, Eisenhower Library.
55. Burns Papers, Box 14, Eisenhower Library.
56. Saulnier to Schultze, October 18, 1956, CEA Papers, Box 11, Eisenhower Library.
57. Long to the CEA, September 26 and October 3, 1956, CEA Papers, Box 11, Eisenhower Library.

their suggestions that inflation be featured in the forthcoming report in subsequent memorandums.[58]

The CEA decided to include a section in the 1957 Economic Report dealing with the experience of using fiscal and monetary policies as stabilization devices, and the chief responsibility for drafting this was given to Leo Grebler. This draft contained a section on the "responsibilities of private enterprise,"[59] which was recast to form a section, "Public and Private Responsibilities in a High-Employment Economy," for the final version. The last two paragraphs of this section, which were finally prepared by Saulnier and Irving Siegel, went as follows:

Economic developments in recent years show the basic role that monetary and fiscal restraints must play if the excesses that often accompany prosperity are to be avoided. At the same time, this experience suggests that fiscal and monetary policies must be supported by appropriate private policies to assure both a high level of economic activity and a stable dollar. When production, sales, and employment are high, wage and price increases in important industries create upward pressures on costs and prices generally. To depend exclusively on monetary and fiscal restraints as a means of containing the upward movement of prices would raise serious obstacles to the maintenance of economic growth and stability. In the face of a continuous upward pressure on costs and prices, moderate restraints would not be sufficient; yet stronger restraints would bear with undue severity on sectors of the economy having little if any responsibility for the movement toward a higher cost-price level and would court the risk of being excessively restrictive for the economy generally.

These are not acceptable alternatives to stable and balanced economic growth. The American economy possesses the potentials for expansion and improvement. If these potentials are supported by proper fiscal and monetary policies on the part of Government, and by appropriate private policies, our economy can achieve and maintain high levels of production, employment, and income with stable prices.[60]

The first draft of the State of the Union Message for 1957 contained only a general appeal for "patriotic leadership ... in the hands of those

58. Norton to Burns, October 4, 1956; Norton to Saulnier, October 11, 1956; Schultze to the Council, October 11, 1956. CEA Papers, Box 11, Eisenhower Library.

59. Burns Papers, Box 14, Eisenhower Library.

60. Economic Report of the President, January 1957, p. 44. The same theme was contained in the opening chapter of the report, which Saulnier drafted himself (CEA Papers, Box 11, Eisenhower Library), called "Opportunity and Responsibility in a Free Economy."

who possess economic influence and power," noting that "leaders of agriculture, industry and labor, by their position, owe the American people a vigilant guard against the inflationary tendencies that are always at work in a dynamic economy."[61] But sometime between this date, December 29, 1956, and January 7, 1957, when the draft of the message was submitted to the cabinet, the decision was made to sharpen this point considerably. Revisions in this section of the message were made up to the morning of January 10, the day it was delivered to Congress. The passage is worth quoting in full:

I have often spoken of the purpose of this administration to serve the national interest of 170 million people. The national interest must take precedence over temporary advantages, which may be secured by particular groups at the expense of all the people.

In this regard I call on leaders in business and in labor to think well on their responsibility to the American people. With all elements of our society, they owe the Nation a vigilant guard against the inflationary tendencies that are always at work in a dynamic economy operating at today's high levels. They can powerfully help counteract or accentuate such tendencies by their wage and price policies.

Business in its pricing policies should avoid unnecessary price increases, especially at a time like the present when demand in so many areas presses hard on short supplies. A reasonable profit is essential to the new investments that provide more jobs in an expanding economy. But business leaders must, in the national interest, studiously avoid those price rises that are possible only because of vital or unusual needs of the whole Nation.

If our economy is to remain healthy, increases in wages and other labor benefits, negotiated by labor and management, must be reasonably related to improvements in productivity. Such increases are beneficial, for they provide wage earners with greater purchasing power. Except where necessary to correct obvious injustices, wage increases that outrun productivity, however, are an inflationary factor. They make for higher prices for the public generally and impose a particular hardship on those whose welfare depends on the purchasing power of retirement income and savings. Wage negotiations should also take cognizance of the right of the public generally to share in the benefits of improvements in technology.

Freedom has been defined as the opportunity for self-discipline. This

61. "State of the Union Draft," December 29, 1956, Special Assistant, Box 25, Eisenhower Library.

definition has a special application to the areas of wage and price policy in a free economy. Should we persistently fail to discipline ourselves, eventually there will be increasing pressure on Government to redress the failure. By that process freedom will step by step disappear. No subject on the domestic scene should more attract the concern of the friends of American working men and women and of free business enterprise than the forces that threaten a steady depreciation of the value of our money.[62]

Of the two statements on the responsibility of leaders, the milder one in the Economic Report received the most attention from economists, some of it highly critical. Milton Friedman wrote to Saulnier, saying:

You will not be surprised that my one really serious disagreement is with the assignment of responsibility to business and labor for restraining inflation. This seems to me not only analytically wrong, but politically dangerous. Heaven preserve us from a world of business men and labor leaders conducting their affairs in terms of "social" responsibility.[63]

Neil Jacoby, who served as a member of the CEA until 1955, wrote to Saulnier, with a copy to Burns, expressing approval of the decision to emphasize the danger of inflation in the report, but added:

If I were to criticize the Economic Report, I would argue that it is not sufficiently bold and specific regarding a long-term Federal program to minimize the danger of further price inflation. The Report lays undue emphasis upon individual and group "responsibilities," "appropriate private policies," and "self-discipline" in setting prices and wage-rates that are non-inflationary. It is, of course, proper for the President to say these things; but history teaches that they will not get us very far per se. You will recall that the speeches and Economic Reports of Truman and his Council of Economic Advisers were larded with exhortations to businessmen to hold down prices (and much less frequently with advice to labor leaders to moderate wage demands!), yet price levels surged steadily upward.

The hortatory approach to the problem of containing inflation is not merely ineffective; it is also contradictory in the sense that it asks people to behave non-competitively. Faced with booming demand for his product, the businessman's normal (and socially desirable) response is to raise price. Observing a shortage of workers having the skills of his union members, the union leader's natural (and valid) response is to demand higher

62. The State of the Union, Address of the President of the United States, Delivered January 10, 1957, H. Doc. 1, 85 Cong. 1 sess. (1957), pp. 3–4.

63. Friedman to Saulnier, February 8, 1957, CEA Papers, Box 11, Eisenhower Library.

wages. Government should not ask them to do otherwise. Rather, it should set a reasonable employment goal (an unemployment ratio averaging under 4 percent a year), and take definite measures that (1) curb excessive monetary demands for commodities and services, and (2) insure vigorous competition in all markets. Monetary and fiscal measures are the main means of moderating market demands. Antitrust and other similar measures are needed to prevent unduly high costs and prices, and associated unemployment of productive resources resulting from monopoly powers. For this reason, I believe the *Economic Report* should have said that fiscal and monetary policies must be supported by appropriate *public* —rather than private—policies in other spheres to assure both a high level of economic activity and a stable price level. (See page 44.) Of course, private understanding and support of anti-inflationary public policy also are essential.[64]

Burns replied to Jacoby, with a copy to Saulnier, saying: "I agree with your principal criticism of the Report and I have also conveyed it to Steve [Saulnier]. We avoided exhortation in our earlier reports because the old Council had done this for a long time without producing any visible effects."[65] Gabriel Hauge responded to Jacoby's letter to Saulnier, saying that while it would be "a mistake to expect any significant results" from appeals for restraint, the statement seemed to him "a good and desirable thing [for the President] to do in the circumstances."[66] Alfred C. Neal, president of the Committee for Economic Development, wrote to Saulnier saying that the 1957 report was "marred" by the hortatory passages,[67] although the following year a major CED document strongly advocated reliance on "the voluntary exercise of restraint in price and wage policies by business and labor" to prevent inflation.[68] Albert Rees appeared as a witness before the Joint Economic Committee in its hearings on the Economic Report to argue that appeals for voluntary restraint "if heeded, can do much harm" by in effect replacing the price system with some form of

64. Jacoby to Saulnier, January 29, 1957, General Files 7-E-1, Box 172, Eisenhower Library.

65. Burns to Jacoby, February 1, 1957, CEA Papers, Box 11, Eisenhower Library. Burns later expressed a more favorable view; see his *The Management of Prosperity* (Columbia University Press for Carnegie Institute of Technology, 1966), p. 26.

66. Hauge to Jacoby, February 5, 1971, CEA Papers, Box 11, Eisenhower Library.

67. Neal to Saulnier, February 6, 1957, CEA Papers, Box 11, Eisenhower Library. He also made a similar statement on February 1, 1957, before the Joint Economic Committee; CEA Papers, Box 16, Eisenhower Library.

68. CED, *Defense Against Inflation*, p. 15; see also pp. 43 and 16 (note), where three members of the CED indicated reservations on this point.

rationing.[69] In its subsequent report, the committee noted that, while it had been pointed out that voluntary restraints might lead to inefficiency in resource allocation, its main criticism of the idea was that there was a lack of "workable machinery," and even the statistical information, to make it effective. The executive branch was urged to repair these deficiencies.[70] At the 1958 meeting of the American Economic Association, Ben W. Lewis attacked the policy of exhortation, arguing that if it were effective (which he was inclined to doubt) it would undermine the fundamental basis on which a market economy functions.[71]

Though many of these criticisms came from firm friends of the administration and though they pointed out the inconsistency between a voluntary restraint system and the general economic philosophy so often expressed by the President and his colleagues, they seem to have had little effect on administration thinking. There is no evidence that, when the 1957 State of the Union Message was drafted, the appeal for voluntary restraint in price and wage setting was regarded as more than, as Hauge put it, "a good and desirable thing to do in the circumstances," but in subsequent months it was developed into a major element of the administration's anti-inflationary policy. The doctrine of "shared responsibility" for price stability began to appear regularly in administration statements. The need to mobilize the force of "public opinion" as a constraint upon the behavior of labor unions and business became a primary focus of the government's anti-inflation activity.

In the light of developments of recent years, one should note the connection that was made in the 1957 State of the Union Message between wage increases and productivity. The use of the productivity criterion for the determination of noninflationary wage increases was not a new idea; economists in the Truman administration had suggested it as early as 1944.[72] By the mid-1950s it had become, as one critic noted, a "fashionable" solution of the inflation problem.[73] When President Kennedy's

69. Albert Rees, "Recent Price Changes," statement before the Joint Economic Committee, January 31, 1957, CEA Papers, Box 11, Eisenhower Library.

70. 1957 Joint Economic Report, Report of the Joint Economic Committee on the January 1957 Economic Report of the President, 85 Cong. 1 sess. (1957), pp. 6–7.

71. "Economics by Admonition," in American Economic Association, Papers and Proceedings of the Seventy-first Annual Meeting, 1958 (American Economic Review, vol. 49, May 1959), pp. 384–98.

72. See chapter 1, pp. 10–11, above.

73. Kelvin Lancaster, "Productivity-Geared Wage Policies," Economica, vol. 25 n.s. (August 1958), p. 199.

CEA made its celebrated statement on the productivity criterion as the basis of "guidepost" policy, it did little more than make official an old idea.[74]

The difficulties inherent in specifically applying the productivity criterion came in for some discussion both outside and inside the administration.[75] I have found no evidence that the administration made any effort to resolve these problems with a view to developing a specific "guidepost" or similar type of wage constraint policy, but it did take to heart the criticism of the Joint Economic Committee that the statistical data available in this area were inadequate. A cabinet paper of December 23, 1958, suggested that the Office of Statistical Standards of the Bureau of the Budget should be asked to examine the problem of providing additional data on "prices, wages, and productivity." The President approved this and the Budget Bureau reported to him on April 8, 1959.[76]

The administration was forced to think through the implication of its pleas for private responsibility in mid-1958 when a rise in steel prices led to demands that it back up exhortation by more concrete action. The movement was spearheaded by Senator Estes Kefauver. The Subcommittee on Antitrust and Monopoly of the Senate Committee on the Judiciary under the chairmanship of Senator Kefauver became in mid-1957 one of the main public instruments of the "administered prices in key industries" approach to the inflation problem. Over an extended period the hearings of the subcommittee enjoyed wide press coverage, and Senator Kefauver's star was rising in one of the most firmly established orbits in American politics—the populist attack on big business. A major object of this attack was the steel industry.[77] The steel companies raised their prices in 1956 and again in 1957, on each occasion generating some public criticism. In the spring of 1958 rumors again began to fly that the companies were about to announce a general pattern of price increases to take effect on

74. James Tobin acknowledged this in his Buxton Lecture, *The Intellectual Revolution in U.S. Economic Policy-Making* (Longmans for the University of Essex [England], 1966), pp. 16–18.

75. See, for example, CED, *Defense Against Inflation*; James Mitchell to Arthur Larsen, December 17, 1957, and Mitchell to Sherman Adams, April 12, 1958, Mitchell Papers, Box 115, Eisenhower Library.

76. Paarlberg Papers, Box 3, Eisenhower Library.

77. For the industry's responses to this see Roger M. Blough and others, *Steel and Inflation: Fact vs. Fiction* (United States Steel Corporation, 1958). See also Harleston R. Wood, "The Measurement of Employment Cost and Prices in the Steel Industry," *Review of Economics and Statistics*, vol. 41 (November 1959), pp. 412–18.

July 1. Senator Kefauver wrote to the President[78] following the latter's
television address of May 20 (which had featured the issue of inflation and
the private responsibilities of business and labor), urging him to present
a "plan" to curb price increases. His proposal was a general one but it is
not without significance that he argued and illustrated it by reference to
the steel industry. Kefauver acknowledged that no statutory authority
existed for the invocation of wage and price controls and did not advocate
their reestablishment. He proposed that the President marshal public
opinion against inflationary forces by such measures as open requests for
abstention from price increases in specific cases; holding conferences with
industry and labor leaders; issuing statements on the price and profit positions of particular industries; and issuing suggested price ceilings for voluntary compliance. The significance of Kefauver's letter was that it challenged the administration to escalate the anti-inflation battle with its own
chosen weapons of persuasion and public opinion.

The President's reply was cautious and evasive. He took no notice of
Kefauver's proposal that the government issue statements on profits or
that it suggest voluntary price ceilings, and specifically rejected the idea
(which many others had also been urging him to consider) of calling a
general labor-management conference. On June 20 Kefauver sent a telegram to the President noting that a steel price increase was reported by
the press to be imminent and urging him "to use the full powers of your
office in order to prevent this disastrous occurrence" by convening a conference of steel industry leaders and officers of the United Steelworkers.
This telegram was discussed in the administration as a high-priority matter, and the President replied on June 24, rejecting the idea of specific
intervention in the steel industry. At the end of July the steel industry
announced a price increase, and Senator Kefauver again telegraphed the
President urging him to "persuade the steel industry to rescind this latest
and most unfortunate price action" and to call a conference of industry
and labor leaders. Up to this point Kefauver had acted as an individual
senator, but now he sought and obtained authority from his sub-committee to speak in its name. He wrote to the President "at the direction"
of the subcommittee on August 2 expressing "grave concern" over the
steel price increases and urging him to intercede with U.S. Steel, which
had not yet announced a general increase in prices, and to call an industry-

78. Kefauver to President Eisenhower, May 22, 1958, Official Files 114, Box 560,
Eisenhower Library. All correspondence between Kefauver and the President referred to below can be found in this file.

labor conference "to formulate a wage-price program to arrest what appears to be a permanent inflationary trend, which continues unabated regardless of whether the economy is in a state of prosperity or recession." President Eisenhower replied on August 14, ignoring Kefauver's suggestion of direct intervention, and specifically rejecting the idea of a public conference. He informed the senator that the CEA was "continuously studying ways and means of promoting sustainable and vigorous economic growth without endangering the stability of the dollar" and indicated the administration's receptivity to any "constructive suggestions" the senator might wish to make.

The significance of this exchange is its indication that, although the administration had decided to beat the drum loudly and publicly on the issue of inflation and private responsibility, it had no desire to translate the policy of exhortation into specific terms or to intervene in specific cases.

Eisenhower's preference for a policy restricted to general terms is further indicated by his attitude toward the Clark-Reuss bill to amend the Employment Act of 1946. As concern about inflation grew, numerous suggestions were made that the act should be amended to include price stability as a specifically stated responsibility.[79] The State of the Union Message and the Economic Report of 1959 indicated the President's acceptance of this idea and he subsequently approved a bill (S. 2824) introduced by Senator Prescott Bush, which would have added "reasonable price stability" to the objectives enumerated in the act. This was undercut, however, by a much more extensive amendment that had been introduced into the House of Representatives on June 3, 1958, by Congressman Henry S. Reuss, which the House Committee on Government Operations reported out, presumably in preference to the Bush bill.[80] The Clark-Reuss bill would have amended the Employment Act by the addition of reasonable price stability and sustained economic growth but would also have required the CEA to make specific quantitative estimates of the levels of employment, production, and so forth, required to meet these objectives. Beyond this, the amendment would have authorized the CEA to make studies of wage and price increases that would adversely affect

79. Arthur Burns, for example, recommended this in his *Prosperity Without Inflation*, pp. 71–73, 83; and again in his address, "Some Lessons of the Recent Recession," of November 1958, Official Files 114, Box 560, Eisenhower Library. Jacoby was lukewarm to the idea; Jacoby to Saulnier, October 1, 1957, Jacoby Papers, Box 7, Eisenhower Library.

80. A. J. Wickens to the Secretary of Labor, July 9, 1959, Mitchell Papers, Box 143, Eisenhower Library.

these objectives and report these to the President as a foundation for an appeal by him for voluntary restraint. None of these additional responsibilities were to the liking of the CEA or the White House. The bill was strongly opposed by the administration and did not pass.

During 1958, as the inflation continued, the administration came under increasing pressure to adopt a more vigorous policy. In August President Eisenhower established a special cabinet committee under the secretary of labor "to consider the wage-cost-price spiral and possible measures for dealing with it."[81] In addition to amending the Employment Act of 1946 and improving the statistical data on wages, productivity, and prices, the committee's recommendations focused mainly on two proposals: to intensify the campaign to make the public aware of the danger of inflation and to examine the impact of the government's own operations on prices and costs. To carry out the former the committee considered the establishment of a "National Board on Price Stability and Economic Growth composed of five outstanding citizens" to work with itself as a continuing body, but this was rejected by the White House. In January 1959 the President announced that he had created two new bodies as part of his campaign against inflation: the Committee on Government Activities Affecting Prices and Costs, and the Cabinet Committee on Price Stability for Economic Growth.[82]

The Committee on Government Activities (CGA) was established under the chairmanship of the chairman of the CEA, with representatives from the departments of Defense, Post Office, the Interior, Agriculture, and Commerce, the Bureau of the Budget, the General Services Administration, the Atomic Energy Commission, the Federal Aviation Agency, and the Office of Civil and Defense Mobilization. The task of the CGA was to review the programs and operations of the various branches of the federal government, especially those engaged in such activities as procurement, construction, stockpiling, and price support, with a view to recommending changes in practice in the interests of price stability. The CGA's chairman remarked in retrospect, "It must be conceded . . . that [this effort] had a mixed reception in the departments and agencies directly involved."[83] So far as I can tell, this is an understatement. The depart-

81. Secretary of Labor to the President, October 1, 1958, Mitchell Papers, Box 57, Eisenhower Library.

82. Press releases, January 23 and 31, 1959, Paarlberg Papers, Box 4, and Staff Files-Wallis, Box 1, Eisenhower Library.

83. Saulnier, "Anti-inflation Policies in President Eisenhower's Second Term," p. 6.

ments and agencies resented the interference implied in the committee's terms of reference. If the CEA and the Bureau of the Budget alone had been given the responsibility, some dent might have been made in revising government policies and operations, but the CGA as constituted was largely composed of people with a much stronger interest in protecting the policies of their bureaus than in fighting general inflation. There is no evidence that it actually played any role of significance in the administration's anti-inflation policy.

The Cabinet Committee on Price Stability for Economic Growth (CCPSEG) was more important. It was established under the chairmanship of Vice-President Richard M. Nixon and its members were the secretaries of the Treasury, Agriculture, Commerce, and Labor, the Postmaster General, and the chairman of the CEA. Allen Wallis, then dean of the School of Business at the University of Chicago, was appointed to be its executive vice-chairman. The CCPSEG had no staff of its own except for Wallis, and no budget. It had to rely on other agencies of the government to give it staff assistance and provide financing. In announcing it, President Eisenhower indicated that the task of the committee would be twofold: to "conduct such studies, as it finds are needed, of those factors affecting the stability of costs and prices that will help prevent price increases" and to "strive to build a better public understanding of the problem of inflation and of public and private policies that should be followed if cost and price increases are to be avoided."[84]

The activities of the CCPSEG were concerned almost exclusively with the second of these two tasks. It conducted no economic research of its own, nor did it request any specific research studies from other agencies. It issued a number of reports and statements and commissioned a number of distinguished outside economists to participate in the drafting of them (including Arthur Burns, Herbert Stein, Reuben Kessel, Albert Rees, George Shultz, and John Kendrick; Martin Bailey assisted Wallis on a more regular basis), but these were designed, from the beginning, as documents of public tuition. "The task of public education," wrote Wallis to the vice-president in July of 1959, "looms increasingly important as our work progresses."[85]

The first interim report of the committee, which was released by the

84. Press release, January 31, 1959, Staff Files-Wallis, Box 1, Eisenhower Library. Also, the President to the Vice-President, January 28, 1959, Staff Files-Wallis, Box 1, Eisenhower Library.

85. Draft memorandum on a Citizens' Advisory Council for CCPSEG, July 27, 1959, Wallis Papers, Box 3, Eisenhower Library.

President on June 29, 1959, struck a note that can only be described as shrill. It emphasized the grave and insidious dangers of inflation facing the country and urged that the (Democratic-controlled) Congress display more responsiveness to the President's anti-inflationary policies, particularly his pleas for restraint in the appropriation of funds for government expenditure. Since the CCPSEG was a cabinet committee and its chairman was a leading contender for the Republican party's presidential nomination for 1960, it was perhaps inevitable that its activities should take on a partisan color; at any rate, its path was set by the tone and substance of its first interim report and the response to it. John Kenneth Galbraith, then chairman of the Advisory Committee on Economic Policy of the Democratic Advisory Council, issued a vitriolic statement condemning it, and Walter Reuther of the AFL-CIO issued a less artistic but equally critical one.[86] The political battle lines were formed. Whether the gauntlet was flung at the feet of the opposition by intention or by inadvertence, the CCPSEG became identified (in the Congress and the press) as an instrument of Republican party politics. The political debate that developed as the presidential election loomed did not cast the Republicans in the role of opponents of inflation and Democrats as defenders of it; rather, each party tried to outdo the other in stressing the firmness of its own anti-inflation resolve and the weakness of the other's, a game of tu quoque in which the CCPSEG was a leading participant.

Allen Wallis was wholeheartedly dedicated to the task of rousing the nation to the danger of inflation and, it seems, to promoting the Republican party image on the issue. Between the last week of April 1959 and the end of the year he made some fifty speeches on the subject before various groups all over the country.[87] Perhaps on this account he was greatly upset when, at the end of July, a Gallup poll carried a report that 38 percent of its sample identified the Democrats and only 23 percent the Republicans as the "party . . . most interested in keeping prices down," and that this gap was widening. On this occasion he wrote directly to the President to explain the failure of public understanding and to provide him with suggestions for more effective public statements on inflation.[88] Two weeks later he became very annoyed with the press for interpreting

86. July 9 and July 1, 1959, Wallis Papers, Box 1, Eisenhower Library.
87. A list of these speeches and the texts of some of them are in Wallis Papers, Box 1, Eisenhower Library.
88. Wallis to President Eisenhower, July 31, 1959, Wallis Papers, Box 1, Eisenhower Library.

the CCPSEG's statement, "What Do We Really Want from Our Economy?" as a falling-off in the committee's anti-inflation emphasis,[89] and he wrote a statement for Senator Bush to read in the Senate for the purpose of correcting this erroneous impression.[90]

Although the President was not warmly disposed to the idea of calling a labor-management conference on inflation, he was persuaded by Allen Wallis and the CCPSEG that a more general public meeting would be a useful step in promoting public awareness. Wallis organized this Economic Conference,[91] which was held on November 2, 1959, at the Hotel Statler in Washington. It was a blue-ribbon affair, attended by almost one hundred senior officers of national organizations representing all major groups except labor (which had evaded invitations to attend), and was addressed by the President, the vice-president, and Senator A. Willis Robertson of Virginia. The purpose of the conference was, in Wallis's words, "to organize a broadly based citizens' movement to combat inflation."[92] The conference did not culminate in any specific organization or policy, and if one looks for substantive results of this sort it must be regarded as a nullity. But its main purpose, in the eyes of the administration, was to sound the tocsin on the dangers of inflation, which, more than specific acts, had become the heart of the administration's anti-inflation policy.

Wage Determination and Government Intervention

The term "wage-price policy" is usually taken to denote specific and public actions on the part of the government to modify the determination of wage rates and prices in the economy. Although the Eisenhower administration did not adopt any system of direct wage and price controls, the policy of exhortation may be viewed as a "wage-price policy" in that one of its aims is to modify price and wage determination processes by

89. Wallis to James C. Hagerty, August 18, 1959, Staff Files-Wallis, Box 1, Eisenhower Library.

90. Wallis to Bush and enclosure, August 27, 1959, Official Files 114, Box 560, Eisenhower Library.

91. Formally, the organizers were H. Burns Palmer, president of the National Benefit Life Insurance Company, and D. Tennant Bryan, president of Richmond Newspapers. Wallis Papers, Box 3, Eisenhower Library.

92. Wallis to President Eisenhower, October 29, 1959, Official Files 114, Box 562, Eisenhower Library.

focusing the constraining force of public opinion, presumably on labor and product markets that are not fully competitive. Another form in which a "wage-price policy" can be pursued is by direct government intervention (which may be secretly carried out) in wage and price setting, again presumably in noncompetitive markets. Not only was the President urged to engage in such intervention in the matter of steel prices in 1958, but on numerous other occasions it was suggested, both publicly and privately, that the administration should "use its influence" to constrain private decision-making in these matters. Recognizing that a "wage-price policy" can indeed be carried out by the exercise of such influence widens the scope of this inquiry enormously. At the least, one would have to examine the role of the Department of Labor in the wage disputes of the period and, beyond this, the activities of the White House and other government agencies that had a bearing on specific cases of wage and price setting. Such an investigation runs far beyond the reasonable limits of this study, but I think it is worthwhile to devote brief attention to the matter.

The two-year contract negotiated between General Motors and the United Automobile Workers in 1948 was notable in that it departed from the established pattern of annual wage negotiations. This was the first of the long-term wage contracts that became common in major industries in the mid-1950s.[93] There has been some dispute among economists as to the net effect of such contracts on wage trends[94] (especially since 1953, when the UAW adopted a "living document" interpretation of its current five-year contract and successfully pressured the automotive companies to renegotiate the terms of a wage agreement that still had two years to run). The growth of long-term contracts tended to sharpen public interest in wage negotiations, since the resulting agreements produced a more durable, and therefore more significant, commitment to and indicator of wage trends. Many of these contracts involved intraterm wage adjustments linked to the consumer price index and to "annual improvement factors." The first of these raised the issue of whether a "price-wage" spiral was be-

93. See James J. Bambrick, Jr., and Marie P. Dorbandt, "The Trend to Longer-Term Union Contracts," *Management Record*, vol. 18 (June 1956), pp. 206–08; Jules Backman, *Wage Determination: An Analysis of Wage Criteria* (Van Nostrand, 1959).

94. See the discussion of this in William G. Bowen, *Wage Behavior in the Postwar Period: An Empirical Analysis* (Princeton University, Industrial Relations Section, 1960), pp. 47–51.

ing closed,[95] and the second linked wages to productivity increases, which became a central element in later discussion of wage-price policy.

Neither the general public nor the mass media can maintain a general review of wage bargaining in the whole economy. By reason of limited information alone, one would expect public discussion of such a question to focus on the behavior of "key industries." This tendency is reinforced by the very nature of collective bargaining. In nonatomistic markets where wages are determined by two-party negotiation, specific contracts are much affected by wage comparisons.[96] Representatives of both labor and management rely heavily on them, and arbitrators and "fact-finding boards" invariably cling to them as providing the only objective straws in a sea of moral claims. But comparisons have to be made *with* something, and this is where "key industries" enter into the general process of wage determination. The staff report prepared for the Joint Economic Committee in 1959 stated that for this reason "most of the wage increases in the manufacturing industries are traceable back, directly or indirectly, to the bargains negotiated in 1955, particularly in automobiles."[97] The OEEC group of experts awarded the crucial role in the inflation of the late 1950s to the steel industry's wage agreement of 1956,[98] and both their study and Jules Backman's concluded that the steel and automobile unions used the wage comparison argument to leapfrog one another up a spiral of "wage-wage" inflation.[99]

I do not aspire to sort out the analytical merits of these arguments, either as a description of the wage determination process or as an explanation of inflation. Whether wages in the steel and automobile industries were crucial is, for the purpose of this chapter, not as important as that they were perceived to be so. The Eisenhower administration did not adopt any policy toward emergent collective bargaining patterns (such as long-term contracts and escalator clauses) that could be described as an aspect of wage-price policy. Did it adopt a policy, and seek to implement it, toward specific cases of wage bargaining? There is no question but that the administration held a "view"—that wage increases were a

95. This was argued in *Economic Report of the President*, 1959, p. 89.
96. Arthur M. Ross, *Trade Union Wage Policy* (University of California, Institute of Industrial Relations, 1948).
97. *Staff Report on Unemployment, Growth, and Price Levels*, 86 Cong. 1 sess. (1959), p. 157.
98. Fellner and others, *The Problem of Rising Prices*, p. 477.
99. Ibid., p. 487; Backman, *Wage Determination*, p. 299.

(the?) primary cause of inflation and that they should be limited to increases in productivity—but did it attempt to make this view manifest as an effective force at the bargaining table? It was with respect to the steel industry that the Eisenhower administration carried its efforts to affect the substantive terms of collective bargaining furthest.

Steel is an important industry, and a strike or the threat of a strike occasions considerable concern on this account alone. In addition, the American public had, before the Eisenhower period, become sensitive to the potential drama of labor disputes in this industry. President Truman was faced with three major steel strikes between 1946 and 1952. In the 1946 dispute the President virtually ordered the parties to the White House to resume negotiations after they had broken down; he publicly announced terms that he felt would be a fair settlement in the public interest; and he publicly bullied the parties into accepting them. In the 1952 dispute he seized the companies and placed them under public ownership to prevent a work stoppage, and the strike only got under way after the Supreme Court declared this action illegal.

The government played an active role in all steel wage disputes, even before World War II. The 1946 negotiations were fundamentally tripartite in that the price of steel was under control and a relaxation of this was offered by President Truman as a condition for the final acceptance by the companies of the wage increase he had publicly recommended. When the first big contest between the United Steelworkers and the steel companies loomed during President Eisenhower's administration, price control no longer existed but the custom of strong government intervention in industrial disputes in this industry had not yet been disestablished. Contract talks between the union and the companies began to break down in the spring of 1956 and the administration had to decide whether to intervene, and if so, how. The log of Secretary of Labor James Mitchell shows that he initiated intervention on March 2, 1956, by calling David McDonald of the United Steelworkers to a meeting with the President, Secretary of the Treasury Humphrey, and himself, "to impress [McDonald] with the necessity of his exercising statesmanship and responsibility in the steel negotiations because of the possible inflationary tendency of an unrealistic wage settlement."[100] A strike was called on July 1 and lasted for twenty-six days. Mitchell and Humphrey actively engaged themselves in bringing this dispute to an end, and there is little doubt that they

100. Mitchell Papers, Box 51, Eisenhower Library.

exerted whatever influence they could to keep the wage settlement low. They did not, however, bring pressure to bear in any way comparable to President Truman's intervention in the steel strikes of 1946 and 1952.

Although I cannot here enter into the discussion of whether government intervention in steel wage disputes actually had any effect on wage rates and what that effect was, it is worth noting that in the opinion of one of the serious students of the question the effect was to make the settlements of 1949, 1952, *and* 1956 "more generous than private negotiations would have produced."[101]

Whatever influence the administration may have actually had on the settlement of 1956 and whatever influence it *intended* to have, the White House view was that it was politically desirable to keep this aspect of its efforts secret. Throughout the 1956 dispute and after its settlement, the official position was that the administration's role was confined to that of a conciliator, with no interference in the substantive terms of the settlement. I cannot say how successful the administration was in convincing the general public that its role was so restricted, but it is interesting to note what one of the wide-circulation weeklies had to say on this point after the dispute was settled:

Every major contract written in steel since the '30s was written in large part by government boards. The National War Labor Board, the Wage Stabilization Board, special Washington-named fact-finding tribunals, and a Taft-Hartley board had been chief authors, if not White House amanuenses, of steel's new contracts. This time the parties took at face value the Eisenhower Administration's "hands-off" policy in labor disputes. They assumed, and correctly so, that there would be no "recommendations" from the government.[102]

The administration hoped that the new wage contract in steel would not be an occasion for steel price increases, but this was not to be the case. The companies posted a general increase in prices in the summer of 1956 and further increases early in 1957. The wage contract called for still further wage increases to take place on July 1, 1957. With, one suspects, an eye on this date, the President issued a new appeal for wage and price restraint on June 26, but the following day U.S. Steel announced that it would raise prices on July 1. This disappointed some and angered others. Bernard Baruch called the President to say that he thought the steel industry was engaged in "free-booting" and that it should be investigated

101. C. K. Rowley, *Steel and Public Policy* (McGraw-Hill, 1971), p. 170.
102. *Business Week* (July 28, 1956), p. 26.

by the Federal Trade Commission or by Congress.[103] The CEA had earlier
made studies (by Charles Schultze and C. D. Long) of steel wages, costs,
and prices, and in response to Baruch's call to the President, Schultze prepared some information on U.S. Steel's profits.[104] The administration was
not happy about the price increases, and the CEA studies indicated that
those of July 1 were not essential to the maintenance of customary profit
rates, but by the middle of July the President's standard reply to criticism
of the steel company actions was that his economists had informed him
that the increases would have little general inflationary impact.[105]

A tougher test for the administration came in 1959 when contract negotiations in steel broke down again and a strike resulted which shut down
85 percent of the nation's basic steel industry for 116 days, more than
twice the previous record length. The contract between the union and the
twelve major steel companies was due to expire on June 30, 1959. In April
the companies proposed that it be extended for one year, but the union
rejected this, indicating that it would seek a substantial wage increase. By
the end of June agreement was not in sight, and the President asked the
parties to continue negotiations for another two weeks. The strike began
on July 15. Throughout August and September the strike continued, with
little activity on the negotiation front. President Eisenhower called the
parties to the White House on September 30 and, meeting separately with
each, urged resumption of negotiations. This they agreed to, but the talks
broke down again on October 5 and the President appointed a board of
inquiry under the Taft-Hartley Act. This board attempted to mediate the
dispute as well as to inquire, but on October 19 it reported to the President that the parties were far apart on all important issues. Thereupon the
President invoked the emergency provisions of the Taft-Hartley Act, and
on November 7 the steelworkers were ordered back to work for the eighty-
day period provided for in the act. By the end of the year the parties still
seemed to be far from a settlement and Vice-President Nixon and Secretary of Labor Mitchell undertook to mediate between them. A new contract was agreed to on January 4, 1960, on terms proposed by Nixon and
Mitchell.

At a press conference in March, before initial negotiations had begun in steel, the President was asked whether he could do anything "to head off this new injection of price-wage inflation." The President replied that he hoped that labor and management would "show statesmanship" in the matter and that the measure of this would be "that there be no advance in the price [of steel]," but he also emphasized that "it has been the policy of this Government to keep outside the business of collective bargaining, and not inject itself in the process, so far as any specific recommendation is made."[106] These two themes were frequently reiterated in the ensuing weeks by the President and other members of the administration. When the strike began and negotiations between the parties were suspended, the demands for government intervention increased sharply. Some of the senior advisers continued to recommend a noninterventionist policy,[107] but as the strike continued, with no visible progress toward a settlement, this position began to erode. Secretary Mitchell reported to the President on the state of the negotiations early in September, whereupon the President sent an open letter to the president of the United Steelworkers and the representatives of the industry urging resumption of bargaining and saying, significantly, "The Secretary's report has demonstrated clearly that there is a reasonable basis for a settlement that will be responsive to the requirements of the public interest as I have previously outlined them in public statements."[108]

The President resisted early suggestions that he call the parties to the White House, and when he finally did so on September 30, after having stated publicly that he was "getting sick and tired" of the "intolerable situation" and that he would "use every conceivable personal and official influence available . . . to break the impasse,"[109] he took a cool and conciliatory line, urging the parties to negotiate and stating that it was not his intention to intervene.[110] Nonetheless, the administration was clearly in favor of the companies' taking a firm stand against large wage increases, and the companies considered themselves to be in harmony with the government in emphasizing their intention to strike a blow at inflation. When the settlement was reached, U.S. Steel and other companies spe-

106. Press conference of March 25, 1959, Wallis Papers, Box 2, Eisenhower Library.

107. See, for example, Wallis to the President, August 7, 1959, Staff Files-Wallis, Box 1, Eisenhower Library.

108. *Public Papers, 1959*, p. 643.

109. Statement by the President, September 28, 1959, Official Files 124-D, Box 636, Eisenhower Library.

110. "Memorandum of Conversations," September 30, 1959, same file.

cifically announced that they would not raise prices, and there is little doubt that, unlike the 1956 settlement, this was an element, if not an explicit commitment, in the discussions with Nixon and Mitchell that led to the new contract agreement.

Throughout the episode the administration was concerned about the politics of the issue. Public pressure on the government was intense—both to intervene and to produce a noninflationary result. The presidential election of 1960 was fast approaching. The administration, especially Vice-President Nixon, was pleased with the final settlement.[111] The wage increase amounted to about 3.5 percent a year over the three-year period covered by the agreement, which was considerably less than previous increases in the steel industry, and the announcement that there would be no immediate price increase seemed to sustain the wisdom of the administration's strategy.[112] But politics is even less predictable than economics. The announcement of the settlement was followed by widespread criticism of the administration for permitting a new round of inflation to begin. Don Paarlberg kept an accounting of letters received on the issue by the White House, the vice-president, and the secretary of labor; they were overwhelmingly unfavorable to the settlement—98 percent so in the vice-president's office.[113] The steel companies themselves do not seem to have been especially pleased with the settlement, at least publicly. Roger M. Blough of U.S. Steel commented that, while the 1960 settlement was better than previous ones, "we have *not* yet learned one thing: How any industry—ours included—can, under present-day circumstances, and with or without the intercession of government, reach a non-inflationary wage agreement."[114]

The Politics of Exhortation

The main thrust of the wage-price policy of the Eisenhower administration was the development of the doctrine of "shared responsibility"—that

111. Vice-President Nixon to Alexander F. Jones, January 21, 1960, Wallis Papers, Box 2, Eisenhower Library. This letter, to the executive editor of the *Syracuse Herald-Journal*, was reprinted in the press; see *New York Times*, January 24, 1960.

112. See *Public Papers*, 1960–61, pp. 24–25.

113. Paarlberg to General Wilton B. Persons, January 18 and 28, 1960, Official Files 124-D, Box 636, Eisenhower Library. There are also numerous letters in Mitchell Papers, Boxes 205, 206.

114. Blough, "Aftermath in Steel," speech delivered to the National Canners

business and labor, in particular big business and big labor, must accept substantial responsibility for price stability. The policy of exhortation, which was the only substantial addition made by the administration to the traditional weapons of fiscal and monetary policy, was founded on the shared responsibility doctrine. This idea was not new with the Eisenhower administration. It can be traced back to the populist movement of the late nineteenth century, and beyond this to such ideas as the medieval Christian doctrine that the economically powerful should be stewards and trustees of the public welfare. This is clearly not the place to embark on such an examination of the history of economic ideas, but it is certain, as some of the critics of the 1957 Economic Report perceived, that the shared responsibility doctrine has wide economic, political, and philosophical implications. It is a more fundamental departure from the general theory of a market economy than is the doctrine of government intervention, for it calls upon private entities, as well as public ones, to guide their specific actions by the criterion of social interest. Although the doctrine of shared responsibility was never fully articulated by the Eisenhower administration or subjected to a searching public discussion, the administration's use of exhortation wove it more tightly into the fabric of American public policy. In this way, the conservative Republican administration of President Eisenhower provided philosophical foundations for the "guidepost" type of policy that was pursued by the succeeding Democratic administrations.

Did the policy succeed in combating inflation? All that one can say with confidence is that the Eisenhower administration ended in a time of price stability. Whether this was the result of the use of traditional weapons of stabilization policy, whether the policy of exhortation or the specific event of the 1959 steel dispute played a role in it, or whether it was the result of the sustained sluggishness of the economy from 1958 on is not clear. Econometricians have not yet been able to demonstrate that wage-price policies, even more definite and concrete ones than those pursued in the late 1950s, have any long-term effect on the price level.

The history of the Eisenhower administration does, however, have something more definite to contribute to our understanding of the politics of stabilization policy. It supports a thesis, which could be documented as well from other periods in American history, that the political benefits of an anti-inflationary policy are derivable only from its verbal aspect. An

Association Convention, January 18, 1960 (New York: United States Steel Corporation, Public Relations Department; processed), p. 16.

administration gains public support and favor by expressing a firm resolve to fight inflation and by exhorting others to do likewise. But to act against it with any of the weapons in the stabilization armory, whether fiscal policy, monetary policy, controls, or intervention in labor and other markets, will surely bring a net political loss. In these terms, the Eisenhower administration's policy of exhortation was politically optimal (or nearly so); it preached against evil, and even evildoers have no great objection to that.

III

The Kennedy Years: Purposeful Pedagogy

PROFESSIONAL OPINION among economists in 1960 was far from unanimous in appraising the condition and prospects of the American economy. Was the economy vulnerable to a "new" inflation and to a novel form of structural unemployment? Was the "stagflation" of the last part of the 1950s so distinctive that it deserved to be regarded as "a phenomenon in search of a theory"?

Though economic thinking tended to divide sharply in diagnosing recent wage-price behavior, unanimity was approached on one general proposition: that the standard goals for the American economy—full employment and an accelerated rate of growth, balance-of-payments equilibrium, decentralized wage and price making (from which government generally stood aloof), and price stability—were not simultaneously achievable. Consensus on the reality of conflicting objectives did not mean, however, that agreement could readily be reached on the weights to be assigned to the several goals; on the contrary, discussions on the ordering of national economic priorities revealed major cleavages. In view of the division of opinion throughout the country, it would have been remarkable if those who advised President-elect Kennedy on economic issues had spoken with one voice. In fact, they did not.

Divergent Initial Perspectives

From the economists in the entourage of the President-elect, two distinct perspectives on the national economic agenda, and on the place of

Note. Most of the material used in this study is drawn from the collections in the John F. Kennedy Library, Waltham, Massachusetts. I am grateful for the valuable assistance provided by its director, Dan H. Fenn, Jr., and by its able archivists, particularly Edward W. Johnson, William W. Moss, Lawrence J. Hackman, and Megan F. Desnoyers. I am also indebted to Walter W. Heller for authorizing access to his papers.

wage-price policies within it, emerged. For one of these schools of thought, Paul A. Samuelson (who chaired a special task force on economic conditions appointed by the President-elect) may be regarded as a representative spokesman. In his view, the most important goal of the new administration's economic policy should properly be the restoration of full employment and the narrowing of the gap—aggravated by the "sluggishness" of the late 1950s—between actual and potential output. Although he recognized that a vigorous program of domestic expansion was subject to two possible objections—the balance-of-payments position might thereby be complicated and inflationary pressures might be renewed—neither of these considerations would justify any compromise in a primary commitment to deploy fiscal and monetary weapons to promote domestic expansion.

In this interpretation, wage-price policy was some distance removed from center stage. It was held to be a matter worthy of study, especially in sectors in which market power could impose upward pressure on the price level before high employment had been reached. Special attention to inflation defenses could, however, be deferred until the momentum of expansion was much more pronounced. A more serious concern was that premature worry about price behavior associated with full-employment activity would itself frustrate the implementation of expansionary programs. The report of the Samuelson task force set forth the issue in a concluding note, captioned "A Final Caution":

If there is indeed a tendency for prices and wages to rise long before we reach high employment, neither monetary nor fiscal policy can be used to the degree necessary to promote desired growth.

What may then be needed are new approaches to the problem of productivity, wages and price formation. Will it not be possible to bring government influence to bear on this vital matter without invoking direct controls on wages and prices? . . . Just as we pioneered in the 1920's in creating potent monetary mechanisms and in the 1930's in forging the tools of effective fiscal policy, so may it be necessary in the 1960's to meet head on the problem of a price creep.[1]

From a second perspective, for which Walt W. Rostow was a representative spokesman, wage-price policy deserved higher priority. Shortly

1. Report, "Prospects and Policies for the 1961 American Economy: A Report to President-elect Kennedy," January 6, 1961, Economy–Samuelson Report folder, Box 686, Transition files, Kennedy Library, p. 11.

after the election, Rostow reminded the President-elect of the basic ingredients of this case:

I cannot emphasize too strongly that the capacity of the new Administration to do what it wants to do at home and abroad will depend on promptly breaking the institutional basis for creeping inflation, notably in the key steel and automobile industries; and on driving hard to earn more foreign exchange and to increase domestic productivity over a wide front. Without determined action in these areas it will be extremely difficult to bring the domestic economy back to reasonably full employment without inflation; and this means that we shall not have the federal revenues to give extra needed thrust in military and foreign policy. If we do not evoke American effort and sacrifice for communal goals at home, we run the danger of being forced by the balance of payments position and inflation into substituting rhetoric for action abroad.[2]

In short, governmental initiative in wage and price setting was essential to the management of the balance of payments, the fulfillment of the administration's goals for American leadership in international affairs, and the uninterrupted pursuit of domestic social programs. Otherwise, it was feared that the requirements of balance-of-payments management would impose a "stop-go" pattern on policymaking. Rostow specifically urged the new President to press for a wage freeze and a price rollback in key sectors of the economy; the steel and automobile industries should be the first targets, in the hope that patterns set there would "spread out over the economy." The government's objective should be "to get an agreement to hold the line on existing money wage contracts on the commitment of the industry to pass along productivity increases in lower prices. In this setting measures to increase employment could be taken with greater confidence that they would not promptly yield an inflationary price increase."[3]

The reasoning underlying this position had been spelled out more fully some months earlier in an address (copies of which were in circulation at Kennedy headquarters) Rostow had prepared for the commencement exercises at the Harvard Business School. On that occasion, he had argued that "a large component of the specific inflationary pressure we face lies outside [the] familiar terrains of formal economics" and was to be found instead "in attitudes and institutional arrangements. . . . By assuming that

2. Report, "Action Teams: Military and Foreign Policy," November 17, 1960, Walt W. Rostow, 1960 folder, Box 64, President's Office files, Kennedy Library.
3. "Appendix: Three Domestic Issues Crucial to Our External Position," ibid.

inflation is the normal condition of our economy, business, labor, and government now act to perpetuate inflation, to the cost of the national interest."[4] To avert this danger, he had then proposed that national policy be devised to achieve two results: real wage increases should approximate the average increase in labor productivity for the economy as a whole, and the general price level should be stable or falling. To this end, wage-price "treaties" were proposed in which labor would agree to forgo increases in money wages on the understanding that productivity gains would be converted into price reductions.[5]

These two schools of thought clearly approached the broad questions of economic strategy, as well as the narrower issues of wage and price policies, from quite different directions. In weighing their relative merits, the new President was necessarily alert to a range of considerations that extended well beyond the domain of economics. Politics, as John Kennedy well understood, is the art of the possible, and the range of the possible in January 1961 was bounded by factors not immediately subject to presidential control. A Congress conditioned to the alleged virtues of budget balancing was unlikely to be enthusiastically receptive to Keynesian prescriptions for domestic expansion. But another constraint on policy maneuverability was equally formidable: the exposed position of the dollar and the drain on the gold reserves (which had accelerated in late 1960) obliged the executive branch to be mindful of the effects of its actions on international confidence.

So it was understandable that the President-elect should seek counsel from outside his inner circle, especially on the international dimensions of economic policy. None of the members invited to serve on the pre-inaugural task force on the balance of payments could have been regarded as close to Kennedy; indeed, that they were not was a significant recommendation for their appointment. The report of the task force, whose chairman was Allan Sproul (former president of the Federal Reserve Bank of New York) and which included Paul McCracken (former member of the Eisenhower Council of Economic Advisers) and Roy Blough (former

4. Draft of Commencement Address to the Harvard Business School, June 11, 1960, Walt W. Rostow, 1960 folder, Box 64, President's Office files, Kennedy Library, p. 4.
5. A version of this "treaty" idea had been explored during the campaign and discussed with George Meany, president of the AFL-CIO, but it was not pursued in depth at that time; see the submissions of Rostow to Archibald Cox, c/o Senator Kennedy's Office, July 22, 1960, Walt W. Rostow, 11/60–5/61 folder, Box 65, President's Office files, Kennedy Library.

member of the Truman Council of Economic Advisers), was designed to reassure the international community of the firmness of the new administration's resolve to defend the dollar. While the group recognized that there were "substantial differences of opinion about the extent of probable inflationary pressures, and on the extent of damage to our economy that would occur if we did have some chronic inflation," it urged that attention be given to steps to improve productivity, to strengthen price and product competition in international markets, and to devise measures to restrain increases in wages within limits allowable by productivity gains.[6] The task force further recommended that "quiet explorations" be undertaken by management and labor on the "inter-related subjects of productivity, costs, and prices without the publicity and pressure of a wage contract deadline." The government was counseled, however, to avoid a doctrinaire approach to these matters and to resist any temptation to create formal mechanisms to review privately determined wage and price decisions. The only effective policy mechanism, it was alleged, was "the considerable power of restraint inherent in public opinion."[7] The alertness of public opinion to the issues at stake might be increased by legislation that amended the Employment Act of 1946 to indicate that price stability was on a par with high employment as an official objective of the administration.

Administration Debate on Economic Priorities

By design, divergent perspectives on economic strategy were brought into the administration through the allocation of appointments to economic policy positions. Senior posts in the Treasury, for example, were filled with an eye to engendering the confidence of the business and financial community (both at home and abroad) and to acquiring expertise in the management of the balance of payments. The Council of Economic Advisers, on the other hand, was staffed with domestic expansionists drawn from academic life.

In the early intra-administration sparring over what should be the objectives of economic strategy, the opening rounds went to the balance-

6. Report, "The Economic Situation and the Balance of Payments," January 18, 1961, Economy–Current Situation folder, Box 688, Transition files, Kennedy Library, pp. 20–21.

7. Ibid., p. 22.

of-payments stabilizers. The Kennedy rhetoric had proclaimed that sacrifice would be asked of the American people; this posture, as he had warned
his nominee for the chairmanship of the Council of Economic Advisers
before the inauguration, could not readily be reconciled with recommendations for tax relief.[8] Even so, the CEA was not prepared for the
news, which its members learned only after the fact, that Kennedy had
promised congressional leaders he would submit a balanced budget for
fiscal year 1962. A Keynesian might count seven loopholes in one cumber-
some sentence in the State of the Union Message: "Within that framework [i.e., that of the revenue estimates prepared by the outgoing Eisenhower administration], barring the development of urgent national
defense needs or a worsening of the economy, it is my current intention to
advocate a program of expenditures which, including revenues from a
stimulation of the economy, will not of and by themselves unbalance the
earlier Budget."[9] There was no ambiguity, however, in another message:
that the political climate for an aggressively expansionary fiscal program
was not markedly favorable.

Nor could domestic expansionists draw much comfort from the prospects for monetary policy. At least in part, the balance-of-payments situation tied the Federal Reserve's hands in setting interest rates. But even
if provision for an interest rate structure attractive to foreign holders of
dollars had been less compelling than it was then perceived to be, the receptivity of central bankers to recommendations for an expansionary
monetary policy was slight. The reigning orthodoxy at the Federal Reserve
—as articulated by Chairman Martin—was that the nation faced a serious
problem of structural unemployment which would not yield to conven-

8. Walter Heller, Kermit Gordon, James Tobin, Gardner Ackley, and Paul Sam-
uelson, recorded interview by Joseph A. Pechman, August 1, 1964, Fort Ritchie,
Maryland, Kennedy Library Oral History Program, p. 121. Hereafter Fort Ritchie
Oral History Interview.

9. "Annual Message to the Congress on the State of the Union. January 30,
1961," Public Papers of the Presidents of the United States: John F. Kennedy, 1961
(1962), p. 22. Hereafter Public Papers.

Of this episode, Walter Heller has observed: "As economists, we were shocked
when we were told in one of our first White House meetings that the antirecession
battle would have to be fought within the bounds of a balanced budget. But relief
followed shock when, with our help, the commitment was watered down . . . in the
State of the Union Message. . . . We counted seven escape hatches." Walter W.
Heller, New Dimensions of Political Economy (Harvard University Press, 1966),
pp. 30–31.

tional techniques to increase aggregate demand. Instead, such measures would touch off another bout of inflationary pressures:

While the unemployment that arises from cyclical causes should prove only temporary, there are, however, forces at work that have produced another, structural type of unemployment that is worse, in that it already has proved to be indefinitely persistent—even in periods of unprecedented general prosperity. . . .

To have important effect, attempts to reduce structural unemployment by massive monetary and fiscal stimulation of overall demands probably would have to be carried to such lengths as to create serious new problems of inflationary character—at a time when consumer prices already are at a record high.[10]

Meanwhile the President made clear that his central concern in economic matters lay in bringing the balance of payments under control. Wage and price behavior that would ensure international competitiveness was therefore regarded as crucial. As he stated early in February:

All of us must now be conscious of the need for policies that enable American goods to compete successfully with foreign goods. We cannot afford unsound wage and price movements which push up costs, weaken our international competitive position, restrict job opportunities, and jeopardize the health of our domestic economy.[11]

International competitiveness was indeed to become a watchword. Government intervention in some areas held promise for this; for example, tax adjustments to encourage modernization of plant and equipment for the purpose of accelerating productivity improvement (a task with which the tax experts in the Treasury were charged) and programs to raise the export-consciousness of U.S. firms (an assignment given Luther Hodges at the time of his appointment as secretary of commerce).[12] But it was not intended that the government should intervene directly in the processes of wage and price making. Instead, it was hoped that the formation of a labor-management advisory committee, which was announced before the new administration was a fortnight old, would create a mechanism

10. Statement of William McChesney Martin, Jr., in *January 1961 Economic Report of the President and the Economic Situation and Outlook*, Hearings before the Joint Economic Committee, 87 Cong. 1 sess. (1961), p. 470.

11. "Special Message to the Congress: Program for Economic Recovery and Growth, February 2, 1961," *Public Papers*, 1961, p. 52.

12. Luther Hodges, recorded interview by Dan Jacobs, March–May 1964, Kennedy Library Oral History Program, p. 15.

through which the public stake in price stability could be effectively transmitted. The committee had broad authority. It was directed to submit recommendations for measures that would contribute to responsibility in wage and price setting and to productivity improvement. The formation of the committee was to be seen internationally as evidence that the Kennedy administration was in earnest about wage and price discipline to ease the balance-of-payments problem.

Though the White House had early and unmistakably assigned top priority to the internationalist aspects of economic strategies, the President did assure domestic expansionists that the state of the economy would be given a "second look" in mid-April. If evidence on the economy's performance during the first quarter failed to indicate that recovery from the recession was under way, policy could then be reassessed. This opportunity to reorient the administration's economic strategies was seized upon eagerly by the Department of Labor and the CEA. Both organizations set about formulating arguments to demonstrate that statistical evidence of an upturn, though welcome, should not be decisive. The problem before the country should be understood as a longer-term narrowing of the GNP gap (the gap between actual and potential gross national product) and not merely one of engineering recovery from the latest recession.

The Department of Labor's submission at the time of the "second look" concluded that "the prognosis for the long-run as well as the immediate months ahead is for a seriously high level and rate of joblessness."[13] While total employment had reached a record high in March, unemployment had "failed to decline even in accord with reasonable expectations." Moreover, the Labor Department estimated that the achievement of a 4 percent unemployment rate within the next year would call for the creation of 7.3 million additional jobs and that this task, in turn, would require an increase in GNP of approximately $60 billion. As a first step in attacking this problem, Secretary Goldberg proposed that the administration recommend passage of legislation drafted by the Department of Labor to be called the "Full Employment Act of 1961." This bill would first identify the central objective of policy. "The paramount criterion for judging the success of national economic policy," it declared, was a "level of unemployment consistent with full employment which, presumptively, under present circumstances, is a seasonally adjusted un-

13. Arthur Goldberg to the President, April 14, 1961, Microfilm Copies of Records of the Department of Labor, Roll 49, Kennedy Library.

employment rate less than 4 percent of the civilian labor force." To enable the executive branch to fulfill this commitment, it was further proposed that the President be afforded discretion in varying tax rates and expenditure allocations.[14]

The Council of Economic Advisers was more specific in its recommendations. Walter Heller counseled the President in mid-March that a major assault on the problem of unemployment should no longer be delayed. The CEA estimated that the task would require a $10 billion deficit in fiscal 1962.[15] Heller was under no illusion that this medicine would be easy to swallow for an administration that, in its first two months, had carefully cultivated an image of caution and fiscal responsibility. Two anticipatable criticisms of deliberate deficits—fear of the consequences for price stability and for international reserves—were thus addressed at some length:

Inflation dangers are at their lowest point in years. With less than 80 percent of industrial capacity in use, with over 5½ million unemployed, and with a lot of sluggishness in the private economic outlook, we have plenty of slack to take up before inflationary inhibitions will call a halt to further government stimulus. This gives us a lot of leeway to introduce fairly long lasting government recovery programs (18 months seems quite safe) without the stultifying fear that they will aggravate an inflationary boom. . . . As for the alleged dangers to our gold stock in expansionary fiscal measures, many informed foreign observers are now beginning to worry about a continued U.S. recession. Fears that the Kennedy Administration would be too inflationary have now been put to rest. . . . Recovery, though it will increase imports, will also tend to keep U.S. long-term capital at home to take advantage of more profitable domestic investment opportunities. Meanwhile, the measures under way to correct the basic deficit, assisted by actions of other Western countries and by programs in burden-sharing and in international monetary cooperation, will be taking effect.

The "gold outflow" problem will be used to oppose all bold expansion-

14. "An Act to Implement the Employment Act of 1946," discussion paper prepared by the Department of Labor, April 13, 1961, Microfilm Copies of Records of the Department of Labor, Roll 49, Kennedy Library.

15. Heller to the President, "The Economics of the Second-Stage Recovery Program," March 17, 1961, Walter W. Heller, 2/61–8/62 folder, Box 63, President's Office files, Kennedy Library.

ary measures by people who oppose them anyway. But our policy can and should be made in Washington, not by bankers in Zurich or Frankfurt or London or even New York.[16]

The CEA outline of the imperatives of economic policy did not at this time lose sight of the significance of price stability. As its members observed in their presentation to the Joint Economic Committee in March 1961, renewal of the price creep of 1955–58 might thwart efforts to restore balance-of-payments equilibrium. An attitude of watchfulness, which should include a more vigorous commitment by the Justice Department to "pro-competitive" policies, would be useful. In addition, the Council expressed the hope that the newly formed Advisory Committee on Labor-Management Policy would aid in enlisting voluntary cooperation in wage and price restraint. But it was also noted that policy should aim to create a higher rate of productivity increase "because a highly progressive economy is able to absorb steadily rising wage rates into a stable price level."[17] The alleged incompatibility between economic expansion and price stability might thus be reconciled.

It was soon apparent that a proposal to move boldly on the fiscal front was unlikely at this stage to win presidential endorsement. Nevertheless, the CEA was persistent. On March 21 Heller submitted an alternate plan which was designed to remove in part any political stigma for reckless deficit financing that might be attached to the Kennedy administration. Under this scheme, 1960 taxpayers would receive a "once and for all" rebate on their 1960 income tax before July 1. As a bookkeeping matter, the resulting deficit would thus appear totally in the 1961 budget returns.[18] Though this recommendation also failed, the CEA had one other resource at its disposal: intervention by Paul Samuelson. His memorandum reinforced the CEA analysis of the economic situation, though it conceded that "if a temporary tax cut made no *political* sense in January, it probably won't in April either (however great its true economic merits)." Samuelson concluded with his proposed response to a hypothetical question that his grandchildren might raise about his contribution to the New Frontier:

16. Ibid.

17. Statement of Walter W. Heller, chairman, Council of Economic Advisers, accompanied by Kermit Gordon and James Tobin, in *January 1961 Economic Report*, Hearings, p. 306.

18. Heller to the President, "Retroactive Income Tax Cut for 1960," March 21, 1961, Memos to JFK, 3/61 folder, Kennedy-Johnson files, Papers of Walter W. Heller, Kennedy Library.

I shall sadly reply: "I kept telling them down at the office, in December, January, and April that, WHAT THIS COUNTRY NEEDS IS AN ACROSS THE BOARD RISE IN DISPOSABLE INCOME TO LOWER THE LEVEL OF UNEMPLOYMENT, SPEED UP THE RECOVERY AND THE RETURN TO HEALTHY GROWTH, PROMOTE CAPITAL FORMATION AND THE GENERAL WELFARE, INSURE DOMESTIC TRANQUILITY AND THE TRIUMPH OF THE DEMOCRATIC PARTY AT THE POLLS."[19]

Fiscal expansionists emerged from the second-stage campaign no more successful than they had been in the first. Their educational efforts in the administration had been neutralized by the behavior of the economy itself. The first-quarter results seemed to indicate that the trough of the recession had passed. When the economy could be seen to be moving in the right direction, the urgency of extraordinary measures to close the GNP gap was increasingly difficult to sell. Theodore Sorensen captured the dilemma of domestic expansionists at that moment with his remark in the White House staff dining room: "There are the Council of Economic Advisers contemplating the dangers of an upturn."[20]

Convergence on Wage-Price Policy in the Administration

The domestic expansionists had lost both round one (in January) and round two (in late March and early April). A rethinking of tactics appeared to be in order. From the experience of the first hundred days, two lessons could be drawn: that political constraints on the explicit use of deficits to stimulate the economy were both formidable and likely to be unyielding, at least in the intermediate run, to purely economic argument and that prospects for winning support for expansionary programs might be considerably brightened if assurances could be made that price increases would not result. A plausible posture on wage-price stability thus assumed significance in the weaponry of expansionary advocacy, even to those who, on the merits of the case, were far from persuaded that inflationary pressures were either a present or an imminent danger. It was now apparent that fiscal remedies for closing the GNP gap were unlikely to be

19. Samuelson to the President and the Council of Economic Advisers, "That 'April Second Look' at the Economy," March 21, 1961, Council of Economic Advisers, 1/61–3/61 folder, Box 73, President's Office files, Kennedy Library.

20. As reported in the Fort Ritchie Oral History Interview, p. 220. In slightly different phrasing, this episode is also recounted by Walter Heller in *New Dimensions of Political Economy*, pp. 31–32.

acceptable to the White House or the Treasury unless such measures could be reconciled with increased international competitiveness. Similarly, the cooperation of central bankers in expansionary programs was likely to be contingent on the availability of plans to deal with upward pressures on wages and prices before the full employment threshold had been crossed. Arguments that concern about inflationary pressures was largely misplaced—at least until the recovery of the economy was much further advanced—had been tried and had failed.

The initial disappointment of the domestic expansionists thus tended to produce a shift in the style and substance of advocacy. By late March CEA members were prepared to assign greater importance to wage-price issues. Kennedy had first commended Rostow's views on these matters to Heller's attention at a preinaugural conference at the Carlyle Hotel in New York.[21] When this suggestion was made again in March, it was pursued. On presidential instruction, Rostow had already conveyed his proposals for wage-price "treaties" in major industries to Secretary Goldberg at a luncheon meeting on February 1, 1961.[22]

Rostow's position in the spring of 1961 was the same as it had been the preceding autumn—that the administration's influence should be directed to achieving wage restraint and price reduction in major industries. In his view, the wage negotiation in the automobile industry (scheduled for late summer) would be "a crucial event for both our domestic and foreign policies." It was therefore of the utmost importance that the administration "use every device at our command to persuade the two parties to go for a wage freeze and price cut." This settlement would be significant because

European bankers are holding dollars and not drawing gold from us in an act of self-discipline. They are waiting to see if we are capable of dealing with the hard core of our balance of payments problem, which centers

21. Fort Ritchie Oral History Interview, p. 181.
22. Rostow reported to the President ("Memorandum of Conversation with Secretary of Labor Goldberg," February 1, 1961, Labor, 1/61–5/61 folder, Box 81, President's Office files, Kennedy Library) that Goldberg indicated his support for a "responsible" price-wage policy, but that he "oppose[d] an immediate price-wage agreement on two grounds:
"—First, neither labor, industry, nor the public understands as yet the seriousness of the world situation and the relationship between price-wage policy and the ability of the U.S. to perform either on the world scene or at home;
"—Second, the problem itself is more complex than any of those who have considered it have yet grasped. In his view an effective proposal has not yet been formulated."

around American prices and productivity. A wage freeze and price cut in
the auto industry would go some distance in making them feel we are serious and making progress; an inflationary settlement might set in motion
a gold drain which could upset our present tenuous equilibrium.[23]

If a pattern could be set in the automotive industry, there was some hope
that it might be transferred to other crucial sectors. As for the prospects
of negotiating the suggested labor-management "treaty" in the automotive industry, Rostow held the view that there was some ground for optimism: it was his impression that Walter Reuther, president of the United
Automobile Workers, was sympathetic to such an arrangement.[24] It is not
clear, however, that Rostow and Reuther had a common understanding
of the rationale for the recommended strategy.[25]

The subject of wage-price policy was close to the President's heart, and
this was made clear to senior economic policymakers at White House
meetings in May and June. Kennedy characterized his view in a special
message to Congress on May 25:

As recovery progresses, there will be temptations to seek unjustified
price and wage increases. These we cannot afford. They will only handicap
our efforts to compete abroad and to achieve full recovery here at home.
Labor and management must—and I am confident that they will—pursue
responsible wage and price policies in these critical times. I look to the

23. Rostow to the President, April 5, 1961, Walt W. Rostow, 11/60–5/61
folder, Box 65, President's Office files, Kennedy Library.
24. On February 1, 1961, Rostow had indicated in a memorandum to Goldberg
(a copy of which was initialed by Kennedy) that "Walter Reuther has already indicated his support for some such course." Rostow to Goldberg, February 1, 1961,
Labor, 1/61–5/61 folder, Box 81, President's Office files, Kennedy Library.
25. It seems, for example, that Reuther attached much greater weight to the
distributive implications of a wage freeze and a price rollback than to their counter-
inflationary implications. Writing to Kennedy at the President's request (following a
conversation between them after the March meeting of the Labor-Management
Advisory Committee), Reuther offered a comparative analysis of postwar income
gains of automobile workers and of Ford and GM stockholders, with results indicating
massively higher rates of growth in dividend incomes than in wage incomes (Reuther
to the President, April 5, 1961, same file). In Reuther's judgment:
"The question of the relative equities of wage earners and stockholders raised by
these comparisons is more than a matter of economic justice. . . .
"The American economy is in serious trouble and we shall continue to be plagued
with high levels of unemployed workers and idle facilities so long as the competing
equities of workers, stockholders, and consumers are not worked out on a more economically rational and socially responsible basis. So long as any of the three basic
groups are [sic] shortchanged, we shall feed the forces of imbalance into the economy with economic dislocation and recession as the inevitable results."

President's Advisory Committee on Labor-Management Policy to give a strong lead in this direction.[26]

To the inner circle, Kennedy was more direct in stressing the need "to try hard to bring the wage-price problem under control."[27] This presidential position was clearly in harmony with the Treasury's reading of the larger economic situation. Though the balance of payments had shown an apparent improvement in the first quarter of 1961, overall equilibrium was not yet in sight. Reductions in imports had been responsible for most of the recorded improvement in the merchandise trade accounts. As Treasury Secretary Dillon pointed out to Kennedy in early May: "These reductions were in turn due to the recession. Imports will increase from here on as our economy picks up steam."[28] The major test of international competitiveness thus lay ahead.

Differing views on the most important goals of economic policy, however, had not evaporated. The CEA held firm to its conviction that the economic situation called for fresh fiscal stimulation and that this could be undertaken without the risk of unmanageable inflationary pressures. But the usefulness of thinking through defenses against cost-push inflation was also given greater prominence. Walter Heller wrote to the President: "Cost-push inflation? There's always danger here if labor and management exercise their full market power as business activity moves up. It will require all our ingenuity to cope with this."[29] In the same context, an alert was sounded about another danger: *"Our powerful tax system and large latent surplus*—plus a Federal Reserve System with an eye typically cocked if not glued on the dangers of gold outflow and inflation—*are likely to exert a strong drag on recovery."*[30]

By mid-June a workable consensus had been approached on the importance of wage-price policy in the overall strategy. Meetings with the

26. "Special Message to the Congress on Urgent National Needs. May 25, 1961," *Public Papers*, 1961, p. 398.

27. Kermit Gordon, "Notes on Meeting with the President on Monetary Policy," June 12, 1961, General File, 6/1/61–6/15/61 folder, Kennedy-Johnson files, Heller Papers, Kennedy Library.

28. Douglas Dillon to the President, "First Quarter Balance-of-Payments Situation," May 5, 1961, Microfilm Copies of Records of the Treasury Department, Roll 39, Kennedy Library.

29. Heller to the President, "Economic Background of the Second-stage Economic Program," May 10, 1961, Memos to JFK, 5/61 folder, Kennedy-Johnson files, Heller Papers, Kennedy Library.

30. Ibid.

President had helped to catalyze some movement from the initial positions. The Federal Reserve, as Chairman Martin noted at a June 12 meeting in the White House, would be prepared to adopt more aggressive policies if assured that any threat to price stability would be taken seriously.[31] Similarly, there was some indication that anxiety at the Treasury about the possible consequences of expansion for the balance of payments would be relieved if measures could be taken to ensure that international competitiveness would not thereby be compromised. As the flow of internal debate evolved, it became apparent that the cause of domestic expansion would be well served if an effective wage-price strategy could be devised. To reallocate energies in this direction—as the CEA was to do— in no sense implied a retreat from the pursuit of expansionary policies. On the contrary, these dimensions of policy could now be seen to be linked: the lack of a firm wage-price position was itself a constraint to expansionary programs. Moreover, there was another link. As Walter Heller reminded the President, the acceptability to labor of requests for wage restraint was likely to be contingent on an administration commitment to attack unemployment more aggressively.[32]

Thus, for different reasons, groups within the government that had originally approached the wage-price issue from different directions now tended to converge. All of the central parties were persuaded of the need —indeed the *instrumental* necessity—for a common commitment to price stability.

Groping for a Strategy

Though by the summer of 1961 there was agreement on the importance of wage-price policy, its specific content and the institutional mechanisms through which it could be effected had yet to be determined. Was the Labor-Management Advisory Committee likely to be as useful for these purposes as the President had publicly hoped it would be? Its early meetings had not been altogether reassuring. The discussions, though lively, had tended to be diffuse and unstructured—a shortcoming perceived by some of the participants, who suggested that the CEA take the

31. Kermit Gordon, "Notes on Meeting with the President on Monetary Policy."
32. Ibid.

lead in organizing an interagency task force to prepare background papers on which future committee discussions could be focused.[33]

In preparation for this role—and, in particular, for the July meeting of the Labor-Management Advisory Committee at which wage-price policy was the scheduled item—the CEA convened its own sessions with consultants drawn largely from the academic community. Walter Heller explained the purpose of the June 13 gathering as, "We need to know which direction to give to the deliberations of the Labor-Management Committee."[34] And Kermit Gordon added when taking the chair for these sessions that the Council was "groping for a strategy."[35]

If nothing else, these discussions demonstrated that the task of formulating an effective wage-price policy capable of commanding broad support would be a formidable undertaking. Within this group of economists a sharp division emerged over whether a government position on wage-price policy was needed at all. The skeptics, however, did not speak with one voice. One line of dissent argued that the history of government intervention in labor-management negotiations had, on balance, been inflationary in that it tended to produce wage settlements higher than those private parties alone would have accepted; another maintained that vigorous economic growth—and the accelerated rate of productivity increase associated with it—would be sufficient in itself to ease inflationary pressures. And among those who accepted the need for an official position on wages and prices, the ranks divided on the form it should take. Should intervention be directed primarily toward wages (with the hope that public opinion would then mobilize against price increases) or should even-handed treatment of both labor and management be adopted? Should the objective of policy be comprehensive coverage or should government involvement be reserved for selected sectors? Was it realistic to expect that without direct controls, potentially inflationary behavior could be policed either by aroused public opinion or by unpublicized presidential com-

33. Kermit Gordon to Heller and Tobin, "Report on May 1 Meeting of the President's Committee on Labor-Management Policy," May 2, 1961, General File, 5/1/61–5/17/61 folder, Kennedy-Johnson files, Heller Papers, Kennedy Library.

34. Minutes of the Economic Consultants' Meeting with the Council of Economic Advisers, June 13, 1961, Heller Council, 5/61–6/61 folder, Kennedy-Johnson files, Heller Papers, Kennedy Library. The participants included Gardner Ackley, William Bowen, E. Cary Brown, Gerhard Colm, James S. Duesenberry, Richard Goode, Aaron Gordon, Alvin H. Hansen, Seymour E. Harris, Edwin Kuh, Mark Leiserson, Richard Lester, Richard A. Musgrave, Robert R. Nathan, Joseph A. Pechman, Albert Rees, Paul Samuelson, Charles L. Schultze, and Lloyd Ulman.

35. Ibid.

munications with leaders in business and organized labor?[36] Though no fully satisfying answers to these questions were immediately forthcoming, many of the crucial issues had at least been identified.

The CEA largely bypassed these matters in the working paper (prepared jointly with the Commerce and Labor Departments) for the July meeting of the Labor-Management Advisory Committee. Instead the paper sketched the statistical background of postwar wage-price experience in the United States and summarized significant theoretical literature on the mechanisms of inflation. But a position of studied neutrality was maintained throughout. A concluding section on anti-inflation policy offered no explicit recommendations but confined attention to a review of proposals that had already entered the stream of public debate.[37]

To the President, on the other hand, the CEA spoke more pointedly. Reminding him that the July meeting of the Labor-Management Advisory Committee would address the wage-price issue "head-on," Walter Heller was pessimistic about the outcome. The chances, he estimated, were "less than 50-50" that the committee would "make a positive contribution to price level stabilization."[38] To improve the prospects, he suggested that the President might indicate a framework within which private wage-price decisions compatible with the national interest could be made. On prices, he recommended the following position:

The national interest requires stability of the general level of prices. In industries where the increase in productivity is less than the national average, prices may have to increase. Hence stability of the price level requires offsetting price reductions in industries where productivity is growing more rapidly than the national average. We cannot have price level stability without reductions in many individual prices.[39]

Productivity was thus introduced as a test of responsible price making. Symmetrical use of a productivity standard for wage determination was not proposed, however. The recommendation for the income side was cast in the following form:

36. Ibid.

37. "Summary of Working Paper: Wage and Price Policy," prepared for use by the President's Advisory Committee on Labor-Management Policy, June 1961, Wage-Price Guideposts, Genesis folder, Kennedy-Johnson files, Heller Papers, Kennedy Library.

38. Heller to the President, "Meeting of the President's Labor-Management Committee," July 10, 1961, Memos to JFK folder, Kennedy-Johnson files, Heller Papers, Kennedy Library.

39. Ibid.

Our economy should continue to yield an ever increasing level of real wages and salaries for our labor force. It must also yield over time an increasing volume of profits, if industry is to attract investment capital to expand and modernize its operations. With steady growth, both of these goals are obtainable. But in the bargaining and decision making which influence the relative size of wages and profits, both sides must accept the principle that the outcome will be consistent with overall price stability. The Federal Government is not intruding in the processes by which wages, salaries, and profits are determined. It is simply asking that those who make these bargains or decisions consider themselves limited to results which will not generate inflation.[40]

Though guidance to the private sector was not highly specific, the "groping for a strategy" had begun to yield some initial returns.

Meanwhile, the Labor-Management Advisory Committee was proceeding along a different route. Its July session was dominated by discussion of a proposal introduced by Walter Reuther, who called for the creation of a "mechanism, not to set prices or wages, but before which labor and management in key situations with a broad impact would have to defend their positions on wages and prices. Such an agency could have public hearings and enlist public opinion behind a sound policy in the relationship of wages, prices and profits."[41]

Both the rationale for this proposal and its substance were spelled out more fully in a paper prepared shortly thereafter by a team of consultants to the committee whose work was coordinated by George Shultz. The labor consultants in this group parted company with the majority in asserting the need for "some form of restraining influence on price-making to substitute for the absent restraint of price competition" in those sectors of the economy in which prices could be administered. In their judgment, informed public opinion would serve this purpose but "only through hearings in which all pertinent facts are available and thoroughly ventilated and analyzed."[42] This could be accomplished through the creation

40. Ibid.
41. Minutes of the President's Advisory Committee on Labor-Management Policy, July 10, 1961, Microfilm Copies of Records of the Department of Labor, Roll 72, Kennedy Library, pp. 2–3. A similar proposal had been introduced by Congressman Henry S. Reuss in 1959 but had failed to reach the floor of the House.
42. "Statement on Sound Wage and Price Policies," Report of Consultants to Sub-Committee 5 of the President's Advisory Committee on Labor-Management Policy, August 4, 1961, Wage-Price Guideposts, Genesis folder, Kennedy-Johnson files, Heller Papers, Kennedy Library, p. 11.

of a board charged with conducting public hearings on significant price and wage increases and by the appointment of a consumer counsel to act as the public's advocate. The board's authority would be restricted, however, to corporations whose sales amounted to 25 percent or more of the total sales within a given industry. Firms fitting that definition would be obliged to submit advance notice of an intent to raise prices; the consumer counsel would also be empowered to initiate hearings should he have reason to believe that price reductions were justified. The board, however, would be prohibited from passing judgment on the propriety of any proposed price or wage increase. As the labor consultants put it:

This restriction is necessary because, unlike public utility situations, there are no consensus standards of proper price behavior in the kinds of industries here under consideration. In time, standards of publicly acceptable behavior might evolve as a result of hearings. Such standards could have an important influence on price-setting decisions. Meanwhile, the prospect of public exposure would be sufficient in itself, despite the absence of standards, to minimize the danger of flagrant abuse of private price-making power.[43]

Industry representatives were outspoken in their opposition to this proposal. They warned that it would be "only too easy for such hearings procedures to create a 'witch hunting' atmosphere in which each party involved tries to assume the mantle of hunter and force on the other the garb of the witch. We have had all too much experience with this process in the United States. . . . It may also lead to undesirable wage and price controls when, as is all too likely, the results of the hearings procedure are judged to be ineffective."[44]

If consensus was beyond reach on the machinery through which the public stake in wage and price making could be asserted, the group was closer to agreement on a procedure that should not be adopted. General preachments by public officials were held to be futile. The consultants asserted:

Exhortation has been tried on earlier occasions and has not yielded satisfactory results. Private parties will not act against their own interests over any extended period of time, nor would it be desirable for them to do so. It is difficult, for example, to imagine unions in the peacetime role of policemen, telling their members not to take wage increases that are available. Union leaders advocating such policies would not last for long, even

43. Ibid., p. 14.
44. Ibid., p. 9.

though they were praised as "responsible" by leaders in management and government. Nor can we visualize business leaders yearly calling to the attention of stockholders how management, through its price policies, has successfully curtailed profits and thereby reduced the dividends to be paid by the corporation.[45]

Though these exchanges exposed major cleavages, they nonetheless engendered the recognition that "soundness" in wage and price making called for improvements in the quality of economic data relevant to informed public judgment and for innovations in the method of communication. In the view of industry representatives (as well as some of the public members of the committee—notably, Arthur Burns), a large step in this direction might be taken by using the President's Economic Report as the vehicle by which materials pertinent to informed public discussion could be conveyed. The subsequent hearings before the Joint Economic Committee—and perhaps also an annual conference of labor and management leaders on the Economic Report—could ensure that issues were publicly aired.

This round solved no problems. But it did signal the importance of perfecting the government's statistical instruments if an official strategy was to move beyond the hortatory and the abstract.

Improvised Skirmish Lines: Automobiles and Steel

By mid-1961 wage-price issues had clearly moved up the scale. Nevertheless, a coherent view of what should be done—as opposed to general agreement that a concerned attitude would be useful—had yet to be reached. That uncertainty persisted was reflected in Walter Heller's choice of words when addressing a question to his colleagues in mid-August: "Along what lines could I give the least lame answer to a [possible] MEET THE PRESS question on what we plan to do to hold down the wage-price spiral?"[46] Meanwhile, there were other matters demanding attention on a timetable that had no flexibility.

Two test cases could be expected to ripen in the early future: contract negotiations in the automobile industry (in prospect for August and September) and the even more complicated case of steel. Though the steel

45. Ibid., p. 8.
46. Heller to Gordon and Robert M. Solow, August 17, 1961, General File, 8/61 folder, Kennedy-Johnson files, Heller Papers, Kennedy Library.

contract would not expire until midsummer 1962, the agreement concluded in 1959 had stipulated that a wage increment be paid from October 1, 1961. Rumors were already circulating that the steel industry would use this occasion to increase its prices. The automobile case had precedence in timing, and thus special significance for pattern-setting that might be imitated elsewhere. But in steel the stakes were higher. A study by Eckstein and Fromm found that steel prices had contributed greatly to 1955–58 inflationary pressure;[47] this and their contribution to the deterioration in the U.S. balance of trade in the late 1950s had made an impression on the administration.

In approaching these specific situations, the administration was handicapped because general battle lines on the wage-price front were not yet well prepared. But accidents of timing had also given some unexpected strength to its bargaining hand. The Berlin crisis in midsummer 1961 and the semimobilization that accompanied it meant that the administration could call for extraordinary civilian discipline and expect to receive a favorable response. The call for sacrifice, as perceived in the White House in July, might properly include a recommendation that Congress vote tax increases justified by enlarged defense expenditures—indeed, a presidential request to this effect was only narrowly averted. In this matter, the President yielded to the persuasiveness of domestic expansionists, who argued that tax increases—despite the case that could be built in their favor on political and psychological grounds—would tend to abort the economy's recovery. Retrospectively, members of the CEA were to regard their success in this instance as their first significant fiscal policy victory.[48]

Behind the scenes, discussions of wage-price policy in this period also took a different turn. In an atmosphere of emergency it was pertinent to ask whether authority should be sought to introduce controls such as those of the Korean War. Though this approach was rejected, it was seriously canvassed. There was still sufficient slack in the economy to justify the conclusion that direct controls would be unnecessary. Moreover, data available on consumer behavior in the late summer yielded no evidence of the panic buying that would have threatened price stability.[49]

47. Otto Eckstein and Gary Fromm, *Steel and the Postwar Inflation*, Study Paper 2, Prepared . . . for the Joint Economic Committee, 86 Cong. 1 sess (1959).
48. Fort Ritchie Oral History Interview, p. 433.
49. Gordon to Heller and Tobin, "Talk with Joe Fowler on Emergency Controls," September 20, 1961, General File, 9/10/61–9/29/61 folder, Kennedy-Johnson files, Heller Papers, Kennedy Library. While it was the "firm conviction" of the

The national climate was thus unusually favorable to official requests for restraint in the bellwether sectors that would be widely regarded as tests of the administration's commitment to price stability. Moreover, the groundwork in the first of these cases—the automobile settlement—had been carefully, though discreetly, laid. As early as June 20 Rostow, at the President's suggestion, had met with Walter Reuther to explain why it was in the national interest to have a wage settlement in which increases were confined to a range justified by advances in productivity, or roughly 2.5 percent. On that occasion Reuther indicated that the proposition might be entertainable, but only if the administration used its weight to persuade the United Steelworkers to proceed along a similar line in their 1962 wage negotiations. But another essential condition was attached: restraint by labor in steel (and automobiles, which "he could look after") would not be exploited by those industries through their pricing policies. Subsequently Reuther met with Kennedy, on August 4 and August 16. The understanding reached by them appears not to have found its way into the written White House record; Walt Rostow, who had been instrumental in setting the stage for these conversations, believes that the framework constructed during his June 20 meeting with Reuther shaped the White House discussions.[50] At any rate, the negotiations produced the desired outcome. The only publicly visible presidential intervention was a telegram to participants in the General Motors negotiations urging them to exercise "industrial statesmanship" to "achieve a settlement which is fair and reasonable to both shareholders and workers and which preserves price stability in the industry."[51]

In steel, the immediate worry was an industry initiative on the price front. In contrast to the quiet backroom work that had preceded the automobile settlement, the effort to contain the steel industry was accompanied by maximum publicity. The first steps were taken through the

Treasury that the President ought to have "standby control authority for use in national security emergencies," it was not held to be either feasible or desirable for such powers to be sought from Congress before the adjournment of the 1961 session. There was in fact some risk that the mere request at that moment for authority to impose direct controls would touch off inflationary behavior. Henry H. Fowler to the President, September 20, 1961, Treasury folder, Departments and Agencies, Box 88, President's Office files, Kennedy Library.

50. W. W. Rostow, *The Diffusion of Power: An Essay in Recent History* (Macmillan, 1972), especially pp. 140–42.

51. "Telegram to Labor and Management Leaders Urging a Just Settlement in the General Motors Negotiations. September 5, 1961," *Public Papers*, 1961, p. 590.

CEA's enlistment of sympathetic senators, under the leadership of Senator Albert Gore, who would be prepared to speak from CEA-inspired briefs on the importance of stable steel prices and on the problems of concentration and price fixing in the industry. This plan received presidential endorsement in a White House meeting of August 3 between Kennedy, Gore, Heller, and Gordon. On August 18 Heller could report to the President that "this effort is moving ahead nicely." He noted that the CEA had "urged that the tone be one of appealing to the steel industry to serve a vital national purpose, rather than beating them over the head. . . . Also, it occurs to us that the Congressional and Administration efforts to hold steel prices in check should be helpful in appealing to Reuther to accept a reasonable settlement and to get McDonald in a reasonable frame of mind for next summer (since we cannot effectively tamper with the October 1 contractual wage increase)."[52]

The senatorial foray into steel pricing occurred on August 22, 1961.[53] Though this proved a useful exercise in public consciousness-raising, reinforcement was required. An industry rejoinder was to be expected, and came in early September in Senate speeches (in some of which the hand of steel was visible). The general theme of the rebuttals challenged the legitimacy of government intrusion into pricing decisions in the private sector of the economy.[54] Before their intervention, members of the Gore group had been anxious to know what steps the President planned to take after they "had stirred up the animals." In response, Heller had assured them that the President would "do at least two things: (1) make a statement, presumably at a press conference, concerning the whole problem

52. Heller to the President, "Progress Report on Steel Prices, Clark Bill, and Long Range Projections," August 18, 1961, Council of Economic Advisers, 8–9/61 folder, Box 73, President's Office files, Kennedy Library.
53. On the Democratic side, the senators who spoke in the floor debate included (in addition to Gore of Tennessee) Paul H. Douglas (Illinois), Joseph S. Clark (Pennsylvania), Stuart Symington (Missouri), Hubert H. Humphrey (Minnesota), Eugene J. McCarthy (Minnesota), Estes Kefauver (Tennessee), Russell B. Long (Louisiana), Stephen M. Young (Ohio), John J. Sparkman (Alabama), A. S. Mike Monroney (Oklahoma), Gale W. McGee (Wyoming), Maurine B. Neuberger (Oregon), and Frank E. Moss (Utah).
54. Senators who spoke from the Republican side of the aisle in the floor debate of September 7, 1961, included Everett M. Dirksen (Illinois), Jacob K. Javits (New York), Prescott Bush (Connecticut), Barry Goldwater (Arizona), Leverett Saltonstall (Massachusetts), Wallace F. Bennett (Utah), Homer E. Capehart (Indiana), Hugh Scott (Pennsylvania), Thomas H. Kuchel (California), Roman L. Hruska (Nebraska), Gordon Allott (Colorado), Kenneth B. Keating (New York), and Jack Miller (Iowa).

and the special importance of stable steel prices; and (2) . . . speak to some of the key people in the industry urging them to hold the price line on steel."[55]

Kennedy honored both of these commitments. In collaboration with Arthur Goldberg, the CEA drafted a presidential response to a prearranged press conference question on steel prices.[56] Though the ensuing public exchange did not reproduce the phrasing of the prepared answer, it captured the spirit:

Q. *Do you believe that there is anything the Government can or should do to try to head off a hike in steel prices? And if so, what would you plan to do?*

THE PRESIDENT. . . . *The inflation which marked our economy before 1958 was, I think, tied very closely to the increases in steel prices. Since 1958 the steel prices have remained relatively stable. And it is a fact that during that same period the cost of living has remained relatively stable.*

Now my economic advisers inform me that it would be possible for the steel companies to absorb the increase [in wages] . . . without increasing prices, and still insure to the steel companies, and their owners, a good profit.

I am concerned that an increase in steel prices would set off another inflationary spiral, and also make us less competitive abroad, serve as a brake on our recovery, and also affect our balance of payments.

So that I am very hopeful that these private companies will—and I'm sure they will—concern themselves with the public interests that are involved in their decision.[57]

But the President also addressed the leadership of the steel industry more directly. On September 6 he dispatched a letter (drafted by the CEA) to senior executives in each of the nation's major steel companies. Its central argument was that the scheduled October 1 wage increment could readily be absorbed "by the advance in productivity resulting from a combination of two factors—the steady long-term growth of output per man-hour, and the increasing rate of operations foreseen for the steel industry in the months ahead." Holding the price line, it was maintained,

55. Ibid.

56. James Tobin to the President, "Press Conference August 30," August 26, 1961, National Economy, 1/1/61–3/31/61 folder (BE 5 Executive), Box 17, White House Central Subject files, Kennedy Library.

57. "The President's News Conference of August 30, 1961," *Public Papers*, 1961, pp. 576–77.

would itself help ensure a growth in earnings through fuller utilization of capacity. The reasoning underlying this proposition was set out as follows: "A rise in steel prices would force price increases in many industries and invite price increases in others. The consequences of such a development might be so grave—particularly on our balance of payments position—as to require the adoption of restrictive monetary and fiscal measures which would retard recovery, hold unemployment at intolerable levels, and hamper growth. The depressing effect of such measures on the steel industry's rate of operations might in the long run more than offset the profit-raising effect of a price increase." But there was also a hint of another reward for good behavior. "If the industry were now to forego a price increase, it would enter collective bargaining negotiations next spring with a record of three and a half years of price stability. It would clearly then be the turn of the labor representatives to limit wage demands to a level consistent with continued price stability. The moral position of the steel industry next spring—and its claim to the support of public opinion—will be strengthened by the exercise of price restraint now."[58]

Not all recipients of this letter found its argument totally persuasive, particularly as it pertained to profits yet unseen.[59] Its public release (combined with knowledge then available about the shape of automobile wage settlements, which were coming in with increments of approximately 2.5 percent) was the moment for David J. McDonald, president of the United Steelworkers, to pledge to the President that the union would cooperate in ensuring that full recognition would be given to the public interest in the 1962 steel contract negotiations. The President's acknowledgement indicated that protection of the public interest implied "a labor settlement within the limits of advances in productivity and price stability."[60]

The special situations presented by steel and automobiles had not been approached symmetrically. But primary reliance on outside tactics in one

58. "Letters to Leaders of the Steel Industry on the Need for Price Stability, dated September 7, 1961 [Released September 7, 1961. Dated September 6, 1961]," ibid., pp. 592–94.

59. In preparation for subsequent contacts with steel company executives, the President was armed with "a bit of timely economic history." Kermit Gordon drew to Kennedy's attention the fact that Senator Taft, in 1948, had "scolded the steel industry for raising prices" and had then argued that "unless steel held the line on prices, 'we will never stop increasing the spiral of wages and prices.'" Gordon to the President, September 16, 1961, Steel, 9/12/61–9/25/61 folder, Box 39, Papers of Theodore Sorensen, Kennedy Library.

60. "Letter to the President, United Steelworkers of America, on the Importance of Price Stability. September 14, 1961," Public Papers, 1961, pp. 604–05.

case and on inside tactics in the other had, for the time being at least, led to satisfactory outcomes. There was, however, some lingering uncertainty about whether the results, particularly of steel pricing decisions, would have been much different if there had been no official rhetoric. Some sources close to the industry reported that softness in its markets had meant that steel leaders were disinclined to raise prices in the autumn of 1961.

Renewed Search for a Broader Strategy

Apparent successes in dealing with the automotive and steel industries afforded some breathing space. But the larger problem remained: how could the public interest in price stability be articulated so as to be neutral between sectors and industries as well as between bargaining parties? In the search for an answer, the President instructed his economic aides to embark on a program of public education. He ordered that the problem be put before the "old guard," forcing them to think about it "without necessarily suggesting solutions."[61] It was in this vein that Walter Heller spoke before a series of business audiences in 1961. To a group in Chicago, he explained the rationale for "holding the price line": "if we succeed, the way is open for private and public policies of expansion; if we fail, then we may be prevented in the short run from pursuing the very policies that may solve our problems in the long run. Price stability, unlike virtue, is not its own reward. But the rewards are great."[62] Further, he asserted that "every person who wants the United States to continue to discharge its world responsibilities, and every person who favors full recovery and a faster rate of economic growth, is tied by the bonds of logic to the cause of price stability."[63]

At the same time, he reassured his listeners that the solution to this problem would be neither sought nor found in direct wage and price controls. Nor, at the other extreme, was mere exhortation—at least at the level of "vague and generalized appeals"—likely to be effective. Recent presi-

61. Heller, "Memorandum for the Files: Meeting of Thursday, October 19, with the President," General File, 10/16/61–10/30/61 folder, Kennedy-Johnson files, Heller Papers, Kennedy Library.

62. Remarks of Walter W. Heller before the American Life Convention, Edgewater Beach Hotel, Chicago, Illinois, October 13, 1961, p. 5, General Files, 10/1/61–10/14/61 folder, Kennedy-Johnson files, Heller Papers, Kennedy Library.

63. Ibid., p. 12.

dential intervention to discourage a possible increase in steel prices was notably different from the general category of admonitory rhetoric. The President's communications with steel executives and union officials were characterized as a "persuasive appeal for specific actions."[64]

But the very specificity—at least in defining the target area—of official correspondence with the key participants in wage and price making in the steel industry was itself troublesome. No administration could comfortably sustain for long a position that individual industries should be singled out for ad hoc treatment. Even though the characteristics of the steel industry were widely acknowledged to be "special" in a number of respects, defensible administrative practice still recommended an even-handed governmental approach to the private sector. This consideration, however, had to be balanced against the remarkable potential of the steel industry to disrupt price stability. The situation called for a general formula to deal with a particularly worrisome case, though one that would not be industry-specific in its incidence.

Tailoring a general formula to the requirements of a specific circumstance is always an unenviable challenge. Yet the task is easier when one can turn to a recognized body of doctrine for guidance. The domestic expansionists in the Kennedy administration were predominantly neo-Keynesian in analytic orientation with their sights originally set on the macroeconomic variables. Ironically, the position in which they shortly found themselves was one in which their aspirations to deploy the fiscal weapons of the "new" economics were likely to be frustrated unless fears of inflationary pressures before full employment was realized could be neutralized. To cope with this problem, guidance from another body of theory was called for. Since the inflation risks in an underemployed economy could largely be traced to sectors that were less than perfectly competitive, a general rule to guide policy might readily suggest itself. The public interest, it could plausibly be argued, would be best served if perfect competition could be simulated in sectors where it did not exist. Without much more direct government intervention than anyone was then prepared to recommend, this could not be achieved. But it could be used as the basis for setting standards that were both universal and neutral. The role of government in these matters could be interpreted conventionally, as creating a climate in which private decision-making could proceed responsibly without direct official intervention.

Within the CEA thinking had begun to crystallize along these lines

64. Ibid., p. 11.

in October—particularly in connection with planning the structure of the annual Economic Report. This occasion was another pedagogic opportunity to supplement the appearances of Council members before business audiences and the informal briefings of labor leaders on broader economic issues (a practice revived in November 1961 after a lapse since the days of Truman). Heller had already won presidential approval for a format in which the Economic Report would be divided into two sections: the first would be the President's report and as such would reflect official policy; the second would be the Council's report, which could be constructed as a discussion of issues. In the latter, and longer, part of the document, the CEA had license to speak for itself without committing the President. (The President stipulated only one condition: that the cover of the Report be green.)[65] This procedure was obviously compatible with the Kennedy presidential style as well as with the educational talents of CEA members. Moreover, the use of this document to broaden the discussion of wage-price issues in particular was consistent with opinions expressed by the Labor-Management Advisory Committee to the effect that the Economic Report and the related hearings of the Joint Economic Committee were the appropriate vehicles for public enlightenment on these matters.

But a problem remained. Formulations of noninflationary behavior derived from competitive theory might have the desired properties of neutrality and generality, but unless quantified, they might lack sufficient bite to deal with the immediate practical concern—the 1962 steel negotiations. The President had introduced a productivity criterion as the standard for a responsible wage settlement in his September correspondence with McDonald. Was not a number therefore needed, and, if so, which one? Lloyd Ulman of the CEA staff concluded in mid-November that the case for a "Mount Sinai caper" was strong:

This would consist in publication by the Administration of some productivity figure, to be regarded by private parties as setting a maximum value on the outcome of their wage decisions. . . . This approach does not envision the establishment of a specific agency and for this reason may lack . . . coercive potential. . . . Nevertheless, it appeals to me on several grounds, assuming that we do not favor the establishment of controls in

65. Heller, "Memorandum for the Files on the Meeting of Thursday, October 19, with the President," General File, 10/16/61–10/30/61 folder, Kennedy-Johnson files, Heller Papers, Kennedy Library.

the foreseeable future. It does not smack of controls and could not seriously be regarded as a backdoor approach; the Administration is completely justified in a further development of its arguments in favor of voluntary wage restraint. It would certainly serve to educate and mobilize public opinion which, in the final analysis, will impose the effective limits on the bargaining process. . . . Finally, the publication of a number would apply to all wage changes, steel need not even be cited in this connection—although some honorable mention might not be out of order.[66]

Ulman suggested that the CEA endorse a figure for productivity increase of 2.9 percent (the Bureau of Labor Statistics calculation of average annual change in manufacturing output per man-hour, 1947–60), though this figure was biased downward in that it ignored capacity effects. Nevertheless, he maintained,

This might be regarded as rough-and-ready New Frontier justice. Moreover, it would give the Steelworkers just about as much as the Auto Workers will get in the second (and third) year(s) of their current agreement. . . . And, while the publication of a general standard might result in some union leaders feeling obliged to obtain larger settlements than they would otherwise be willing to settle for, this particular number should not furnish the basis for a rise in the price of steel which is regarded as sui generis in its inflationary potential.[67]

The treatment of wage-price issues in the 1962 Economic Report took a somewhat different tack. This section of the document—for which Kermit Gordon had overall responsibility—was at once less precise and more comprehensive. The "guidelines" set out in the text for noninflationary behavior contained no reference to numbers; instead a variety of measures of annual rates of growth of output per man-hour was reported in tabular form. Attention was drawn to the fact that the results varied with coverage, with whether the calculations referred to productivity growth in the total private economy, the nonagricultural economy, or manufacturing exclusively; with the choice of time period (estimates were reported for 1909–60, 1947–60, 1947–54, and 1954–60); and with the conceptual basis of calculation (notably on whether performance in manufacturing was adjusted to take account of varying rates of capacity utilization). The

66. Ulman to the Council, "Some Alternative Approaches to the Encouragement of Restraint (Controls we abhor . . .)," November 17, 1961, Microfilm Copies of Records of the Council of Economic Advisers, Roll 71, Kennedy Library.
67. Ibid.

CEA drew back from committing itself to a single figure with the observation that "several measures are given because none of the single figures is clearly superior for all purposes."[68]

At the same time, this approach included prices as well as wages within its frame of reference—a move accomplished by drawing on insights from competitive theory. In the first instance, the statement of the wage-price guideposts was an analytic exercise in describing "how prices and wage rates would behave in a smoothly functioning competitive economy operating near full employment." This perspective permitted the formulation of two broad behavioral norms: (1) for wages, "that the rate of increase in wage rates (including fringe benefits) in each industry be equal to the trend rate of over-all productivity increase"; and (2) for prices, that price reductions ought to occur "if the industry's rate of productivity increase exceeds the over-all rate—for this would mean declining unit labor costs," while "an appropriate increase" in prices would be expected in industries in which productivity performance fell short of the overall trend but which, nonetheless, would be subject to increases in unit labor costs if their wage rates were adjusted as suggested by the wage guidelines.[69]

But was it legitimate to suggest that normative propositions deduced from a competitive model could usefully be employed as standards for appraising behavior in a complex economy which, in its structure, was anything but ubiquitously competitive? That the CEA anticipated this challenge was apparent in its formulations of several categories of exceptions. Adaptations in the general guidelines, it was pointed out, should be expected in situations in which wage or profit rates had been noncompetitively distorted. Thus, prices should fall more rapidly or rise more slowly than suggested by the general guide in industries in which "excessive market power has resulted in rates of profit substantially higher than those earned elsewhere on investments of comparable risk." Similarly, wage increases should fall short of the overall trend when "wage rates are exceptionally high compared with the range of wages earned elsewhere by similar labor, because the bargaining position of workers has been especially strong." By the same token, departures from the general guidelines should be encouraged if their strict observance would tend to frustrate the allocative efficiency associated with a competitive system. Thus in expanding sectors factor rewards might rise at rates in excess of the guidepost suggestions. Wages ought properly to exceed the general guide rate "in an in-

68. *Economic Report of the President, January 1962*, pp. 185–88.
69. Ibid., pp. 188, 189.

dustry which would otherwise be unable to attract sufficient labor" and prices might "rise more rapidly, or fall more slowly, than indicated by the general guide rate in an industry in which the level of profits was insufficient to attract the capital required to finance a needed expansion in capacity."[70] Wage and price movements in declining industries should depart from the overall norm in the opposite direction.

This approach to a strategy had the desired properties of neutrality and generality. A broad base for informed public judgment, it was maintained, had now been laid, and displayed no overt concern about any particular industry. But the guidepost formula also permitted detachment from another potentially volatile issue: no judgment was passed on the distribution of income. If translated into practice, the guideposts would maintain constancy in relative shares, but this feature, the CEA insisted, did not imply that the existing distribution of income was either optimal or immutable. It was recognized as "desirable that labor and management should bargain explicitly about the distribution of income of particular firms or industries"; it was held to be "undesirable," however, for them to "bargain implicitly about the general price level."[71]

The theme of neutrality in this approach also extended to the role of the government, whose central function in wage and price making was construed as that of an educator committed to the enlightenment of the public.[72] The CEA emphasized that the guideposts did not constitute "a mechanical formula for determining whether a particular price or wage decision is inflationary. They will serve their purpose if they suggest to the interested public a useful way of approaching the appraisal of such a decision."[73] The state itself was not disposed to construct machinery to enforce compliance with the guideposts. The disciplinary agent, if there was to be one, would be an informed public.[74]

70. Ibid., p. 189.
71. Ibid., p. 188.
72. However, the CEA sensed the need to educate some echelons of the bureaucracy—particularly the mediators and arbitrators in the Labor Department—on the criteria for socially responsible wage setting. Remarks of James Tobin, transcript of the Conference on the Development of Wage-Price Policy in the United States, Boston, November 1–2, 1974, vol. 1, p. 132.
73. *Economic Report of the President, January 1962*, p. 188.
74. The noncoercive intent of this approach was decisive in the very selection of the term "guideposts." In the discussion of nomenclature, "guidelines" was the rival candidate, but was rejected because "lines" might be regarded as more constraining than "posts." Remarks of Lloyd Ulman, transcript of the Boston Conference on the Development of Wage-Price Policy, vol. 1, p. 130.

That this educational mission would not be easily discharged was apparent in December. Persuasion had not succeeded in winning support for the guidepost statement from the CEA professional staff. With but one exception (Robert Solow, who had contributed significantly to the guidepost formulation), members of this group were adamantly opposed to its publication—largely out of fear that the suggestions of a comprehensive formula might destroy collective bargaining and invite a regime of direct controls. These objections were overriden by the presidentially appointed members of the CEA.[75]

If the CEA staff had doubts about the wisdom of the guideposts, many others in the administration did not. Senior officials in the Treasury in particular welcomed this statement of doctrine and regarded it as a potentially significant buttress to their efforts to bring the balance of payments under control.

The Dual Strategy—and Some Ambiguities

Even before the guidepost approach had been publicly aired, it was being disseminated within the administration in preparation for the forthcoming steel negotiations. Walter Heller opened the campaign on December 29 with a memorandum to Arthur Goldberg, who had been designated the administration's principal contact with the key parties, to supply him with the new ammunition. The objective was set out as follows:

In seeking a non-inflationary settlement we are really aiming at a dual economic target: (1) avoiding a price rise in steel itself; and (2) avoiding wage-induced price rises in other industries whose wage settlements (and materials costs) will be affected by the basic steel settlement. Achieving the first objective means limiting the percentage increase in steel wages to the percentage increase in output per manhour in steel (as measured over some suitable period of time). Achieving the second objective means limiting the steel increase to the overall increase in output per manhour throughout the private economy. Thus if we are to achieve both objectives, the basic steel settlement should yield an increase in hourly employment costs no greater than the smaller of these two productivity changes.[76]

75. Walter Heller and Kermit Gordon, recorded interview by Joseph A. Pechman, July 20, 1965, Kennedy Library Oral History Program, especially pp. 31–37.
76. Heller to Goldberg, December 29, 1961, CEA, 11–12/61 folder, Box 74, President's Office files, Kennedy Library.

Heller conceded that there was "no single engraved estimate of productivity increase, either in steel or in the broader sectors of the economy, which [could] be regarded as final and authoritative." For the task at hand, however, the lowest figure with any relevance was 2.4 percent—the estimated annual increase in output per man-hour in the basic steel industry. However, this figure, when adjusted for capacity utilization, yielded an estimate of about 3.4 percent. Meanwhile, the best estimate of productivity gains in the total private economy was 3.1 percent. Heller took the latter figures to represent "the upper end of the plausible range."

But it was also pertinent to ask whether any special features in steel warranted departures from the guidepost approach. Surveying this part of the terrain, Heller observed:

Taking into account that the steel companies have probably been squeezed a bit in absorbing the last three wage increases, that economy-wide productivity has probably risen less rapidly in the second half than in the first half of the postwar period, that steel wages already look pretty high in relation to wages in other basic manufacturing industries, that there is heavy unemployment among steel workers, and that employment costs per manhour will probably go up faster than the contract requires because of upgrading and the shift to salaried employment, I would find it hard to regard as non-inflationary any settlement in excess of 3 percent. At the same time, I would think that a settlement below 2.5 percent would indicate the possibility of a price reduction.[77]

On balance, he concluded: "Not only would a settlement within the 2.5–3.0 percent range give steel management no license for price increases, but it should also have a fighting chance of meeting the steelworkers' tests of reasonableness and equity." Moreover, "a settlement between 2.5 and 3.0 percent should silence the critics and make a major contribution to checking the price-wage spiral."[78]

Thus the dual strategy was launched. Whether a macro formula could successfully be brought to bear on an industry with a troubled history was far from certain. But the stakes seemed high enough to make the effort worthwhile. A new line of argument could still be conveyed by old-fashioned methods. Armed by the CEA, both Secretary Goldberg and the President appealed to the principal parties to reach a noninflationary settlement. At a meeting in the executive mansion on January 23, 1962, with David McDonald, president of the United Steelworkers, and Roger Blough, chairman of the United States Steel Corporation, the President

77. Ibid.
78. Ibid.

(accompanied by Secretary Goldberg) specifically asked that a 3 percent wage increase ("based on productivity factors") be regarded as a ceiling. McDonald reportedly replied: "I don't think it's right. You asked me. I will do it."[79] Blough, however, made no commitment on prices.

But another problem in interpreting the guideposts lay outside before a wider audience. The press conference convened when the Economic Report was published made it clear that the message could easily be misconstrued. Indeed, much of the time at that session was devoted to explaining what the guideposts did *not* mean. From the questions asked, it was apparent that fears of direct governmental intervention in the wage and price setting process needed to be dispelled. To clarify this matter, Heller observed: "We, as a Council of Economic Advisers, are not the ones who are to apply these guidelines to a particular wage negotiation. Indeed, the purpose . . . is to provide guides within the overall rule of holding wage increases in the economy *in toto* within the bounds of the increases in productivity, to develop these guidelines which can be applied by the parties to the negotiation and by the public in judging these negotiations. We do not, after all, have, nor do we want, direct control over wages."[80] Not surprisingly, the press also questioned the implications of the guideposts for the steel negotiations. In response, Kermit Gordon indicated that it would be "improper and inappropriate" to comment on individual cases.[81] When pressed further on whether the Council would be prepared to suggest specific guides to bargaining parties privately, Walter Heller replied: "Certainly if called upon to give our opinion on this subject in terms of the interpretation of the available facts, we would make these available either directly to the parties or to anyone the parties called on in government for such information."[82] But the nub of the matter was touched by a reporter for *Business Week*: "What we all want, obviously, is an easy 'do it yourself' kit for separating the good guys from the bad guys after the steel contract is signed. Is economic science ever going to be able to provide that sort of thing?"[83] In reply, Kermit Gordon indicated that "it would be irresponsible to suggest a single simple tight

79. David McDonald, recorded interview by Charles T. Morrissey, February 15, 1966, Kennedy Library Oral History Program, pp. 13–14.

80. Transcript of the press briefing by the Council of Economic Advisers in the Treaty Room of the Executive Office Building, January 20, 1962, CEA, 1/62–2/62 folder, Box 74, President's Office files, Kennedy Library, p. 25.

81. Ibid., p. 24.

82. Ibid., p. 25.

83. Ibid., p. 26.

formula that you can tattoo on your arm that would automatically give you the answer to every collective bargaining situation. Nevertheless, I do feel that the considerations that are developed in these pages do provide, with careful use, considerable illumination on these matters, and do, in many cases, provide a basis for judgment."[84] The systematic ambiguities of the dual strategy, it had begun to appear, did not always contribute to its comprehensibility.[85]

A potentially more serious set of misunderstandings surfaced at the February 6 meeting of the Labor-Management Advisory Committee. In the course of the committee's discussions, it was discovered that not all members of the group had fully absorbed the "first approximation" character of the guideline statement. One of the public members apparently regarded the guideposts as stipulating a uniform 3 percent increment for all wage changes—a formula that would mean radical restructuring in collective bargaining institutions and in mediation and conciliation procedures.[86] Those who had read with care the qualifications attached to the guideposts did not share these fears. Yet it would be idle to pretend that the basic presupposition of the guideposts—that the social responsibility of private wage and price decisions could be tested against an objective standard, though one with some elasticity—had not given rise to them.

84. Ibid., p. 27.
85. The guideposts per se did not figure prominently in the discussion of the Economic Report during the Council's appearance before the Joint Economic Committee. The CEA was congratulated by members of the committee for demonstrating concern for price stability and Council members were invited to comment on whether legislation should be introduced to amend the Employment Act of 1946 by making stable prices an explicit national goal. In response, Walter Heller maintained that such action would be redundant because the 1946 act stipulated that the maintenance of maximum purchasing power should be a central objective. Though Kermit Gordon, in the CEA appearance before the Joint Committee, alluded to the importance of price stability to the balance of payments, it was Secretary Goldberg who emphasized the significance of the guideposts to the committee: "We want to preserve free collective bargaining in the United States, and we don't want the Government to dictate the terms of settlements in steel or elsewhere. But the Council has done a very valuable job in defining national goals and guidelines. . . . I feel that one of the important functions of Government is not to dictate or impose terms of settlement, but to define the public interest. I do not think we have done enough in that area in the past." Statement of Secretary of Labor Arthur J. Goldberg, in *January 1962 Economic Report of the President,* Hearings before the Joint Economic Committee, 87 Cong. 2 sess. (1962), pp. 212, 238.
86. Ulman to the Council, "Labor-Management Committee's Discussion of 'Statement on Sound Wage and Price Policies' (Report of Subcommittee No. 5, Draft of November 3, 1961)," February 21, 1962, Wage-Price Guideposts, 1/62–9/62 folder, Kennedy-Johnson files, Heller Papers, Kennedy Library.

At the same meeting a number of those present politely scolded the CEA for bypassing the Labor-Management Advisory Committee—and it was registered as the sense of the committee that henceforth its membership should be afforded an opportunity to discuss such matters with the CEA before public pronouncements were made.[87]

At the same time, there was also a hint that the White House needed reassurance on the wisdom of the guidepost approach. Some indirect support could be drawn from recent British policy (materials on which the President had drawn to Walter Heller's attention). As Heller noted in mid-February, there was "an uncanny similarity—in purpose, approach, and even in specifics" between the British official posture and the CEA guideposts.[88] Both used an overall productivity formula for wage settlements and recognized much the same types of exceptions. But there were also differences, one of which was particularly noteworthy: "The British are tougher in some respects. We use the cautious subterfuge of addressing our guidelines, not to labor and management, but to the public—so that the public may judge whether particular wage and price decisions are consistent with overall price stability. The British come right out and say that labor should abide by the guidelines." Heller concluded that the initial reception of the guideposts had been promising: the steel workers had reacted constructively and contacts with officials in the communications union had left him with the impression that they welcomed the guideposts as a means of restraining some of their militant members.[89]

By the end of March it appeared that the dual strategy had begun to pay off. The crucial wage negotiation of the year had been concluded on terms fully consistent with guidepost standards: indeed the 2.5 percent wage and fringe benefit settlement in steel was at the low end of the recommended range. The President personally congratulated the principal negotiators in a telephone message that conveyed his assessment of the results: "It is obviously not inflationary and should provide a solid base for continued price stability."[90]

87. Ulman to the Council, "Forthcoming 'National Economic Conference' of Labor, Management, etc.," February 8, 1962, Microfilm Copies of Records of the Council of Economic Advisers, Roll 71, Kennedy Library.

88. Heller to the President, "The British White Paper on Wage Policy," February 14, 1962, CEA, 1/62–2/62 folder, Box 74, President's Office files, Kennedy Library.

89. Ibid.

90. White House transcript of the telephone conversation of the President with first, David McDonald, president of the United Steelworkers of America, and then

The Steel Confrontation and Its Aftermath

Though an understandable mood of satisfaction settled over government circles with the outcome of the steel negotiations, a cloud remained
on the horizon. Labor had certainly picked up the official cues from the
wage guideposts, but there was some indication that the steel industry
had read the price guideposts in its own way. Press reports in early April
suggested that the industry regarded the wage settlement as justifying a
price increase.

In a memorandum prepared for the President, Heller sketched the
basis for divergent interpretations of the implications of the guideposts
for steel prices:

*While everybody admits that the 2.5 percent settlement is well within
the economy-wide productivity trend, the steel companies claim that steel
productivity has been rising only 1.7 percent. If this were true, it would
make steel eligible for a price increase under that section of the wage-price
guidelines which allows price increases to industries with below-average
productivity trends.*

*Our researches indicate that the 1.7 percent productivity figure esti-
mated by the industry is too low, and that steel has been getting a productivity trend on the order of double that figure—between 3.0 and 3.4
percent. The steel statisticians ignore official Census data which show a
higher trend in productivity than the data compiled by the steel trade
association. They also fail to correct for the downward effect on recorded
productivity caused by slack activity of recent years, which masks the
extent of the underlying upward productivity trend.*

*Thus far, the steel industry's productivity estimate has held undisputed
sway in the press. We think it would be helpful, if you are to go down
in history as the Man who Broke the Wage-Price Spiral, for the press to be
let in on the fact that the correct figures, properly interpreted, do not
justify a price increase.*[91]

As this analysis was being completed—but before it reached the Presi-

---

with R. Conrad Cooper, executive vice president of the United States Steel Corporation, March 31, 1962, National Economy, 10/1/61–4/30/62 folder (BE 5 Executive), Box 17, White House Central Subject files, Kennedy Library.

91. Heller to the President, "The Steel Industry's Case on the 'Need' for a
Price Increase," April 10, 1962 ("5:00 P.M." in Heller's hand), CEA, 4/62–5/5/62
folder, Box 74, President's Office files, Kennedy Library. The copy of this document

dent—calm on the wage-price front was abruptly shattered. Roger Blough
called at the White House to inform the President that U.S. Steel was
releasing a public announcement at 7 P.M. of its decision to raise prices by
$6 a ton (roughly 3.5 percent). The President did not conceal his dismay.
Shortly after Blough's departure, Kennedy telephoned David McDonald
in Pittsburgh. By McDonald's account, the President's words were:
"Dave, you've been screwed and I've been screwed."[92] Kennedy's outrage
was only slightly more restrained at his press conference the following
day—by which time other steel producers had announced matching increases. The action of Big Steel was then characterized as a "wholly un-
justifiable and irresponsible defiance of the public interest." The American people, he asserted, had a right to expect "a higher sense of business
responsibility for the welfare of their country than has been shown in the
last 2 days. Some time ago I asked each American to consider what he
would do for his country and I asked the steel companies. In the last 24
hours, we had their answer."[93]

Most of the events of the next few days have been described elsewhere.[94]
The tactics employed in what came to be known as "the Battle of Blough
Run" were not altogether routine. Persuasive leverage was applied to firms
that had not joined the price parade—an exercise informed by responses
to the President's letter of the preceding September. With the aid of this
intelligence, the firms most likely to be receptive to suggestions that they
spurn the lead of Big Steel could be more readily identified. Quiet education on criteria for responsible wage and price making had now been abandoned. Government was waving the big stick with threats of antitrust actions and a hint (conveyed by the President in his press conference of
April 11) that the eligibility of the steel industry for tax benefits in the
Treasury's forthcoming revision of depreciation schedules might be subject to review.

White House intervention in steel pricing achieved its immediate

in the President's Office files has an attached handwritten note from Walter Heller
to the President: "4/10/62—10:00 P.M. An ironic note, now mainly of historical
interest."

92. David McDonald, recorded interview by Charles Morrissey, February 15, 1966,
Kennedy Library Oral History Program, p. 15.

93. "The President's News Conference of April 11, 1962," Public Papers, 1962,
pp. 315–17.

94. See, for example, Roy Hoopes, The Steel Crisis (John Day, 1963), and John
Sheahan, The Wage-Price Guideposts (Brookings Institution, 1967).

objective: prices were rolled back. Nonetheless, the episode was at best a somewhat ambiguous victory for the administration. It had shown that the administration meant business on price stability in key sectors— though the vigor of Kennedy's response was largely a reaction to behavior considered insulting to presidential authority and dignity. While the outcome was the desired one, it had required techniques not anticipated at the time the dual strategy was formulated.

It was again a time for reflection. To the extent that the dual strategy depended on executive muscle, it was a failure. In disciplining bad behavior, what alternatives were available? Talents in the Department of Labor focused on a legislative solution that would give the President the power to petition for an injunction to restrain "unwarranted price increases" when they were determined to be "inimical to the public welfare." A bill was drafted, along lines reminiscent of the Taft-Hartley Act, that would confer that power. A court-directed price freeze would then be supplemented by the appointment of a board of inquiry which would report to the President, who in turn would make "recommendations with respect to the action which should be taken by the parties in the public interest."[95] Along similar lines, the Treasury—through Acting Secretary Henry H. Fowler—recommended on April 13 that the President (in the absence of a rescission of steel price increases) should seek legislative authority permitting him to establish maximum prices or wages whenever the "prices of iron and steel commodities, or wages affecting them, have risen, or threaten to rise, in a manner which threatens national economic stability" for a period not to exceed eighty days.[96]

The CEA, on the other hand, turned elsewhere in search of a new direction. On April 19 it convened a team of consultants to review the longer-range price problems in steel. Summarizing the results of these deliberations for the President's benefit, Kermit Gordon reported that several of the options canvassed had been judged unpromising; for instance, a "yardstick" approach (a proposal that the federal government "build and operate an integrated steel plant to provide a yardstick by which to measure the cost and price performance of the private companies") and a public utility solution (an approach rejected on grounds

95. Steel Price Emergency Statute, April 12, 1962, Microfilm Copies of Records of the Department of Labor, Roll 48, Kennedy Library.

96. Fowler to Sorensen, April 13, 1962, Steel, 4/10/62–4/12/62 folder, Box 39, Sorensen Papers, Kennedy Library.

that pricing practices subject to the jurisdiction of a federal regulatory agency would tend to reduce efficiency in steel). On one line of action, however, "striking and unexpected" consensus was approached, though it fell short of unanimity: "the Justice Department should proceed aggressively under the antitrust laws to seek the dissolution of U.S. Steel and perhaps of Bethlehem Steel as well."[97] Though it was recognized that this would involve extended litigation (and thus offered no prospect of early relief) and that success was far from assured, the overwhelming opinion was that "the degree of market power in the steel industry is excessive and should not be allowed to persist; that the breakup of U.S. Steel (and Bethlehem) into six or eight independent companies would substantially increase the vigor of competition in steel; and that dissolution of the Big Two could be accomplished without impairing productive efficiency."[98]

On this occasion, another idea was thought to warrant further study: the price notification and public review proposal that had been urged for some time by Walter Reuther (among others). Note was taken, however, of difficulties inherent in this approach:

a. Companies might thwart this procedure by abandoning across-the-board price increases and substituting small but frequent increases in the prices of different products. This might make it extremely difficult to decide when to lower the boom.

b. . . . a similar procedure would have to be established for major wage settlements if price increases were to be subject to this kind of public scrutiny.

c. The danger was seen that if this device proved ineffective in one or two key cases, it would either disintegrate or the Government would be forced to move toward more coercive forms of control.

d. The procedure would have to be sufficiently removed from the Presidency so that the President would not have to select the cases in which the machinery was to be employed.[99]

But the CEA also looked further afield for inspiration. At this time,

97. Gordon to the President, "Steel: The Longer-range Problem," April 21, 1962, CEA, 4/62–5/5/62 folder, Box 74, President's Office files, Kennedy Library.
98. Ibid. The outside consultants included Edward S. Mason, Paul Samuelson, M. A. Adelman, James W. McKie, Ben Lewis, Joseph A. Pechman, and Richard Heflebower.
99. Ibid.

with presidential encouragement, the experience of European countries with wage-price policies was canvassed more systematically. These investigations yielded some interesting findings on the steel industry. The French government, James Tobin noted, had successfully fought off steel companies that had signaled their intention to raise prices—but only because stock and bond issues had to be approved by the Ministry of Finance, which had indicated that this approval would be unlikely in the event of a price increase. In Germany, on the other hand, the government had "exhorted steel not to raise prices, but they went up 6 percent anyway." Tobin concluded that "moral suasion" was "more effective in the USA!"[100] As for the broader issue of European experience with wage-price policy and its potential lessons for the United States, Walter Heller summarized the results of the preliminary canvass with the observation that "American industrial relations institutions are probably less amenable" to official manipulation than in most of the seven countries surveyed. Even so, European success with price stabilization programs was judged not to have been outstanding. Thus there were grounds for a perverse optimism ("in the Chas. Addams sense"), at least "with respect to the future of our international competitors."[101] This inference was elaborated at greater length by James Tobin when the study was completed. Its central conclusions were:

1. *Most Western European governments have more power over wages and prices than the United States government....*

2. *In spite of these controls, most Western European countries have not been remarkably successful in holding down wages....*

3. *The prospects are that wages and prices will rise faster in Europe in the next few years than in the 1950's, and that the U.S. competitive position will improve, to the benefit of our balance of payments.*[102]

Nevertheless, the search continued. Arthur Goldberg paid a visit to Sweden for a look at the centralized wage-setting machinery there. This trip was reciprocated by the appearance of delegations from Swedish trade unions and from the Swedish Employers Federation at the October 1962 meeting of the Labor-Management Advisory Committee.

100. Tobin to the President, "Prices in Europe," April 21, 1962, CEA, 4/62–5/5/62 folder, Box 74, President's Office files, Kennedy Library.

101. Heller to the President, April 26, 1962, Memos to JFK, 4/62 folder, Kennedy-Johnson files, Heller Papers, Kennedy Library.

102. Tobin to the President, "Wages and Prices in Europe," May 12, 1962, CEA, 5/7–31/62 folder, Box 74, President's Office files, Kennedy Library.

Reordering Priorities

While part of the fallout from the steel confrontation was a reappraisal by the administration of the apparatus of wage-price policy, there were other reactions with greater public visibility. A reading from much of the business community was not long delayed: the tactics used to achieve the steel price rollback were perceived as a form of immoral suasion. Tremors in the stock market also reflected shakiness in business confidence—and charges that the Kennedy administration had demonstrated that it was "antibusiness" did not improve the atmosphere. Presidential rhetoric in late April and May was addressed to refuting this charge and to assuring both business and labor that the administration had no intention of fixing prices or wages and certainly did not propose to intervene in every labor-management dispute. Meanwhile, reconciliation with the steel industry was under way—a decision that had been made on April 16 in a meeting of the President and Heller, Goldberg, Sorensen, Robert Kennedy, and Clark Clifford. Heller had earlier set out the possible elements of an attitude toward steel that would be "constructive and cooperative rather than gloating or punitive":

Emphasize the area of common interest between Government and the steel industry, especially:

(a) the need for improvement and modernization of plant and equipment, as aided by our moves on the investment credit, depreciation guidelines, and interest rates;

(b) the need for more profits—profits generated by a more fully employed economy rather than by premature price rises in a slack economy and slacker steel industry. Here, the industry should begin to recognize that it has a stake in government expansionary policies just as government has a stake in expansionary steel industry policy;

(c) the interest in labor peace and wage moderation, already manifested in the recent steel settlement.[103]

Some personal signals were sent to the steel industry as well. Roger Blough —who had been cast as the devil during the confrontation—was appointed to chair the Business Advisory Council's Committee on Balance of Payments Policy, and arrangements were quietly made for discussions be-

103. Heller to the President, "Steel: Where do we go from here?" April 14, 1962, Steel, 4/10/62–4/12/62 folder, Box 39, Sorensen Papers, Kennedy Library.

tween the CEA and industry representatives to narrow their differences on productivity measurements in steel.[104]

But a larger question loomed: was a Kennedy recession in the making? The CEA had indicated in March that the path of the economy was already below its projections.[105] The stock market tumble after the steel confrontation did nothing to brighten the picture. The market's performance, however, could also be read as a symptom of strength on one front. John Kenneth Galbraith supplied the President with the following interpretation:

The cause of the drop is that people have ceased to see an unlimited prospect for capital gains. This is partly out of respect for the Administration anti-inflation measures. That means that common stocks will not rise forever for reasons of inflation. And as the inflation danger lessens, so does the demand for stock as an inflation hedge.[106]

Meanwhile there were signs that Kennedy—with the steel price episode behind him—was prepared to worry less about inflation dangers. Walter Heller, who was asked to brief him on "the possible benign effects of a 'little inflation,'" replied that "the answer depends in good part on the *kind* of inflation and on its impact on our *relative* position in world markets. The more prices rise abroad, the less serious price rises here become."[107] In elaboration, he distinguished demand-pull from cost-push inflation. Of the former, there was no current risk: "it would be unsound economics and unsound politics to choke off recovery and slow down our growth . . . for the sake of absolute price stability—especially now, when we have plenty of slack in the economy."[108] This doctrine, to be sure, had been circulated for some time. But now intervention in steel had also relieved worries about cost-push inflation. In Heller's judgment, there was room for "added stimulus—without harm to our international position—with policies which contribute substantively and directly to the

104. Heller to the President, "Industry-Government Differences on U.S. Steel Statistics," May 14, 1962, CEA, 4/7–31/62 folder, Box 74, President's Office files, Kennedy Library.

105. Heller to the President, "What It Takes to Get to Full Employment," March 3, 1962, CEA, 3/62 folder, Box 74, President's Office files, Kennedy Library.

106. Galbraith to the President, "The Stock Market," May 29, 1962 (dictated by telephone from Newfane, Vermont), J. K. Galbraith, 3/2/62–11/15/63 folder, Box 30, President's Office files, Kennedy Library.

107. Heller to the President, "Care and Feeding of Inflation," May 8, 1962, CEA, 5/7–31/62 folder, Box 74, President's Office files, Kennedy Library.

108. Ibid.

pace of the recovery, in short, more permissive fiscal and monetary policies." Space had been opened by intervention in steel: "In fact, had you not acted as you did, the clamor for a really balanced budget and a tougher monetary policy might have eventually become louder, as other firms and industries followed suit and the price indexes rose."[109]

That Kennedy was receptive to this line of argument was confirmed in his comments to the May 21 White House Conference on National Economic Issues (a gathering promoted by the Labor-Management Advisory Committee). He there invited his audience to distinguish between myth and reality in economic life. To illustrate the point, he noted the "alarm and concern" that federal deficits would produce inflation. That view, based on an impression "hung over from years ago," had failed to identify the real problems.[110] The same theme was developed more eloquently and at greater length in his commencement address at Yale University on June 11, 1962. This was pedagogy on a broadened scale, but it was not yet a specific commitment to a detailed program.

At the same time, the behavior of the economy suggested that there was a strong case for immediate fiscal stimulation. Paul Samuelson and Robert Solow (now returned to the Massachusetts Institute of Technology) painted a stark picture for the President in early June: "now, for the first time, the prudent odds for a so-called Kennedy recession, allegedly brought on by a so-called stock market crash (attributable to antibusiness governmental attitudes impinging on inflated values and ebbing fears of inflation), have ceased to be negligible.... There is right now a substantial possibility that you will go into the 1964 election with the highest average unemployment rate of any post-war administration." As for antibusiness sentiment: "More can be done for confidence by expansionary policies—early tax cuts—than by any feasible alternatives. . . . Under present circumstances only an early tax cut appears to be capable of giving the economy the stimulus it needs in time to be really effective."[111] The CEA was less alarmist about the forecast. Even in late June Heller, when reviewing the gloomy views circulating among business and academic economists, noted: "We're not this bearish yet, but we're no

109. Ibid.   '
110. "Remarks to Members of the White House Conference on National Economic Issues. May 21, 1962," *Public Papers*, 1962, p. 422.
111. Paul A. Samuelson and Robert M. Solow to the President, "The Changed Mid-Year Outlook," June 6, 1962, Memos to JFK, 6/62 folder, Kennedy-Johnson files, Heller Papers, Kennedy Library.

longer pawing the ground."[112] Nevertheless, the CEA urged an early presidential announcement of plans to recommend a net tax reduction.[113] Kennedy took a long step in this direction in his prepared remarks at the press conference of June 7, when he indicated his intention to recommend to the next Congress the enactment of a tax cut to become effective January 1, 1963.[114]

Although the domestic expansionists had scored a signal success, victory was not complete. Arguments in midsummer that the President accelerate the pace of a tax cut with a "quickie" reduction fell short. The balance of payments was again proving worrisome, and the Treasury made clear its opposition to any hasty action that might complicate its plans to bring a tax reform program before Congress in 1963. Meanwhile, the softening of the economy—combined with the apparent slippage in business confidence following the steel confrontation—directed attention away from wage-price issues. In mid-July the White House requested the heads of departments and agencies to take careful note of programs designed to help business. On presidential instruction, cabinet- and subcabinet-level officials were directed to "avoid the wrong kind of speeches or press conference remarks—no commenting now on the stock market, a tax cut, gold, business ethics, wage price intervention, or anti-trust laws."[115]

By the year's end the economic policy ranks within the administration had again begun to close.[116] The Cabinet Committee on Economic

112. Heller to the President, "Storm Signals," June 27, 1962, CEA, 6/62 folder, Box 74, President's Office files, Kennedy Library. This observation is a handwritten postscript on the copy of this document in the President's Office files.

113. Heller to the President, "Comments on Washington Post Editorials," June 2, 1962, CEA, 6/62 folder, Box 74, President's Office files, Kennedy Library.

114. "The President's News Conference of June 7, 1962," Public Papers, 1962, p. 457.

115. Memorandum for Members of the Cabinet from T. J. Reardon, Jr., special assistant to the President, July 30, 1962, Business and the Administration, 7/22–8/19/62 folder, Box 39, Sorensen Papers, Kennedy Library.

116. One distant dissenter failed to rally round the Keynesian banner. Galbraith, writing from India on August 20, 1962, to applaud Kennedy's decision not to press for a "quickie" tax cut, set out his views as follows: "you gave the tax-cutters enough support to qualify as the most Keynesian head of state in history. Do put a picture of the Master in your bathroom or some other suitably secluded place. As a charter member of the worshipful following this should give me more pleasure than it does. For, alas, I am left with the thought that the orthodoxy is as always one step behind the problem. And so it is now that Keynes is official." Galbraith to the President, August 20, 1962, J. K. Galbraith, 3/2/62–11/15/63 folder, Box 30, President's Office files, Kennedy Library.

Growth (on which the Treasury, Labor, and Commerce Departments, the Budget Bureau, and the CEA were represented) could report unanimously: "Our main hope for restoring full employment and thus meeting *the* basic prerequisite for faster growth is to remove the tax-over-burden on aggregate demand and the tax drag on incentive." The committee recommended a $7 billion to $12 billion net reduction in taxes as promptly as possible.[117]

The dual strategy with which 1962 had opened had not worked as planned. But the flow of events had created a situation in which there was at once an increased need for expansionary programs and a reduced fear that their consequences would be inflationary. Policy had thus found a new focal point.

Wage-Price Policy on the Back Burner

As 1963 began, the energies of economic policymakers in Washington were concentrated on planning for the tax cut program. Though the administration had consolidated in support of an expansionary fiscal policy, its precise shape had yet to be determined. The White House had specified the constraints to which the operation would be subject: (1) expenditures should not exceed $100 billion (there was thought to be no political mileage in penetrating this barrier before the next election); and (2) the projected deficit should not exceed the peacetime record set by the Eisenhower administration in fiscal 1959.[118] Within these limits, many of the practical details had yet to be worked out.

This preoccupation was sufficient justification for putting wage-price issues in abeyance, but there were other reasons as well. The record of the recent past had, after all, been generally satisfactory. Labor costs per unit of output in all manufacturing were calculated to have declined by 4.5 percent between February 1961 and December 1962. Moreover, increases in average hourly earnings in manufacturing had been lower than in any comparable period since 1955. Though the consumer price index had

117. Report to the President from the Membership of the Cabinet Committee on Economic Growth, as transmitted by Walter Heller, chairman of the committee, December 1, 1962, CEA, 11/16/62–12/31/62 folder, Box 75, President's Office files, Kennedy Library.

118. Theodore Sorensen, sixth recorded interview by Carl Kaysen, May 20, 1964, Kennedy Library Oral History Program.

moved upward by 1.3 percentage points during 1962, this was well within the range of price stability as officially defined (that is, within allowances for quality changes not captured by the index makers).[119] Nor was any immediate threat to price stability thought to be in prospect. Even with the most optimistic assumptions about congressional action on the tax cut program, the CEA estimated that the unemployment rate would not fall to 4 percent before the fourth quarter of 1964. Demand-pull inflation, in short, was still remote. Although the possibility of agitation on the cost-push side could not be totally dismissed, 1963 seemed likely to be an off year for major labor contract negotiations.

The treatment of the guideposts in the 1963 Economic Report reflected this mood. While it was asserted that the guideposts would "gain in importance" as the "margin of unemployed labor and idle capital narrows," no changes in the 1962 formulation were introduced.[120] One break from the pattern of the earlier report was noteworthy, however: no calculations of overall trends in productivity were included in the discussion of the guideposts.

A breathing spell on the wage-price front was welcome. Though the guideposts had survived 1962, the weather had not been completely calm. There had been indications (of which the White House was aware) that the Federal Mediation and Conciliation Service regarded the official enunciation of a formula on appropriate wage changes as complicating its task in reconciling labor-management differences.[121] The change in command at the Department of Labor with Arthur Goldberg's nomination to the Supreme Court in August 1962 also indicated that an intra-administration educational effort was in order. Willard Wirtz brought to the secretaryship insight developed during a distinguished career as an arbitrator in bargaining disputes. In addition, the drama of steel had obscured the stretching of standards that had occurred in less conspicuous

119. N. J. Simler, "Wage-Price Developments" (CEA Briefing Paper), January 26, 1963, Wage-Price Guideposts, 10/62–12/63 folder, Kennedy-Johnson files, Heller Papers, Kennedy Library.

120. *Economic Report of the President, January 1963*, pp. 85–86.

121. In June 1962, for example, Special Assistant Reardon sought clarification and explanation of comments in the reports of the Federal Mediation and Conciliation Service to the effect that the guideposts were encouraging a " 'let the government tell us what to do' attitude on the part of many employers, especially those negotiating with strong unions otherwise willing to settle for less." A "confused collective bargaining situation," it was maintained, had resulted. Reardon to Steve Shulman, June 6, 1962, National Economy (BE 5 Executive), Box 17, White House Central Subject files, Kennedy Library.

negotiations. The settlement recommended by the Railway Emergency Board (which increased hourly wage costs by 4.1 percent) was a case in point. As Walter Heller had noted at the time: "It accepts the guidelines in principle but justifies deviations in terms of additional criteria, notably (1) cost-of-living and (2) 'equity'—or 'catching up' with some handy reference group.... [This] reminds one of our friend's diet meal—his regular lunch plus a side order of cottage cheese 'for my diet.' "[122] Pressure for guidepost compliance was clearly not being applied uniformly. Nor was it reasonable to expect that it could be. The CEA, though available as a monitoring agent, neither possessed nor sought any formal enforcement authority; its staff was small and already spread too thin. Moreover, White House enthusiasm for the guidepost approach was not unrestrained. Kennedy was quite content with the division of responsibility worked out for the 1962 Economic Report (and repeated for the 1963 report): the guideposts were the CEA's, not the President's. In these circumstances, government intervention in wage and price making was necessarily highly selective.

In 1963, as in 1962, the major disturber of the peace was steel. There were a few minor troubles, such as the East Coast dock strike and the New York newspaper strike settlements, in which results not readily reconcilable with the guideposts were obtained. The administration refused to join battle in these cases and treated them as special situations best resolved by bargaining parties on the spot. The decision of the Wheeling Steel Corporation to increase prices on a range of its products (with effect from April 10, 1963) could not be dismissed so easily. It was expected that a number of other companies in the industry would announce similar decisions within a matter of days.

Presidential rhetoric at this time contrasted sharply with the tone of a year earlier, and was far more moderate than the language recommended to him by the CEA. The Council's notes for a presidential statement suggested that this kind of behavior be branded as "even less justified" than it had been in 1962—for "even apart from the dangers of touching off a new price-wage spiral and worsening our gold position, the steel industry itself is stronger today than a year ago."[123] The President's actual state-

122. Heller to the President, "The Railway Emergency Board (Wallen)—Summary and Comment," May 14, 1962, Memos to JFK, 5/62 folder, Kennedy-Johnson files, Heller Papers, Kennedy Library.

123. Notes for Draft of Presidential Statement on Steel, Council of Economic Advisers, April 11, 1963, CEA, 3/1–4/14/63 folder, Box 76, President's Office files, Kennedy Library.

ment, however, was more conciliatory and careful to differentiate 1963 from 1962:

I realize that price and wage controls in this one industry while all others are unrestrained would be unfair and inconsistent with our free competitive market—that unlike last year the Government's good faith has not been engaged in talks with industry and union representatives— and that selected price adjustments, up or down, as prompted by changes in supply and demand, as opposed to across-the-board increases, are not incompatible with a framework of general stability and steel price stability and are characteristic of any healthy economy.[124]

The White House obviously had no appetite for a replay of April 1962. The situation needed to be attended to, but on this occasion the treatment was to be private and discreet. At a White House meeting on April 10, it was decided to avoid confrontation with the steel industry if possible and to dispatch Walter Heller and Roswell Gilpatric, deputy secretary of defense, as the administration's emissaries to the industry.[125]

By April 17 all but one of the top twelve companies in the industry had announced some price increases, though an equilibrium had not been reached. The Heller-Gilpatric visit to the U.S. Steel representatives at the Carlton House in Washington had produced some movement. The result of the item-by-item negotiation in which they participated delighted Kennedy: Big Steel's previously announced price increments were reduced by some 40 percent.[126] As of that date, the CEA judged that Big Steel had exercised restraint and had apparently attempted to "stay within the boundaries" of the President's statement of April 11. But the Council also told the President that the "price increases do not significantly affect the steel products we *import*, but they do hit the steel products we *export*. Although your statement last Thursday referred to steel price stability and 'adjustments up and down' there have been *no real adjustments downward*." Heller concluded: "In short, we have come off well, but not unscathed. To put the whole matter in a perspective that will accentuate the positive and minimize the negative effects, it is important to get an agreed Administration posture."[127]

124. "Statement by the President on the Need for Price and Wage Stability in the Steel Industry. April 11, 1963," *Public Papers*, 1963, pp. 321–22.

125. Walter W. Heller, Kermit Gordon, and Joseph A. Pechman, recorded interview by Larry J. Hackman, September 14, 1972, Kennedy Library Oral History Program, p. 29.

126. Ibid., p. 31.

127. Heller to the President, "A Summary of the Steel Situation: 5:00 P.M.

The central position was indeed in need of repair. The President indicated as much when requesting background material for questions he anticipated at his next press conference. He wrote to Heller on April 22: "I think we should be prepared to discuss the prospects of inflation and should be considering if a warning statement should be made."[128] In reply Heller indicated that the overall impact of recent price changes was inconclusive; some prices had gone up, others down. The "basic economic environment," however, was "*not* favorable to a surge of inflation."[129] In industries where there was "a certain amount of price discretion"—steel being a case in point—the guidepost standards needed to be reaffirmed. He added:

The guideposts have inevitably been bloodied a bit by decisions not fully consistent with their prescriptions—most recently by the steel price increases. But in no sense can you be said to have "retreated." Whereas last year there was an attempt for a major across-the-board steel price increase, this year selective and moderate price increases have occurred.[130] The covering note transmitting this analysis was more direct in its suggestion for an administration posture: "I don't think we should overdo the spectre of inflation, lest we give aid and comfort to price increases and to the Federal Reserve Board."[131]

When the final returns on the April 1963 round of steel price increases were in, the administration's restraint could be interpreted a bit differently. On April 23—when prices had been equilibrated throughout the industry—it appeared that the average price increase for all products was about 1.1 percent (or 3.4 percent on the average realized prices of items in the product lines that were directly affected).[132] The following day the Council reported to the President that testimony by the Bureau of Labor Statistics before the Joint Economic Committee's steel hearings indicated that "steel industry employment costs have increased *slightly* faster than productivity since the price boosts in 1958—this evidence would suggest

Wednesday," April 17, 1963, Memos to JFK, 4/63 folder, Kennedy-Johnson files, Heller Papers, Kennedy Library.

128. The President to Heller, April 22, 1963, CEA, 4/15–30/63 folder, Box 76, President's Office files, Kennedy Library.

129. Heller to the President, "Inflation (a response to your April 22 memorandum)," April 23, 1963, Memos to JFK, 4/63 folder, Kennedy-Johnson files, Heller Papers, Kennedy Library.

130. Ibid.

131. Heller to the President, April 23, 1963, same file.

132. Heller to the President, "Steel Settles Down," April 23, 1963, same file.

that a slight price adjustment (of the kind made to date) would fit within our wage-price guidelines."[133]

With the aid of this information, face could be saved all around. The new evidence was not conspicuously proclaimed. In its public statements, the administration was again careful to emphasize that the steel price episodes of 1962 and 1963 were not comparable. The guideposts had not forestalled a 1963 price rise, although as talking points they had been useful in producing an outcome less unsatisfactory than would otherwise have been the case.

But there was still an awkward corner to be turned: the steel labor contract was due for renewal before June 30, and the administration's hand had lost some of its strength. In advising the President on how best to proceed in this matter, the CEA recognized that there were more than trivial arguments in favor of governmental detachment in this instance. In particular: "The 'guideposts' do not give unambiguous guidance in the steel case. We could get ourselves into an unnecessary fight with the union about the interpretation of the guideposts, creating hostility by the union and the labor movement toward the Administration." And further: "The steel price increase was difficult to justify as within our guideposts for prices; why should we try to restrain the union?"[134]

At the same time, patterns in steel had both a real and a symbolic significance for the economy as a whole. The case for an informal recommendation to the union was summed up as follows:

With the economy hopefully narrowing the gap between demand and capacity, especially with a tax cut, we can expect an intensification of wage-price pressures during the next twelve months. Particularly for balance of payments reasons, the Administration is going to have to grapple hard with the problem, and this is a good time for it to start (non-ostentatiously) digging in its heels.[135]

On balance, Heller concluded that guidepost reasoning—as adapted to the special circumstances of the industry (including the need to avoid giving the companies a pretext to raise prices further)—warranted an administration suggestion that a wage increment of "not more than 2 percent" was appropriate. The package negotiated in June was appraised as

133. Heller to the President, "Late Returns on the Price and Wage Front," April 24, 1963, same file.

134. Heller to the President, "Issues in the Steel Wage Settlement," May 21, 1963, CEA, 5/11–31/63 folder, Box 76, President's Office files, Kennedy Library.

135. Ibid.

follows: "the actual rate of increase in hourly employment costs is just over 1.5 percent a year. . . . In short, it is a real contribution to continued price stability."[136]

Though it was useful to "accentuate the positive," there was no way to camouflage the fact that the guideposts—on the price side—had been dented by steel in the spring of 1963. The damage, to be sure, had been minimized. Nevertheless, this round conveyed a potentially ominous signal that the guideposts were vulnerable to "salami tactics."

Some Symptoms of Disarray

From the inception of the guidepost strategy for inflation defenses, action in the steel sector was held to be crucial. Events in the first half of 1963 indicated some shakiness in the administration's position. If, in fact, steel was the bellwether it had so often been alleged to be, other attacks on prices could certainly be expected.

By midsummer the consumer price index had begun to pick up some disturbing signals. The June and July increases in the CPI marked the largest two-month rise in prices in several years. Much of this increase (which amounted to 0.9 point for the two-month period) could be accounted for by special factors (particularly as they affected food prices). At the same time, though a considerable number of price advances had been announced, their impact was not fully reflected in the indexes: for instance, aluminum, finished brass and copper, electrical and electronic equipment, wood products, furniture, petroleum products, automobile tires, and plastics. Walter Heller, who reported to the President in early August that his "viscera" had "been agitated a bit about prices," offered the following interpretation:

These actions can best be explained as probes by corporations to see whether markets will yet bear cost-based price increases that their standard price-making rules would have dictated some time ago but have been postponed because of market sluggishness. . . . All of this . . . doesn't add up to much yet, but if the economic expansion proceeds as it should, more and more of these upward price adjustments are likely, and we shall be watching them with—to coin an expression—a steely eye.[137]

136. Heller to the President, "Steel Prices and Wages," June 21, 1963, CEA, 6/63 folder, Box 76, President's Office files, Kennedy Library.

137. Heller to the President, "What's Happening to Prices?" August 2, 1963, CEA, 8/63 folder, Box 76, President's Office files, Kennedy Library.

In late August Gardner Ackley resurveyed the terrain, reporting that the CEA was "talking quietly with other agencies about strengthening and integrating our early-warning system."[138] But, in his judgment, the main problem lay ahead:

We are still so far short of full-capacity operations that there is little or no present evidence of bottleneck price pressures. By next Spring, if a January 1 tax cut already is providing direct stimulus to demand and has fortified expectations of continuing expansion, cost-justified price raising is likely to be somewhat more prevalent than now. And later in 1964, if we succeed in substantially narrowing the underproduction gap, we may indeed begin to encounter some bottlenecks.

Thus, price policy may very well be a troublesome item on our 1964 agenda (assuming we succeed in avoiding the bigger problem of recession).[139]

For the time being, Ackley counseled, "we'll do well to remain visibly unruffled over the subject of prices. . . . It would be most unfortunate for the Administration to express any alarm about inflation that would give aid and comfort, either to opponents of the tax bill or to tight-money partisans within the Federal Reserve System."[140] This tactical consideration had taken on increased importance because of the latest steps to bring the balance of payments under control. The announcement of the new measures (which included the recommendation for the interest equalization tax) in mid-July had been accompanied by an increase in the discount rate. With monetary policy tightening, the momentum of expansion was even more dependent on fiscal stimuli. Agitation about inflation that might jeopardize support for the tax cut would serve no worthwhile purpose.

But there was to be yet more action on the price front in 1963, much of it again centered in steel. Several firms in the industry touched off another round of selective price increases in late September. By the time the industry as a whole had adapted to this latest set of changes, price increases had been effected on about 78 percent of the total tonnage produced, with the result that prices had risen by about 2.2 percent of the total value of steel shipped.[141] There was no ambiguity about whether

138. Ackley to the President, "More Price Rumbles—Next Week's Rise in the CPI—and Our Posture on Prices," August 24, 1963, same file.

139. Ibid.

140. Ibid.

141. John P. Lewis to the President, "Background for Talk with Jim Patton, Republic Steel," November 6, 1963, CEA, 11/63 folder, Box 77, President's Office files, Kennedy Library.

these cumulative increases were consistent with the guideposts: "the 1963 price increases," the CEA asserted, "simply don't wash in terms of the price guideposts."[142] Nevertheless, steel pricing during the year presented an interpretative problem in relation to the approach taken in April: namely, "when does a cumulation of 'selected' increases become 'across-the-board'?" John P. Lewis, writing to the President as acting chairman of the CEA on November 6, concluded that the steel increases—though they clearly could not be justified under the guideposts—represented "no heinous violation. It's a case of an open-and-shut misdemeanor, but no felony."[143]

How best should this situation be handled? There were weighty arguments to support administration silence, among them, as Walter Heller noted in October:

Calling attention to price increases may play into the hands of tax-cut opponents who have been claiming that the tax cut will be inflationary. . . .

Government-business relations are better than in a long time; any condemnation of steel, or intimation of possible "future price crackdowns," could impair confidence, with possibly bad economic and political effects. . . .

Unless we think there is some prospect that something can be accomplished by speaking out, we are wasting our ammunition and run the danger of appearing futile.[144]

But there was also a potent case for speaking out, which, in addition to the obvious relation of price stability to the balance of payments, contained the following ingredients:

Despite our ability to avoid demand-pull inflation because of unused manpower and plant capacity, some cost-push pressure on prices is in the cards as we head toward full employment. For both domestic and international reasons, we are going to have to resist it, by word and perhaps by deed. Our wage-price policy will have to become tougher in the months and years ahead if we are to preserve and extend our international competitive advantage. It would have been good to have the tax cut (and the election!) behind us before facing this whole issue, but we may be unable to wait for the first, and almost surely will be unable to wait for the second. Steel is a good place to start.

142. Lewis to the President, "Third Quarter Steel Profits," November 2, 1963, same file.

143. Lewis to the President, "Background for Talk with Jim Patton."

144. Heller to the President, "Administration Posture on Steel—and other—Price Increases," October 2, 1963, CEA, 10/63 folder, Box 77, President's Office files, Kennedy Library.

Labor is very restive about our wage guideposts, which they say we have tried to enforce on them—with considerable success—while giving no evidence of recent concern for the price side of the guideposts.

On balance, Heller concluded, the administration should "express responsible concern without raising the spectre of inflation."[145]

This assessment had the authority of a remarkable record of price stability to recommend it. Of the industrial countries, only Canada could claim better price performance than the United States during the Kennedy years. From January 1961 through September 1963, the consumer price index advanced at a rate only slightly in excess of 1 percent a year and the wholesale price index actually declined.

Maintaining a low profile did not, however, exclude taking other steps. In its internal assessments of the situation in October, the CEA had determined that the "price adjustments of the past few months represent no flagrant abandonment of the guideposts. But, rather plainly, managements, wherever markets have looked to be receptive, have been probing for increases in a fashion that tends to be unjustified by guidepost standards and would entail a progressive abandonment of the guideposts if it became the rule rather than the exception."[146] To help minimize the exceptions, an organization formed in March 1962 for other purposes (the Consumers' Advisory Council) was nudged to issue a statement deploring price increases. Meanwhile, the Justice Department moved to reopen grand jury investigations of pricing procedures in the steel industry. For public consumption, the official line on this activity was that the steel industry should not be exempt from normal investigative procedures simply because it had raised prices.[147]

Preparations for the longer term were also in order. Walter Heller had indicated to the President in October that further development of the wage-price guideposts appeared to be necessary—with particular attention to "ways and means of putting the spotlight of public opinion on specific

145. Ibid. Secretary of the Treasury Douglas Dillon (to whom a copy of this memorandum had been sent) concurred with this general position. While he favored a "statement of concern," he added: "It should carefully avoid any tone of belligerency and should be geared largely to balance of payments considerations rather than inflation. The latter point . . . could provide an argument for opponents of tax reduction." Dillon to Heller, October 3, 1963, Microfilm Copies of Records of the Treasury Department, Roll 59, Kennedy Library.

146. "Lines of Action on Price Increases," CEA memorandum, October 6, 1963, CEA, 10/63 folder, Box 77, President's Office files, Kennedy Library.

147. Lewis to the President, "Background for Talk with Jim Patton."

unjustified price and wage increases."[148] The 1964 Economic Report was suggested as one vehicle by which this might be accomplished. Preliminary planning for the report indicated a "shift in emphasis . . . away from the aggregative and toward structural and sectoral problems—away perhaps, from Keynesian toward neo-classical problems and policies."[149] This shift was occasioned by the prospect that favorable congressional action on the tax cut would bring the 1964 economy much closer to full employment. Similarly, the fiscal dividends promised by a higher rate of growth would open new space for socially constructive expenditure programs. As early as June, Heller had indicated to the President that an "assault on poverty" might usefully become a focal point of the 1964 economic program. By late October, Kennedy reportedly was "aroused" by the idea.[150] But the fate of this proposal might very well be linked with a rethinking of wage-price strategies. In his allocation of preliminary work assignments for the preparation of the 1964 Economic Report, Heller noted:

The price and wage problems are almost bound to come to the fore if the economy pushes on towards high—indeed, we hope, full—employment. The early signs of upward price push are already in evidence. So, whether as part of a series of Administration moves to discourage price increases or as a further natural development of the wage-price guideposts, or both, we will want to have a very careful job on this subject.[151]

The Evolution of Wage-Price Policy in the Thousand Days

During the abruptly abbreviated term of the Kennedy administration, thought and action on matters pertaining to wage-price issues passed through a number of phases. In the first, the administration was divided within itself about the importance of an official position on wages and prices. Those who assigned top priority to alleviating the distress of the

148. Heller to the President, "Administration Posture on Steel—and other—Price Increases."

149. Heller to the CEA professional staff, "Initial Assignments for the 1964 Annual Report," October 10, 1963, Heller Council, 7/63–12/63 folder, Kennedy-Johnson files, Heller Papers, Kennedy Library.

150. Heller, "Confidential Notes on Meeting with the President," October 21, 1963, Meetings with JFK, 1963 folder, Kennedy-Johnson files, Heller Papers, Kennedy Library.

151. Heller to the CEA professional staff, "Initial Assignments for the 1964 Annual Report."

nation's international accounts attached high importance to price stability for reasons of international competitiveness; those inclined to give major weight to expansion of the domestic economy, on the other hand, tended to regard worry about inflation as premature and a matter of secondary concern. Both the flow of events and the dynamics of intra-administration debate on the priorities of economic policy worked to produce an effective concurrence on the need for a wage-price strategy. The rationale for that need was not perceived identically by all the parties involved. To the domestic expansionists in particular, a plausible position on price stability was valued more highly as a solvent to constraint on expansionary programs than as an objective in its own right.

A second phase opened with a search for a strategy that would achieve this purpose, though the search was itself constrained: direct government controls, at least in circumstances short of a national emergency, could not be seriously considered. The doctrine that emerged, however, was shaped with more than a passing glance toward one industry, steel, which was held to be singular in its capacity to spark price increases in an underemployed economy. The formulation of the dual strategy of the guideposts was a high tribute to analytic ingenuity, and it succeeded for a time in achieving one of its objectives: steel price increases were temporarily suppressed, even though some unconventional reinforcements to policy were invoked.

This set the stage for a third phase, in which plans for expansionary programs could move forward. But at this point, the roles were reversed. Mobilization of support for expansionary programs now precluded monitoring of errant price or wage behavior. Meanwhile, the hope that an informed public would act as a spontaneous disciplinary agent seemed not to have been fulfilled.

A fourth phase was in process at the time of Kennedy's death. Success in moving the economy toward full employment was in sight, and at that point the wage-price problem could be expected to assume yet another form. The rethinking initiated in the early autumn of 1963 had not crystallized by November 22. Should the guideposts be redefined in a way that would make the standards for voluntary compliance more explicit (as Gardner Ackley was to suggest)? Or should strategy be redirected to selected, but significant, targets toward which presidential persuasive powers could be aimed (as John P. Lewis was to suggest)?[152] These questions were to be part of the inheritance of President Johnson.

152. For details of the Ackley and Lewis memorandums, see chapter 4 below.

IV

The Johnson Administration: Moral Suasion Goes to War

JAMES L. COCHRANE

LYNDON BAINES JOHNSON continues to be thought of as a war President. Certainly much of the story to be told here is inextricably linked to U.S. military activities in Southeast Asia, activities that extended Kennedy policies. But if LBJ inherited the war, he also inherited the extraordinary Kennedy apparatus. He moved quickly to try to make both the political and governmental components of this apparatus his own. With the important exception of Robert F. Kennedy and the people who would at one time or another associate themselves with him as the leader of *their* Democratic party, LBJ was successful in this conversion process, more so than most people would have predicted. The integration of his own political lieutenants and advisers into the apparatus, coupled with the normal turnover in line and staff federal jobs, eventually produced a Johnson administration. But the process took time. Nevertheless, LBJ did acquire an effective, ongoing administration—complete with rivalries, political practices, tacit and formal operating policies, links with various constituencies, and a legislative program.

Note. Much of this paper is based on materials in the Lyndon Baines Johnson Library, Austin, Texas. I am indebted to the Library's director, Harry J. Middleton, and his staff, especially Claudia W. Anderson, Charles W. Corkran, John T. Fawcett, Sharon K. Fawcett, Christina Lawson, and Dorothy P. Territo, for their patient, gracious, and knowledgeable assistance. Most of the archival digging was done during the spring semester of 1974, a visit made possible by James W. McKie and Stephen L. McDonald of the University of Texas as well as James F. Kane of the University of South Carolina.

I am grateful to the following for reading and commenting on at least one earlier version of this essay: Gardner Ackley, Stanley W. Black, Joseph L. Block, James Bouknight, Royall Brandis, Joseph A. Califano, Jr., Susan H. Cochrane, Paul Dragoo, Otto Eckstein, Kermit Gordon, Walter W. Heller, Thomas M. Humphrey, Myron L. Joseph, Randolph Martin, Harry J. Middleton, Willard F. Mueller, Hugh S. Norton, Arthur M. Okun, Joseph A. Pechman, William S. Rawson, John E. Robson, Robert Rosen, Stanford G. Ross, Walt W. Rostow, Charles L. Schultze, Ronald P. Wilder, and C. Glyn Williams.

Many portions of the Kennedy economic program required almost immediate acceptance or rejection by the new President. Late November is a critical time for economic policymaking in any administration and 1963 was no exception. The Great Keynesian Tax Cut, for example, was on the floor of Congress. Would the new President follow JFK's lead? Also, there was the uncertain status of the so-called guidepost principles, the Kennedy administration's wage-price policy. The principles can be simply put. The rate of increase in wages should equal the national productivity increase. Prices in an industry should be reduced (increased) if the industry's rate of productivity increase is greater than (less than) the national productivity increase. The issue was how to firm up this pair of generalities a little (or a lot).

After the transition jitters had subsided and President Johnson had begun rolling JFK's legislative program through the second session of the Eighty-eighth Congress, administration efforts on the wage-price front were concentrated on the automobile industry, with a rather disappointing outcome. But the landslide victory over Senator Barry M. Goldwater in 1964 provided a powerful mandate and a friendly Congress. The Johnson administration moved forward boldly in many directions, including a series of generally successful attempts to apply the guidepost principles to the metals industry. By the end of 1965 more and more U.S. ground forces were committed to Vietnam, and the economy reached the Kennedy-Johnson interim goal of 4 percent unemployment. But the price indexes were on the move, and the administration realized that any wage-price policy for 1966 would be tough to enforce. To complicate matters, Johnson decided not to ask Congress to raise tax rates to yield the revenue required by the Great Society programs and the war. The year 1966 was a period of defeat for administration wage policy, marked by a highly publicized, above-guidepost settlement in the airline industry. Because the administration had stuck with its 3.2 percent wage guidepost for its 1966 program, price fighting in 1966 was fairly successful, especially until August 1966, when an army of problems—the airline settlement, a credit crunch, an out-of-control budget, and a rise in steel prices—simultaneously battered administration policy. During the remainder of 1966 the administration sought new fiscal programs and possible replacements for the guideposts. During 1967 the administration fought for its tax surcharge proposal and battled some price increases. But with a spiraling deficit, moral suasion on the price side was ineffective. And with price indexes on the move, moral suasion on the wage side was met by derision from the leadership of organized labor. In early 1968 the Johnson administration established a Cabinet Committee on Price Stability, which emerged, after the surcharge became law in late June, as a fairly effective apparatus for analyzing the sources of inflation and proposing what the administration could do about them. But the Nixon-Agnew Republican team won in November 1968 and the incoming administration would have little respect or use for the wage-price wisdom, policies, or apparatus accumulated during the Kennedy-Johnson years.

The Transition

I like the way you write memoranda—crisp, to the point and concise. Work-think-work-think hard. . . . I depend on you.
            —LBJ to Walter Heller, December 23, 1963

When Kennedy was assassinated on Friday, November 22, 1963, Walter Heller, chairman of the Council of Economic Advisers (CEA), and six cabinet members were en route to Japan. The aircraft refueled in Honolulu and returned to Washington. By the time Heller got to his office, the other two members of the CEA, John P. Lewis and Gardner Ackley, together with some of their staff and Joseph A. Pechman, had completed a lengthy "Summary Review of the Economic Situation and Pending Issues," which was on LBJ's desk Saturday morning. The CEA informed the new President of the state of the economy and of the important unfinished business he had inherited, including preparations for the Kennedy Round of trade negotiations scheduled for Geneva in May 1964[1] and the proposed interest equalization tax to improve the U.S. balance of payments. The CEA informed LBJ that the chronic deficit in the balance of payments had worsened during the first half of 1963 and that on July 18 JFK had informed Congress of the agreement struck between the administration and the Federal Reserve to raise short-term interest rates while lowering long-term rates, in an attempt to diminish the incentives to move short-term capital to Europe while promoting the expansion of domestic industry. Kennedy told Congress that he remained

---

1. Of course it took the new President time to master the complexity of issues: "One day he turned to Bromley Smith, an assistant on McGeorge Bundy's National Security staff in the White House, and asked plaintively: 'Can you tell me in one clear sentence what the Kennedy Round is?' " Rowland Evans and Robert Novak, *Lyndon B. Johnson: The Exercise of Power* (New American Library, 1966), p. 356.

concerned about the increasing outflow of long-term U.S. capital and asked them to enact the interest equalization tax, which would have in effect added a penalty of about 1 percent to the interest paid by foreign borrowers in the United States, retroactive to the date of his request. When Johnson became President, the bill was still in Wilbur D. Mills's House Ways and Means Committee, but the balance-of-payments deficit was improving, perhaps because of uncertainty about how the retroactive feature of the law was to work.

A major section of the CEA's Summary Review was devoted to "Wage-Price Developments and Policies":

Wage increases have been moderate in the past 3 years, while productivity has been rising nicely. As a result, labor costs (per unit of output) have been relatively stable. . . . Hourly earnings in manufacturing have increased about 3 percent in 1963. High profits and labor restlessness make somewhat larger wage increases likely in 1964.

Prices have been quite stable since early 1961. The wholesale price index is slightly lower today than it was in 1961. The consumer price index has increased about 1 percent a year, with prices of consumer services the main culprit.

In the second half of 1963 business has been experimenting with price boosts, but the increases have not yet been enough to raise the price indexes, and there is little indication of a general price movement. However, it can be expected that more firms will test the market with higher prices. Although labor costs have been generally stable, there may be upward cost pressure from higher prices for some basic raw materials.

Undoubtedly the recent record of stable prices is partly due to high unemployment and excess productive capacity. But partly it results from the opposition of the Administration to inflationary wage and price decisions as spelled out in the 1962 and 1963 Annual Economic Reports, statements by President Kennedy, and the Big Steel episode. As the economy approaches fuller utilization of capacity, it will be more difficult to restrain prices and excessive wage increases. Thus the Administration may have to strengthen its anti-inflation policy to meet future price and wage pressures.[2]

But the main theme of the Summary Review was the need for a major

2. "Summary Review of the Economic Situation and Pending Issues," November 23, 1963, Memoranda for the President, 1963, Papers of Arthur M. Okun. I am grateful to Mr. Okun for letting me go through his personal files and talking with me about the Johnson years.

tax cut to stimulate the economy. After the assassination, the CEA continued to be the major force pushing the tax cut proposal.[3] The tax bill was apparently on its way out of Harry F. Byrd's Senate Finance Committee, but administration officials could take neither the new President nor the Congress for granted. Johnson was informed that, although the 1963 gross national product was on the high side of the forecasts, the unemployment rate for October 1963 was 5.5 percent (just below the 5.6 percent average for 1962). Even without the tax cut, the forecast was favorable for modest expansion until the second half of 1964, when, without the tax cut, a slowdown or even a downturn could be expected. (LBJ did not have to be told that this would be election time.)[4]

After the assassination, Johnson sought advice on fiscal policy from outside the apparatus he had inherited. The three most influential outsiders were Donald C. Cook, a utility executive; Dwight D. Eisenhower; and Robert B. Anderson, a fellow Texan and secretary of the treasury under Eisenhower. Although Eisenhower and Anderson offered conservative fiscal advice, Cook suggested that the new President go with his advisers' tax program but cut the federal budget. On the night of November 25, LBJ met with his internal economic advisers, the principals and deputies at the Treasury, the Budget Bureau, and the CEA: the "troika" pairs —C. Douglas Dillon and Henry H. Fowler, Kermit Gordon and Elmer B. Staats, Walter Heller and Gardner Ackley. The discussion centered on

3. "The lead on the Great Tax Cut was taken by CEA and . . . it was a long, hard job to bring the Treasury up from its initial objective of a $2 to $3 billion tax cut to 'lubricate tax reform' to the $10 billion-or-so target [the CEA] set up in the spring of 1962." Heller to the author, August 19, 1974.

4. On December 2, 1963, Seymour E. Harris, senior consultant to Treasury Secretary Douglas Dillon, reported to Heller that the consensus at a November 6 meeting of Treasury consultants was that "without the tax cut the rise [in real GNP would] flatten out and unemployment might well rise by 1 percent and there would be trouble in the second half of 1964." On December 5 Harris told Heller that the tax cut would really be needed "after the first quarter of 1964" because, among other reasons, "monetary policy tends to be restrictive just before elections." Box 13, Heller Papers, John F. Kennedy Library. I am grateful to Professor Heller for granting me permission to go through his papers.

Harris became an important transition issue. The term of James L. Robertson, a friend and ally of Chairman William McChesney Martin, Jr., on the Federal Reserve Board of Governors would soon end, but he was eligible for reappointment as since 1952 he had been serving out the remainder of someone else's fourteen-year term. JFK, however, had promised Harris that this position was his. After a great deal of pressure from Robertson's allies and Harris's enemies, LBJ appointed Robertson to his own full fourteen-year term, building credit with the current voting majority at the Fed.

fiscal policy. The President told the group that his cabinet ("nine salesmen and a credit manager") would have to get the administrative budget
down to around $100 billion to get the tax cut through Congress.

In late November and early December, Heller led administration liberals in trying to preserve the Kennedy target figure for fiscal 1965 expenditures of $102.1 billion. The day the troika pairs met with the Presi-
dent, Heller had presented him with a "case for a $101–102 billion
budget."[5] That same day he also gave LBJ his assessment of "the general
economic effect of holding the FY 1965 budget below $100 billion." Hel-
ler assumed "that this would be a real cut—that very little of it could be
gotten from inter-year switches in outlays, asset sales, changes in government loan financing mechanisms, or other 'gimmicks.'" The effect "would
not be massive" but "would be in the wrong direction, and sizeable."[6] On
December 5 Heller reported that the jump in the unemployment rate to
5.9 percent during November "can't be all explained away."[7]

Nevertheless, on January 21, 1964, LBJ sent a $97.9 billion administra-
tive 1965 budget to Congress. It was achieved through Robert S. McNamara cutbacks and Kermit Gordon gimmicks, some real cutting coupled
with a little creative accounting. The administration estimated that a
GNP of $623 billion would produce tax receipts of $93 billion, cutting
the expected no-tax-increase deficit in half, and that personal and corporate tax liabilities would, with the cut, be $9.1 billion and $2.4 billion
lower respectively, with two-thirds of the impact occurring in 1964 and
the remaining one-third in 1965. Fortunately, Johnson was able to draw
attention away from the fact that fiscal year 1965 requests for new obliga-
tional authority came to $103.8 billion.[8] On February 7, 1964, the Great
Keynesian Tax Cut received 77 yeas in the Senate. Countercyclical fiscal
policy had come a long way from the June 1958 vote on Senator Paul H.
Douglas's antirecession tax cut, which got only 23 yeas, primarily because
Senate Majority Leader Lyndon B. Johnson had been talked out of sup-

    5. Heller to the President, November 25, 1963, Memos to LBJ, Box 6, Heller
Papers, Kennedy Library.
    6. Heller to the President, November 25, 1963, same file.
    7. Heller to the President, December 5, 1963, same file.
    8. Reports of the charade did appear in the press. Bernard D. Nossiter reported
the story in the January 8, 1964, *Washington Post* under the headline, "Budget Not
as Austere as It Seems, Administration Economists Say." Nossiter had gotten Heller
"to interpret the figures on a for-his-information-only basis." Heller told LBJ that
the story was "an almost classic example of a back-fire and a double-cross." Heller
to the President, January 8, 1964, EX FI 4/Budget App., 11/22/63–1/31/64, Johnson Library.

porting the Douglas bill by Treasury Secretary Robert B. Anderson. Since the law called for an *immediate* reduction in withholding, the multiplicative effect on the economic aggregates would begin working immediately. The impact on GNP was expected to be fully felt by the November elections. As Heller apparently told Nossiter of the *Washington Post*, "You can bet [LBJ will] have the economy going up like a Roman candle at election time." This fiscal program, plus the dazzling legislative execution of JFK's programs, dominated media coverage of the new President as political economist and operator. But meanwhile an alarming problem had quietly emerged on the wage-price front, one that buttressed the November 23 Summary Review point that the administration "may have to strengthen its anti-inflation policy."

Automobiles and Guidepost Failure

Without the shield of a Presidential call for responsible action Donner and Reuther wouldn't have the defense they need against GM stockholders and UAW members to justify sharing productivity gains with consumers.
—Harold L. Korda to LBJ via Walter Heller, June 24, 1964

On December 5, 1963, Walter P. Reuther gave government officials an ominous warning of UAW (United Automobile Workers) plans to go all out in the forthcoming negotiations.

In our long meeting yesterday morning Walter Reuther told us in the most emphatic terms possible that UAW is going for a whopping wage increase next summer, especially from GM. He mentioned no numbers, but it is clear that what he's after would give a big shove to the price-wage spiral. He says they're going to "unburden" GM (whose after-tax profits in the 12 months ending in September were $1.6 billion) of the biggest chunk of profits any company ever parted with.

Our arguments about socially responsible collective bargaining, the need for price stability, and so on, made no apparent dent. He claims rank-and-file pressures require a dramatic settlement; that the AFL-CIO have been good boys long enough; that labor's share of income has been slipping while the corporations have been racking up unwarranted price increases.

He's confident he'll have a good case with the public. According to UAW, GM has declared extra dividends this year equivalent to 73-cents-an-hour for the company's whole work force. And he's tired of remaining

moderate while the irresponsibles in the labor movement like Hoffa and
the Building Trades are pushing inflationary wage increases with im-
punity.[9]

The CEA's internal reaction to this sobering conversation and a flurry
of recent price increases was led off by John P. Lewis. To Lewis it was
"clear that 1964 will contain more inflationary danger than any year since
1957."[10] He recognized that "the wage-price guideposts of 1962 and 1963
. . . had very little testing as operating restraints" and that "we have a new
President with a different style."[11] Lewis worked through the pros and
cons of the existing policy and a few alternatives. He concluded that wage-
price policy should remain vague in "theory" but tough and specific in
"fact."

Gardner Ackley, a veteran wage-price controller (with the Office of
Price Administration during most of World War II and assistant director
of the Office of Price Stabilization during the Korean War), reacted to the
Lewis memorandum the next day. Ackley advocated retention of the
guideposts as the centerpiece of wage-price policy.

This approach (a) would attempt to spell out the guideposts more fully
than at present . . . in order to make them reasonably self-executing by
anyone who wanted to respect them; (b) would not change their status as
voluntary restraints and would not ordinarily involve the President's prestige in efforts to enforce them; (c) would realistically (though not publicly)
recognize that there would be many violations; (d) would warn in the most
serious terms that wholesale violations will mean a revival of inflation; (e)
would set up some reasonably low-level group of government technicians
who would (if asked) freely interpret ex post whether, in their judgment,

9. Heller to the President, "Prices and Wages in 1964," December 6, 1963,
EX FI, 11/22/63–12/14/63, Johnson Library.

10. Lewis to Heller, "Price-Wage Policy for 1964," December 10, 1963, CEA
History, vol. 2, Documentary Supplement, part 2, Johnson Library.
Toward the end of his administration, President Johnson ordered all agencies to
prepare histories of their activities under his leadership. Each history is essentially an
"administrative review" of events, accompanied by photocopies of critical documents.

11. Ibid. A month after the assassination, CEA consultant Otto Eckstein suggested that wage-price policy should take into account "Johnson's persuasiveness on
the telephone." Eckstein also offered the prescient observation that "Johnson would
want to have 'weapons' at his disposal. Marshalling those 'weapons' would be [an]
immediate assignment for us." Susan J. Lepper (CEA staff member) to the Council,
"Consultants Meeting," December 21, 1963, Papers of Gardner Ackley, Michigan
Historical Collections, University of Michigan. I am very grateful to Mr. Ackley for
letting me go through his papers and talking with me about his experiences at the
CEA.

*based on publicly available data, any important wage or price change was
or was not consistent with the guideposts. . . . There would be no moral
judgments expressed, simply factual statements.*

*The basic idea would be to make the guideposts a matter of private
conscience, encouraging firms and industries or unions to publish their
justifications for price or wage increases (or to remain silent on peril of
seeming to have no justification). It would be designed to create an informed public opinion, which would know what's going on. If the method
does not hold down prices and wages (as it probably wouldn't), it would
place the onus where it belongs, and build up the case for a later change to
ex ante evaluations (under some scheme requiring advance notice of proposed changes), if that should ever become necessary.*[12]

Ackley went on to suggest that the CEA publish its figure for overall
trend productivity as the basis for a wage guidepost, spelling out reasonable and specific definitions of exceptions. He also suggested a more operational price guidepost, keying the rule for permissible increases to changes
in overall unit cost, "disallowing wage rate increases less than one year
old to the extent that they clearly exceed the wage guidepost (a pious but
for the record necessary exception, to keep pressure on employers not to
accede to inflationary wage changes)."[13]

A bit earlier, on November 12, CEA staff member Fredric Q. Raines
had also proposed "operational guideposts." Rules establishing exceptions
to the price guidepost were suggested, keyed to an industry's rate of return
on equity and unit material costs. Also given were rules establishing exceptions to the wage guidepost based on an industry's unemployment situation, wages paid compared to those paid the same types of labor in
other industries, and "elasticity of substitution." The third exception was
meant to immunize the guideposts from part of a theoretical objection to
them lodged by CEA consultant Kenneth J. Arrow in a memorandum he
had prepared on the long-run consequences of the administration's inflation policy.[14]

12. Gardner Ackley to Walter Heller, "Price-Wage Policy for 1964," December
11, 1963, CEA History, vol. 2, Documentary Supplement, part 2, Johnson Library.
13. Ibid.
14. "Wage-Price Guideposts and Economic Growth," August 1963. Arrow's
critique was based on the "elasticity of substitution." Assume that there are only
two inputs, labor and capital. The elasticity of substitution measures the relative
responsiveness of the capital–labor ratio to given proportional changes in the ratio of
input prices. If the elasticity of substitution for the economy as a whole were unity,
a 3 percent increase in the relative price of labor would lead to a substitution of cap-

Raines's proposal and Arrow's memorandum do not appear to have much influenced CEA thinking, although the Council must have supported the Lewis position that vagueness might be a virtue in the wage-price section of the 1964 report. Neither the CEA nor the economics profession had much information in 1963 about industry elasticities of substitution; the memorandums slipped into the files.[15]

Heller wanted to get both the Lewis and Ackley memorandums and the problem itself into the economic policymaking machinery. In late 1963 his best bet was the semimoribund Cabinet Committee on Economic Growth, set up by JFK at Heller's suggestion to develop a consensus on the size and composition of the tax cut; that is, to provide the CEA with an instrument to bring the Treasury Department around to the CEA point of view. The committee included the budget director and the secretaries of the treasury, commerce, and labor. Committee Chairman Heller called a meeting for December 18. As stated in the Lewis and Ackley memorandums, the central issue was the choice between concentrating "on a few key price- and/or wage-making jurisdictions that are both (a) important and (b) relatively susceptible to influence" versus striving for "a comprehensive policy that in fact affects all offenders uniformly."[16] Put another way, the issue was how "activist" Johnsonian wage-

---

ital for labor and, specifically, to a 3 percent increase in the capital–labor ratio. It follows that the relative share of labor would remain constant, as implied by the CEA's exposition of the guideposts. But if the elasticity for the economy as a whole were two-thirds, as Arrow suggested it was (about), a 3 percent increase in the relative price of labor would result in only a 2 percent increase in the capital–labor ratio and the relative share of labor would increase. Thus Arrow pointed out that one side feature of the guideposts, the constancy of relative input income shares, would probably be neither obtainable nor—more important—desirable.

Raines's third wage guidepost exception recognized that *industries* with elasticities of substitution of less than one *and* rapidly increasing capital–labor ratios should be permitted to increase wages at above-average (above-guidepost) rates.

15. My copies of the Arrow and Raines documents are from the Papers of Stanley W. Black, to whom I am very grateful for letting me go through materials from his CEA staff days. I also thank Professor Arrow for talking with me about his memorandum.

16. CEA, "Issues for Decision," prepared for meeting of the Cabinet Committee on Economic Growth, December 18, 1963, CEA Microfilm, Roll 21, Johnson Library.

In 1965 LBJ became concerned about historians and his presidency. This concern manifested itself in many ways, from improved filing practices to plans for a library. Following the precedent set by the Kennedys, LBJ made arrangements in 1965 for the General Services Administration (GSA) to microfilm agency files from his administration for eventual deposit at his library. The microfilming began in early price policy should be. The decision was to compromise. Although the pricing side of Ackley's suggestion did not go anywhere, the soon-to-be-famous five-year annual average increase of output per man-hour (3.2 percent) appeared in a table in the 1964 CEA report; it was not mentioned in the text.[17] (Throughout LBJ's tenure in office government officials recognized that he thought a range was for cattle rather than numbers.) The CEA identified total compensation per man-hour as the appropriate definition of labor cost. There were now "do-it-yourself" wage and price guideposts, one quantitative and the other qualitative or directional. The only additional information required for voluntary compliance in applying the price guidepost was *industry* trend productivity. Anyone with access to published data could apply the guideposts to particular cases and get the same answer. This was the "Ackley orientation." But the 1964 report could also embrace the "Lewis orientation": if the administration wanted a firm objective basis for intervention in particular important cases, there it was in print. In chapter 4, "Price and Wage Policy for High Employment," of their 1964 report, the CEA asserted that "there is considerable room for discretionary decision making in most major industries" and boldly claimed that the "guideposts can cover the vast majority of wage and price decisions." The guideposts would enable the economy to avoid the Phillips-curve inflation-unemployment trade-off: "If cost and price pressures should arise through the exercise of market power while the economy is still climbing toward high output and employment levels, we would be forced once more into the dreary calculus of the appropriate trade-off between 'acceptable' additional unemployment and 'acceptable' inflation." In *his* 1964 Economic Report, President Johnson specifically endorsed the guidepost principle, something JFK had done by his actions but never in so many words.[18]

1968 and took many months. The results are uneven in quality. Properly done, it would have been an extraordinary boon to research.

17. The CEA's 3.2 percent would take on more and more weight as the years went by. Even though LBJ's economists knew that "scientific economy" was incapable of producing *the* trend of productivity, "political economy" required *a* number.

18. "At the end of the thousand days he [JFK] wasn't saying a great deal about the guideposts. When President Johnson jumped in and in effect permitted us to have him say what he did in the economic report and the economic message in January '64, we did feel that that went beyond what Kennedy would have permitted." Walter W. Heller, with Kermit Gordon, recorded interview by Joseph A. Pechman, July 20, 1965, Kennedy Library Oral History Program.

With the 1964 report published and "defended" before the Joint Economic Committee,[19] the CEA needed to touch base with the President about what the economic-policy machinery had undertaken. On February 1 Heller met with the President and was told to contact Secretaries Willard Wirtz (Labor) and Robert S. McNamara (Defense) on the automobile situation. A few days later he reported back to the President.

Running the kind of price-wage policy we have adopted for 1964 will involve 2 functions, each of which can be reflected in our behind-the-scenes organization. This applies not only to the automobile case but to others we may encounter.

1. Identification and Analysis of Difficult Situations: Here . . . we have already set in motion early-warning, screening, and evaluation machinery, to consist of

—Early-warning procedures whereby industry specialists in Commerce and collective-bargaining specialists in Labor regularly feed us earliest possible across-the-board notification of new and impending price and wage changes.

—A technical "task force" set-up whereby working parties composed of Commerce, Labor, and Council staff (possibly sometimes reinforced by other agencies) make intensive efforts to assemble and appraise comprehensive price, wage, other cost, profit, and productivity data on particular industries where trouble may be a-brewing. (In the past such compilations have been made for steel and aluminum. One is now under way for autos, and one is contemplated for construction.)

—An interagency watch-dog committee at the Assistant Secretary level, chaired by a Member of CEA, to ride herd on this fact-gathering, analytical activity. This group should screen the tough cases, identify those that invite off-the-record jawbone action by the Administration, and suggest the lines such action should take along with supporting data.

19. Part of Walter Reuther's testimony on the 1964 report was a critique of the guideposts, focused on the failure of real wages to match the growth in productivity. January 1964 Economic Report of the President, Hearings before the Joint Economic Committee, 88 Cong. 2 sess. (1964), part 2, pp. 17–31. Paralleling his testimony, Reuther and UAW Special Projects Director Nat Weinberg corresponded with Heller about productivity, wages, prices, and the 1964 report. The CEA had the job of convincing the UAW that the guideposts should be stated in nominal not real terms: a "real" or constant purchasing power "guidepost" would justify all combinations of wage-price changes corresponding to a particular "real guidepost." CEA Microfilm, Roll 13, Johnson Library.

2. *Jawbone Operations:* Following the lead of your instructions to me on Saturday and Bill Wirtz today, this Cabinet-level group would
—*review the recommendations of the watch-dog committee;*
—*decide whether and when consultation with the parties to wage and price decisions is in order;*
—*determine whether it should (a) undertake some quiet consultation itself, or (b) recommend that Presidential influence be brought to bear directly on one or both of the parties.*
Action:
1. We would like to have your *approval of the above.*
2. Are we right in assuming that you want the Cabinet group to go beyond the auto case to other major industries as required?[20]

The "cabinet-level group"—some of the Committee on Economic Growth and Defense Secretary McNamara—was very informally established to work on the automobile problem during 1964, although mostly this would be a joint Heller-Wirtz venture. The administration did not establish longer-run wage-price policy machinery with broader authority.

As explained in the February 3 "organization" memorandum, the CEA, aided by contacts at the Departments of Labor, Commerce, and State, the Office of Emergency Planning (OEP), the Federal Trade Commission (FTC), and so forth, began tracking major price developments. A routinized flow of price information, "Early Price Warnings," came to the CEA from the Commerce Department's Business and Defense Services Administration. Attention was focused on producers' goods such as copper, zinc, sulphur, and machine tools.[21] By later standards, some fairly modest attempts were made to ward off price increases in this segment of the economy. But Lewis, responsible for these efforts as well as for the automobile case, counseled caution: "We cannot, I think, encourage the

20. Heller to the President, "Price-Wage Watching and Influencing—The Organization of Our Effort," February 3, 1964, EX BE 5, 11/22/63–6/11/64, Johnson Library.

21. This scrutiny of producers' goods was not surprising in view of the results of the widely known and highly regarded study of the 1955–57 inflation by Charles L. Schultze. Schultze concluded that the *rapid* change in the *composition* of total demand led to increases in prices of semifabricated materials and components, particularly those consumed by the capital goods and allied industries—price increases of materials in heavy demand were not matched by price decreases of materials in excess supply. "Recent Inflation in the United States," Study Paper 1 in *Study of Employment, Growth, and Price Levels,* Materials Prepared for Consideration by the Joint Economic Committee, 86 Cong. 1 sess. (1959).

President to wade in on a great variety of individual price questions—there are just too many individual prices and there is too much detailed industrial lore that one has to know before he can be sure that he is not going off half-cocked."[22]

The main job of the "interagency watch-dog committee," chaired by Lewis, was to take on the problem industry of 1964—automobiles. The government at this point faced an unusually straightforward policy problem. Following the release of the 1964 Economic Report, Reuther wrote a long letter to the President about the automobile situation. Reuther pointed out that the price guidepost principle explicitly called for price cuts in industries where productivity exceeded the aggregate trend. He challenged the administration to enforce the price guideposts in the automobile industry. If the UAW was to acknowledge the wage side of the guideposts, it was only fair that the price side be made to work. As in the tax *increase* part of countercyclical fiscal policy, however, the price *decrease* part of guidepost policy would turn out to be medicine that decision makers preferred to avoid.

While the Lewis task force was hard at work, others in the administration actively pursued personal diplomacy. On March 23 Heller visited Ford to make firm contact and get data for the Lewis study. Data from General Motors was solicited by a letter to Chairman Frederic G. Donner, answered by George Russell, GM's executive vice-president. On April 7 Reuther had a meeting with Wirtz and on April 9 with Heller to inform them that he would "*call for an auto price cut* in his opening presentation to the companies" but could not treat it as a bargaining subject since "that would only lead to charges that he is trying to 'run the industry.' "[23] The administration's best link with the industry was Secretary McNamara, who met with Chairman Henry Ford II and Ford President Arjay Miller on April 10. A continuing problem emerges in this conversation: the company believed that the industry's productivity gains were "so close to the national average that no price reduction is justified and any wage increase over approximately 3.2% should be accompanied by a price increase." Furthermore, Ford could not "justify a price reduction because the company's profits as a percentage of net worth have been falling."[24]

    22. Lewis to Heller, May 13, 1964, CEA Microfilm, Roll 9, Johnson Library.
    23. Heller to the President, "Meeting with Walter Reuther," April 9, 1964, EX BE 4/Auto, 11/22/63–5/29/64, Johnson Library.
    24. Robert S. McNamara to the President, "Meeting with Ford Executives," April 10, 1964, CF BE 4/Adver.-Aviation, Johnson Library.

By April 15 the Lewis task force had gotten a preliminary memorandum together and, at McNamara's request, a delegation met with him.

His [McNamara's] basic concern is the failure of the price-wage guideposts to differentiate between a firm that has made a large investment to achieve a higher level of productivity and one that has had the same increase in productivity without making a similar investment. He is concerned that, in the auto case at least, application of the guideposts would imply a lower rate of return.[25]

The Lewis group agreed that "adoption of guideposted pricing would indeed probably mean a lower rate of return" but that the decline was a side effect of executing an economically desirable policy.

Mr. McNamara [warned] that the industry—especially GM—is mighty jealous of its rate of return; that it will resist any attempt to talk down its RoR; and that we must be sure the President is fully apprised of what he's getting into if and when he tries to do so.

Mr. McNamara also does not consider the collective bargaining trade-off (a smaller wage increase for a price cut) very attractive from the companies' point of view.[26]

In May Labor Secretary Wirtz had almost given the game away via a "back-grounder" in which a "high Government source" viewed "chances of *price cuts for autos as pretty remote.*"[27] Nevertheless, the Lewis task force report was sent to the President on May 29. It was fairly detailed, running to more than fifty pages. Gardner Ackley, acting chairman of the CEA at the time, signed a four-page summary. The bulk of the study was an attempt to make the previously qualitative and directional price guidepost *operational* and then to apply the technique to automobiles to get a *numerical* estimate of the appropriate cuts in model year 1965 products.

25. Lewis to the Auto Task Force, April 15, 1964, CEA Microfilm, Roll 2, Johnson Library.

26. Ibid. LBJ's personal intervention in a labor problem during the spring of 1964 indicated to the nation his perception of the relation between the presidency and the economy. On April 8, 1964, 7,200 workers struck the Illinois Central Railroad. This was not really a wage case, but rather went back to at least the February 1959 Association of American Railroads' announcement that it wanted revisions of "outmoded and wasteful work practices." On April 22 LBJ appeared on live TV, flanked by railroad labor and management leaders, to announce the settlement hammered out in the Executive Office Building. The main result of this episode was that the country, including government, union, and management leadership, now knew that an economic activist occupied the Oval Office, a man willing to concern himself *directly* and *enthusiastically* with the economic affairs of the day.

27. Heller to the President, "Press Conference: Bill Wirtz on Autos and the Guideposts," May 15, 1964, EX FG 11-3, 2/1/64–5/20/64, Johnson Library.

With the Lewis report, the cabinet-level group (excluding McNamara) "reached agreement on auto price cuts."[28]

The guideposts fully justify an auto price cut averaging $60 at whole-sale (as applied to the GM—it would average less for the others, who sell relatively more low-priced cars). Taking account of the standard markups, this would mean cuts in manufacturers' suggested retail prices ranging from about $50 on Corvairs, Ramblers, Valiants to about $150 on the bigger Cadillacs, the Continental, etc.

- The guideposts would justify an average cut of $28 in just one year.
- But if the industry had been "guideposting" throughout the past 5 years it would have lowered average prices about $65 more than it actually has done.
- And we're talking about a price change in advance of a 3-year wage contract.
- So the $60 price cut—worth about 2 years' guideposted price reduction —certainly isn't too much to ask.

The Committee's judgment is that the proposed price cuts of $50–$150 at retail would significantly restrain union wage demands.

- The UAW would dismiss a $25 cut as "token" window-dressing.
- Even a $50 average cut might be only a borderline proposition.
- But the cuts we propose would surely shake the union significantly.

The companies—all of them—can afford to make such cuts.

- For the industry as a whole, of course, profits and cash flow are lush. In 1963 after-tax return on equity was 19.5% compared with 10.3% for all manufacturing, and in the first quarter this year it rose to 24.4%.[29]

The Lewis task force recognized that "there are no official productivity data for the motor vehicle and equipment industry." Using five different measures, they estimated the trend to be from 4.9 to 7.4 percent; a "conservative" estimate of 6 percent was used in their calculations.[30] The

28. Ackley to the President, "The Case for Auto Price Cuts," May 29, 1964, EX BE 4/Auto, 11/22/63–5/29/64, Johnson Library.

29. Ibid.

30. The actual equation employed was

$$\Delta P/P = [(a - b)/(1 + a/100)](1 - m/s),$$

where the left side is the appropriate percentage reduction in price, a is the percentage trend productivity increase in the industry, b is the percentage trend productivity increase in the private economy (3.2 percent), m is total material costs, and s is total sales before any price reduction. The m/s ratio was assumed to be 50.5 percent.

Discussion later in the summer led to further analysis of the equation. Some outside readers of the report argued that the equation "assumes that material costs go price cuts were assumed to be potentially palatable to the industry since, although the Lewis task force recognized that there were "a variety of estimates of price elasticity of the demand for new cars," they "converged" on a figure of about −1.1. That is, a 10 percent cut in automobile prices could be expected to result in an 11 percent increase in the number sold, thus having a modest but positive impact on automobile industry revenues.

On June 5 the President sent the study out for review to Edward S. Mason, dean of Harvard's Graduate School of Public Administration, and Clark Kerr, president of the University of California. Neither consultant would commit himself as to whether the evaluation of Reuther's preferences in the report was correct, although both urged that an attempt be made to sell the proposal to the companies.

The CEA and Wirtz took the Lewis report to the industry. A not insubstantial part of the CEA's effort in the summer of 1964 was devoted to this missionary work at various levels of the automobile industry. By early June Heller and Wirtz were convinced that General Motors was the key and that direct presidential intervention with Chairman Donner was a necessary though perhaps not sufficient condition for GM to cut prices. The President, in a politically circumspect decision, was not willing to take this step. Apparently the candidate did not want to press automotive industry management in an election year.[31]

On July 11, 1964, Lewis and Heller met at the Defense Department with Secretary McNamara and Harold L. Korda, a New York businessman.[32] By this time, it was fairly clear that this attempt to make the price

---

down in proportion to automobile prices." The task force economists argued that the equation was based on the more "conservative assumption" that "material costs per unit of output remain constant." Myron Joseph to John P. Lewis, August 28, 1964, CEA Microfilm, Roll 2, Johnson Library.

31. In an interview Heller said: "It's just worth a footnote that we thought we had LBJ persuaded to intervene with General Motors and in effect say, look, we can get you a low wage increase from Reuther if you'll cut the prices on the cars. And up to a point, LBJ seemed to be going along with us. One day in June of '64 LBJ simply said, 'I don't want to hear any more about it.' It wasn't long after that Henry Ford declared for LBJ. Now, I'm not suggesting there's any causal relationship. [Laughter.]" Walter W. Heller, Kermit Gordon, and Joseph A. Pechman, recorded interview by Larry J. Hackman, September 14, 1972, Kennedy Library Oral History Program.

32. "[Korda], who has his finger in many business and financial pies (and is a good Democrat besides), is a continuing source of economic intelligence for me." Heller to the President, "Economic Intelligence," April 1, 1964, CF BE 5-4, Johnson

guidepost work was probably not going to come off, but Korda and Mc-Namara offered some insight into the anatomy of the failure.

The full-time management people have been hostile to price cuts since the time the question first began to be raised several months ago. . . . Despite the successive phases through which GM's thinking on the subject has passed, according to Mr. Korda, they remain essentially opposed. The "phases" have involved attempted interventions by outside and/or retired directors more favorably disposed toward price cuts and also a significant impact on two GM vice presidents made by Secretary Wirtz and you [Heller]. But GM management, like Ford, remains opposed unless Donner can be converted—and (see below) this sounds like a hard job, not only because he is substantively resistant but because he is very hard to reach. . . .

Korda and McNamara agreed completely, first, that *GM's viewpoint of the world is a thing unto itself that makes the company an exceptionally difficult one for informal Government influences to penetrate and, second, that the difficult key to the present problem is, overwhelmingly, Fred Donner who is a creature of, the personification of, and presently the sole arbiter of this GM milieu. . . . McNamara doubts that those outside directors who are now in a good-guy's role have much influence on him. He thinks Donner's old mentor, Albert Bradley, could exert effective influence on him, but also thinks that, while Bradley would oppose price increases, he would not press Donner for price reductions—reasoning that, according to the GM scheme of things, pricing is Donner's baby. There was emphatic agreement that Donner is indeed GM's price-maker, that he has been doing it for many years and does not effectively delegate in this field, that he recognizes (as does Secretary McNamara, who used to do the same job for Ford) that pricing is the key decision in the whole GM management process. Somewhat oddly . . . Henry Ford II has a good bit of influence with Donner; but his public statements alone make it unlikely that Ford can be converted into an advocate of price reductions.*

Library. Korda continued to transmit information between the administration and the business community until he died of throat cancer in 1967. "His background was a mystery even to intimates." *New York Times,* May 3, 1967.

Korda had been introduced to Heller by Charles Bartlett, the columnist. Both Heller and Ackley "were drawn to him as were many others by his warmth and his concern for the public interest," although they did not fully understand him. Heller to the author, August 19, 1974.

The one most promising communicator with Donner would be the President himself, but the President is rightfully reluctant to risk his prestige.[33]

Regardless of how the automobile price story would eventually turn out, it was clear that organized labor was freshening its general opposition to the guidepost philosophy. AFL-CIO President George Meany, not shy about telling LBJ that "they're your guidelines and not mine,"[34] explained his personal position on March 26 at the UAW convention in Atlantic City.

Let me say just a few words on the subject of free collective bargaining.

I want to make it quite clear that I am not attempting to advise the United Automobile Workers how to conduct their free collective bargaining. Walter Reuther and his associates are quite capable of taking care of that job.

I do want to discuss with you this so-called idea of guidelines on the part of the Federal government. These are guidelines that are laid down by the President's Council of Economic Advisors. I question this whole idea of guidelines.

We were told several years ago by a member of the President's cabinet that the government had a responsibility to assert the public interest in collective bargaining. At that time I challenged that statement, and I challenge it now.

Who said that the government has this responsibility? Who said that guidelines should be laid down on the question of prices and wages in order to protect the public interest? And if the public interest is to be protected by government, by what branch of government? Executive? Legislative? Judicial? How do they arrive at these guidelines?[35]

33. Lewis to Heller, July 13, 1964, CEA Microfilm, Roll 2, Johnson Library.

34. George Meany, recorded interview by Paige E. Mulhollan, August 4, 1969, Johnson Library Oral History Program.

35. A transcript of the relevant portion of Meany's remarks was attached by Heller to his memorandum to the President, "George Meany's Attack on the Price-Wage Guideposts," March 27, 1964, EX BE 5, 11/22/63–6/11/64, Johnson Library.

Meany may have been stronger on this issue than he had planned. "We hear that Meany was not getting much response to his comments on foreign policy. When he switched to the attack on the guideposts, the audience warmed up to him. And he warmed up to the subject and really played to the galleries" (ibid.). Nevertheless, on May 19 the AFL-CIO Executive Council strongly denounced the guideposts, refusing even to let Wirtz present the administration's request to tone down the resolution.

Actual contract negotiations had begun in late June. A month later the CEA was still trying to convince the President that the case was, if anything, stronger than ever for "direct Presidential persuasion to achieve auto price cuts." Profits in the first half of 1964, "up a huge 28% over the excellent first half of 1963," were "even better than expected when the late-May 'task force' price cut study was made." "The UAW, not surprisingly, has been smacking its lips."[36]

On August 17 GM's George Russell telephoned his bargaining offer to Heller. GM's view was that the offer was so generous it precluded any chance for a price cut. But the CEA staff, working with the Bureau of Labor Statistics, "made its own 'quick and dirty' estimate" and came to the conclusion that it was "a pretty lean offer." In a "friendly exchange with Russell," Heller "suggested that the good sales outlook should make a price cut easier than ever—and it would sell Reuther a lean package at the same time and give the Nation insurance against a wage-price spiral. [Russell] took it well, but didn't bite!"[37] The consensus within government was that, although Reuther was "talking mighty tough,"[38] automobile strikes were unlikely.[39]

The Chrysler contract was settled first, on September 9, and set a pattern for the others. The CEA estimated the rate of wage increases to be between 4.3 percent to 4.7 percent a year, with the cost-of-living adjust-

36. Heller to the President, "Auto Profits and Price-Wage Prospects," July 29, 1964, Memoranda for the President, 1964, Papers of Arthur M. Okun.

37. Heller to the President, "GM's Wage Offer and Auto Sales Prospects," August 17, 1964, EX BE 4/Auto, 5/30/64–7/21/65, Johnson Library.

38. Heller to the President, "Auto Prices and Wages, Again," August 21, 1964, CF BE 5-4, Johnson Library.

A note from this day brushed against the future. On August 21, following a brief but intense exploration of what the CEA ought to do if the "Viet Nam flare up" (leading to the Tonkin Gulf Resolution) really developed into something, Lewis informed Heller that "the heat having gone out of the issue for now, we have not followed thru." CEA Microfilm, Roll 9, Johnson Library.

39. On August 20, 1964, Arthur Goldberg, then a Supreme Court associate justice, suggested that the President take steps "similar to those which the Labor Party in Britain has taken, to minimize serious strikes during this campaign." Five steps, including private presidential talks "with Meany, Reuther, other labor leaders and politically friendly industrialists," were recommended. The President gave it to Press Secretary George E. Reedy for comment. Reedy approved of most of the five suggestions but drew the line at presidential contact. "If Meany, Reuther et al. are so immature as to call strikes at this period, they are too immature to risk discussing the matter with them." Reedy to the President, with Goldberg memorandum, August 26, 1964, EX LA 6, 11/23/63–12/12/66, Johnson Library.

ment thought to add another 0.7 or 0.8 percent.[40] The settlement was "generous" and, "in the absence of auto price cuts ... no surprise." Now the government faced the "unbelievable" situation of trying to fight off auto price *increases:* "George Russell (GM executive vice president) told me yesterday on the phone: 'I don't see how we can give that big a labor increase without having it affect prices.' "[41]

Secretary Wirtz urged (and LBJ apparently agreed) that no further *public* statements be made regarding the automobile situation "until all negotiations were completed." Wirtz argued that any statement right after the Chrysler settlement might be interpreted as "the Administration 'let the unions make a big wage grab but then clamped down on the companies' prices.' " (Heller and McNamara disagreed, urging the President to put the companies on notice about prices.) Wirtz also pointed out that there were "acute sensitivities *within* the union. The assumed, but not certain, successor to Walter Reuther is Leonard Woodcock. He handles the *General Motors* negotiations. He feels, right now, a little overshadowed—and would react negatively to any statement that might imply publicly that the case is all over. Woodcock is a good and valuable man."[42] The GM settlement came hard, after a thirty-one-day strike. But money was not the issue. UAW leadership had been pressed very strongly by "*local* union leaders on some 'rules' issues (involving handling of grievances, disciplinary rules, etc.) on which GM has historically been tighter than the other companies."[43] The companies held the line on prices although they increased revenue per car through various marketing devices, such as making "standard" engines bigger at higher cost to the consumer.

Now that the automobile fight was over, the President's economists had the job of puzzling out the implications of this fracture of both sides of the guidepost principle. They chose to update an earlier, widely circulated study done in response to the inflation scare talk that had accompanied passage of the tax cut in February. Following usual CEA practice,

40. Heller to the President, "The Auto Settlement," September 10, 1964, EX BE 4/Auto, 5/30/64–7/21/65, Johnson Library.

41. Ibid.

42. Wirtz to the President, "Automobiles," September 12, 1964, EX BE 4/Auto, 5/30/64–7/21/65, Johnson Library.

43. Wirtz to the President, "Autos: General Motors and UAW," September 24, 1964, EX LA 6/Auto, Johnson Library. Ford suffered a series of local shutdowns in November.

a fairly technical, detailed document was prepared for circulation inside and outside the government and a terse summary was prepared for the President. The situation was a bit alarming.

The high auto settlement lessens the chances for maintaining our near-perfect price record, but we do not expect a repeat of the 3%-a-year crawling inflation of 1956 and 1957, much less the trotting inflations of the Korean War or 1945–48.

Luckily, the wage negotiations calendar is not as crowded as it was in 1955, when autos led a big-settlement parade that included nearly every major industry.

But the auto settlement will set the pattern for some of its traditional followers—farm equipment and some other machinery industries—and will influence, a bit less strongly, such other followers as auto parts and rubber.

The big question is the influence of the auto settlement on steel. Steel wages can be reopened January 1, and they may be under active consideration by steel's Human Relations Committee before then. *Steel wage demands will be high after the lean settlement of 1961. To be sure, Dave McDonald's bargaining power won't match Walter Reuther's:*

- Unemployment has been higher in most steel centers than in auto areas.
- Steel profits—while greatly improved—are lower than auto profits, so company resistance will be stronger.
- Workers may be reluctant to strike after their bitter experience of 1959.

Nevertheless, left to itself, the steel settlement may come out not too far below autos, and the steel companies are less able to absorb rising labor charges.[44]

Heller came away from a preelection meeting of the Business Council in Hot Springs, Virginia, on October 15–17 with the impression that business was for LBJ but that the automobile settlement was being perceived by management as a pattern setter which, if carried to their industries, would necessitate price increases. Also, Heller noted, *"the drums are being beaten for a steel price increase—Blough's crying towel was wringing wet with the woes of trying to expand and modernize with such miserable profits. In a friendly exchange, I cited the figures on the great advances in steel profits and cash flow as a direct and indirect result of sound government actions—but he was unmoved: 'It's not enough.'"*[45]

44. Heller to the President, "The Outlook for Price Stability in 1964—A Second Look," October 8, 1964, EX BE 5, 6/12/64–10/31/64, Johnson Library.
45. Heller to the President, "Hot Springs and Steel," October 18, 1964, CF BE 5, Johnson Library.

Victories in Metals

At Hialeah Park on Thursday, a horse named Moral Suasion won in a three-horse photo finish and paid $76.

—Ackley to LBJ, February 27, 1965

Armed with the moral authority provided by Johnson's victory over Goldwater, the postelection administration moved forward boldly in all areas, including efforts to minimize the impact of the automobile settlement. From the standpoint of wage-price policy, 1965 was a metals year, dominated by a very public steel settlement, negotiated in part during a palace guard revolt within the union. The administration's focus on metals in 1965 has to be placed against a background of the deterioration of the U.S. balance of payments. By 1964 the United States had run deficits for sixteen consecutive years, excluding 1957. In August 1964 Congress passed the interest equalization tax bill, designed to curtail U.S. purchases of foreign securities. Because of uncertainties the tax apparently worked before it was passed, but once it was enacted Americans rushed into the markets for foreign securities, buying with gusto. During the fourth quarter of 1964 net capital outflows were $9 billion at an annual rate, and on November 23 the British raised their bank rate from 5 to 7 percent. (The U.S. Federal Reserve raised its discount rate from 3.5 to 4 percent, an action incompatible with LBJ's attempt to keep interest rates down by "jawboning" the major banks.) In January 1965 the President asked Congress to repeal the gold cover required on Federal Reserve deposits, to free about $5 billion of U.S. gold to meet foreign demands. In a special message on the balance of payments on February 10, 1965, President Johnson outlined a largely voluntary program designed to keep U.S. dollars at home, repatriate liquid funds from abroad, and attract foreign capital. "Guidelines" were established by the Cabinet Committee on Balance of Payments, chaired by Treasury Secretary Dillon. Banks would try to get 1965 foreign loan balances below 105 percent of levels prevailing at the end of 1964 while nonbanks were to generate intracompany trade balances 15 to 20 percent more "favorable" than they were in 1964. Compliance would be "checked" by the Federal Reserve and the Commerce Department. Activities in "less developed" countries as well as in Japan and Canada were exempt.

These *financial* measures were expected to bring some relief and they apparently did; the U.S. balance of payments improved in 1965. But the CEA was well aware that to a certain extent symptoms rather than diseases were being treated. The *real* (goods and services) side of the U.S. international situation was not healthy.

Steel

Steel in particular seemed covered by a terminal pall, as in 1961 when the guideposts were originally formulated.

The American steel industry has lost most of its traditional export markets in the last seven years. It is now in deep trouble at home, losing ground to imports.

- Until 1959 we were a net exporter of steel, and one of the world's major suppliers.
- In 1955–57 our exports averaged about 4½ million tons, and *exceeded imports by 3.4 million tons a year.*
- This year, partly reflecting strike worries, imports were 4.8 million tons in the first half; may total close to 9 million for the year. *That's about 10% of the steel we use.*
- Our exports in the first half were down to 1.2 million tons. They *mainly go to captive customers* under tied foreign aid.
- At first, the imports were mainly specialty items like barbed wire and nails. Imports of the big staple items were largely in coastal areas. By now imports have penetrated most markets. Two of the *major auto companies have begun to import basic sheets. It is even said that new schools in Gary, Indiana, are being built with imported steel.*

The loss to our balance of payments has been enormous.

- In 1955–57 the industry earned an *export surplus* averaging $645 million a year.
- By 1964, the U.S. was spending $146 million a year more for steel imports than we got from exports.[46]

Unfortunately, the steel industry's trade weakness had developed even

46. Gardner Ackley to the President, "Steel Imports and Exports," August 27, 1965, EX TA 6/ST, Johnson Library. Ackley, who had replaced James Tobin as a CEA member in August 1962, replaced Heller as chairman after the November 1964 election. Otto Eckstein and Arthur Okun rounded out the 1965 Council, with Okun taking on the forecasting responsibilities and Eckstein assigned the wage-price job.

Heller came close to being drafted as a part-time "Special Consultant to the President in Economic Affairs" in an effort involving the new vice-president, Heller's fellow Minnesotan Hubert H. Humphrey. LBJ hated to let good men go, but Heller could appreciate better than anyone that the arrangement would have put Ackley in an anomalous position. So Heller declined but he nonetheless continued to assist the Johnson administration, internally and in the news media. I am grateful to though the United Steelworkers of America (USW) had not had a wage increase since October 1961. In the 1963 contract, USW President David McDonald bargained for nonwage improvements; but he also got a January 1, 1965, contract reopener. McDonald's bargaining attitude was hardened by the high UAW settlement and by USW Secretary-Treasurer I. W. Abel's announcement of his own candidacy for the union presidency in November 1964. Even though McDonald's predecessor, Philip Murray, had advised union officials to wear ties and go first class, McDonald's appearance and apparent life style (home in Palm Springs and so forth) made him vulnerable. His summit bargaining, during which he was flanked only by his technicians, was focused on by Abel as undemocratic. The Human Relations Committee, one of the fruits of the bitter 116-day 1959 steel strike, was a forum for continuous labor-management discussion. Abel and the majority of district directors who supported him considered it to be a poor replacement for traditional collective bargaining. In short, the union was going to be a problem this time around.

While the preliminary skirmishing was going on within the union and between the union and the management negotiating team led by U.S. Steel's R. Conrad Cooper, the industry began nudging up some prices. Ever since the April 1962 confrontation between President Kennedy and Roger Blough, steel companies had raised prices very modestly and generally matched increases in some lines with cuts in others. (Cynics joked that some companies' "price cuts" were in lines they did not produce.) Although there had been rumbles of steel price increases in the financial press in August 1964 during the automobile negotiations, things were peaceful until December 22, when Inland Steel raised the price of galvanized sheets and coils by almost 3 percent, an important increase but in part justifiable by increases in zinc prices.[47] After a few days, U.S. Steel followed suit with an increase.

U.S. Steel announced today that it will raise its prices on the day after

---

Walter Heller for supplementing the materials in the Johnson archives germane to this issue with "Comments on LBJ's Attempt to Persuade WWH to Serve as His Economic Consultant After Leaving the CEA Chairmanship," memorandum to the author, August 19, 1974.

47. Six months later, at a White House dinner attended by members of the President's Advisory Committee on Labor-Management Policy (LMAC) and other business and labor leaders, Inland Chairman Block focused on this episode in a brief speech: "Last December my company raised its price on a relatively minor steel product—galvanized sheets. We did this because the cost of the coating material—zinc—had gone up considerably and we regarded our profit as inadequate. It was in reality a minor matter, yet based on the government reaction, one would have thought

Christmas on galvanized steel by $6 a ton (except at its California mill).

The action appears to match Inland's increase earlier this week. We expect the other companies to follow quickly now.

We are only surprised that it took U.S. Steel 3 days to make up its mind. They may have started their vacations early—or they could have been listening for government's response.[48]

The relation between the price increase and the wage negotiation was not a subtle one:

The following item appeared on today's UPI ticker:

United Steelworkers President David J. McDonald said the developments [the recent price increases] augured well for the union in its current contract negotiations with the industry.

"The price increases should put the industry in an even better position to meet the urgent needs of steelworkers," McDonald said.

"Even before the price increases were announced, the industry was in an excellent position to meet the needs of its employees as well as reward them for their increased productivity."

The further "selective" price increases the industry apparently expects to make will put the union in a still better position to demand—and probably to get—a truly inflationary wage settlement that will bring even higher steel prices.

Back in the 1950's, the steel companies repeatedly raised prices to meet their profit targets only to have the union take the gains away in higher wages. When the game was over, steel prices had been raised 47% and wages 64% in just 7 years. In those years, steel was the focal point for the inflation that largely created the balance-of-payments problem we have been fighting ever since.

Apparently, the industry never learns.[49]

Ackley was worried that the steel industry would be emboldened by

---

we had dropped an atomic bomb. We were told that we might trigger inflation. We were told we might induce Mr. Abel here to increase his wage demands. We were told we would lose business to foreign steel. We were told we would lose business to competitive materials. Now all this would seem to indicate that we must have been thought pretty dumb not to have considered such matters in advance of our action. And perhaps we were. But, Mr. President, I know you are a strong believer in our free enterprise system. As such, sir, my request is that you permit us the freedom of making our own mistakes without scolding us." Papers of Joseph L. Block (to whom I am grateful for letting me review papers pertaining to his LMAC tenure).

48. Ackley to the President, "U.S. Steel's Christmas Gift to the Nation," December 24, 1964, EX BE 4/Steel, 6/22/64–2/3/65, Johnson Library.

49. Ackley to the President, "Footnote on Steel," December 28, 1964, EX BE 4/Steel, 6/22/64–2/3/65, Johnson Library.

this minor victory to go for across-the-board increases. He wired some Korda information and advice to the President at his Texas ranch.

[Korda] reports a division of opinion within the industry about the wisdom of higher steel prices. (With much new capacity coming in 1967–68, the more far-seeing people want to hang on to their markets, not lose them to other materials.) But the majority feels that higher prices must be obtained now, before the labor settlement is completed.

The industry believes that there will not be effective government opposition to excessive demands by the steelworkers. They rather anticipate a strike, and fear that the government will then pressure them to settle on any terms to end the strike. At that point they think that there will be government opposition to a price increase to keep the settlement from appearing too inflationary.

Nevertheless, Korda anticipates another steel price increase, on a "selective" basis, within 6 months or so after the wage settlement.

He feels that only Presidential intervention is likely to be successful in avoiding a steel price increase prior to the wage settlement. Such intervention can be most effective if it emphasizes the determination of the government to resist an excessive increase in steel wages and fringes.

Presidential intervention could occur either through a strong public statement or through private discussions with one or two of the industry leaders, or both. Roger Blough would be the obvious person to talk to first.

Several points can be made in private conversations that could not be put in a public statement.

a) It could be pointed out that the government would be in no position to resist effectively an inflationary wage increase if the companies have already raised their prices. This is like the automobile case, where the government could not take a strong stand on wages because the companies refused to reduce prices as the guideposts so clearly required.

b) In any conversation, an implied threat could be made to hold up the tax concessions that the Treasury is about to announce through a revision of the "reserve ratio test." This measure could mean as much as $100 million to the steel companies, by staving off the day when their investment practice has to correspond to their large depreciation claims under the 1962 liberalization. We understand the Treasury plans to announce the revised regulations early in January.[50]

On December 29 Roger Blough apparently proposed that the administration help the companies with the labor settlement. But Korda, via

50. Ackley to the President, "Steel Prices," December 27, 1964, Memoranda for the President, 1964, Papers of Arthur M. Okun.

Ackley, advised the administration to "make no direct or implied commitment to pressure the union to settle on any particular terms. (We could not deliver on such a commitment anyway.)" Although Korda forecast a settlement "within or near the guideposts," he recommended that "the President should publicly request the CEA to make a factual study of prices, wages, costs, and profits in the steel industry."[51] On January 1, 1965, LBJ directed the CEA to undertake such a study. As in the automobile case, the CEA chairman was to use personal diplomacy to get data from the industry. Otto Eckstein was assigned responsibility for the study. An earlier Bureau of Labor Statistics estimate of 2.2 percent for the 1957–64 trend in steel productivity had been rounded off by the companies and used in their presentation of a 2 percent wage offer. The Eckstein report recognized that this period was also characterized by great year-to-year variations. During 1961–64, for example, a period without strikes or recessions, the trend average was 4.9 percent, probably associated with higher operating rates. Using data from public and private sources, plus the results of a questionnaire sent to the eight major steel companies, Eckstein corrected the 1957–64 data on steel output per worker for variations in operating rates and seasonal factors. He estimated the adjusted trend productivity to be 3 percent, close to the guidepost. The report urged both sides to accept a noninflationary labor cost settlement, based on this number.[52]

Steel management (Cooper) and McDonald had already agreed to an extension of the strike deadline, with a thirty-day reopener. The union now had to serve notice on August 1 if it was going out on September 1. The companies would put 11.5 cents (2.6 percent) per hour in escrow for later disposition. The results of the February 9, 1965, USW election were announced on April 30. Out of 600,000 votes cast, Abel won by about 20,000. Meanwhile, after a short strike, the USW concluded its negotiations with the can industry in March, getting about 3.5 percent. On May 31 USW and Alcoa signed at about 4.1 percent.

The steel negotiations were not going anywhere, but the government had some good examples to point to. In April the printing trade unions

51. Ackley to the President, "Advice on Steel," December 30, 1965, EX BE 4/Steel, 6/22/64–2/3/65, Johnson Library.
52. The author of the report has noted that it "was an attempt to develop a model for such studies, pulling together a wide range of government information, and striving for an even-handed, objective approach. The report also demonstrated that a tiny staff such as the economists at CEA could not really handle a large number of such cases if the work were to be done in this detailed way." Eckstein to the author, August 13, 1974.

and the New York City newspapers agreed to a guidepost settlement, while the rubber workers' settlement came "to a nice guidepost settlement of 3.1%."[53] By the end of August the government would also be able to point with pride to the 3.2 percent maritime settlement of a dispute which had tied up East and Gulf Coast shipping from mid-June to the end of August. The strike itself had little to do with the guidepost *principle* in the sense that both "sides agree that it should be a 'guidepost' settlement of 3.2%, but the *union ignores the future costs of pensions and the potential loss of productivity on overmanned ships* in its figures."[54] As he would be later at the Federal Communications Commission, Maritime Administrator Nicholas Johnson was being a maverick.

Because that part of the Maritime Industry which is involved in the strike is subsidized, no money agreement between labor and management is worth anything unless Nick Johnson approves it.

The tentative agreement which Secretary Wirtz can negotiate will not be approved by Johnson.

What Johnson will approve cannot be negotiated, according to Secretary Wirtz.

In general, this situation arises because Johnson is, quite properly, taking the position that the Subsidy Board should be much more than a rubber stamp handing out taxpayers' funds through joint agreements between industry and labor. His position is absolutely sound. The only difficulty with it is that the Board has been a rubber stamp for 30 years and the new found independence is something that was not asserted forcefully until negotiations had actually started this year.[55]

On June 22, 1965, Ackley, Wirtz, Bill Moyers, and two new cabinet members, Henry H. Fowler (Treasury) and John T. Connor (Commerce), met to discuss the guideposts. Otto Eckstein prepared a background memorandum.

The Price Indexes are moving up, mainly because of food prices. These increases are likely to continue for the next few months and will produce a public reaction and new fears of inflation.

Industrial prices are inching upward, by 1.2% over the last 12 months, by 0.3% in the last three months. Industrial increases are still concen-

53. Ackley to the President, "Wage Moderation," April 22, 1965, EX BE 5-4, 3/1/65–5/31/65, Johnson Library.
54. Ackley to the President, "Economics of the Maritime Dispute," July 24, 1965, EX LA 6/Maritime, Johnson Library.
55. George E. Reedy to the President, August 3, 1965, CF BE 4/Maritime, Johnson Library. The 1965 maritime case is discussed by John Sheahan, *The Wage-Price Guideposts* (Brookings Institution, 1967), pp. 51–52.

trated on non-ferrous metals, recently also in paper and rubber. These material price increases so far have led to only small increases in finished goods.

The Consumer Price Index was up 1.4% in April over a year earlier, still within the narrow 1.2 to 1.5% range of the last seven years. But the rise of food prices could edge the 12-month comparisons a bit above that range for May and June. There will be a small feedback on wages through escalator clauses.

Total employee compensation is still generally moving within productivity trends, with a gradual shift from wages to fringes.[56]

Eckstein concluded that the economy was "still close to price stability —hence guideposts stand a chance to be effective," but that it was "especially important now to leave the Administration firmly on the record and visibly fighting any inflation."[57]

During the summer Ackley tried to keep the President aware of the importance of a favorable disposition of the steel situation.

The next strike deadline in steel is September 1. But it is not too early to think about the Government's role in this crucial situation.

This will be the key test of the guideposts—both for wages and prices. Government influence could make a real difference.

- Abel will be anxious to get off to a good start not only with his members, but also with the Government.
- The companies will be tougher if they feel they cannot pass on the increases in higher prices.
- Without guidepost intervention, the parties will interpret the usual Government mediation efforts as an Administration blessing on the outcome, whatever it is. That's what happened in aluminum.

If the steel settlement is close to guideposts, and the companies hold the price line, then industrial prices generally can't move up very much. It will be a lot easier to pursue policies that keep the expansion going.[58]

On August 25 Ackley advised LBJ that "steel remains our major test." Its importance was emphasized by the price indexes:

Our price record is no longer perfect.

- The wholesale price index has risen 2.5% in the past 12 months, after 5 years of complete stability.

56. Eckstein to Ackley, June 19, 1965, EX BE 5, 1/30/65–6/19/65, Johnson Library.

57. Ibid.

58. Ackley to the President, "The Steel Labor Negotiations," June 14, 1965, Memoranda for the President, 1965, Papers of Arthur M. Okun.

- *The consumer price index in June was 1.9% above a year earlier, compared with an average increase of 1.3% over the previous 5 years.*[59]

The steel negotiators bargained the summer away. The USW served notice that it would strike on September 1 if a settlement was not reached. William Simkin, director of the Federal Mediation and Conciliation Service, as well as LBJ's special envoys to Pittsburgh, Senator Wayne Morse and Under Secretary of Commerce LeRoy Collins, were unsuccessful. On August 30 the President sent an aircraft to Pittsburgh to gather up the major negotiators and bring them to Washington. The union accepted the ride; management traveled in its own aircraft. But Marines collected both sides and carried them by helicopter to the White House. LBJ gave the negotiators the "Let us reason together" blessing from Isaiah and, after an eight-day extension of the McDonald-Cooper truce had been negotiated, hard bargaining continued.[60] The steel company officials were reported to be very unhappy with this turn of events; they had tried for years to remove their negotiations from public view. First, USW President Abel successfully attacked the Human Relations Committee, a forum for continuous and private discussions to study problems and present facts, as undemocratic. Then LBJ put the 1964 negotiations in the news as they had never been before.

While discussion of local issues continued in Pittsburgh, the primary negotiators in Washington bargained intensely. An hour-by-hour description of the activities of these negotiators as well as the many official and unofficial arbitrators would be out of place here, but the following memorandum gives an indication of how seriously the government took the affair.

Arthur Goldberg [U.S. Ambassador to the United Nations] has made his contact with the Union negotiators. He informs me that the Union is willing to give, as a result of your meeting this morning. He believes that the problem now is to get the Company to give.

He recommends against bringing Eisenhower into the picture now. He believes, however, that Ike should be brought in at the time of any Taft-Hartley action.[61]

59. Ackley to the President, "The Price Situation and Outlook," August 25, 1965, Memoranda for the President, 1965, Papers of Arthur M. Okun.

60. LBJ had received his first taste of the Executive Office Building style of collective bargaining, complete with presidential pressure and intense media coverage, during the April 1964 railroad crisis.

61. Joseph A. Califano, Jr., to the President, August 30, 1965, EX LA 6/Steel, Johnson Library. Califano had been recruited from Thomas E. Dewey's law firm for the Kennedy administration Defense Department by Cyrus R. Vance. In July 1965,

The administration was confident that Abel could be gotten down to the 3.2 to 3.4 percent range. The problem was to get the companies to come up, without a price increase. The President had at least three basic tools he could use to get both sides to agree to a noninflationary settlement. First, there was the threat of executive branch support for a proposal by Senator Jacob Javits for a thirty-day extension of the strike moratorium plus the commissioning of a fact-finding panel. This panel might make suggestions neither side wanted. Second, the Department of Justice was making the usual preparations "in the event the President should invoke the Taft-Hartley Act injunction procedures."[62] Third (and there is no currently accessible evidence in the public record that this was used), sentencing in a major steel price-fixing case was coming up. The 1962 price battle grand jury had been released but another one was impaneled in October 1963. By April 1964 indictments were returned against seven major steel companies. Nolo contendere pleas had been accepted (helping the companies avoid civil damages), but two officials—William J. Stephens, president of Jones and Laughlin, and James Barton, manager of sheet and strip sales for U.S. Steel—were about to be sentenced. The degree to which this antitrust aura affected the outcome of the 1965 steel negotiations cannot be judged.[63]

One point of view about steel management's true objective was offered by George Reedy. This comment was part of a set of observations offered after three days of watching the negotiations.

The issues under discussion do not accurately represent the real objectives of management and labor even though they reflect them. The figures that are being thrown around are basically talking points and can be dressed up by any competent statistician to indicate whatever the partisans wish them to indicate. If some means can be found of satisfying the real objectives of labor and management, the settlement itself should go very quickly.

after a successful round of jobs in Defense, he took over Bill D. Moyers' duties when Moyers was made press secretary. LBJ assigned Califano three areas of responsibility: domestic legislative programs, domestic crises, and domestic economic affairs. (Califano had been advised by McNamara to get the latter in his portfolio.) His success in the steel case gave him a strong position with President Johnson, which never diminished.

62. John W. Douglas to Lee C. White, "Possible Steel Strike," September 3, 1965, EX LA 6/Steel, Johnson Library.

63. See, however, the interesting speculations in George J. McManus, *The Inside Story of Steel Wages and Prices, 1959–1967* (Chilton, 1967), pp. 178–82.

There is every indication that the real objective of the steel companies is to get some freedom in determining steel prices. The steel companies over the past few years have become hemmed in by the popularization of economics so that almost anybody on a street corner can repeat the phrase that steel is basic to the whole economy and that any increase in steel prices automatically means inflation. The companies are afraid that they will get clobbered if they increase the price of anything and they are looking for some release from this fear. They have made it quite clear that they will settle for almost anything if they can get some guarantees of price freedom. The economics of keeping a lid on steel prices are probably valid but they make it very difficult to settle a labor-management dispute in that industry.[64]

On September 3 agreement was reached, although none of the parties ever agreed on exactly what the wage settlement was in annual percentages. Computing the cost of the contract back to May 1, 1965, when the last contract expired, the CEA (which had served as statistical referee during the negotiations) arrived at an annual cost of 3.2 percent, a perfect guidepost settlement. Heller's pessimistic prognosis made before the 1964 election was not realized.

As part of general 1965 wage-price policy and, in particular, the ongoing effort to keep the steel industry from raising prices, the administration again tried to get the automobile companies to obey the price guidepost. In May some thought was given to using proposed excise tax reductions as a lever on the industry.[65] Although this ploy apparently was not used, by September private negotiations with the companies were in full swing and Walter Reuther was urging the administration to press for price reductions to "help sell more cars and create more jobs."[66]

Although the rate of return on equity of the big four manufacturers was above 25 percent, the government now seemed to be struggling to keep prices from being increased. In its September 13 issue, *Newsweek* quoted industry sources as saying it would take a "miracle" to keep this from happening. Chrysler, the first to announce prices, was approached by Fowler, Wirtz, and Connor. Although the announced prices were

64. Reedy to the President, September 1, 1965, CF LA 6/Steel, Johnson Library.

65. The CEA had endorsed these reductions because they understood that Vietnam "spending will not be raised above the levels already in the budget." Ackley to the President, "Excise Tax Reduction," May 11, 1965, Papers of Gardner Ackley, Michigan Historical Collections.

66. Califano to the President, September 16, 1965, EX BE 5-2, 4/14/65–11/16/65, Johnson Library.

difficult to interpret (because, for example, previously optional safety equipment had become standard), Chrysler had apparently nudged prices up a bit. But General Motors and Ford followed with clear reductions, not big ones but, in Ackley's words, "a small step in the right direction."[67] GM's action could not have come at a better time, from the viewpoint of the steel and balance-of-payments story.

An informant in the New York business community today reports two items of interest:

1. The opinion is widely held in business circles that the new GM prices are the direct result of your influence on Fred Donner. The story is vague whether you intervened directly on the specific matter of GM's prices, or whether the prices merely reflected the respect that Donner paid to your well-known views on price stability. In any case, you get the credit.

2. GM's reductions definitely killed any prospect of a steel price increase at the present time. My informant insists he knows this as a fact.[68]

Eight months before the steel settlement, Harold L. Korda had predicted that a price increase would follow six months after the settlement. It came early, during the end-of-the-year holidays.

Bethlehem Steel today announced a $5 a ton increase on structural steel shapes and piling. This is an increase of 4 percent, and applies to 7 percent of the industry's shipments. This is not an across-the-board increase, but it is big enough to be important. (Last year it was U.S. Steel that gave us the Christmas present of a price hike of similar scope.)

Probably it is also a test of your reaction. If they are able to make this increase stick, there will probably be a lot more of them.[69]

Ackley and Califano held a backgrounder for the press on January 2 during which they hinted at various available government sanctions. Califano informed the President that "Ackley couldn't bring himself to use the 'word' (profiteering)," but he, Califano, "managed to get it in."[70] A few of the documents in the White House central files from this period

67. Ackley to the President, "GM Car Prices," September 22, 1965, EX BE 4/Auto, 7/22/65–8/15/66, Johnson Library.
68. Ackley to the President, "GM's Prices," September 24, 1965, EX BE 4/Auto, 7/22/65–8/15/66, Johnson Library.
69. Ackley to the President, "A New Year's Present from Bethlehem," December 31, 1965, BE 4/Steel, 8/27/65–1/2/66, Johnson Library.
70. Califano to the President, January 2, 1966, EX BE 4/Steel, 8/27/65–1/2/66, Johnson Library.

give clues about the flavor of arguments brought to bear during this round with the industry: "The Anti-Trust Record of the Steel Industry," "Defense Actions in the Steel Episode of 1962," and "Comparison of Executive Compensation in the Steel Industry with Military Compensation for Soldiers in Vietnam."[71] On January 1, 1966, the CEA met with Bethlehem Steel officials and President Johnson wired the heads of the seven other major steel firms, requesting they not follow Bethlehem's price lead. On January 3 Inland Steel did follow, along with Colorado Fuel and Iron Corporation, although the latter quickly rescinded.[72] "The conflict was suddenly resolved by the intervention of a conciliatory industrial statesman, disguised as the U.S. Steel Company."[73] On January 5 U.S. Steel raised structural prices by $2.75 a ton, undercutting Bethlehem's $5 increase. It also cut prices on some lines Bethlehem was not interested in. Bethlehem then came down to U.S. Steel's price.

The government had expended a great deal of its energy and moral authority on this industry. Unfortunately, steel imports, which had been about a million tons a year in the mid-fifties, were a million tons a month in 1966. Econometricians can try to wrap their equations around the question of what 1966 imports would have been if the steel settlement had followed the 1964 automobile pattern and if steel prices had shot up before and after the settlement. The public record suggests that this guidepost activity *was* a success, given the tools at hand. This drama in steel was

71. This was one of the first uses of the "while-our-boys-are-dying-in-the-Vietnam-jungles" argument. (According to Califano, it had been used earlier at LBJ's request by Senator Wayne Morse in Pittsburgh during the summer 1965 contract negotiations. Morse's position was that the war was illegal but that steel wages and prices could not be raised in an inflationary manner while U.S. soldiers were fighting it.) Reedy observed: "The current situation involving the Bethlehem Steel Corporation has been complicated by the implication in the backgrounders coming out of official Government sources in Washington that the Steel executives are unpatriotic because they raised structural steel prices while the fighting is going on in Viet Nam. Actually, the real charge is that they were thoughtless but this is not the way it will appear to the average businessman. It will look to him like a revival of the old 'merchants of death' charges which were thrown around so freely in the 30's and which played such an important role in leading the business community to believe that the Government is its enemy." Reedy to the President, January 3, 1966, Office Files of Bill D. Moyers, "Steel Crisis 1965," Johnson Library.

72. The ubiquitous Mr. Korda "helped write their rescission announcement." Ackley to Califano, "Miscellaneous," January 6, 1966, CEA Microfilm, Roll 69, Johnson Library.

73. Sheahan, *Wage-Price Guideposts*, p. 65.

the important price case of the period. Nevertheless, there were two other price fights in metals, aluminum and copper, at roughly the same time, and the government "won" both.

Aluminum

The Johnson administration's November 1965 confrontation with the aluminum industry had its roots at least as far back as November 1964, when the current price of 24.5 cents a pound for ingots had been attained.[74] It should be noted that these list prices were ceilings, with bid and actual prices fluctuating below. As market conditions drove discounts from list to zero, the ceiling was raised, usually by Alcoa. Although there were eight firms producing primary aluminum by the mid-1960s, Alcoa had over one-third of the market.

Alcoa has raised aluminum ingot prices ½¢ per pound, effective tomorrow, bringing the price to 24½¢. Reynolds and Kaiser followed immediately. In a little over a year Alcoa has

—raised ingot prices by ½¢ four times—in September 1963, March, June, and now November of this year;

—successfully maintained its price leadership by vetoing the 1¢ per pound ingot rises by Kaiser last December and Reynolds last January, and by cutting in half the 1¢ increase by Aluminum Ltd. in March;

—brought ingot prices up a total of 2¢ from their nine year low of 22½¢ in 1963, although they are still 1½¢ below the 1960 peak of 26¢ per pound.[75]

At the time of the November 1964 price increase, Gardner Ackley suggested that LBJ consider "placing a call to Alcoa's President, John D. Harper (or to the Chairman, Lawrence Litchfield)" which "could be helpful in restraining further price-raising propensities." Ackley suggested that the President refer in particular to his "problem of restraining, on the one hand, Bill Martin and Al Hayes [chairman of the Federal Reserve System's Board of Governors and president of the New York Federal Reserve Bank respectively; the New York bank being a powerful and nearly

74. A thorough account of the 1965 aluminum episode is provided by John Haas and others, "The Aluminum Price Crisis of November 1965" (University of Pittsburgh, Graduate School of Business, 1966; processed). See also Sheahan, *Wage-Price Guideposts*, pp. 62–65.

75. Ackley to the President, "Another Aluminum Price Hike by Alcoa," November 18, 1964, EX CM/Aluminum, Johnson Library.

independent voice in monetary affairs] who want to tighten money, and, on the other hand, the labor leaders who are pressing for larger wage settlements."[76] In February 1965 there had been reports in the financial press, initiated by Alcoa and Reynolds Metals officials, that aluminum prices were "unsatisfactory." Following instructions he had solicited from the President, Ackley called Joseph H. McConnell, president of Reynolds, to express administration concern. Ackley believed the call was effective; the company would "now think twice" before raising prices.[77] The administration maintained contact with the industry. In May Eckstein talked with Stanley V. Malcuit, Alcoa economist, about the industry's price structure. Malcuit followed up the conversation by sending Eckstein data on the industry. On June 7 Ackley and Eckstein met with Alcoa officials to discuss the industry's prices. The administration was grateful that, although prices of fabricated products had been increased following the guidepost-breaking labor settlement in May, the industry was apparently holding the line at 24.5 cents a pound for ingots. Nevertheless, after the settlement the industry engaged in deliberately underestimating its rate of return.[78] Although it was clear that the aluminum industry's rate of return was better than advertised, it *was* relatively low. In November Eckstein wrote the President:

- *Profits of the big 3 [Alcoa, Kaiser, and Reynolds] have been rising sharply since 1961, and particularly this year.*
- *Total profits this year will be second only to the 1956 period.*
- *The rate of return on equity will be 9 to 10%, a little below the 12% average for all manufacturing.*

   The puzzle is: Why isn't the rate of return higher? . . . Here is part of the explanation.

   Back in their mid-fifties heyday, industry profits were extremely high.

- *Capacity was operating at almost 100%, and the big 3 producers had most of it.*
- *Prices were going up steadily.*
- *The Government was taking 10% or more of output off the market to put in the stockpile.*

   76. Ibid.
   77. Ackley to the President, "Aluminum Prices: Call to Reynolds Metals Co.," February 27, 1965, EX BE 4/Alum, 11/23/63–11/15/65, Johnson Library.
   78. "Reynolds said the aluminum industry's return on investment in 1964 was 3½%." *Wall Street Journal*, June 15, 1965. On June 19 Ackley wrote to McConnell, suggesting that regardless of how one defined "rate of return," it was over 7 percent in the aluminum industry. CEA Microfilm, Roll 37, Johnson Library.

The *drop in profits from 1956 to 1961 is no mystery*. Attracted by high profits, *new companies* moved in and raised industry capacity at the end of the 1950's. About the same time, *Government stockpiling eased off and the economy slowed down*. Operating rates of the capacity fell from 100% to 77.7%. *Result: A fall in the rate of return of the big 3 from 18.6% in 1956 to 6.3% in 1961.*

Ingot production is now back at 100% of capacity again. *The rate of return* of the "big 3" has risen again but *not to the level of the mid-fifties*. What is the explanation?

• More liberal depreciation allowances cut reported profits. Depreciation doubled from 1955 to 1960 and continues high.
• More important, the *big three have lost their market position in the fabricating end of the industry*.

Information is very limited, but what there is strongly suggests that *ingot production is again very profitable.* . . .

The *high profits on ingot are diluted by low profits or losses in fabricating.* . . .

Many small companies are now *in fabricating, and competition is extremely keen. The big companies are doing less of the business, and have to match the efficient specialized operations of small producers.*[79]

During this period, the industry continued to negotiate with the government about the disposition of surplus aluminum in the national stockpile. By 1965, the government held 2.1 million tons of aluminum although only 700,000 tons were currently considered necessary to meet strategic requirements. The industry had been unenthusiastic during the protracted negotiations with the government over the disposition of the 1.4 million tons of surplus.[80]

Stockpile disposition had been fairly orderly. A 135,000-ton disposal program initiated in 1963 was completed in May 1965. Negotiations now centered on a long-term plan for the 1.4 million tons. On August 26, 1965, as the Vietnam War was being escalated, President Johnson directed Califano to speed stockpile sales in general. On September 2 Califano and an

79. Eckstein to the President, "Further Analysis of Aluminum Profits," November 4, 1965, Papers of Stanley W. Black.

80. The negotiations were complicated by the fact that portions of the surplus acquired early in the program were of lower quality than was now standard. Also, some of the ingots had begun to oxidize and needed to be reworked in a buyer's furnace. But the key to the negotiations seemed to be the reluctance of primary producers who had entered the industry *after* the stockpile had been built to recognize responsibility for its disposition, while the older firms wanted surplus elimination to be an industry-wide effort.

ad hoc stockpile policy group decided to put initial emphasis on a short-run aluminum agreement with a 1966 disposal goal in excess of 200,000 tons, but the companies wanted a long-run, twenty-year program for the entire surplus, not a partial deal.

On October 29 a small producer, the Ormet Corporation (jointly owned by Olin Mathieson and Revere), muddied the stockpile *and* guide-post waters by announcing a price increase on ingots of ½ cent a pound and increases on fabricated products. Two of the big three, Reynolds and Kaiser, followed. Although there had been four identical increases since September 1963, the government decided this one was not to be permitted. The administration's mission was to keep Alcoa from "codifying" the increase by matching it. Acting CEA Chairman Eckstein[81] reported the increase to LBJ, in a six-point memorandum. The juxtaposition of the last two points was not without importance:

5. We have 1.2 million tons of aluminum in the stockpile, including 500,000 tons we can sell without legislation.

The Government and the producers have not been able to agree on a deal, but we understand negotiations are still going on. Releases might ease the pressure in the market.

6. When Alcoa's President John Harper was in to see Gardner Ackley at your request last June, he was reassuring on ingot prices. He told us that your tax policies "made it possible to keep ingot prices stable."[82]

Unfortunately, communications during the first few days of this episode were made difficult by at least three factors—Ackley was recuperating from surgery, Alcoa President John D. Harper was in Japan, and LBJ was at his Texas ranch recovering from a gall bladder operation. The administration's initial strategy focused on the chairman of Alcoa's board:

McNamara, Ackley, Fowler, Schultze and I have developed the following plan:

Ackley will call Litchfield [Alcoa's chairman] tonight and invite him to come down on Monday [November 1] to discuss the aluminum situation (prices and stockpile), as a result of the newspaper story concerning aluminum.

If Litchfield comes down, Ackley, Fowler and McNamara will state that

81. The Kennedy-Johnson CEA chairmen designated another CEA member "acting chairman" when they went abroad or were indisposed.

82. Eckstein to the President, October 29, 1965, "Aluminum Price Increase," Papers of Otto Eckstein. I am grateful to Professor Eckstein for opening his files to me as well as talking and corresponding with me about Johnson economic policies.

if Alcoa holds the price at 24½ cents, the Government will agree to sell 70,000 tons of aluminum per year for seven years (a deal the companies have been trying to negotiate). If, however, Alcoa does not hold its price at 24½ cents, then the Government will dispose of its aluminum stockpiles (1.4 million tons surplus) as rapidly as possible.

We are developing a plan, which should be ready Monday, to begin selling stockpiles as rapidly as possible, in case Litchfield refuses to come down. McNamara believes we can almost surely sell enough aluminum to bring the price back down to 24½ cents.

If Litchfield refuses to come, it may be desirable to leak to the press on Sunday that the Government intends to dispose as rapidly as possible of its 1.4 million ton aluminum surplus.[83]

The administration's initial Litchfield strategy was revised in a two-hour meeting of administration leaders (but not LBJ) in the Cabinet Room on Monday morning, November 1. There were to be two "prongs" of attack, "defense" and "balance of payments."[84] The administration's public position throughout this episode was that there was no connection between the stockpile discussions and the price hike. (It was arguable that the administration's use of the stockpiles as a weapon of wage-price policy was in violation of, among other things, the Defense Production Act of 1950.)[85] Meanwhile, on November 2 Harper called LBJ and apparently told a presidential assistant that he would do nothing for forty-eight hours, then match the increase if he heard no objections. Having heard none, Harper on November 5 raised the price. To add insult to injury from the government's point of view, Alcoa raised the price of fabricated products more than the others had.

83. Califano to the President, October 30, 1965, EX BE 4/Alum, 11/16/65–, Johnson Library.

84. "Notes on Aluminum Stockpile Meeting," November 1, 1965, EX BE 4/Alum, 11/16/65–, Johnson Library.

85. On November 2, 1965, Bill Moyers had the following colloquy with a re-porter at his news conference at LBJ's ranch:

Q. Well, have you talked to the President about this [the connection between the aluminum meeting in the Cabinet Room the day before and the price increase]?
MR. MOYERS. Yes.
Q. And he said there is none?
MR. MOYERS. There is none.
Q. He said that?
MR. MOYERS. There is none.
Q. Does he say that?
MR. MOYERS. There is none.
Q. I'm still asking the question?
MR. MOYERS. Keep on asking it. The answer will be the same.
Q. Thank you.

EX BE 4/Alum, 11/16/65–, Johnson Library.

On November 4 Califano informed LBJ that administration strategy was to press the industry on the stockpile negotiations, "scrupulously avoid[ing] discussing prices (Fowler and McNamara state that the validity of our Defense-balance of payments position and the fact that we are not mentioning prices is placing the industry in an untenable position)."

Lawson Knott [administrator of the General Services Administration] should call the companies tonight and tell them to come to Washington tomorrow to discuss disposal of the stockpile in terms of either 200,000 tons next year or the entire 1.4 million tons in a 5–7 year deal. Under this deal, the 770,000 tons we are authorized to sell would be sold in the first 2½ to 3½ years. The contract for the sale of the remaining 630,000 tons would be signed subject to the required legislative approval. We should let the industry know that our only other alternative is that McNamara issue his order to dispose of 200,000 tons in the next year. The industry would have to make its decision by Friday.

We recommend this course of action because we believe it places you in the excellent posture of having tried to work this out with the industry. If the industry accepts the deal, fine. If the industry does not accept the deal, they have been given full opportunity to work with the Government prior to unilateral action to dispose of the stockpile. While the next 24–48 hours pass, Moyers and/or the GSA press officer can state that (a) we are meeting with industry on an expeditious basis to work out an orderly method of disposing of the aluminum stockpile, and (b) get to the public our record of prior negotiations over the past several months. Such action is typically LBJ in style and avoids the mistakes Kennedy made in handling the steel industry.[86]

On Saturday, November 6, McNamara, Ackley, and Fowler held a news conference, at which the White House Press Office issued three separate press releases on aluminum: a McNamara "defense-needs" release, a Fowler "balance-of-payments" release, and an Ackley "aluminum-guideposts" release. McNamara announced that 200,000 tons of stockpiled aluminum would be released in 1966, 115,000 tons directly to contractors producing finished goods (the government would then pay only the "value added" to fabricators of, say, airfield matting extruded from raw aluminum or bombs containing powdered aluminum and TNT) and 85,000 tons at market prices.

McNamara's statement in the following interchange made clear the relationship between the 85,000 tons and the new list price of 24.5 cents:

86. Califano to the President, November 4, 1965, EX BE 4/Alum, 11/16/65–, Johnson Library.

Q. *Mr. Secretary, you say you will dispose of this at the current market price?*

SECRETARY MC NAMARA. *Yes.*

Q. *Is this the new price that was just established by the aluminum industry?*

SECRETARY MC NAMARA. *The market price would be the price at which buyers and sellers in the market dealing at arm's length would agree on the one hand to buy and on the other hand to sell.*

Q. *In other words, the price increase just announced by the industry would be reflected in your price?*

SECRETARY MC NAMARA. *Not necessarily. Many transactions take place at other than the published price.*[87]

Administration officials spent a great deal of time this day on missionary work with journalists and the Congress. The administration apparatus, from Ackley and Califano in the White House, to McNamara at the Defense Department, to Henry Wilson and Lawrence F. O'Brien at Congress, tried to sell the government's point of view and undermine that of the companies.

On November 8 Alcoa's executive vice-president, Leon E. Hickman, held a press conference. He accused administration officials of speaking about negotiations in the past tense. (This was a correct view on his part. He was negotiating with Paul R. Ignatius, who really wanted to negotiate but was under orders that this was "a non-negotiable negotiation.")[88] The administration escalated its attack on the industry. One issue within the administration was over the amount of aluminum that would have to be released to break the price increase. The CEA advised McNamara that the incentive for the big three producers to absorb whatever the government released at the now-higher producers' price was "now inevitably a part of the tactics of their struggle with the government." One alternative open to the companies was not to buy but rather to sue the government for trying to sell at less than the producers' price. But "they could not count on winning" such a suit. The administration had decided to release "standard material, in no way inferior to ordinary commercial grade." (Earlier releases had been in part low-grade aluminum, and some were still unsold.) Nevertheless, the CEA argued, there were a number of economic reasons for independent users *not* to pay the producers' price for

87. Califano to the President, "Complete Text of This Afternoon's Press Conference," November 6, 1965, EX BE 4/Alum, 11/16/65–, Johnson Library.

88. Interview with Joseph A. Califano, Jr., September 26, 1974.

the released ingots, including the fact that the government could not "be counted on as a regular source of supply."[89] That same day, after the director of the Office of Emergency Planning, which had statutory responsibilities for the stockpiles, announced that 300,000 tons of aluminum would be released, the first 100,000 tons to be "offered for sale immediately," Alcoa officials met with McNamara at the Department of Defense. Alcoa's President Harper agreed to "see what he could do about the price question." At this meeting the linkage between the stockpile and the price increase is clear:

Mr. Hickman opened the meeting by saying that if the Government was interested in disposing of the entire stockpile of 1,400,000 tons, he was certain that Alcoa and other aluminum producers would be able "to move it.". . .

Mr. McNamara replied that the immediate problem which faced us was the disposition of the 200,000 tons of aluminum ingot which it had been previously announced would be sold, and that we should address ourselves to that problem. . . .

Mr. McNamara then said perhaps he was in error, but he had understood from Governor Ellington [director of the OEP] that Messrs. Harper and Hickman were interested in discussing a possible roll back in prices in conjunction with a plan for acquisition of the stockpile of 1,400,000 tons. Mr. Hickman asked whether the Government's primary concern was rolling back ingot prices or fabricated prices. Mr. McNamara replied both.[90]

Besides the stockpile, the government explored alternative levers on the industry. In a Justice Department summary of available tools, Attorney General Nicholas deB. Katzenbach noted that there were some legal possibilities.

There is one case in which aluminum companies could well be concerned. This is a damage suit against Alcoa, Kaiser, Reynolds, Olin Mathieson, Anaconda Wire and Cable and General Cable. Like the electrical suit, it involves simple price fixing to which the defendants pleaded nolo contendere in a criminal case. We estimate damage to the Government to be about $1,000,000; they have offered $170,000 in settlement. We could double the amount of damage by including a false claims allegation which has never before been litigated.

89. Ackley to McNamara, "The Aluminum Market," November 8, 1965, Papers of Otto Eckstein.

90. Summary of meeting by Cyrus Vance, November 8, 1965, EX BE 4/Alum, 11/16/65–, Johnson Library.

What is most important is the fact that there are at least fifty private utility companies who can sue for treble damages the same defendants. Their capacity to do so would be greatly improved if the Government litigated rather than settled this case, and it could cost the defendants several million dollars.[91]

On November 10 McNamara held a press conference and announced Alcoa's price rescission, five minutes before the company did so in Pittsburgh. The other three companies quickly fell into line. On November 15 the General Services Administration and McNamara struck a deal with the aluminum industry covering the entire stockpile. Only two meetings were needed.[92]

Why was the government fighting this particular aluminum price increase so hard? After all, the industry's rate of return *was* weak. This aluminum case was inextricably linked to the late 1965–early 1966 steel price episode. Again, we hear from Mr. Korda:

Korda reports that Richard Mellon—whose family remains the principal stockholder in Alcoa [and its banker]—was not consulted on the increase, and is unhappy about it. If any effort is made to head off the Alcoa increase, Korda advises working through Mellon (he is said to be Mike Monroney's brother-in-law).

Korda says that steel has been ready to go with the price increase announcement all week, awaiting the Alcoa move. He does not know how large an increase is contemplated, but believes that it will cover something like 60% or more of total steel output. Korda's closest contacts are with U.S. Steel, so I assume that it is U.S. Steel that will be making the first move.[93]

A bit later on November 5 Ackley had passed along some more news to Califano:

Korda says the decision will be made this afternoon on steel increases although the announcement is likely to be delayed for several days.

91. Katzenbach to Califano, "Government Action with Respect to Aluminum Price Increases," November 9, 1965, EX BE 4/Alum, 11/23/63–11/15/65, Johnson Library.

92. That month Secretary "McNamara showed up at a costume party for Averell Harriman with his head wrapped in aluminum foil. No one, needless to say, had any difficulty guessing his identity." Henry L. Trewhitt, *McNamara* (Harper and Row, 1971), p. 266.

93. Ackley to the President, "Aluminum and Steel Prices," November 5, 1965, Papers of Henry H. Fowler. I am grateful to Mr. Fowler for letting me go through his papers at the National Archives. In 1979, they will be jointly accessioned by the Johnson and Kennedy Libraries.

He insists that if only the U.S. Steel people are told firmly and clearly that the President is opposed to an increase, there will be no increase. The message could be sent through him, or through Bob McNamara, or in any other way, so long as it is unambiguous. The contacts on the other end should be John Meyer (member of the Executive Committee), and/or Bob Tyson.

What is essential, he says, is that the companies don't get a different answer from Jack Connor or Bob Anderson. If they know the President is opposed to an increase, they won't do it. (Korda insists, incidentally, that the aluminum companies got—or thought they got—a private green light from Connor.)[94]

This episode had absorbed a great deal of the administration's resources. After the dispute was over, Califano supplied LBJ with a chronology of the affair which, though lengthy, did "not record the literally hundreds of informal calls and contacts." He told the President that "you and I, for example, discussed stockpiles in more than 25 separate telephone conversations. Between the 1st and the 9th of November, Fowler, McNamara, Connor, Katzenbach, Knott, Ellington and I met 8 times in the Cabinet Room. McNamara and I had numerous separate discussions. McNamara himself held a number of separate discussions with the aluminum industry, many more than the 2 or 3 he mentions in his November 10, 1965, press conference."[95]

Copper

Another metals victory, in copper, had more to do with the peculiarities of domestic and world copper pricing and with U.S. foreign relations than with the guidepost principle.[96] In November 1965, 200,000 tons of

94. Ackley to Califano, "Korda Reports Further on Steel," November 5, 1965, CF FG 11-3, Johnson Library.

95. Califano to the President, November 16, 1965, EX BE 4/Alum, 11/16/65-, Johnson Library.

96. "The guideposts could never have been used to justify the attempt to hold down copper prices in 1965 and 1966. This experience is discussed in the 1966 Annual Report of the Council on page 82 under 'Selected Problem Areas,' but *not* on pages 88 and 89 where guidepost actions are reviewed. The guidepost actions in the aluminum, steel, and other industries [but not copper] were always carefully supported by staff analysis of past productivity growth, costs, profits, prices, and capacity utilization." Stanley W. Black, "Comments on the Wage-Price Guideposts During 1965–1966," memorandum to the author, January 1974.

Sheahan, *Wage-Price Guideposts*, pp. 67–71, reviews this copper episode.

stockpiled copper were used, with the industry's blessing, to help the copper market. Copper had been scarce for several years, and the producers' price had risen from 36 to 38 cents a pound. (The price on the U.S. secondary copper market at this time was over 50 cents and copper was quoted on the London Metals Exchange at about 70 cents.) The domestic producers' price was cut back to 36 cents after the stockpile release. The industry placed a premium on price stability and the government helped them get it. But one country, Chile, was unhappy since most of its foreign exchange earnings came from copper. The output of its American-owned mines was sent to the United States for sale at the "controlled" producers' price. From November 1965 through the summer of 1966, various deals were made between the U.S. Department of State, the Chilean government, and the mining companies.

This episode involved suspension of the U.S. tariff on copper, new Chilean tax arrangements, a soft $10 million AID (Agency for International Development) loan to Chile, Chilean miners striking to protest President Frei's "generosity" to the companies, efforts to impeach Chile's minister of mines, an increase negotiated by the Treasury Department in the copper futures margin requirements at the New York Commodity Exchange, export controls, and a quiet trip to Chile in November by W. Averell Harriman, LBJ's roving ambassador, and Anthony Solomon, assistant secretary of state for economic affairs. The situation was exacerbated by production problems in the Congo and Zambia (for the latter these were further complicated by the Rhodesian independence movement).

Ackley offers a clue to the reason for the government's initial entry, in November 1965, into what would become a thicket of intrigue, resulting in an even more complex set of multiple prices and informal supplier rationing throughout late 1965 and 1966. Copper was linked to aluminum and both were tactically peripheral to steel.

On narrow economic grounds, a rise in the price of copper has merit. There simply is not enough copper to go around, and there is little prospect that the situation will improve, even in the long run. An increase in the producers' price makes users economize on copper, eliminating the least valuable uses, and switching to substitute materials. By reducing the extent of producer rationing, it also gives the little fellow or the new business a fairer chance to get copper at the same price as the traditional customers of the companies.

On the other hand, we can't welcome a copper increase in the middle of the aluminum crisis. Moreover, the big copper companies are far more *profitable than the aluminum companies, and their profits are rising faster.*[97]

Lessons of These Episodes

Although this aspect of the story has not been emphasized in this chapter, the deeper one digs into the 1965 victories in metals, especially the aluminum story, the more they appear to be one-act satires on the inability of human beings to communicate. Pro-administration legislative aides, the spear carriers of the Great Society, were confused during the aluminum episode, for example, about just what it was they and their employers were supposed to do. They understood that a general mobilization had been called and that the aluminum industry was the enemy, but they had few clues about the order of battle or even about who their commanding officers were. The absurd situations that can be produced by the mutual mental telepathy upon which men of affairs sometimes rely is bad enough. But "translations" of an adversary's language and actions are often more than slightly wrong. These victories in metals illustrated the need for a small, permanent group, which would be "at the highest level" and careful with its use of language, to manage administration activities during wage-price adventures. Everyone in labor, business, and government needed to know who had authority to speak and, if something were said, what it really meant.

These episodes also demonstrated that this administration, if it chose, could, as Califano would have put it, play very hard ball. The question remained for 1966: what type of ball did they want to play? Should the administration have a wage-price policy that would put it in nose-to-nose confrontations with industries or should the game be more subtle, with less contact?

Policies for 1966

If expenditures follow the path that Bob McNamara now visualizes as likely, they could provide a significant stimulus to economic activity during the first half of next year.

—Ackley to LBJ, July 30, 1965

While the administration was successfully battling the metals industry, it was also being pressed by the economic consequences of foreign policy.

97. Ackley to the President, "The Copper Price Increase," November 8, 1965, EX BE 4/Copper, Johnson Library.

As late as June 1, 1965, CEA consultants discussed a "strategy for tax reduction." They were "generally agreed that a strong fiscal stimulus was needed in fiscal 1967 to reverse the drift toward slower expansion."[98] But in late July, LBJ committed U.S. forces to major combat; the "strong fiscal stimulus" came on the spending side rather than on the taxation side. The costs of the expanded effort in Southeast Asia for the fiscal year just begun on July 1, 1965, had not been anticipated. Military expenditures increased by over $3 billion in the third and fourth quarters of calendar 1965 and would increase by $13 billion (25 percent) in calendar 1966. By December 1965 the economy was at the Kennedy-Johnson "interim goal" of 4 percent unemployment. Although the Federal Reserve served notice that monetary policy would be countercyclical by raising the discount rate from 4 to 4.5 percent on December 5,[99] there was great concern within the Johnson administration that the economy was in danger of being thrown out of balance by a surge of aggregate demand. Two key questions were the 1967 defense budget and the possible need for increased rates of taxation. On December 17 Ackley responded to Johnson's request for his "private preliminary view of the policy implications of FY 1967 budgets of $110 and $115 billion." Ackley argued that the lower number would "probably" necessitate a tax increase while the second would require *a significant tax increase.*"[100] About a week after receiving what he characterized as Ackley's "gloomy report," Califano wired a summary of the issues to LBJ at his Texas ranch.

I have discussed the Defense Department budget with [Deputy Secretary] Vance and Schultze.

Vance believes that you should go for $60 billion rather than $57 billion. He said that if we budgeted for long lead time items and some other things beyond December 1966 and tried to avoid having a supplemental,

98. Susan Lepper and Frank W. Schiff to the Council, June 28, 1965, CF FG 11-3, Johnson Library.

99. Harmony between the Federal Reserve and the President faded during 1965. On June 1 William McChesney Martin, Jr., frightened the financial community with a "1965-is-1929" speech. Ackley advised LBJ not to take the speech too seriously: "Some people—especially central bankers—just can't stand prosperity, and keep looking under the bed for ghosts. Bill has taken to conducting the search in public." Ackley to the President, "Martin and Money," June 3, 1965, SP/FG 233, Johnson Library. On October 4, 1965, Budget Director Charles L. Schultze informed the President that, contrary to past practice, his staff would not discuss the budgetary outlook with the Fed and suggested that "a discussion of budgetary totals at the Quadriad" be avoided lest they be "used as an excuse to tighten up on monetary policy." "Monetary Policy and the Budget," EX FG 110, Johnson Library.

100. Ackley to the President, "Policy Implications of the Budget," December 17, 1965, EX FI 11, 6/29/65–3/16/66, Johnson Library.

the budget would be roughly between $63 and $65 billion. (I am sure you are aware that even with McNamara's detailed procedures for preparing the budget, Defense estimates have always been lower than the amount eventually needed.)

Schultze prefers the lower budget number of $57 billion. He believes he can bring the total budget in for $110–111 billion with the lower Defense figure. If the excise tax reduction is deferred and there are accelerated corporate payments, he says revenues might reach $108 billion. This would leave you with a deficit of only about $3 billion. Schultze firmly believes that eventually a tax increase will be necessary. He would go for a large Defense supplemental in May or June and at the same time go for a tax increase of some sort.

As you probably already know from Joe Fowler, Wilbur Mills had the same political judgments that you had. As I read what Joe Fowler told me, Mills would prefer going for the lower budget figure of $57 billion. McNamara, when he called to wish me a Merry Christmas, reiterated his strong personal view that we go for the higher figure of $60 billion. He is very concerned about our credibility both in budget terms and in terms of Vietnam if we go for the lower figure.[101]

Thus even the lowest budget estimate fell into Ackley's "probably yes" tax-increase range. But the administration chose to go with the lower defense number and a "bits-and-pieces revenue package."[102] LBJ asked for and got restoration of the excise taxes that had been reduced the previous year. Personal tax withholding was increased and corporate tax payments were accelerated. (The latter policy caused many firms to go into the money market to raise cash for advance tax payments while the Fed was tightening the market, helping to set the stage for what would become the "credit crunch" of 1966.) The CEA was painfully aware that the administration's fiscal policy would place a greater burden on the guidepost principle than it had ever borne before.

During the report-writing season in 1965, the CEA began to realize that a wage-price section of the 1966 report would be difficult to write, regardless of how the tax, budget, and monetary issues were resolved. It wrestled with the questions of enlarging the scope of wage-price activities and sharpening its tracking of market developments.

One idea receiving a fair amount of attention was "prior notification."

101. Califano to the President, December 23, 1965, EX FG 110, 12/4/65–1/26/66, Johnson Library.

102. Arthur M. Okun, *The Political Economy of Prosperity* (Brookings Institution, 1970), p. 70.

Eckstein noted that this had "been a logical next step beyond guideposts" in other countries.[103] The administration's problem was that wage increases (settlements) could be anticipated; the government could, if everyone cooperated and got mobilized in time, weigh in on the side of wage restraint before and during the negotiations. But in the case of prices, the government was generally fighting accomplished facts. The thrust of the debate for a 1966 price policy was to find ways of *achieving* prior notification without *requiring* prior notification. The hope was that the government could get the increases tempered, postponed, or canceled.

By mid-November, a few days after the aluminum price fight was over, Ackley recommended that the President "establish a Cabinet Committee on Price-Cost Stability."[104] For different reasons, Commerce Secretary Connor had proposed a similar "national economic council" a few weeks earlier. But Connor's suggestion was a reaction to his discontent with the CEA's handling of the aluminum case:

Consistent with recent practices you received a memorandum last week from the CEA on the aluminum situation that in my opinion was one-sided and quite misleading and in no sense an objective statement of relevant facts. Quite obviously, the memorandum was designed to get you excited so that you would take immediate action.[105]

On November 18 LBJ asked Treasury Secretary Fowler to chair a price-stability group, to include McNamara, Connor, Wirtz, Ackley, Schultze, and Califano. The group's first report to the President, on December 27, was fairly general and Califano's conclusion was that "the group is not an effective apparatus for handling specific price situations at this time."[106] On January 7, 1966, the Fowler group reported again and for the last time. The President was advised to speak to representatives

103. Eckstein to the Council, "Organizing to Make Guideposts Work," September 9, 1965, CEA History, vol. 2, Documentary Supplement, part 2, Johnson Library.

A bit earlier, LBJ's ally Marshal Ky had offered his own, Diocletian-style proposal for price fighting. If South Vietnam's leading rice merchants did not reduce prices sufficiently, Ky explained, "one of their number, chosen by lot, would be shot. This procedure would be continued until the price reached a satisfactorily low level or until all the merchants were dead." "A Dashing Flier Stirs Worry as He Assumes Premiership in Saigon," *Wall Street Journal*, June 24, 1965.

104. Ackley to the President, "Guideposts in the New Environment," November 13, 1965, EX FG 11-3, 10/23/65–12/9/65, Johnson Library.

105. Connor to the President, "Improved Organization for Government Handling of Domestic and Foreign Economic Policy Matters," November 3, 1965, CF BE 5, Johnson Library.

106. Califano to the President, attachment to Fowler report, December 28, 1965, EX BE 5-2, 11/17/65–12/28/65, Johnson Library.

from special economic interest groups explaining the situation the country faced in avoiding inflation during stepped-up U.S. involvement in Southeast Asia. Also, labor and management were to be asked to practice *voluntary* prior notification.

Perhaps the main issue for 1966 inflation policy was the guidepost number. The success of Johnson's domestic policies coupled with Vietnam-generated demand had pushed the economy near full capacity. Efficiency would probably decline because older, standby equipment and less-skilled, "marginal" workers would be used. Specifically, the *expected* productivity increase for 1966 was less than 3 percent. But the guidepost was based on past performance. The CEA estimated that for "the next couple of years" trend productivity would be above actual productivity gains. (It was arguable "that the 'correct' guidepost target is not trend productivity at all, but rather the best forecast of the expected productivity gain.")[107] Ackley explained the guidepost number issue to LBJ:

In the 1964 and 1965 Reports, a table was included with one column labelled "Trend productivity," which showed a "trend" computed simply by averaging the productivity gains of the most recent 5 years. . . . In both 1964 and 1965, the current figure in that column was 3.2%. This is the only source of the 3.2% guidepost figure—it is nowhere mentioned in the text.

If we compute "trend productivity" in the same way for 1966, the figure comes to 3.6%. This is why:

- Until this year, the average productivity gain for the most recent 5 years has included the very low (1.8%) productivity gain of the recession year 1960 balanced off by the very high (4.8%) productivity gain in the recovery year 1962. This time, the 5-year average will drop out the low 1960 figure (1.8%) and will include instead the 2.8% productivity gain in 1965. This raises the 5-year average by 0.2 percentage point.

- The remaining 0.2 percentage point increase comes from a statistical revision that Commerce made last summer in all the figures.[108]

Although a number of labor economists suggested that the CEA should

107. Stanley W. Black to the Council and Wage-Price Group, October 12, 1965, Papers of Stanley W. Black.

108. Ackley to the President, "Wage Guidepost for 1966," December 28, 1965, CEA Microfilm, Roll 64, Johnson Library. When they were first released, Commerce's revision of the national income and product statistics were a source of pleasure: "*They throw an even more favorable light on our recent record.*" Ackley to the President, "New GNP Numbers," August 14, 1965, EX BE 5-4, 6/1/65–8/26/65, Johnson Library.

not worry too much since 1966 was expected to be an unimportant bargaining year, with few major contract negotiations, Ackley solicited opinions on this problem from union economists ("raise it"), corporate economists ("keep 3.2"), outside consultants ("raise it," "keep it," "throw it out"), and his colleagues in government. The Fowler group suggested keeping 3.2. The only exception was Labor Secretary Wirtz, who argued that they would "have a great deal of trouble with labor" unless the 3.2 was *"part of a general austerity program."*[109] On Ackley's cover memorandum, LBJ checked the line next to "approve sticking to 3.2%." The guidepost number no longer had a computational foundation; 3.2 percent had taken on a life of its own. When the 1966 Economic Report was released (a week late, because anguishing over a budget for 1967 had absorbed a great deal of time) business was delighted: "an act of true economic statesmanship," according to the U.S. Chamber of Commerce. Labor was angry and hostile.[110]

Price Fighting

"What is the magic of 3.2?"
Asked Quill and Blough of Ackley.
"Them guidelines' good for other folks
But not for us exactly."
—Excerpted from "Owed to 3.2" by G. B. Hotchkiss, Jr.,
The Foggy Bottom News, January 1966

The administration's strong stand on 3.2 percent made at least the first half of 1966 a good period for price fighting. The CEA had coupled

109. Ackley to the President, "Wage Guidepost for 1966," December 28, 1965, CEA Microfilm, Roll 64, Johnson Library.

In a personal memorandum to LBJ, Wirtz argued for "a *new* wage *and price* approach," centered on a remobilized LMAC, coupled with "tax increase and reform." He argued that "defense build-up pressures" were causing the enactment of certain policies (e.g., the 3.2 guidepost and no expansion of the anti-poverty program) which "affect organized labor . . . adversely." He warned that the AFL-CIO was "much more divided privately about our foreign and military policy" than public appearances would suggest. Wirtz to the President, "Domestic Economic Policy," December 21, 1965, CF BE 5, Johnson Library.

110. The January 28, 1966, *Wall Street Journal* reported that I. W. Abel argued for a "cost-of-living escalator" in the guideposts. In other words, the guideposts should include the trend or expected change in, say, the CPI. The CEA refused to accept this. It would result in a mechanization of the wage-price spiral. This proposal, which the CEA would see again as the price indexes began moving, would "build an engine of inflation." CEA Memorandum, "A Cost of Living Escalator for Guideposts?" January 28, 1966, CEA Microfilm, Roll 52, Johnson Library.

their retention of 3.2 as a guide to labor with an appeal to business managers to absorb cost increases from the high profits they were enjoying. One of the major thrusts of Ackley's efforts during the late 1965–early 1966 steel price crisis and the Fowler group discussions had been to try to broaden the foundation (and roof!) of wage-price policy. If the administration was to reap the price-fighting benefits of 3.2, all parties had to sign on and do their share.[111] Unfortunately the departments with strong interests in economic affairs, such as Commerce and Labor, had difficulty sustaining enthusiasm for wage-price policy.[112]

By early 1966 the Johnson administration had a much more thoroughly staffed price-fighting apparatus than would have been obvious to outside observers. In late 1965 a group of three—Eckstein from the CEA, Alexander B. Trowbridge from Commerce, and James J. Reynolds from Labor—provided deputy-level staff work for their principals in the Fowler group. A larger version of this deputies' group—including Andrew F. Brimmer from Commerce, Arthur M. Ross from Labor, as well as officials from Interior and Agriculture—operated as the Interagency Working Group on Price and Wage Statistics. Their mission was to improve the early warning system for important price and wage changes and, in general, improve the internal communication of information needed to formulate and execute sensible wage-price policy. Ackley and Califano acquired the partial services of John W. Douglas, assistant attorney general, civil division. Douglas provided some legal and operational strength to the CEA's analytical capabilities. Also, a three-man price staff, two economists and a lawyer, set up shop in the Executive Office Building. They had been recruited by Ackley from AID, the Budget Bureau, and the Justice Department. An Interagency Staff Price Committee, led by Saul Nelson, the price staff member Ackley had acquired from AID (and who had

111. "Unless Jack [Connor] is willing to do some of the no-saying, every case will wind up either in the White House or in the Council—or with a price rise. I have no objection to being the bastard; but, in the long run, it may weaken the usefulness of the Council to you." Ackley to the President, "A Small Sulphur Company Tries for a Price Rise," January 14, 1966, EX BE 4/Sulphur, Johnson Library.

112. In mid-1966 LBJ directed Walt W. Rostow to have a short session on wage-price policy with Wirtz, Connor, Ackley, and Califano. Rostow emerged with the following impression: "The battle we are now engaged in to hold both prices and the wage guidelines is *not* a battle merely for the next six months until we have a political base for a tax increase. It is the kind of battle that will have to be fought on a systematic basis for the long pull, if we are to hold this economy up close to full employment without inflation. I don't think this is clear to Connor and Wirtz—or only half-accepted, if it is clear." Rostow to the President, June 14, 1966, CF BE 5, Johnson Library.

been his deputy during the Korean effort), met regularly to provide the higher-level, more operational groups with staff work. Nelson, whose mind was crammed with the "industrial lore" John P. Lewis had worried about in early 1964, was also responsible for a never-completed guidepost manual (a "do-it-yourself-kit"). The CEA itself divided pricing problems into ten categories and allocated "first line" and "second line" responsibilities, parallel to those of the Nelson group, for tracking price developments.[113] Reports from the various departments and agencies were sent to the CEA by noon each Thursday. Ackley and Califano would "meet each Friday morning to discuss developments in the price situation."[114] "Weekly price reports" were now going to the President, summarizing price changes and actions taken or contemplated. In the first half of 1966 this multilayered mechanism would achieve what in retrospect appears to have been the high-water mark for Johnsonian price-fighting. In March alone the administration had successful rounds in hides and shoes, newsprint, residual fuel oil, and cigarettes. Following LBJ's appeal for voluntary prior notification, other companies came to the administration and explained why they had to raise prices. In May 1966 this activity was buttressed by a letter from Commerce Secretary Connor to the chief executive officers of more than 26,000 U.S. corporations asking them for restraint during "a time of challenge to our country, both on the battlefront of freedom in Vietnam and on the economic front at home."[115]

The price confrontations were generally private affairs. Successful battles in hardwood lumber, cotton textiles, and sulphur were not widely publicized. (Raw materials were drawing so much attention because they were leading the 1965–66 inflation.) Often the price discussions were coupled with actions, suggested by the Nelson group, such as changes in government purchasing practices or sales from stockpiles or changes in foreign trade regulations, to break a bottleneck or help producers meet contracts. Timely releases of tungsten, vanadium, rubber, and a large number of stockpiled products helped to ease pressure on prices, just as timely changes in the training programs of the Departments of Labor and Health, Education, and Welfare (HEW) and the Office of Economic Opportunity (OEO) were directed toward supplying workers to

113. Eckstein to Ackley, "Staff Responsibilities in the Price Field," January 31, 1966, CEA Microfilm, Roll 55, Johnson Library.

114. Califano to the President, February 11, 1966, EX BE 5-2, 12/29/65–2/20/66, Johnson Library.

115. From text of letter, attached to Robert E. Kintner to LBJ, "Response to Secretary Connor by Business on Economic Restraints," June 27, 1966, CF BE 5, Johnson Library.

break specific labor bottlenecks. The administration "tried to limit temporary bulges in farm prices, through appropriate sales of farm commodities from excessive Government stocks, through the judicious programming of PL 480 [Food for Peace] exports, and through adjustment of the timing of purchases by the Defense Department and other agencies."[116] In its 1967 report the CEA would state that it had become involved in the prices of about fifty product lines during 1966. This direct effort on prices was supported by more general anti-inflationary moves, such as trying to get both business and all levels of government to curtail capital expenditures, particularly on construction, and trying to monitor and occasionally limit the issuance of debt instruments by agencies of the federal government.

In July there was a major exception to this low-profile approach. By this time, the administration had an airline fight on its hands and needed a public price victory, and molybdenum, used chiefly as an alloy in high-strength and high-temperature steels, looked "like a good situation for a confrontation."[117] On July 8, 1966, Climax Molybdenum, a division of American Metal Climax (AMAX), increased its list price by about 6 percent; "80% of the 1965 Free World supply of molybdenum . . . was produced in the United States" and "70% of the U.S. supply" was extracted from "one mine located at Climax, Colorado" and owned by the offending company.[118] Even though the nonproducer and export prices of molybdenum were considerably above this administered domestic price, the government was afraid that this list price increase would put direct upward pressure on steel prices. The administration possessed an almost embarrassing surfeit of levers it could use. AMAX was being helped by the U.S. government in a number of copper, aluminum, and iron ore ventures around the world, from Australia to Zambia. The government was currently negotiating with AMAX about the release of stockpiled molybdenum. The government could remove the 30 cents a pound import duty. (AMAX allegedly wanted protection from Canadian imports.) The company was the subject of current investigations by the Antitrust Division and the Federal Bureau of Investigation. The company was worried about the imposition of export controls. In short, the price fighting

116. Ackley to Califano, August 15, 1966, EX BE 5-2, 7/13/66–9/17/66, Johnson Library.

117. Ackley to the President, "Molybdenum Prices," July 8, 1966, EX CM/Molybdenum, Johnson Library.

118. William N. Lawrence, "Molybdenum," February 2, 1966, CEA Microfilm, Roll 53, Johnson Library. Lawrence, of the Office of Emergency Planning, had met with steel officials to listen to their complaints about the molybdenum industry.

mechanism could obtain an armory of weapons from the Departments of Interior, State, and Justice that Ackley could have with him at his meeting with the company. At a meeting with the CEA on July 11 officials of AMAX argued that, as their output increased, productivity declined, thus justifying a "guidepost" price increase. Ackley responded: "I am sure that everything that you have said today is sincere and accurate. But our point is that the price increase is badly timed."[119] On July 13 the price increase was rescinded. Government officials took the rescission news to the media with enthusiasm, trying to get major columnists to link the story with the administration's firm stand in the airline dispute.[120] This sort of inflation control bore little resemblance to the guidepost philosophy of 1962.

The CEA would not have considered 1966 complete without its now-traditional autumnal price fight with the automobile industry. Since 1967 would be a labor contract year, the 1966 season began early, with a February 12 letter from Walter Reuther to LBJ supporting restoration of excise taxes (part of the "bits-and-pieces" fiscal program) and suggesting that the government renew its efforts to get the industry to cut prices. Ackley explained the problem to the President:

The source of the problem is fantastic automobile profits.
- *In 1965, the four big companies earned over $3 billion after taxes.*
- *General Motors alone earned over $2 billion, or a 26% after-tax return on equity (a figure more reasonably associated with a newly opened gold mine).*
- *Ford and Chrysler also did extremely well. American Motors is having trouble, with profits down to 2% of equity.*
- *There has never been a profit record like this in the history of American industry.*

These companies are the prime example of failure of the guideposts. If we can't pull their prices down, Reuther will go after their profits in 1967 with a huge wage demand. And he will get it. Workers in other industries will surely try to follow him, touching off a massive wage-price spiral.[121]

Ackley suggested (and LBJ approved) that "Katzenbach, Califano,

119. "Meeting of Gardner Ackley and James Duesenberry with officials from American Metal Climax," July 11, 1966, CEA Microfilm, Roll 53, Johnson Library.
   After the 1966 Economic Report was out of the way, Duesenberry had replaced his Harvard colleague Eckstein.
   120. On January 10, 1967, the price of molybdenum was increased with a passing statement (in another context) by Ackley, praising AMAX for holding off for six months.
   121. Ackley to the President, "The Solid Gold Cadillac," March 6, 1966, Papers of Stanley W. Black.

and Ackley" discuss the several ways of getting a substantial price cut—ordering a CEA or Federal Trade Commission study of the industry, having a friendly congressional committee hold hearings, or giving the companies an indication of "renewed interest on the part of the Anti-Trust Division."[122]

The main difference between this and earlier rounds was the level of cooperation and seriousness demonstrated by General Motors. Chairman Donner and Executive Vice-President George Russell met Ackley and Connor in Washington to discuss the issues.[123] Another apparent indication of GM's seriousness was a visit to the CEA by former Kennedy aide Theodore C. Sorensen.

After initial pleasantries, Ted remarked that in his law practice he was now representing General Motors. They had asked him to come out to Detroit next week to sit with them while they reached decisions on their new model prices. It occurred to him, he said, that while he was in Washington on other business he might drop by and see what thoughts we had on the subject. He pointed out his long interest and involvement in guidepost questions while he was in the Government. He naturally retained a great interest in this subject, and it had occurred to him he might be able to convey our views to the company. He was aware that Donner and Russell had been in to see us but didn't know the substance of the conversation. He either said or implied several times during the conversation that this was all his own idea.

He said it had occurred to him that he might render a useful service both to his old loyalties and his new ones if he could help achieve a price result that the Government would find itself able to approve and that the company could live with. He referred to some damage in the past year to the images both of the Corporation and of the guideposts, and hoped that both might be simultaneously repaired.

He asked what kind of a price announcement the Government might be able to greet with approbation. I told him that the result we could approve would be the holding of nominal prices—which would mean a reduction in prices as measured by BLS [Bureau of Labor Statistics].[124]

Ackley interpreted the conversation to mean "that Ted was an emissary

122. Ibid.

123. But "[Donner's] tactics were to challenge about every sentence—with either relevant or irrelevant observations—in what probably was a deliberate effort to keep things fuzzed up." Ackley to the President, "Meeting with Fred Donner on Auto Prices," August 20, 1966, EX BE 4/Auto, 8/16/66–5/5/67, Johnson Library.

124. Ackley, "Memorandum for the Files," September 17, 1966 (sent to LBJ by Ackley), EX BE 4/Auto, 8/16/66–5/5/67, Johnson Library.

from the company; that the company is anxious not to put itself in the position in which the government will be critical; and that they would like to negotiate a pricing decision that we can approve."[125]

In discussions with the government, the automobile companies argued that price increases were necessary to cover the higher unit costs that had resulted in part from the safety equipment mandatory for 1967 models. Ford announced average increases of $107 over standard 1966 models; Chrysler, $92. GM's $56 increase caused the other two firms to cut their increases to $82 and $79 a few days later. After adjustment for safety items, "the BLS figured that the real price increase was only 0.2 percent" for the industry as a whole.[126]

Although at the beginning of the year steel was a major issue because of the episode begun with Bethlehem's New Year's Eve price increase, the government's relations with the industry were uneventful until August. (In July 1966 the New Year's Eve offender made a cordial approach to by-then former CEA member Eckstein to help them "improve business-government relations."[127]) Steel prices were being inched up, but in amounts too small to justify a major confrontation. But on August 2, 1966, Joseph Block's Inland Steel announced a price increase of $3 a ton on sheet and strip steel, which was used in automobiles, construction, appliances, and a broad variety of industries. American exports of this line were negligible and imports were growing rapidly. Although the government hoped a successful rollback strategy could be developed, exploiting the fact that "some of the industry boys *hate Joe Block's guts* for having spiked the 1962 increase,"[128] U.S. Steel and the rest of the industry matched the increase. Ackley denounced the companies as irresponsible.

By August 1966 the Vietnam War was expanding and the price indexes were rising. Nevertheless, the overall experience with the large, visible, "cost-push" sectors had not been too bad, and efforts in these sectors could reasonably be expected to remain fairly successful. But the administration recognized the need to continue operating in the problem areas, such as foods, raw materials, services, construction, and medical care. The Nelson interagency committee was unsuccessful; it met with less and less frequency during the summer of 1966. It was operating at too low a level.

125. Ibid.
126. Lawrence J. White, *The Automobile Industry since 1945* (Harvard University Press, 1971), pp. 131–32.
127. Otto Eckstein to Gardner Ackley, "Visit to Bethlehem Steel," July 18, 1966, EX BE 4/Steel, 3/24/66–7/31/68, Johnson Library.
128. Ackley to the President, "Suggested Strategy on Steel," August 3, 1966, EX BE 4/Steel, 3/24/66–7/31/68, Johnson Library.

The problem was Califano's responsibility, and he wanted some way of marshaling the resources of the federal government to tackle these problem areas. He did not have time himself but sought to delegate the power resulting from his proximity to the President. The bureaucracy had to respond to commands with a sense of urgency. Someone needed to cut through the barriers imposed by divided agency responsibilities and loyalties. Califano recruited his Harvard Law classmate John E. Robson, a Republican from Illinois, as his inflation lieutenant. (John Douglas, who had been doing some of this work on loan from Justice, had resigned from government to work in his father's unsuccessful senatorial reelection campaign against Charles H. Percy.) Robson was formally on the payroll of the Budget Bureau and occasionally had some duties there, but his real mission was to help Califano, Ackley, and Duesenberry with the legal and operational aspects of the inflation-fighting effort.[129] Robson received the early price warning reports from Commerce's Business and Defense Services Administration (BDSA). Typically, he would then analyze the situation (with help from the CEA, especially Duesenberry) to see if intervention of any type—telegrams, calls, requests for data, or requests for visits by company officials—would be fruitful. Robson's immediate superior, Califano, was consulted and, in major cases, became directly involved. Robson also served as "stockpile liaison" between the White House and all interested parties. (Generally his mission was to produce revenue and relieve industrial bottlenecks.) He worked with the Departments of Agriculture, Interior, Justice, and State and other federal agencies to obtain maximal and consistent government reactions to problems the BDSA early warning system and other sources of information suggested as trouble spots.[130] By mid-October Robson was able to report to Califano that he had been involved in "principal price actions" in seventeen areas, from eggs to air conditioners.[131]

The administration now had a modest but, for a voluntary program,

129. LBJ's habit of "borrowing" people for specific tasks, to minimize the visible "White House staff," makes it difficult to reconstruct a true organization chart for a particular time.

130. Sometimes the suggestions would come from above: "Jake [Jacobsen] called early yesterday (from the President's bedroom) with respect to the attached article in the *Wall Street Journal*. It deals with rising food prices. Jake wants you to call Ramsey Clark first thing and ask him to get some Grand Juries to investigate food prices in about a half-dozen big cities. Ramsey is going to be reluctant to do this and should be talked to 'sweetly.'" Lawrence E. Levinson to Califano, October 13, 1966, CF BE 5-2, Johnson Library.

131. "DOD has switched from large to medium eggs, with price-depressing effect (and some WPI [wholesale price index] relief too since only large eggs get into the

sufficient price-fighting apparatus. And it *was* a success, at least until August 1966, a crucial month for administration economic policy. U.S. Steel's successful price hike in that month was simply one symptom of a general collapse in wage-price policy.

Wage Defeats

Perhaps we've bragged too much about how profits are up 88% since early 1961.
—Ackley to LBJ, May 2, 1966

Economic historians will recognize 1966 to have been a vintage year, a rich and lively monograph subject. For the Johnson administration, it was *the* key year; the year events overran policies. From the point of view of wage policy, 1966 began badly and then deteriorated. The failure of real disposable income to rise as expected coupled with the January 1966 adjustment of the old-age, survivors, and disability insurance tax and taxable base, shifted the orientation of collective bargaining from fringe benefits toward wages.[132]

WPI)." Robson to Califano, "Price Actions," October 12, 1966, Office Files of Joseph A. Califano, Jr., Pricing, Johnson Library.

The egg case was actually more complex than Robson indicated in this one sentence, as Califano knew only too well. Defense's decision raised a storm of protest from midwestern farmers producing large eggs. There was a long and rather bitter discussion of this issue among several congressmen, Paul R. Ignatius (assistant secretary of defense, installations and logistics), Califano, and Robson.

In early 1967 Robson's duties would be taken over by another lawyer, Stanford G. Ross. Ross had practiced law with Califano at Thomas E. Dewey's firm in New York. He had returned to New York to teach law after having worked in the Kennedy administration. Just as it smooths over the ragged edges of the period to think of Robson as John Douglas's "successor," Ross did not come into government and assume some well-defined "Robson job." In fact, because the administration "thought that these [inflation-fighting] activities might no longer be necessary after a tax increase was proposed," Robson "had been nominated to be General Counsel of the [new] Department of Transportation." He was working at his new job when Ross arrived on the scene. I am grateful to Robson and Ross for talking with me about their activities during this period. The quoted material above is from a Ross memorandum of October 31, 1968, summarizing his experience: "Wage-Price Problems and Economic Coordination Activities," Papers of Stanford G. Ross.

132. In their 1966 report, the CEA stated that the increases (effective January 1, 1966) in employer payroll taxes to finance Medicare and additional social security benefits were not included in "the definition of employee compensation for purposes of the guideposts" because the increases were incurred by law rather than collective bargaining.

The first disaster of the year was the 6.3 percent transit settlement in New York City. The federal government did not openly intervene. It was a case "shot full of politics and personalities,"[133] an early crisis for John V. Lindsay, the newly elected Republican mayor. The Johnson administration blasted the settlement as inflationary.

The statements (yours, Gardner's, mine) made after the settlement had to be made. Industry and the press would have howled to high heaven at anything less.

The price was high, though, in solidifying the opposition of labor and the mediation profession (government and private) to a guidepost policy expressed as a specific decimal point policy.

- *George Meany and Co. are ready to declare open war on the guideposts.*
- *There was a fairly formal meeting of leading private mediators in New York Saturday to work out a program to protest the "strait-jacketing" of collective bargaining. This will be carried further at the annual meeting of the National Academy of Arbitrators which is being held later this month in Puerto Rico.*[134]

Wirtz's comments illustrate a recurring issue. Throughout the Johnson administration, the "CEA's guideposts" were a problem for the labor establishment—the fraternity of union officials, labor economists, arbitrators, negotiators, labor lawyers, and their advocate, the Labor Department. It was natural that the conflict between this "distinct club"[135] and the guideposters would be greatest in 1966, when strong pressures to increase wages met the administration's "decimal point policy." This fra-

133. Wirtz to the President, "New York Transit Case," January 5, 1966, EX LA 6/Transit, Johnson Library.

134. Wirtz to the President, January 17, 1966, CF LA 6/Transit, Johnson Library. This case stimulated a strong interest in national emergency disputes legislation. There was some hope that a bill could be introduced by a Democratic administration and passed by a Democratic Congress, particularly if passage could be coupled with repeal of section 14(b), the "right-to-work" section, of the Taft-Hartley Act. (Labor leaders were angry that this rather symbolic part of the Democratic program had not been delivered.) In his 1966 State of the Union Message, LBJ told Congress that he intended to introduce legislation to solve the strike problem. For the next year or so a great deal of energy was spent searching for ways to modify the appropriate statutes, the Taft-Hartley and Railway Labor Acts, to make them more effective, especially the "cooling-off" periods. The administration and its outside consultants sought *institutions* to make these periods conflict-resolving rather than conflict-postponing.

135. W. W. Rostow, *The Diffusion of Power: An Essay in Recent History* (Macmillan, 1972), p. 322. I am grateful to Professor Rostow for conversing with me about Johnsonian economic policy.

ternity, sometimes playfully called "The War Labor Board Protective Association," seemed to have its own version of the 1946 Employment Act trilogy. In early 1966 the director of the Federal Mediation and Concilia- tion Service (FMCS), William E. Simkin, sent a thorough critique of the guideposts to Califano. It was based on three interrelated objectives: "stability, full employment, and preservation of collective bargaining."[136] To believers in the guidepost principle, this was another illustration of what they perceived to be the fraternity's true motto—LABOR PEACE AT ANY PRICE LEVEL. But to Simkin, the FMCS was a neutral third party. Its mis- sion was to offer assistance in cases generally characterized by multiple objectives on both sides. Wages were just one, easy-to-quantify aspect of a bargain. The single (productivity) standard was, from the mediation point of view, inconsistent with collective bargaining, which would be capable of reflecting the *structure* of wages, by skill and by industry. James S. Duesenberry, who replaced Eckstein on the Council and became the CEA's wage-price specialist, responded that the FMCS could, at the onset of negotiations, "explain the logic of the guideposts and the public inter- est in noninflationary settlements."[137]

But sincere criticism of the guidepost principle from the FMCS was not its greatest threat. In 1966 the guideposts were used by union leaders needing a visible dragon to slay, especially a dragon that would not just quietly die after the coup de grâce but would thrash about.[138] In mid-July Ackley explained this problem to the President.

Labor's objections to the guideposts are, in principle, no different than before. But now the unions know that the economic situation would per- mit them to get a lot more. Only the guidepost stands between them and the kind of settlements they haven't known in 6 or 8 years.

136. Simkin to Califano, "Appraisal of the CEA Wage Guideposts from a Medi- ation Point of View," April 12, 1966, LA 8, 4/5/66–12/31/66, Johnson Library.

137. Duesenberry to Califano, "Comments on Memo from W. Simkin," April 18, 1966, EX BE 5-2, 3/24/66–5/20/66, Johnson Library.

138. Two illustrations: "He [W. A. (Tony) Boyle, president of the United Mine Workers] has internal union trouble. . . . He could very well decide that 'taking on the Government' is just what he needs within the Union." Wirtz to the President, "Stabilization—Coal," January 20, 1966, CF BE 4/Coal, Johnson Library.

"Joe [Joseph A. Beirne, president of the Communications Workers of America and former friend of the guidepost principle] is *very* much interested in the eventual Meany succession, and will be trying to lead the anti-guidepost parade." Wirtz to the President, "Beirne Letter," March 25, 1966, CF BE 4/Steel-Telephone, Johnson Library.

The same economic situation has made *management more friendly than before* to the guidepost. But its increased support—largely silent—is no offset to labor's offensive.

The recent rise in the cost of living provides powerful ammunition for labor's case. If consumer prices were to continue rising at their recent 3% a year rate, a guidepost settlement would mean little or no real gain.

Labor's unhappiness is intensified by its obvious loss of political muscle and of prestige in the liberal community. Therefore it is flailing around in all directions and the guidepost is one good target.[139]

The wage guidepost collided with more than just the labor fraternity in 1966. It also produced conflicts in three areas of major concern to the government: the minimum wage, federal salaries, and federal contracts.

In 1961 Congress had extended coverage of the Fair Labor Standards Act (FLSA) and approved a staged increase of the hourly minimum to $1.25. Organized labor and the Labor Department did not wait long to argue for more. Further FLSA amendments became part of the 1964 legislative program, but failed. The CEA fought a steady internal battle against the amendments throughout 1964 and 1965. But an FLSA bill was finally reported out of the Select Subcommittee on Labor of the House Committee on Education and Labor in August 1965. It called for an increase in the minimum as well as a further extension of coverage. The CEA was publicly silent on this issue; it was not mentioned in the 1966 report.[140] But within the administration family, the CEA argued that "too rapid an increase in the minimum wage" would "contribute to inflation" and "keep some poor workers from getting jobs."[141] It was generally agreed that the hourly minimum would be $1.40 following passage, then $1.60 sometime later (x). There was much discussion of the political-inflationary trade-offs involved in alternative dates for x. Ackley pointed out that the CEA had "*never said exactly what the low-wage exception* [to the guidepost principle] *means, numerically.*" But a "reasonable interpre-

139. Ackley to the President, "The Wage Guidepost," July 11, 1966, EX FG 11-3, 6/22/66–8/12/66, Johnson Library.

140. "The great reconciler of loyalty and integrity is silence." Comment by Arthur M. Okun in a panel discussion at the annual meeting of the Allied Social Science Associations, 1973; printed in *Challenge*, vol. 17 (March–April 1974), p. 33. Okun illustrated his obiter dictum with the 1966 minimum wage case.

141. Ackley to the President, "Minimum Wages and the Guideposts," February 22, 1966, EX LA 8, 11/2/65–4/4/66, Johnson Library.

tation" was that "low-wage people could advance about twice as fast as the general public." This ruled out x being in 1967, but the CEA "could probably stretch the rule" to make it sometime in 1968.[142] The Ackley-approved measure was passed by Congress, and in a splendid ceremony, complete with bickering over the guest list and a Mary Wells speech flown in from Acapulco, the President made the 1966 FLSA amendments law on September 23.

Another policy collision was between the guideposts and the Federal Salary Reform Act of 1962.[143] This act, an attempt to upgrade pay scales of federal civilian employees to make them equal to what people in the private sector would receive for comparable work, led to above-guidepost pay increases. This situation was generally thought to be consistent with the exceptions to the guideposts explicated in the various CEA reports. It did not cause a major problem until the administration faced a hostile private-sector labor movement. The government was forced at least to give the appearance of keeping its own salaries down if its moral suasion policy was to be credible. The CEA's response to this issue over three successive years is illustrative of the diminishing optimism and self-belief that one discovers while going through any chronological slice of the Johnson administration's written record. In 1964 Chairman Walter Heller was able to say yes, the federal pay bill is above the guidepost, but it is a legitimate exception: "Indeed, by making Federal pay more comparable with private pay, they will *help us attract and retain the top level talent needed to make your government operate wisely, effectively, and frugally.*"[144] In 1965 Ackley was asked to review the salary bill and, in a formal memorandum, stated that in his judgment "the present bill meets the guidepost criterion." But in a handwritten cover note he had to acknowledge that "this memo goes about as far as possible. The *fact is that the bill really does exceed the guideposts a bit.*"[145] The 1966 version, by Acting Chairman Okun, was similar: "The Federal Government will once again be setting a good example for private wage settlements in giving full recognition

142. Ackley to the President, "Minimum Wages and the Guideposts," March 5, 1966, CF LA, Johnson Library.

143. See Sheahan, *Wage-Price Guideposts*, pp. 54–57.

144. Heller to the President, "The New Federal Pay Bill and the Wage-Price Guideposts," August 6, 1964, EX BE 5-2, 11/22/63–4/13/65, Johnson Library.

145. Ackley to the President, "Civil Service Pay Bill," October 17, 1965, EX LE/PE 11, Johnson Library.

to the importance of non-inflationary conduct."[146] But at the bottom of the CEA's file copy was: "Written at Joe Califano's orders."[147]

The third point of policy collision, government contracts, was only a potential one. They were never fully exploited by the administration to enforce the wage side of the guidepost principle. The guideposters came close to getting LBJ to unsheathe what probably would have been a very effective weapon, but they did not succeed. The CEA, Budget Director Charles Schultze, and Civil Service Commission Chairman John W. Macy, Jr., argued that application of the guideposts to federal salaries, federal "wage board" employees, and to the military was politically difficult if employees of federal contractors were not equally "covered." Ackley, Schultze, and Macy attempted to get the President's agreement to require federal contractors to pay guidepost wages. This proposal was discussed at length within the administration, with the Justice Department pointing out that "it would require a waiver of a number of statutory wage provisions such as the Davis-Bacon Act."[148] The discussion ended with Defense Secretary McNamara's strong argument that "we should not implement this proposal."[149] At a meeting on July 21, 1966, "McNamara convinced everyone that the ... proposals were administratively impossible of execution."[150] McNamara was apparently afraid of losing his defense industry labor force.

Another case involving potential use of federal contract power was the administration's unfortunate public battle in 1966 with a tiny corner of the construction industry. Since the early days of the Johnson administration, the CEA had recognized that construction industry wages were "high and rising too fast."[151] In early 1966 the administration was alert to all phases of the inflation problem, and construction seemed to be one phase

146. Okun to the President, "Federal Pay and the Guideposts," May 25, 1966, CEA Microfilm, Roll 69, Johnson Library.

147. "After the minimum wage and federal pay bill episodes, I wrote a memo to the President (maybe to Califano asking him to tell the President) I'd resign if ever again ordered to do this." Gardner Ackley to the author, August 26, 1974.

148. Leon Ulman to Califano, "Contract Stipulation Against Pay Raises in Excess of Wage Guidelines," March 23, 1966, Office Files of Joseph A. Califano, Jr., Economics, Box 10, "Executive Controls," Johnson Library.

149. McNamara to Califano, "Application of the Wage-Price Guideposts to Defense Contracts," undated and unsigned [July 21, 1966], Office Files of Joseph A. Califano, Jr., Economics, Box 8, "Wage-Price Guideposts," Johnson Library.

150. Ackley to the Council, July 23, 1966, CEA Microfilm, Roll 64, Johnson Library.

151. Heller to the President, "Construction Wages: A Tough Nut to Crack," May 23, 1964, EX FG 11-3, 5/21/64–7/20/64, Johnson Library.

completely out of control. Many solutions to the problem were explored. Labor Secretary Wirtz tried personal diplomacy with the unions, asking them to agree to a national construction wage review board. They refused. The one actual confrontation between the government and the construction industry was on terrain the administration would probably not have chosen. Pressure from contractors and the media forced it to get involved in a dispute between the Associated General Contractors (AGC) of New Jersey, largely engaged in highway construction, and Local 825 of the International Union of Operating Engineers. (Contrary to rumors, New Jersey had *not* already been paved over.) As Sheahan has noted, the government was driven to take action "by criticism implying that inability to act here was a confession of defeat" for the wage guidepost.[152] Unfortunately, the AGC had already agreed to a high settlement (drawing attention to the case), which Local 825 President Peter Weber had rejected. Also, Weber was under federal indictment.

The union problem is particularly severe in New Jersey because of (probable) collusion between Weber, local contractors, and local political forces. The Contractors Association is very weak, and it is virtually impossible to get contractors to serve on local committees of the AGC. The contractors even hire lawyers to do their negotiating, "just to avoid the humiliation of sitting at the table with Weber." The contractors have "gotten licked every time, and see no reason to resist the union."[153]

Of course, the administration's main weapon was to withhold federal highway contracts. This course of action was explored in depth but the President "concluded that it would not be desirable to withhold Federal funds."[154] A settlement was achieved by Wirtz in two stages, the wage increase in March and, after arbitration, the fringe benefits in September. The union eventually got what it wanted. What the CEA did not want or need was the kind of media reaction exemplified by the *Newark Evening News* headline of March 22, 1966: "Weber in Labor Spotlight— Newarker Gets Kudos for Challenging Guidelines." The construction industry would continue to be a nemesis for Johnsonian wage policy and federal contract power would remain an idle tool.

All of these 1966 wage activities were of minor importance compared

152. Sheahan, *Wage-Price Guideposts*, p. 52.
153. Harold Richman to Philip Arnow, May 17, 1966, Department of Labor Microfilm, Subject File, Roll 19, Johnson Library.
154. John T. Connor to W. Marvin Watson, April 1, 1966, EX BE 4/Const, 11/22/63–7/10/66, Johnson Library.

to what became the big, explosive case of 1966: the International Association of Machinists (IAM) versus Eastern, National, Northwest, Trans
World, and United airlines (the "Five Carriers"). It was an extraordinary
battle, one in which the guideposts were believed to have been destroyed.

The case began in August 1965, when negotiating procedures were established by the two sides. The existing contract was scheduled to expire
on December 31, 1965. In January both parties applied to the National
Mediation Board, which provided continuous help through March. On
March 18 the NMB suggested compulsory arbitration of the remaining
eight common and forty local issues; the carriers accepted, but the IAM
refused. With a strike set for April 23, President Johnson had to decide
whether to appoint an emergency board.[155] Ackley and Wirtz submitted
arguments for and against the creation of a board. Ackley offered six symmetrically balanced arguments on each side but focused on the guideposts. He noted that "arbitrators of stature are bound to be independent,
and many of them don't approve of the guidepost policy." But "if the
board were *carefully selected* [Califano used the phrase "presidentially
oriented" in his covering note to LBJ], there could be *strong probability*
of a settlement at or very close to the guideposts. This would *give the
guidepost principle strong support* at a time when such support is badly
needed."[156] Ackley made no overall recommendation. However, Wirtz
and the NMB favored creation of a board, although Wirtz advised the
President that the Five Carriers had dug in at 3.2 percent and the IAM
would "*never, under any circumstances, settle here for 3.2%.*"[157] He suggested three reasons for the IAM's determined stand. First, IAM President P. L. Siemiller had "been one of the two or three most bitter public
critics of the guideposts." Second, the IAM vice-president in charge of the
airline division, who was responsible for this negotiation, "*is a strong and
outspoken Republican. He is retiring later this year and considers this case
his monument.*" Finally, Wirtz pointed out that the IAM and the Transport Workers Union are strong competitors. The TWU represented the

155. As amended in 1936, the Railway Labor Act of 1926 gave the President
power to create such a board in airline labor disputes. Strikes were not permitted
during the thirty days the board had to investigate and report or during the thirty
days after the submission of its report.
156. Ackley to the President, "Arguments For and Against Appointing an Emergency Board in the Airline Case," April 20, 1966, EX LA 6/Air, 11/22/63–7/8/66,
Johnson Library.
157. Wirtz to the President, "Airlines Case," April 20, 1966, EX LA 6/Air,
11/22/63–7/8/66, Johnson Library.

mechanics of American and Pan American airlines. Negotiations with those two lines were under way, with the TWU demanding over 10 percent a year. Wirtz suggested that the IAM had "to make as strong a play here as Mike Quill [TWU president] did in the New York Transit case."[158]

LBJ decided to create a board, a distinguished one, consisting of Senator Wayne Morse (chairman), David Ginsburg, and Richard E. Neustadt.[159] The board got its thirty-day life extended and, on June 5, reported to the President. Its wage recommendation was 3.5 percent with a cleverly designed cost-of-living reopener, requiring an exceptionally large burst in the CPI to reopen the contract. Ackley approved.

We would be extremely lucky to get a settlement along these lines. The problem is to devise a strategy that maximizes the chances of getting it.
* *If we endorse it too warmly, the union will be scared off.*
* *On the other hand, we can't expect a better settlement. If we denounce it, and the final settlement is this or higher, it will appear as a defeat for wage moderation.*
. . . Every possible pressure should be put on the union to get the quickest possible acceptance.
The longer the time that elapses
—the more pressure there will be for CEA to say what the settlement amounts to; and
—the better the union will be able to figure out that it's really a pretty tight proposal.
We ought to nail this down before labor knows what hit them.[160]

Secretary Wirtz estimated that "the odds are overwhelming that the Union will reject the proposed settlement."[161] Everyone Califano consulted, including the Morse board as well as Secretaries McNamara and Fowler, agreed "that any knowledge by the Union that Ackley could live

158. Ibid.
159. David Ginsburg played an increasingly important role in the Johnson administration from 1966 to the end. He had argued the Roosevelt administration's case for the constitutionality of what became the Emergency Price Control Act of 1942 before Congress. During World War II, he was general counsel of the Office of Price Administration.
160. Ackley to the President, "Emergency Board Report in Airlines Case," June 6, 1966, EX LA 1-1/Airlines, Johnson Library.
161. Califano to the President, June 6, 1966, EX LA 1-1/Airlines, Johnson Library. An important but neglected piece of information was transmitted to the President at this point: "The IAM has rejected every major settlement the first time it was presented to it during the past 12 months since Siemiller has been President." Ibid.

with this settlement would kill off any chance of acceptance by the Union."[162] But the IAM did reject and, on July 8, struck the Five Carriers. At this point, Presidential Assistant Califano used the lever of the Civil Aeronautics Board "to put some spine in the carriers," making it clear that there would be no letup in the "drive for lower fares on the basis of any high settlement."[163] As the strike continued, there was the expected mounting pressure for "the government to do something." But "the government" had ceased to be a neutral party. The strike was really against the administration's wage policy. Although the Five Carriers were losing $8.2 million a day, they stood behind the recommendation of the Morse board.

On July 22 an angry Senator Morse proposed giving the President authority to place the airlines in government receivership. Neither the Five Carriers nor Senator Everett M. Dirksen cared for this proposal and three days later Senator Morse formally offered a more modest proposal: a 180-day "cooling-off" period. Against the background of angry noises from Congress and the continuing hostility of the inconvenienced airline-using public, negotiations moved to the Labor Department on July 28 and, the next day, to the Executive Office Building. Apparently, however, LBJ had decided on July 26 to cave in and on July 29 at 9:52 P.M., on live TV, the President announced a settlement, arguing "this settlement that has been reached will not be inflationary" because "productivity has advanced so rapidly in the airline industry."[164] This, of course, was inconsistent with the guidepost principle, something the CEA quickly clarified. The contract called for a 4.3 percent annual increase in wages.

After midnight on the day LBJ decided to capitulate, Ackley wrote a very long and thoughtful analysis to him about "the decision I think you have made."

Every free industrialized country which tries to maintain full employment faces this problem: strong unions have the power to push wages up faster than productivity and thereby to inflate costs and prices; and semi-

162. Ibid.
163. Califano to the President, July 8, 1966, CF LA 6/Airlines, Johnson Library. The CAB was thought by many to be the villain of the piece because it had failed to take appropriate action which might have reduced fares to bring the carriers' actual rates of return near the 10.5 percent set as a reasonable average for the industry. Most of the carriers were doing handsomely: if the Five Carriers' common stock had been bought at their 1962 highs and sold at their January–June 1966 lows, capital gains would have ranged from 190 to 442 percent.
164. LA 6/Airlines, 7/23/66–7/29/66, Johnson Library.

monopolistic industries have the power to push up prices even if costs are stable. No country has really solved it. Sooner or later we will have to come to grips with it. Now may not be the time. But if not now, soon.

I think it is obvious that—with our balance of payments situation—we cannot afford inflation, even if it could be tolerated domestically. The polls don't suggest it can be tolerated domestically. This either means abandoning full employment or finding a way to live with it.

This is not a problem for the next six months or two years but for the decade. The end of the war won't solve it. A tax increase won't solve it (though it could help). It will have to be approached head on. Sometime, somewhere, we will have to find a way to convince the unions they cannot continually push wage costs up, and to convince business that profit margins cannot continually rise.

The airlines case may not be the place to begin. All the points we made yesterday afternoon against drawing the line here and now are correct and relevant. But can we be sure the next case, or the one after that will be a better place to start? . . .

Maybe it can't be done. [Harold] Wilson didn't do it. Or maybe things have to get worse before they get better. But history suggests that once they get worse, the job is twice as difficult.[165]

The denouement of the story began on July 31. By a 3–1 vote, the rank and file rejected the settlement LBJ had so proudly announced to the national television audience. On August 1 the Senate passed a new Morse bill and the House Interstate and Foreign Commerce Committee reluctantly took it up. Negotiations continued until August 15 when Under Secretary of Labor James Reynolds came out of a session at 6:22 A.M. and announced, "We've got a settlement." In a letter to his membership urging approval, Siemiller asserted that the settlement (4.9 percent a year) "destroys all existing wage and price guidelines now in existence."

The administration from this point on had a great deal of difficulty

165. Ackley to the President, "A Longer-Run View of the Airlines Case," July 27, 1966, 12:30 A.M., EX BE 5, 7/15/66–8/24/66, Johnson Library.

It is interesting to juxtapose Ackley's memorandum against one written by Nicholas Kaldor after he had suggested the guidepost principle to the British Chancellor of the Exchequer on June 21, 1950: "The unfettered freedom of wage bargaining of individual unions is one of the most cherished rights of the trade union movement; and a policy which, however guardedly, limited this freedom would certainly have met with outright rejection only a few years ago. Since that time, however, the experience of the post-war period has taught a great deal. The institutions which grew up over the last century were appropriate to an unemployment economy." Nicholas Kaldor, *Essays on Economic Policy*, vol. 1 (Norton, 1965), p. 116.

trying to establish a defensible position from which to intervene in labor settlements. In May 1966, after an eighteen-month lapse and twelve months to the day after Ackley had suggested it to LBJ, the tripartite LMAC was revived. The LMAC endorsed the "productivity principle" in August, but by then it was too late. Beirne's Communications Workers of America settled above the guidepost with AT&T. The TWU did "better" against American and Pan American Airlines than Siemiller had done against the Five Carriers. Also, the 3.2 percent guidepost became enmeshed in an unsuccessful defense by General Electric of its "Boulwarism doctrine" ("our first offer is our last offer"), resulting in White House and Pentagon intervention. GE used 3.2 percent, but settled at about 5 percent. Wirtz advised the President that the word from the AFL-CIO Executive Council meeting in Chicago was not good: "Everybody is assuming 5% is the new guideline."[166] Put another way, the productivity guidepost no longer existed. The administration no longer had an operational wage policy.

Policies for 1967

Anybody with open eyes can see what is coming. No guesswork is necessary. If we can see what is coming, if we know what we must do, then I think we ought to do it right this time—and do it fast.

In both World War I and World War II, we bumbled and bungled our way through the battle of the home front. We started late. We worked without a plan. We didn't know just where we were going—or how to get there. Surely we can profit from the errors of the past.
—Excerpted from a speech by Senator Lyndon B. Johnson, radio station WBAP (Fort Worth, Texas), August 6, 1950

While the administration was battling wages and prices during 1966, it also had the dual problem of developing new fiscal policies and, as they became battered, possible replacements for the guideposts. As the year progressed, it became clear that the Defense Department had greatly underestimated the costs of the Vietnam War. (Korea was a misleading example; expenditures for that war were lower than forecast.) In late 1965 and early 1966 President Johnson chose not to ask Congress for a tax increase for the war and for his Great Society programs. This decision has been explained by Charles L. Schultze, budget director at the time. Except

166. Wirtz to the President, August 24, 1966, EX LA 6, 11/23/63–12/12/66, Johnson Library.

for a misguided effort in the 1930s, Congress had never passed a general tax increase in peacetime. But 1965–66 was a gray period, a time of neither war nor peace. Schultze's view is that President Johnson could have "wrapped himself in the flag" and gotten a full-fledged war in Vietnam. This would have entailed, among other things, calling up the National Guard, instituting mandatory wage-price controls, and asking Congress for a war tax. Schultze argues that LBJ did not follow this course of action for two reasons. First, the generals would have gotten out of hand; LBJ's approach of measured escalation was a restraining force on the military's strategy and tactics in Southeast Asia. And the second session of the Eighty-ninth Congress was LBJ's last chance to bring decades of social and economic ideas to legislative harvest. One cost of "formalizing" the war would have been the loss of the domestic legislative program.[167] (Also, the President may have been unwilling "to loose the flood of debate on Vietnam for which a tax increase proposal would provide the tempting occasion."[168])

In late March, when LBJ asked a large group of businessmen at a White House dinner if any of them would call for a tax increase, no hands were raised.[169] In May, five months after his "gloomy report" to the President advising a tax increase, Ackley, strongly supported by Budget Director Schultze, began an intense campaign to convince the President of the need for a responsible fiscal program. On May 7 Ackley, Califano, Fowler, McNamara, and Schultze met to discuss the tax increase–defense budget supplemental situation. After the meeting, LBJ decided to postpone a decision. McNamara had said he simply would not know about his fiscal 1966 and 1967 outlays until mid-June. Fowler, who apparently shared the

167. Interview with Charles L. Schultze, August 1, 1974.
168. Walter W. Heller, *New Dimensions of Political Economy* (Harvard University Press, 1966), p. 94.
169. But a month later Otto Eckstein reported to the President that a number of businessmen at a Harvard Economics Department Overseers Committee meeting expressed "general *agreement* on the need to raise taxes." "*Why didn't the business leadership make its views felt? And why did their friends just sit there when you asked them* about tax action at your dinner? . . . They were caught *flat-footed*, with their *tongues tied*. If a candid man-to-man poll had been taken, *a clear majority would have favored a tax rise.*" Eckstein to the President, "The Tax Question and the Business Leadership," April 29, 1966, EX BE 5-4, 4/30/66–5/21/66, Johnson Library.
    There is further evidence of support: "If it were not for resistance by Bill Wirtz and me, the LMAC *would have given you a formal expression of opinion on a tax increase*. The recommendation would have been divided, but with a *majority in favor*." Ackley to the President, May 5, 1966, EX FI 11, 3/17/66–8/20/66, Johnson Library.

Ackley-Schultze view "but [did] not feel as strongly about it," pointed out that postponement by McNamara would mean that if the Ackley-Schultze view did prevail in mid-June "nothing would go to Congress until July 15. Fowler believes that this may be too late to present a tax bill to the Congress for passage in this session and that Congress might be quite annoyed at receiving a tax bill at that time."[170] Ackley and Schultze did not give up. A few days later they sent separate detailed fiscal proposals to the President. Both called for "a 10% tax increase on personal and corporate income, accompanied by suspension of the investment credit and of accelerated depreciation on nonresidential building."[171]

Ackley and Schultze kept up their arguments throughout the eventful summer of 1966. But they were prescribing medicine the decision maker was very reluctant to take. The advice from outside economists was the same. Richard E. Neustadt had established an informal study group: Otto Eckstein, John T. Dunlop, Derek Bok, Carl Kaysen, Robert M. Solow, Lester C. Thurow, and John R. Meyer. Califano informed LBJ that "this group has been quietly meeting for the last three months in Cambridge on the economic situation, with a view towards making recommendations to you, on their own, for a program for January 1967."[172] McNamara, Ackley, David Ginsburg, Fowler, and Califano met with the group in Cambridge on August 22. Eckstein gave a summary of the group's proposals to Califano, who passed it along to the President. Many areas of the economy were covered, but the "group was agreed that a personal and a corporate tax increase was absolutely essential, and the sooner the better."[173]

The Cambridge group's advice matched that which LBJ had solicited and received from Kermit Gordon, Schultze, and Ackley.[174] But the President realized that congressional elections were coming up in November.

170. Califano to the President, May 7, 1966, CF BE 5, Johnson Library.

171. Ackley to the President, "The Case for Higher Taxes," May 10, 1966, and Schultze to the President, "The Effect of a Tax Increase," May 11, 1966, EX FI 11, 3/17/66–8/20/66, Johnson Library.

172. Califano to the President, August 16, 1966, EX BE 5, 7/15/66–8/24/66, Johnson Library.

173. Otto Eckstein, attached to Califano to the President, August 23, 1966, EX BE 5, 7/15/66–8/24/66, Johnson Library.

174. Gardner Ackley was not exactly underemployed in August 1966. The following request, dated 9:30 A.M., Friday, August 12, 1966, might, to weaker men, have been grounds for justifiable homicide: "I am getting up a history . . . [and] need a chapter, written in simple form, on the 'mass prosperity' created during the first thousand days of President Johnson. . . . I would hope that you would have the material in my office by noon on Monday, at the latest." Robert E. Kintner to Ackley, CF FG 11-3, Johnson Library.

Could he ask the House, especially the sixty-nine freshman Democrats
he had carried with him during the 1964 landslide (who might be facing
tough elections in "marginal" districts), to vote for increases in personal
and corporate taxes before going home to campaign? The question was
answered in the negative, but by now there were good economic reasons
for doing so.

By August 1966 the economy was at the peak of a credit crunch. (In
December 1965 housing starts had been 1,770,000 at an annual rate; by
October 1966 the rate was 850,000.) The Federal Reserve was compensating for the President's failure to enact proper fiscal policy. It was also
taking a terrific public beating for its policies, especially from Congress.
According to Ackley, the executive branch should be grateful. "So far the
Administration has been able to maintain silence on monetary policy—
neither blessing it [n]or blasting it. We should continue that successful
strategy as long as we possibly can."[175]

A fiscal package was finally agreed upon and submitted to the President in a remarkable page-and-a-half document, initialed by Fowler,
McNamara, Katzenbach, Lawrence O'Brien, Schultze, Ackley, Ginsburg,
and Califano. They agreed on budget cuts, a request for temporary suspension of the investment tax credit, and "a statement of your [the President's] intention to ask, at an appropriate time in the future, for whatever
tax measures are necessary to raise the money to cover add-ons to the
budget by Congressional action or by the Generals in Vietnam."[176] Congress approved the President's request on the investment tax credit and
the President signed the bill into law on November 8, 1966. By then the
Federal Reserve had already provided additional reserves to "un-crunch"
the liquidity crisis; and on November 22 the Open Market Committee of
the Federal Reserve voted to move toward easier money. From January
1967 to the Nixon inauguration the Fed presided over the fastest sustained rate of money stock growth since World War II. On January 9
McNamara, Fowler, Wirtz, Connor, Schultze, Ackley, Clark Clifford,
and Califano initialed and sent a one-page fiscal program to the President.
They advised LBJ to call for a 6 percent surcharge in the Budget Message

175. Ackley to Marvin Watson, July 29, 1966, CF FG 11-3, Johnson Library.
176. Fowler and others to the President, September 2, 1966, EX BE 5, 8/25/66–
9/26/66, Johnson Library. The procedure for these documents was for Califano to
dictate a memorandum, following discussion. Then, before leaving, everyone would
initial it. One day Attorney General Katzenbach drolly inquired if Califano "had a
notary coming in." Interview with Joseph A. Califano, Jr., September 26, 1974.

and to "continue to press for easier money."[177] But forecasts for 1967 were anomalous: very large budget deficits in an economy that seemed to need no real restraint. The fourth quarter of 1966 had been a period of massive inventory accumulation, the largest since the spring of 1951. It was anticipated that 1967 would be soft. In his January 1967 Budget Message LBJ did propose a 6 percent tax surcharge but did not send a tax message to Congress. He also approved a strong presentation of the need for tax increases in the CEA's report and let Ackley and the Treasury start preparing the groundwork for an eventual increase.

While everything else was going on in 1966, the administration was involved in seemingly perpetual evaluation of its wage-price philosophy. Criticism had intensified in early 1966. Friends and enemies of the guideposts had an opportunity to proselytize at three conferences during the spring. (The most substantive one was a premature wake organized by George Shultz at the University of Chicago.) The festivities marking the twentieth anniversary of the Employment Act of 1946 also served as a useful forum.

Congress was the source of two proposals for altering the administration's inflation program. Congressman Emanuel Celler proposed an amendment to the Sherman Antitrust Act which was a sixty-day compulsory prior notification scheme for "basic industries."[178] An alternative proposal was offered by a senior House Democrat on the Joint Economic Committee, Henry S. Reuss. Reuss and Celler were reacting to the January 1966 steel episode, which had begun with Bethlehem's New Year's Eve price increase. Reuss suggested amending the Employment Act to codify the guideposts. The CEA would be required to transmit its guideposts to the Joint Economic Committee each January 20. The committee would then review them. If it did *not* approve, it would send its own guideposts to Congress. The CEA's guideposts would remain in effect unless and until Congress agreed on an alternative. The CEA would be required to study actual or imminent violations and report them to the committee, which would be given authority to subpoena "offenders" to appear, with their records, at public hearings. Needless to say, Reuss was suggesting quite a departure from the original nonoperational roles of the CEA and the committee. Administration officials had mixed feelings about the

177. McNamara and others to the President, EX FG 11-3, 1/6/67–2/4/67, Johnson Library.

178. H.R. 11870, *Congressional Record*, vol. 112, pt. 1, 89 Cong. 2 sess. (1966), pp. 77–78.

Reuss bill, but at the hearings on the 1966 Economic Report and at the hearing in September 1966 on the Reuss bill, they argued that legislation of specific guideposts and public hearings on specific cases of guidepost violation would be a mistake. According to Ackley, for the guidepost policy to work in the long run, it had to "remain a matter of understanding and freely volunteered cooperation."[179]

The executive branch under the Johnson administration would not look to Congress to broaden the base of support for wage-price policy, but other departures from the 1962 voluntary guideposts were discussed. At the 1958 Joint Economic Committee hearings on the relationship of prices to economic stability and growth, which had been so instrumental in crystallizing the views of the men who would take over responsibility for making Kennedy-Johnson policy, a proposal was offered whereby Congress would establish a permanent wage and price commission, charged with formulating general standards, collecting the information required to enforce these standards, and making public its findings. The author of this proposal was University of Michigan economist Gardner Ackley.[180] Not surprisingly, the idea of a permanent commission was under active consideration at the CEA. A number of variants of this idea were proposed —by the CEA, Walter Reuther, Wirtz, David Ginsburg, and Robert R. Nathan. In August 1966 thinking about a price-wage review board had proceeded far enough for Califano to give the President an outline of a possible arrangement, coupled with pros and cons. The proposal was supported by "Fowler, Wirtz, Connor, Ackley, Clifford, [and] Fortas."[181] However, McNamara, Califano, and Katzenbach believed that presidential identification with the program was too great a risk, given a general view that without legislation it probably would not work. The idea died. It was revived in the 1967 Joint Economic Committee majority report. A price-productivity-income (PPI) office was suggested, perhaps to be embedded in the administration's proposed new department, which was to be formed by merging Commerce and Labor. Neither the committee's proposed office nor the administration's proposed merger came off.[182]

The commission idea would not have required legislation. It would

179. *Congressional Review of Price-Wage Guideposts*, Hearing before a Subcommittee of the House Committee on Government Operations on H.R. 11916, 89 Cong. 2 sess. (1966), p. 67.

180. *Relationship of Prices to Economic Stability and Growth*, Hearings before the Joint Economic Committee, 85 Cong. 2 sess. (1958), pp. 394–96.

181. Califano to the President, August 4, 1966, EX BE 5-2, 7/13/66–9/17/66, Johnson Library.

182. The merger had received a highly favorable endorsement by the ongoing

have been an evolutionary change from the guideposts, still "voluntary" but less so. LBJ also had periodic flirtations with more *compulsory* programs, in case events in Vietnam forced the administration to move in that direction. As early as January 1966, the President and Califano discussed the imposition of mandatory controls. Former Budget Director Kermit Gordon was brought into the discussion. He explained to Califano, who passed the information along to the President, "why economists—particularly those who served with OPA or OPS—tend to flinch when mandatory price control is mentioned."[183] Gordon concluded that the situation in early 1966 did not come close to requiring mandatory controls. More important, he reinforced the viewpoint of Gardner Ackley, thus helping to counterbalance the controls orientation of some of the President's other advisers.

Even if it is skillfully administered, general price control inevitably generates serious economic distortions, and the distortions tend to become more damaging the longer price control survives. For example:

—*Price controllers will inevitably maintain tighter control over the prices of necessities than over the prices of luxuries. This causes business firms to curtail the production of necessities and increase the production of luxuries.*

—*Since a price ceiling on a commodity can be precise, but the definition of the controlled commodity cannot be, price control tends to lead sellers to lower the quality of their goods.*

—*Standardized products are easier to control than unstandardized products; thus price control tends to penalize producers of the former.*

—*Price control tends to make the price system unresponsive to changing demands; thus it tends to cause shortages in some areas and gluts in others.*

—*Price control tends to confer windfalls on producers of commodities*

Task Force on Government Organization, whose chairman was Ben W. Heineman. Califano liked it, and at first the two departments attacked the staff-level planning with enthusiasm. But as the weeks passed the upper echelons of both departments cooled on the idea and so did George Meany. The idea also met some congressional resistance and, at a March 17 LMAC meeting, it was killed. The internal politics of the merger story are interesting: there was a trade-off for every affected party involving their perceived "loss" or "gain" associated with the expectation that the new department would be less constituency bound, to be weighed against the "loss" or "gain" associated with the creation of a new and probably very strong voice in the formation of national economic policy. Perceptions of the trade-offs shifted over time, causing most parties to reverse their positions on the merger at least once.

183. Gordon to Califano, "Why Economists Dread Mandatory Price Control," January 25, 1966, EX BE 5-2, 12/29/65–2/20/66, Johnson Library.

whose costs are falling and to penalize producers of commodities whose costs are rising.

—If the political or the economic situation leads sellers to expect that price control may soon be terminated, sellers will withhold their goods from sale, thus creating artificial shortages. . . .

The administrative problems of general price control are staggering:

—It takes an army of federal employees to administer and enforce price control.

—Many of the price control specialists are inevitably recruited from the industry they will regulate, with the result that the integrity of the whole process comes under a cloud.

—Any clever and unscrupulous seller can find loopholes in price regulation; thus general price control tends to reward scofflaws and penalize honesty.

—Under price control the advantage goes to those businessmen who focus their energies on dealing with government rather than to those who devote themselves to producing a good product at low cost.

In my judgment, there are only two sets of circumstances in which the gain from mandatory price control outweighs the harm:

—First, if the government is absorbing so large a share of gross national product that stabilization by fiscal measures would require rates of taxation so high as to be regarded as confiscatory and intolerable, mandatory price control may be the lesser evil. . . .

—Second, if the people think they are on the verge of some sort of military cataclysm, and if they respond with an orgy of price increases and panic buying, immediate imposition of price control and rationing may be the only solution.[184]

By August 1966 the President was again interested in mandatory controls. John Robson had the Justice Department provide a full evaluation of current presidential "authorities in the economy." He also made a detailed study of efforts at voluntary price controls immediately preceding the general wage-price freeze of January 26, 1951. By October a lengthy legal opinion had been prepared for the President by the Justice Department, David Ginsburg, and John Robson (based on a report done earlier at Justice) about the authority to control prices and wages under the Trading with the Enemy Act.[185] Also during this period the President was kept informed of the OEP's plans.

184. Ibid.
185. "There are no copies in Justice because it raises questions about your authority to do this, and Justice wanted to have a free hand to support any such

We have draft legislation for various alternative legislative approaches —ranging from a 90-day freeze of prices to a full-scale stabilization.

We have drafts of some of the basic orders and regulations, including an Executive order to establish an Economic Stabilization Agency.

We have many standby administrative arrangements on organization, staffing, and functions, as well as general location of offices in the field, logistical support, and related matters.

We have kept our work in this area at a low key so as not to create any problems of public awareness or reaction.[186]

Nevertheless, these and other exotic departures from the "voluntary guideposts for noninflationary behavior" were not adopted. The CEA, after a winter of discussion with each other, the Labor and Commerce Departments, its Business Council's Liaison Committee, the President's Advisory Committee on Labor-Management Policy, academic consultants, and union economists, decided that the wage-price policy in the 1967 Economic Report would "retain the productivity principle, although sacrifice the rigidity of the 3.2%"[187] They realized that some allowance was going to be made in contracts for the increase in the cost of living but made "clear it should be far less than 100%" of the increases. The CEA still opposed escalator clauses as increasing inflation, but "on Bill Wirtz's plea," they eliminated from an earlier draft "the suggestion that—if escalators are used—they should be delayed and limited."[188]

No one was really satisfied with this policy, but an acceptable alternative could not be found. Throughout late 1966 and early 1967 one of the CEA's primary missions was to get across the message that the guideposts were not dead. Not surprisingly, the news media focused on the "aban-

---

action if it should be taken." Califano to the President, October 5, 1966, Office Files of Joseph A. Califano, Jr., Economics, Box 10, "Executive Controls," Johnson Library.

186. Farris Bryant to the President, undated but attached to a note from LBJ to Califano, August 13, 1966: "Take this—Study carefully." EX BE 3, Johnson Library.

Earlier in 1966, the CEA and the OEP tangled when Franklin B. Dryden, OEP's acting director, sent LBJ a "Report on the Current Situation with Respect to Production, Manpower, and Prices." Ackley and Budget Director Schultze believed that the OEP was poaching on troika territory and should go back to its traditional duties. Particularly after JFK and McNamara transferred its civil defense functions to the Defense Department, the OEP's mission was rather limited. In the Nixon administration it would blossom dramatically (under the name of the Office of Emergency Preparedness) during the 1971 wage-price freeze, then be killed in 1973.

187. Ackley to the President, "Annual Economic Report," January 19, 1967, EX FG 11-3, 1/16/67–2/4/67, Johnson Library.

188. Ibid.

doned" number. The January 27, 1967, *Washington Post's* bold headline was typical: "Administration Gives Up Its 3.2% Wage Guidepost."

Inflation, Taxes, and Alternative Policies

The 3.2% figure had many more friends after we buried it than it had during its lifetime.
—Ackley to LBJ, February 25, 1967

On January 4, 1967, the President met with about a dozen leaders of the U.S. private sector. The CEA prepared a fairly pessimistic "Briefing Paper on Economic Policy in 1967" for LBJ's use. (In a covering note, Califano advised LBJ not to have Schultze and Ackley attend the meeting because "it could create a problem" if they "talked about their fears of recession.")

A. *The Budget*

    1. *Here is the picture for FY 1967.*

        • Expanded hostilities in Vietnam, and the fact the January budget was based on an assumed end of hostilities by June 30, 1967, require a roughly $10 billion increase of defense spending in FY 1967, to about $67 billion.

        • Tight money and high interest rates also will add about $4 billion we hadn't counted on (increased lending, smaller asset sales, higher interest on debt).

        • Despite the President's $3 billion cutback, total spending will be around $127 billion.

        • With revenues now estimated at $116 billion, the Administrative deficit will be about $11 billion; on the more meaningful NIA [National Income Accounts] basis, around $5 billion. (In FY 1966 the Administrative deficit was $2.3 billion, and there was a $0.9 billion surplus on NIA.)

    2. *For FY 1968, further spending increases will be necessary.*

        • Defense will rise another $6 billion, to about $73 billion (we plan no supplementals).

        • HUD, HEW, interest, and miscellaneous will add another $4 billion, for a total of about $137 billion.

        • Given a GNP of around $785 billion, revenues would be about $119 billion, leaving an Administrative deficit of about $18 billion, and an NIA deficit of about $7 billion. (This assumes no Social Security program, or one that balances benefits with taxes.)

B. The Economy

1. *Fiscal actions in March and September and monetary tightness have slowed down the advance of production to a sustainable pace since March.*

   • *The drop of $9½ billion in construction since March—all due to tight money—is equivalent to the effects of a $10–12 billion tax increase.*

   • *Inflationary pressures have been reduced. The wholesale price index in November was below July. Consumer prices rose only 0.1% in November.*

2. *More recently, there has been some further general loss of momentum, showing up in*

   —industrial production, nearly flat since August;
   —disappointing retail sales, not confined to autos;
   —manufacturers' new orders and shipments;
   —corporate profits;
   —bank credit.

3. *The loss of momentum is likely to persist into early 1967, as*
   —*the further rise of plant and equipment expenditures will be slow,*
   —*defense spending will be growing less than in 1966, and business purchases for inventory will have to turn down.*

   This last factor will be the most depressing element for the next few months. Some are fearful that it could bring on a recession. While that can't be ruled out, we don't believe it.[189]

One of the primary administration wage-price efforts during this early 1967 malaise was a successful tempering of an increase in the price of gasoline. On February 1 Phillips Petroleum raised the retail price 1 cent a gallon. Some other companies, including Continental and Mobil, followed Phillips' lead. After the usual activity—meetings, calls, telegrams, memorandums on the status of current antitrust actions against the industry, and getting an important company (Humble) to hold back—the increases were partially rescinded. Three things are interesting about this case. First, it was the last hurrah for Harold L. Korda, who gave Ackley some advice on a "wonderful lever" to use on a key company. Second, it demonstrated that the government could get the intelligence required to design a strategy even when taking on a relatively diffuse, atomistic industry. The Bureau of Labor Statistics was mobilized to collect the retail

---

189. Ackley to the President, January 4, 1967, CF BE, Johnson Library.

prices of gasoline prevailing on February 1 and in the third week of February in fifty-three cities. Thus the government had a fairly accurate picture of the nature and scope of the problem, with the first returns coming in hours after the mobilization. In Ackley's words, "it was a remarkable enterprise, *and shows what BLS can do when called on*."[190] Third, politically appointed officials at the Department of the Interior assisted the CEA and the White House staff in exploring and delicately using the levers at the government's disposal. One of these levers was a set of possible changes in oil import regulations. Other officials at Interior were unhappy about this activity. Oil Import Administrator Elmer L. Hoehn wrote at length to his superiors about "the objectives and aspirations of the role of Interior that have guided the great and noble minds and aims of its outstanding Secretaries and leaders since 1849." Hoehn concluded that "it should be the role of Interior to join in advocating the causes and protecting the producers of natural resources as agriculture aids . . . the farmer . . . or commerce . . . the business man. It is the hope of many that Interior will completely shed its recently accepted role of 'price policing.' "[191] Thus if the department was to serve its clientele, someone else (apparently) would have to serve the national interest.

In general, the government ran a very "formal" program of price persuasion during 1967, formal in the sense that it centered on well-planned large meetings with officials from potential problem industries. The meetings were managed by the Commerce Department and Stanford G. Ross. Once the information on a given industry was assembled, Commerce Secretary Trowbridge would invite the industry leaders to Washington. News releases were given to the press before and after the meeting. Each participant would receive a nicely packaged folder complete with facts on his industry and the economy in general. On the agenda would be a plea from Ackley. He would explain the nature of the softening in the economy during the fourth quarter of 1966 and the CEA's evaluation of the relatively weak first half of 1967, and then state that the economy was expected to surge in the second half of 1967 and beyond. This surge would have to be coupled with the greatest restraint on prices and wages if it was to be reasonably noninflationary. Ackley and officials at relevant departments would ask the industry people about their prospects and problems, probing for areas in which the government could help. To avoid

190. Ackley to the President, March 3, 1967, EX BE 5-2, 3/1/67–3/31/67, Johnson Library.
191. February 23, 1967, EX NR 6, Johnson Library.

antitrust problems, price specifics were not discussed.[192] This activity reached a peak in August 1967, when "seminars" were held with the chemical industry, machinery manufacturers, and manufacturers of household appliances. In addition to managing these formal meetings, Ross continued to take on specific problems. Besides his stockpile, procurement, and other activities designed to ease pressure on prices, he was responsible for analyses of particularly troublesome sectors. The HEW-CEA study of medical costs is an illustrative case. In April 1966 John Douglas and James Duesenberry submitted an initial report on this sector. In August 1966 LBJ formally directed HEW Secretary John W. Gardner to produce a "major study of medical costs." The results were presented to the President in February 1967 and became the foundation for the National Conference on Medical Costs in June. No one in the administration was really satisfied, however, that this was the way to "fight inflation." It did not produce enough output suggesting *action* by *specific agencies* to solve *immediate and urgent problems.* The gestation period was incompatible with a "problem today–action today–solution today" approach to affairs.[193]

Since 1967 was a contract year in automobiles, this industry received more than the usual amount of CEA time. The average of major collective bargaining settlements in the first nine months of 1967 was around 5 percent. With cost-of-living adjustment, the UAW got over 6 percent. The CEA made no comment on the settlement but, in fact, was happy it was not even larger. In September, after some governmental pressure, the manufacturers announced relatively small price increases. But, as Ackley pointed out, there was "a hooker in all this." GM's prices, the last announced, were lower than Ford's and Chrysler's, but the third sentence

192. Arthur J. Alexander has analyzed the characteristics associated with government success or failure in forty-six price incidents between October 1965 and June 1967, using information gathered primarily from CEA files, in "The Price Guideposts: Application and Effect" (Ph.D. dissertation, Johns Hopkins University, 1969) and "Prices and the Guideposts: The Effects of Government Persuasion on Individual Prices," *Review of Economics and Statistics,* vol. 53 (February 1971), pp. 67–75. I am grateful to Mr. Alexander for letting me go through three notebooks of materials assembled for his dissertation.

193. On his way back to the United Kingdom from the guidelines conference that George Shultz had convened in Chicago in April 1966, E. H. Phelps Brown jotted down a few thoughts on the conference. There were nine points; the second is relevant here: "The quick pragmatic test—to speak of a policy needing 3 or 4 years to take hold is to condemn it out of hand." (The nine points were enclosed by Phelps Brown in a letter to me, December 14, 1973.)

of its press release indicated that the 1968 model list prices were based on *current* material and payroll costs. Ackley feared an upward price adjustment during the model year.[194] On December 27, 1967, GM's George Russell and James Roche, the new chairman, went to Ackley to report a general increase in prices effective January 1, 1968, the first repricing since 1956. Ackley persuaded GM to wait twenty-four hours before making the announcement.[195] The next day Ackley called Roche and argued in the strongest possible terms against the increase. GM decided to increase prices just "$23 to cover the cost of required shoulder harnesses."[196]

As in 1966, the administration spent a great deal of time searching for alternatives to the guideposts. One of the more interesting fruits of this year's search was an "Outline for an Incomes Policy" drafted by Ackley in June. It was circulated both inside and outside government. Ackley argued that there were four requirements for reviving "some kind of reasonably effective wage-price policy":

1. *That it rely on voluntary cooperation, not legislative controls.*

2. *That it appear as different from the old guideposts as possible, though defensible as an evolutionary improvement of them.*

3. *That it face up more explicitly to the problem of income shares, and particularly to the division between wages and profits.*

4. *That it provide a mechanism for enlisting the participation of business, labor, and others in the process of establishing goals.*[197]

Ackley went on to suggest one proposal satisfying these four criteria; "essentially a form of indicative planning." "Some agency—presumably, but not necessarily, CEA—would draw up a provisional set of integrated and mutually consistent targets for income and price developments for the coming year."[198] Business, labor, "groups representing the public," and perhaps the Joint Economic Committee would review the work. On the basis of these consultations, the targets would be revised and published. At the end of the year, there could be a detailed and formal review

194. Ackley to the President, "General Motors Auto Prices," September 15, 1967, EX BE 4/Auto, 5/6/67–12/25/67, Johnson Library.

195. Ackley to the President, "GM's Christmas Present," December 27, 1967, EX BE 4/Auto, 12/26/67–, Johnson Library. Unfortunately for future GM–White House relations, Ralph Nader apparently saw and publicized this memorandum.

196. White, *The Automobile Industry since 1945*, p. 132.

197. Gardner Ackley, "Outline of an Incomes Policy," June 15, 1967, CEA Microfilm, Roll 70, Johnson Library.

198. Ibid.

of what happened. Ackley pointed out that the plan could have varying degrees of detail. He roughed out one version.

For the year ahead, the plan would project a real GNP consistent with full employment (however defined). It would also project a target for prices, involving the lowest price increase which was deemed realistically achievable, given the initial conditions. This would be expressed in terms of the GNP deflator, and, consistent with it, the movement of the WPI and CPI.

For each major producing sector—non-farm business (possibly subdivided into a few major sectors), farms, general government, and other (households and rest of world)—the real GNP originating would be shown as the product of projected employment, hours, and productivity, and the dollar GNP as the product of the real GNP change and a sectoral deflator. The sectoral detail would be consistent with the projected total GNP, real and dollar, and with the income projections, described below.

Starting from the dollar GNP, capital consumption allowances, indirect business taxes, etc., would be deducted to get projected national income. The composition of this would, in turn, be [disaggregated by both factor and productive sectors]. . . . Given the projected CPI, wages, by sector, could be translated into real wages. All income rates, nominal and real, would also be shown as percentage changes from the previous year.

Basically, these projections would outline a pattern of income developments consistent with the target degree of over-all price stability, and with targets for the distribution of income. These targets would have been extensively discussed with, if not agreed on by, the major parties at interest and representatives of the public. By this fact, they would hopefully have achieved some degree of moral authority.

Whether the plan would be realized would depend (among other things) on the wage and price decisions of labor and business. At the end of the year, there would be a careful review which would permit a judgment as to what went wrong—"who dunnit.". . .

The fundamental element of the incomes plan would be the direct involvement of labor and business—and a confrontation between them—in determining consistent targets for wages and prices. This would take place at a level of aggregation in all cases higher than the individual industry, and thus would not become or replace individual bargaining. It does not anticipate that business and labor would fully agree with the targets; but each group could be led to consider more explicitly the implications of its behavior for the over-all result. *If one sector of business sought higher prices, it could be seen to require either raising the over-all price target, or lowering the price target for another sector. The implications of higher wages in a particular sector on prices would become more evident, etc.*

Success would depend almost entirely on the extent to which a real dialogue could be achieved, and business and labor could be persuaded to participate actively in the discussions leading up to the final plan. It cannot succeed as just another purely Governmental operation.

As with any formal apparatus, there are dangers that it could move toward controls, but no more, I think, than under any scheme that tries to be meaningful.[199]

Ackley's proposal got favorable responses, especially from economists who preferred disaggregated analysis. Clopper Almon of the University of Maryland, for example, was favorably disposed to it, noting that "the Council has a reputation for dealing with prices at only two levels. It writes at the GNP-deflator level but swings into action at the pork-bellies level."[200] The CEA was well aware of this criticism. Walt Rostow, for example, had noted "the lack of a systematic way to organize and present sectoral economic data in a sufficiently disaggregated form to grip key structural problems. The statistical categories we do employ in the analyses are so broad that they lard over rather than illuminate critical structural changes, e.g., 'industry'; 'government expenditures'; 'services'; etc."[201] Nevertheless, the Ackley "incomes policy" proposal was too radical. The administration had to search for a more conservative departure from the guideposts.

During the summer of 1967 there was a great deal of agonizing over whether or not to press Congress for the tax surcharge which had been proposed but not pushed in January. While the economy was soft during the first two quarters of the year, the CEA held back, waiting for the signs of an upturn that would signal the need to push Congress to act. By June all of the President's economic advisers except Wirtz and Ginsburg agreed that the time had come. Finally, on August 3 a detailed request was submitted to Congress. By August 1967 it was clear that the prognosis of a weak first half to be followed by a strong second half had been correct.

199. Ibid.
200. Almon to Ackley, July 13, 1967, CEA Microfilm, Roll 70, Johnson Library.
201. Rostow to CEA, AID, CIA, "Sectoral Economic Analysis in the U.S. Government," May 13, 1965, CEA Microfilm, Roll 39, Johnson Library.

And the price indexes had risen even during the sluggish first half. But Congress was in no hurry to act, even though the price outlook was grim.

We are in bad shape. It was necessary to give up the 3.2% standard, and we now have no real influence at all on wage settlements. If we have no quid pro quo to offer management, we cannot expect even verbal adherence to the voluntary restraint notion, unless we scare them with threats of ad hoc Government pressure or price control.

We have continued to send telegrams, hold meetings, and make speeches about price restraint, but our effectiveness is diminishing. We are doing very little about wage settlements. It is clear that we need a new approach. An occasional confrontation will not be sufficient.[202]

The next day Ackley told Califano that he was "not at all sure that we *want* a renewed or stepped up effort in the wage-price field," but, if so, "the activity must be moved out of the CEA." He suggested appointing a "distinguished private citizen" (first choice, David Ginsburg) as full-time executive chairman of a new Cabinet Committee on Price Stability (CCPS). The President would turn "the problem" over to him and the committee, with the expectation that they would operate "independently and without further direction." "White House staff would be conspicuously absent." The executive chairman would "take the heat away from the President."[203] In October Ackley circulated a proposal for the CCPS plus "Executive Secretary," whom the press would undoubtedly come to call a "price-wage 'Czar.' "[204]

This document became the basic discussion instrument for a "supersecret" task force on wage-price policy and organization. (Ackley had suggested such a group to Califano, who obtained the President's permission.) The chairman of the eight-man group was Robert M. Solow of the Massachusetts Institute of Technology. One of the substantive differences between the October CEA memorandum and the task force's views was that the latter believed the 1968 Economic Report should not include explicit guideposts. The CEA memorandum suggested that to be "realistic" the guidepost must be higher than 3.2 percent, but should be clearly described

202. Duesenberry to Califano, "Price Stabilization Program," August 9, 1967, Papers of Gardner Ackley, Michigan Historical Collections.

203. Ackley to Califano, "Government Organization for Price and Wage Stabilization Efforts," August 10, 1967, Papers of Gardner Ackley, Michigan Historical Collections.

204. CEA draft, October 11, 1967, "The Problem of Price and Wage Stabilization," CEA Microfilm, Roll 70, Johnson Library.

as an interim target, consistent with the 1968 target for prices. Even in late December, the CEA retained this view.

For 1968, we face essentially the same dilemma about guideposts we did last year. If we establish a numerical wage guidepost, it will either have to be so high as to appear merely to be placing a stamp of approval on continuing inflation, or too low to appear realistic given the inflationary forces already built into the economy. In the latter case we would immediately be attacked by the unions, and laughed at by the press and public.

Yet the only alternative to a numerical guidepost has appeared to be the kind of essentially meaningless formulation used last year, which restates the productivity principle for wage increases, but clearly says it is not applicable in 1968. No matter how much rhetoric follows about the need for "restraint" by both labor and business, the conclusion will be that we have abandoned the guidepost policy, not just for a year, but for good.[205]

The argument of the Solow task force was that "there is no point in setting an utterly unrealistic target; and any reasonable number will be too large to serve as an official target of the government."[206] Actually, an explicit guidepost was not included in the 1968 Economic Report, although Ackley fought up to the last to get some tangible guide to responsible behavior in it. On January 23, 1968, Ackley took a disputed passage to the President for a decision. The CEA, Commerce Secretary Trowbridge, and Budget Director Schultze wanted to state that the economy would "make a 'decisive' turn back toward stability only if wage settlements should average about 4½ percent in 1968."[207] Wirtz argued that this would be interpreted by labor as a new numerical guidepost. "It will make labor furious, and maybe even make settlements higher than they otherwise might be."[208] The CEA had to settle for one sentence suggesting settlements be appreciably lower than the 5.5 percent average of 1967.

The Solow task force also endorsed the Ackley executive secretary–CCPS idea, but in modified form. They proposed a permanent wage-price productivity review board ("three very hard-boiled and prestigious men") to be assisted by a small permanent staff. Their concept was "not far dis-

205. Ackley to Califano, "A Possible Approach to the Guidepost Discussion in the 1968 CEA Report," December 21, 1967, CF BE 5-2, Johnson Library.

206. Solow to Wage-Price Task Force, untitled and undated memorandum accompanying a letter from Solow to Ackley, December 4, 1967, CEA Microfilm, Roll 70, Johnson Library.

207. Ackley to the President, "Your 1968 Economic Report," January 23, 1968, SP 2-2/1968, Johnson Library.

208. Ibid.

tant" from the PPI office proposed in the 1967 Joint Economic Committee majority report. (If it achieved nothing else, the task force activity must have deepened and broadened the views of two of its members, John T. Dunlop and George P. Shultz.[209])

As late as December 22 a very mild variant of Ackley's incomes policy was discussed at a cabinet-level policy group. This variant would have had the CEA, in its 1968 report, sketch out two alternative wage-price targets as illustrative cases. Then representatives of business and labor, against a background of public and congressional debate, would negotiate on final targets and agree on how they should be applied in individual wage negotiations and price decisions. By the end of December, it was clear to Ackley that nothing this dramatic would be acceptable. "The suggestions contained herein go only a little way toward meeting Secretary Fowler's need for a tough wage-price policy as part of the balance-of-payments program for 1968. However, I have the impression that you and the other members of the Government with whom we have discussed these problems believe that it will be necessary to settle for something substantially less than Secretary Fowler seems to be hoping for."[210]

"Secretary Fowler's need" to which Ackley referred was not a minor point. During 1966 and 1967 there had been little change in total international monetary reserves, while world trade continued to grow by around 7 percent a year. The Johnson administration recognized the need for reform of the existing international monetary system. Nearly continuous International Monetary Fund and Organisation for Economic Cooperation and Development negotiations led to the main result announced in September 1967 at Rio de Janeiro—the principle of special drawing rights to be issued by the IMF. But the problems continued. In late 1967 the international financial picture was a multifaceted disaster. (And not even this set of problems could budge the 10 percent tax sur-

209. At an early November meeting with the CEA, John Dunlop argued that the short-run prospects were grim because the Johnson administration had "been derelict in dealing with the inflation problem." Dunlop concentrated on long-run solutions, including statutory controls: "There are going to be times over the next 3 or 4 decades when wages and prices are going to be moving up suddenly. The standby ability to freeze prices and wages for perhaps 6 months could be a very useful tool in our arsenal." John F. Burton, Jr., "Notes from November 4, 1967, Meeting of Outside Task Force on Wage-Price Guidelines," sent to the task force members on November 9, 1967, Papers of John F. Burton, Jr. I am grateful to Professor Burton for sending me materials from his CEA staff days.

210. Ackley to Califano, "Wage-Price Policy," December 28, 1967, CEA Microfilm, Roll 64, Johnson Library.

charge out of Wilbur Mills's committee.) The fourth quarter U.S. payments deficit (annual rate—liquidity basis) was $7 billion. A major decrease in the usual surplus from sale of goods and services was coupled with an increase in net capital outflows. On November 8 Britain devalued by 14 percent, and on November 22 France made public its withdrawal from the eight-nation gold pool formed early in the Kennedy administration to support the 35:1 dollar price of an ounce of gold. Devaluation by the United States was anticipated since its gold stock was $13 billion, of which all but $3 billion was needed to cover Federal Reserve notes, and about $29 billion in short-term dollar claims were held by foreigners. But by late November, the international financial community became convinced that the remaining seven gold-pool participants would support 35:1. The Johnson administration provided reassurance of the integrity of 35:1 by getting Congress to eliminate the 25 percent gold cover against Federal Reserve notes. But on March 15, 1968, the British closed the London "gold pool" (the institution used to maintain 35:1). That weekend in Washington an agreement establishing a two-tier system was reached: major central banks agreed to buy and sell gold only to each other; the price of nonmonetary gold was to be established by supply and demand. But the need for dramatic revisions in the international monetary mechanism put together during and after World War II would continue beyond 1968.

"Fowler's need for a tough wage-price policy" was not filled. Wage-price policy in 1968 would be based on a relatively weak CCPS. On February 15, 1968, the new CEA chairman, Arthur M. Okun,[211] reported a suggested organizational arrangement for the CCPS to Califano. The "key slot of Executive Secretary" would be filled by someone familiar "with the agencies and relevant programs." The ideal person would be an economist "with this knowledge and the competence to direct research."[212] Thus the CCPS would only be half the mechanism many thought necessary to do the job. There would not be a "czar" or any "hardboiled and prestigious men."

---

211. On February 5, 1968, a reception was held honoring two departing officials. LBJ was in excellent form: "As all of you know, Gardner Ackley is headed for Rome, where he will be my Ambassador to Italy. Charlie Schultze is headed for Brookings, where he will be my Ambassador to Kermit Gordon. In other words, one of them is going off to an embassy, and the other one is going off to an institution." President Johnson, from a transcription of a tape made during the farewell reception, EX FG 11-3, 3/11/68–4/11/68, Johnson Library.

212. Okun to Califano, "Launching the Cabinet Committee on Price Stability," February 15, 1968, Office Files of Joseph A. Califano, Jr., Economy, Box 8, "Wage-Price Guideposts."

The Cabinet Committee on Price Stability

All of the graphs in this report point upward.
                  —LBJ in presenting the Economic Report, February 1, 1968

It is not surprising that little progress was made on economic policy matters in early 1968. The President's mind was on Southeast Asia. The *Pueblo* incident, the siege of Khe Sanh, and the Tet offensive were only major public episodes in a winter of torment for the President and his advisers on military and geopolitical affairs. Also, on March 12 Eugene McCarthy polled 42 percent of the Democratic vote in the New Hampshire presidential primary; and on March 16 Robert F. Kennedy announced his own candidacy in the Senate Caucus Room. The winter culminated in the President's political resignation on March 31.

A substantial portion of the President's March 31 speech was a plea to Congress to act on taxes. The administration's 10 percent surcharge was still bottled up in the Congress. Wilbur Mills's committee wanted the tax increase to be matched by expenditure cuts, but the latter were handled by another committee, Appropriations. The impasse would not be resolved until early spring, when the surcharge, coupled with $6 billion in expenditure reductions, was tacked on in the Senate to an innocuous administration-supported bill (extending some soon-to-expire excise taxes and speeding up corporate and personal tax collections) already approved by the House. This procedure was considered by some to be unconstitutional ("all bills for raising revenue shall originate in the house of representatives"). But it was not protested by Chairman Mills, who was rumored to have had his hand in it as a way out of the impasse. On June 28, 1968, ten months after the administration had sent a tax message to Congress and twenty-nine months after Ackley's "gloomy report" advising a tax increase, LBJ signed the Revenue and Expenditure Control Act of 1968.

The Cabinet Committee on Price Stability got off to a slow start. On February 23 the President formally announced the CCPS's existence; it would include the secretaries of the treasury, commerce, and labor, and the budget director. The fifth member, CEA Chairman Okun, was to coordinate the CCPS as well as recruit and supervise its professional staff. In mid-April the President announced the appointment of Willard F. Mueller, who had been chief economist at the Federal Trade Commission, as CCPS executive director. Four senior economists, a legal counsel, and a supporting staff were hired. During the spring, the CCPS staff and outside consultants were busily engaged in doing or commissioning studies of particularly difficult problems: medical care prices, problems of regulated industries, and construction. Also, work was being contemplated in other areas, such as food prices and government procurement practices. Although the President's instructions were that CCPS not "become involved in *specific* current wage or price matters," Okun asked for and got LBJ's permission to approach his CCPS colleagues about issuing a statement blasting construction settlements, which were averaging 7.5 percent in the first quarter, with all industries averaging about 6 percent. Okun wanted to release the blast to influence a specific settlement that might become a pattern setter: the Detroit-Toledo building trades unions were demanding "a fantastic" 30 percent a year.[213] The only other wage-price activity during this period before passage of the surcharge was an unsuccessful attempt in April by Okun to talk copper producers out of raising prices, a month after a long and bitter copper strike had been settled. During this same period the CEA had to sit back and watch a short telephone strike end with a high settlement.

Ben Gilmer, President of AT&T, called me this morning right after the labor settlement had been reached. He wants you to know that
—the company did all it could to achieve a responsible settlement, but
—militants within the union forced Joe Beirne to take a hard line, and
—there will not be a "general campaign" to raise telephone rates despite the added labor costs.

The 3-year settlement is about 6½% a year, according to information supplied by the parties. This is a disturbing step-up from the first-quarter average union settlement of 5.8%.[214]

There is evidence that LBJ was engaged in one of his periodic searches for information and advice about moving in the direction of mandatory controls. In December 1967 Ackley wrote that he was "severely troubled by the President's recent tendency to refer publicly to the possibility of wage-price controls." Such comments *themselves* caused inflation.[215] Stanford G. Ross explored the Truman experience, as his predecessor Robson had done. Califano talked with Attorney General Ramsey Clark

213. Okun to the President, "Proposed Statement on Construction Costs," April 29, 1968, EX LA 8, 1/1/68–, Johnson Library.

214. Okun to the President, "Notes on the Price-Wage Front," May 2, 1968, EX BE 5-2, 12/19/67–6/30/68, Johnson Library.

215. Ackley to Califano, "Discussion of Wage-Price Controls," December 9, 1967, CEA Microfilm, Roll 69, Johnson Library.

to get his opinion. The administration's view was that, if the President chose to move in this direction, controls would be put in the *Federal Register* and enforced, using the basic powers of the presidency. Simultaneously, Congress would be asked to approve them.[216] In May 1968 Okun conceded that "controls are *surprisingly popular*," but argued, along the lines of the Gordon memorandum sent to LBJ over two years earlier, that they carried heavy economic costs.[217]

In mid-July Okun gave Califano an overview of the situation.

During the period of delay on the tax bill, there was a lull in our efforts to get business and labor cooperation on wage-price restraint. While the Government was the main source of inflation, it was hard to ask business and labor to stem the tide. My statement criticizing the copper price hike and settlement and the Cabinet Committee's plea for responsible settlements in construction are the sum total of our public efforts so far this year. Our record of activity here is considerably below any other period of the Kennedy-Johnson era.

Now that the surcharge is law, the basic question is whether we should resume a more concerted and visible effort. In point of fact, matters are back in the lap of private decision-makers. The President has indicated his attitude by emphasizing the need for private restraint in his signing statement on the tax bill and his comments at the swearing-in of [new CEA member] Warren Smith. Unless we follow through these general statements with specific requests for restraint, we will be backing away from the past policy of activity. And we do not have a good economic rationale for inactivity.

Rather, economic conditions indicate this is the time for an energetic price-wage stance. Surely, the most serious challenge to over-all economic policy in the year ahead is to show that we can get back on the road to price stability without sacrificing high employment and prosperity. If we can't pass this test, there will be increasing demands for a very tight fiscal and monetary policy to keep the economy sluggish and to stop inflation with higher unemployment and idle capacity. If anyone wants to argue that we can afford to relax on inflation, I'd be glad to debate that case on its merits.[218]

---

216. Califano to the President, February 1, 1968, CF BE 5-2, Johnson Library.
217. Okun to the President, "Price and Wage Controls," May 20, 1968, CF BE 5-2, Johnson Library.
218. Okun to Califano, "The Future of Wage-Price Policy," July 15, 1968, Wages, Prices, and Guideposts, 1968–69, Papers of Arthur M. Okun.

Okun got agreement from Califano and his CCPS colleagues to carry out a set of "constructive efforts." On April 25 CEA staffer John Burton had proposed "that the Council send a letter to all unions and companies involved in important negotiations. The guidepost principle would be briefly stated and the national interest in a responsible settlement would be emphasized."[219] Okun took the idea to Califano and to the CCPS. It was decided that the CCPS would issue what the staff called a "Pre-Sin Sermonette" and mail copies to the presidents of *all* major unions and companies. The President's approval was obtained in mid-July and the CCPS released the statement on July 21. It was given wide and thorough coverage in the general and commercial press.

Before the 1968 presidential election, the CEA made several successful attempts at jawboning, although its efforts were hampered by the fact that it often shouldered the burden alone; the constituency-bound departments and agencies remained constituency bound. The CEA had a successful "moral suasion" round with home heating oil, getting Humble to rescind a price increase. A month after a 6 percent labor wage-and-benefit package had been negotiated in July, the steel industry went through a price fight with the government, which was remarkably similar to the late 1965–early 1966 case. Bethlehem raised the price on a major line, the administration reacted (even going back to the White House Central Files for a script), U.S. Steel then undercut Bethlehem's increase by half, Bethlehem cut back, and everyone was satisfied. In 1968 the negotiations with the automobile industry went well. Chrysler led off with a price increase, which was blasted by the CCPS. General Motors and then Ford announced very moderate increases and Chrysler adjusted.

These 1968 price-fighting battles were now rather routine, although in each one the right set of levers had to be found. In the case of the steel industry, the Defense Department was "able to indicate quickly that we intended to shift orders from those companies which had increased prices to those which had not, and that we would persuade our major contractors to take similar action." The case of automobiles could be handled by Defense even though the General Services Administration took care of the department's orders for passenger automobiles, the product at issue. Defense had over $1 billion in contracts with the automobile industry (one typical item: $86 million with GM for 105 mm shells). "The threat

219. Burton to Okun, "A Proposed System to Take the Guideposts to the Natives," April 25, 1968, Cabinet Committee on Price Stability, Papers of Arthur M. Okun.

of a shift might be a coercing factor." Also, new contracts were constantly coming up which were of "special interest to the industry." ("One is for procurement of 13,200 5-ton trucks at an estimated cost of about $345 million. Both General Motors and Ford are competing with Kaiser who is the present producer.")[220]

After the election, the administration wound down its activities. The CEA's only mandatory duty at any time was to produce the January Economic Report and it settled down to this task. On December 6 the LMAC reaffirmed its 1966 endorsement of the guidepost philosophy and then fell on its collective sword. In January 1969 some of the CCPS staff studies were published. In its final report to the President, the CCPS recommended wage and price guideposts for 1969: "new *union settlements should average a little less than* 5% (halfway back from this year's 6½% to the productivity trend of 3.2%)" and "business should *absorb cost increases of* 1% of unit costs without passing these on in higher prices, and should aim at profit margin targets no higher than the 1967–68 average."[221] Two principal aspects of the report have been summarized by CCPS Executive Director Mueller.

First, the CCPS proposed a comprehensive attack on the unemployment-inflation problem. In addition to monetary-fiscal policies and guidepost policies, a number of complementary micro policies were proposed including manpower policies, vigorous antitrust enforcement, freer trade, government actions, reform of regulatory agencies, and special efforts to reduce the inflationary bias of the construction and medical care industries.

Also . . . from the outset [the section on guidepost policy] was the most controversial part of the report. In the many meetings with labor representatives it seemed clear to some of us that price and wage guideposts, alone, would not be sufficient. Before the final report was submitted to the President, the CCPS were faced with three separate versions of the guidepost section: (1) a Labor Department version, (2) a Commerce Department version, and (3) a CCPS staff version, which I believe also essentially reflected the views of CEA Chairman Okun and Budget Director

220. Glenn V. Gibson (Department of Defense) to Clark Clifford to Califano, September 17, 1968, Office Files of Joseph A. Califano, Jr., Economy, Johnson Library.

221. Okun to the President, "Attached Report of Your Cabinet Committee on Price Stability," December 18, 1968, Memoranda for the President, 1968–69, Papers of Arthur M. Okun.

Charles Zwick, and later of Secretary of Treasury Fowler. The Labor version provided for no wage and price guidelines, rather, it would have relied on extensive labor-management dialogue on the issue. The Commerce version provided for a weak form of price and wage guidelines. The CCPS staff version called for wage, price, and profit guidelines. After a somewhat heated debate among the Cabinet members, with Labor Secretary Wirtz objecting most vigorously, Secretary Fowler broke the deadlock by implying that if the Secretaries of Commerce and Labor felt constrained in accepting this position because they felt a special obligation to their constituencies, it would perhaps be in the public interest if they submitted dissenting statements. Secretary of Commerce C. R. Smith said "hell no," he didn't object to a profit guideline. The deadlock was broken and the Committee unanimously agreed in principle to a profit guideline. Secretary Smith said, "just come up with the right number." (The preceding is from notes of the meeting.)[222]

As Mueller mentioned in his first point, the CCPS had proposed (and actually became involved in executing) a good many proposals relating to *micro*economic aspects of inflation. One example of this was LBJ's memorandum of November 13, 1968 (which would probably "have taken the form of an Executive Order had President Johnson not been a lame duck"[223]), proposing that government procurement policies be designed to reduce seasonal variation in construction activity and employment.

But, of course, the Nixon administration was under no obligation to pay attention to any of these policies. One of the costs of the 1968 election was the dismantling of a potentially effective inflation-fighting apparatus, the CEA-CCPS-LMAC triad. This apparatus had finally broken through many of the problems that had kept the Johnson administration from realizing its potential in this area. It is interesting, though out of place here, to speculate about what a Humphrey administration could have done with this apparatus.[224]

222. Willard F. Mueller to the author, October 18, 1974.
223. Ibid.
224. Robert E. Smith, one of the senior staff members of the CCPS, offers some clues: "I had reason to believe at the time that if Humphrey had been elected, we may well have moved in this direction: we talked about establishing industry desks— one for each of the fifteen or so inflation-prone industries. These people would be charged with knowing what was going on and whom to contact. There was also concern that the tripartite meetings be resumed. There was talk of the need for an 'incomes crunch' (a freeze) to supplement a monetary crunch; the function of the former was to break inflationary expectations and give time for macro policies to take hold." Letter to the author, February 19, 1974.

Concluding Reflections

I think that . . . one of the most significant issues for our times . . . is that
of peacetime inflation; its causes and cure.
              —Gardner Ackley, in Relationship of Prices to Economic
                        Stability and Growth, Hearings (1958), p. 394.

In a speech in Chicago on April 20, 1967, Gardner Ackley noted that
voluntary programs, such as the guideposts, will work if the government
is simply providing the leadership "to coalesce the latent agreement" on
what needs to be done. Heller, Ackley, and Okun, together with their
colleagues at the CEA, took the lead in trying to provide that leadership
during the Johnson administration. (The economists had come a long
way from World War II, when Congress passed a law prohibiting persons
from holding policymaking positions in the Office of Price Administration if they lacked experience in business or industry.) On the wage
side, the Johnson administration showed that the public interest could be
injected into contract negotiations. Mediators from even the federal government might be willing to give "the lion's share to the lion," but other
portions of the federal apparatus could try to curb the lions' appetites or
to convince them that big bites were bad for them and for the zoo in
general. On the price side, the effectiveness of many of the interventions
emphasizes both the sensitivity of big business to the political system and
the lack of precision inherent in the cost-markup pricing schemes used by
many firms. That lack of precision *can* be exploited to the public's advantage. It is arguable that it *should* be exploited to compensate for the
fact that people are so much better organized as producers than as consumers. Another benefit of the guideposts was educational, especially the
repeated denial of the idea that payment of "productivity-guidepost"
wages would eliminate increments in profits. Some variant of the following simple example was used: assume that an initial total output of 1,000
is divided between 800 wages and 200 profit. As a result of a 3 percent increase in productivity, output goes to 1,030. A 3 percent increase in wages
(a guidepost increase) would result in a wage increase of 24, with 6 left
over for profits to grow from 200 to 206; that is, to grow by 3 percent as
well. Organized labor should be grateful to the guidepost advocates for
doing so much missionary work in selling this arithmetic to employers
who had argued, "If we pay the 'whole' productivity rate of increase to our
workers, what's left for us?"

But the process of providing this leadership is not costless. Criticism of the guidepost policy—that is, estimates or reminders of its costs—takes many forms. First, there is the unavoidable fact of life that some people are perverse and will do exactly the opposite of what they are advised to do. Ackley made this point, using a homely example, about wages, but his point is equally applicable to prices: "Public preachments about wage restraint by Bill [Wirtz] or me or the President have exactly the opposite effect from that which we intend. It is like telling children not to put beans up their noses."[225] Quite often this perversity may have been due to the failure of the government, back in the Kennedy administration when the guideposts first became public policy, to involve leaders of Congress, labor, and business, as well as public opinion, in the development of the policy. By the time Kennedy was assassinated, they *were* policy. The Johnson administration periodically tried to get endorsements of the policy, but these efforts were rather futile. Once the guideposts were unilaterally promulgated by (a portion of) the executive branch, it was very difficult to enlist others in planning and implementing strategies for their use.

It seems to me undeniable that any successful stabilization system— whether described as "compulsory" or "voluntary"—demands the consent or at least the tolerance of those whose wages and prices are to be stabilized. For this consent to be forthcoming, those regulated—and the general public as well—must see the system as one that is basically fair and equitable, or, at least, that embodies sacrifices by "our side" roughly equivalent to those imposed on the "other side." Moreover, members of each group must believe that the restrictions its members accept on their freedom to do as they please will achieve something important—that slowing the rise in prices is a highly desirable objective, and that this system will be effective in achieving it.

In my view, this consent can only be secured through an active participation by the major groups in society—and particularly by the organizations of labor and business—in the process of recognizing the problem to which the policy is addressed, in planning the strategy to be used, and in formulating the basic standards.[226]

These "basic standards," such as the CEA's 3.2 percent, may "contain an element of arbitrariness, just as a fifty-mile speed limit is arbitrary in

225. Ackley to Califano, "Wage Restraint in 1967," February 28, 1967, Office Files of John E. Robson and Stanford G. Ross, Box 10, "LMAC," Johnson Library.

226. Gardner Ackley, "An Incomes Policy for the 1970's," *Review of Economics and Statistics*, vol. 54 (August 1972), pp. 220–21.

the sense that it is not demonstrably superior to forty-nine or fifty-one."[227] The key is to get society to agree that the standards, although containing "an element of arbitrariness," should be used as guides to responsible behavior.

Second, there are the "legal" arguments. Discarding hopes about altruism and virtue being their own rewards, Johnsonian wage-price policy *did* put the burden on the socially cooperative. It also put the burden on the vulnerable.

Moral suasion is inequitable in that it rewards noncompliance; it constitutes extra-legal coercion by government without judicial review; it is in violation of the "rule of law"; where promises, implicit or explicit, are involved, it entails the danger of an overly familiar relationship between regulator and regulatee; its ad hoc character adds an additional and unnecessary element of uncertainty to business decisions; and it may frequently be used in lieu of (i.e., as an excuse for not implementing) more effective legislation.[228]

The guideposts *were* rules of men rather than rules of law. Milton Friedman has pointed out one of the dangers: "If legal powers granted for other purposes can today be used for the 'good' purpose of holding down prices, tomorrow they can be used for other purposes that will seem equally 'good' to the men in power—such as simply keeping themselves in power."[229] The government's use of stockpiles and government contracts to influence business behavior were in some ways similar to the unusually aggressive use of federal income tax statutes to prosecute people society is convinced are guilty of other crimes (perhaps covered only by state or local statutes) but who, for one reason or another, cannot be convicted in "normal" ways. Justice (or the public interest) may be served, but not the law. Some argue that this sort of moral suasion need not be feared because its effectiveness diminishes with use. But the automobile industry is an important case where just the reverse happened. The point is that the power is there; and it is going to be used. Institutions need to be devised to ensure that it will always be used in the public interest.

Third, there are the critics who take their text from Adam Smith: "I have never known much good done by those who affected to trade for the

227. Okun, *Political Economy of Prosperity*, p. 105.
228. J. T. Romans, "Moral Suasion as an Instrument of Economic Policy," *American Economic Review*, vol. 56 (December 1966), p. 1221.
229. George P. Shultz and Robert Z. Aliber, eds., *Guidelines, Informal Controls, and the Market Place: Policy Choices in a Full Employment Economy* (University of Chicago Press, 1966), p. 38.

public good." But few could have really believed the guideposts to be the Trojan horse for socialism. And of course, by the 1960s it had become even more difficult to separate public and private interests. Eighteenth and nineteenth century liberalism may have been a daily guide to behavior for some of the players in the guidepost drama, but few would fail to recognize that in a world of business council briefings at Hot Springs and LMAC dinners and stockpiles and government contracts, discussions based on separable "public and private sectors" must be rather abstract.

Fourth, the CEA's methods were also a bit out of step with the growing orientation toward "public access," "open meetings," and "participatory democracy"—a juncture where liberals of all centuries have found common cause. Ralph Nader's argument is illustrative.

As you know, General Motors has been reviewing prices in strict secrecy with the Council of Economic Advisers since 1964. I objected to this practice in a letter of January 10, 1968 to Mr. Ackley. Such a government policy, contrary to its usual justification, does not, in my judgment, maximize the government's leverage in combating inflation nor does it serve the public by keeping it in the dark about the issues, the facts and what its government did or did not do. The latter consequence prevents any evaluation of the government's role by its citizenry, misleads the public by not disclosing the reason for government inaction (the reason being that some modus vivendi was arrived at in secret and what appears publicly to be inaction was action of a sort totally immunized from critical public scrutiny) and is not in the direction of furthering a maturer democratic participation.[230]

Fifth, the officials and technicians involved with the wage-price effort could have been doing other things. Energy could have been redirected to the many "tabled" proposals, such as the Heller-Pechman concept of revenue sharing,[231] which could have been sold to the President and the country. But it is not clear that any specific thing was *not* done because staff was engaged in fighting inflation. The small number of people involved worked very long days. Indeed, one important characteristic of the Johnson program was how much was done with so little machinery.[232] But this was achievable in part because of the extraordinary energy of the

230. Nader to Okun, August 12, 1968, Papers of Arthur M. Okun.

231. See prepared statement of Walter W. Heller and Joseph A. Pechman, "Questions and Answers on Revenue Sharing," in *Revenue Sharing and Its Alternatives: What Future for Fiscal Federalism*, Hearings before the Subcommittee on Fiscal Policy of the Joint Economic Committee, 90 Cong. 1 sess. (1967), pp. 111–17.

232. Former Kennedy-Johnson CEA members are fond of pointing out some

President (as well as his economists and operational lieutenants). (The uncharitable view might be that wage-price policy worked better than fiscal policy during the Johnson administration because LBJ excelled at bullying, not biting bullets.) Otto Eckstein, who served on the CEA during a period of high activity (September 1964 through January 1966), has observed that LBJ's energy was a sine qua non for the policy to be effective but was, perhaps, "an unreasonable expenditure."

I would not recommend that such policies become a permanent part of the American economy. The wear and tear created on the President is considerable, only a President Johnson could undertake it, and even for him it meant an unreasonable expenditure of political goodwill and time. Furthermore, the political opposition does mount gradually, and the Congress would bring any such program to an end after a couple of years. In the longer run we will have to devise institutions that can deal with these matters in a more orderly and routine fashion. We will have to also continue to weigh genuine structural reform vis-à-vis the direct price and wage intervention.[233]

The point Eckstein makes at the end of the above paragraph is a final problem with the guideposts. Were the Kennedy-Johnson guideposts treating symptoms and not the disease? This point surfaces continually within the CEA staff. For example, Edwin S. Mills noted that "the only hope for enforcing the wage-price guideposts in the long-run is to bring about a structure of industry in which competition will enforce them automatically."[234] Perhaps if the United States did gulp enough antitrust medicine, the guideposts, extending Mills's argument, would not only be automatic but unnecessary.

A little before the 1968 election, CEA Chairman Okun discussed one aspect of the Johnson legacy: "The Johnson Administration has scored a tremendous victory in showing that prosperity can be the normal state of affairs in the American economy. We leave behind, however, the unsolved riddle of coupling that prosperity with price stability. This will be the biggest over-all economic challenge facing the next Administration."[235] And it was.

---

variant of Walter Heller's observation that the CEA's annual budget is midway between that of the Battle Monuments and Indian Claims Commissions.

233. Letter to the author, December 12, 1973.

234. Mills to Okun, "Anti-Trust," October 30, 1964, CEA Microfilm, Roll 1, Johnson Library.

235. Okun to Califano, "Ideas for Programs," September 20, 1968, Memoranda for White House Staff, 1968–69, Papers of Arthur M. Okun.

V

The First Nixon Administration: Prelude to Controls

NEIL DE MARCHI

RICHARD M. NIXON took office in January 1969 committed to controlling inflation but with the avowed intention of doing so without recourse to guidelines or formal wage and price controls. On August 15, 1971, the President announced a temporary freeze on all wages, prices, and rents, initiating, as it turned out, a series of modified programs of control that extended through April 1974—that is, for just a little longer than his administration had held out against such a policy. The turnaround was remarkable, not only in its apparent completeness, but also because it was sudden, largely unexpected, and marked the very first peacetime use of mandatory wage and price restraints in the nation's history.

This chapter provides an account of that change. In one important respect, of course, the announcement of August 15 did not signal a change. The President and those of his economic advisers who had initially rejected controls remained convinced that they are ineffective except for short periods and are for other reasons undesirable. In another sense, the program of compulsory controls might be regarded as having merely formalized and generalized isolated elements of an incomes policy that the administration had long since appropriated into its arsenal of anti-inflationary devices. Did controls, then, represent the logical next

Note. I acknowledge the generous cooperation of several members of the Nixon administration. I am grateful to Arthur F. Burns, Sidney L. Jones, Marvin H. Kosters, Maurice Mann, Paul W. McCracken, George P. Shultz, Herbert Stein, Paul A. Volcker, Charls E. Walker, and Murray L. Weidenbaum for allowing me to interview them. In addition, I received helpful communications from Roger M. Blough, William H. Branson, Robert L. Joss, William McChesney Martin, Jr., and Louis P. Neeb. Detailed criticisms of the draft by Herbert Stein, Marvin Kosters, and Arnold R. Weber were invaluable, though the final essay perhaps is not the one they would have had me write. Finally, acknowledgment is made to the administrative officer of the Council of Economic Advisers and the librarians of the U.S. Treasury and the Office of Management and Budget for helping me gain access to certain materials, and to Donald Reneau and Clifford Goalstone, who at various times assisted with research.

step in a sequential response to evolving economic circumstances? If not, if in principle other options were still open and controls are to be regarded as in some sense having been thrust upon an unwilling administration, what precise set of pressures produced this result? The task here is to try to find answers to these and related questions.

The reader should be aware that the following account of the events from January 1969 to August 1971 is circumscribed in several ways. First, it had to be written for the most part without access to official records; it therefore does not trace in fine detail the inner decision-making processes of government. Primary reliance on public materials may have resulted also in an account that is misleading in at least two ways: the administration may have intervened in specific wage and price decisions more often than the public record shows; and speeches by administration officials, from which frequent quotation is made here, normally reflect presidential policy and thus tend to understate the degree of uncertainty or internal disagreement that may have existed on a particular policy issue. Second, the focus is on the views of administration economists, to the relative neglect of congressional and general public or professional economic opinion or the views of major constituencies such as organized labor and business. Third, the contribution of decisions and policies to the overall goal of stabilization is only casually assessed. The emphasis is on how ideas and events and the way they were perceived by policymakers shaped the government's strategy for containing inflation, with particular reference to wage-price policy.

The Problem of Inflation

The new administration lost no time in declaring that inflation was the prime problem confronting its economic policymakers in 1969. Paul McCracken, chairman of the Council of Economic Advisers (CEA), presented the common view of the President's economic advisers when he spoke of inflation as "the major current threat to orderly progress of the economy along [the] path of reasonably full employment and vigorous growth and sustained improvement in levels of living."[1] There was gen-

1. "A Policy for Orderly Economic Growth," speech delivered to the Economic Club of New York, March 5, 1969 (Council of Economic Advisers). Similar assessments were made by Herbert Stein, CEA member, in "Economic Policy in 1969," speech delivered to the Executive Seminar on Banking, University of Rochester, April 29, 1969 (Council of Economic Advisers); and by David M. Kennedy, the new

eral agreement also on the origins of the inflationary pressure. The proximate cause was thought to be the rapid increase in federal defense spending in 1966–68, which, together with domestic spending on the programs of the Great Society, had led to increasing budget deficits (unified budget basis) from 1966 through 1968. In addition, Mr. Nixon's advisers felt that stabilization policy had been pursued in the three years after 1965 in such a way that its net effect had been to exacerbate the inflation. Thus, even after cognizance had been taken of the inflation problem, President Johnson for a time balked at calling for a tax increase; and once it was requested Congress delayed passage of the tax surcharge. These actions or inactions, combined with an overestimate of the probable impact of the surcharge and a mistaken though dominant impression that tight credit markets signified monetary restraint, lulled the monetary authorities into doing little to curb the substantial growth of the money supply between mid-1967 and the end of 1968.[2]

---

secretary of the treasury, White House press release, "Statement by Secretary Kennedy in Introducing the Treasury Under Secretaries," January 22, 1969.

It is not always possible to supply the repository for memorandums, press releases, and some of the speeches cited in this chapter. Most of the speeches are on file in the libraries of the various departments or agencies, but in all cases only the sponsoring body is cited here (in parentheses at the end of the citation). This also applies to press releases, which are not consistently filed, and to memorandums and interdepartmental communications.

2. Typical statements can be found in "Statement of Paul W. McCracken," in *Compendium on Monetary Policy Guidelines and Federal Reserve Structure, Pursuant to H.R. 111*, Printed for the Use of the Subcommittee on Domestic Finance of the House Committee on Banking and Currency, 90 Cong. 2 sess. (1968), pp. 472–74, and McCracken, "The Management of Economic Policy," speech delivered to the American Enterprise Institute for Public Policy Research, Washington, D.C., February 20, 1969 (Council of Economic Advisers). Useful accounts of the fiscal and monetary history of the Johnson era are Charles E. McLure, Jr., *Fiscal Failure: Lessons of the Sixties* (American Enterprise Institute, 1972), especially pp. 29–35, and Phillip Cagan, *Recent Monetary Policy and the Inflation from 1965 to August 1971* (American Enterprise Institute, 1971), especially pp. 8–10. Both McLure and Cagan served as senior staff economists at the CEA during 1969. Arthur Burns, presidential adviser through 1969 and from January 1970 chairman of the Board of Governors of the Federal Reserve System, was inclined to see the origins of the inflation in the expansionary policies of the early 1960s, "before Vietnam was of any financial or economic consequence." See "The Perils of Inflation," address given at the Town Hall, Los Angeles, California, April 23, 1968, reprinted in Burns, *The Business Cycle in a Changing World* (Columbia University Press for the National Bureau of Economic Research, 1969), pp. 286–302; also Burns, "Inflation: The Fundamental Challenge to Stabilization Policies," speech delivered to the Seventeenth Annual Monetary Conference of the American Bankers Association, Hot Springs, Virginia, May 18, 1970 (Federal Reserve System).

This three-year experience left two impressions on the minds of Nixon's advisers, both representing departures from the thinking of the early 1960s. First, it seemed that for economic and political reasons fiscal fine tuning could not be relied upon. The government would not necessarily accept the prescriptions of modern fiscal policy, and Congress might not pass the enabling legislation when it was called for. Moreover, the stabilizing effects of fiscal measures, while not zero, were "probably slower and smaller than commonly assumed and probably also difficult to predict." Second, the experience appeared to confirm that monetary policy is more important than allowed by the New Frontier economists. This was not to say that its effects could be forecast very precisely, but at least the chances of erroneous responses by the monetary authorities, with their attendant destabilizing consequences, could be much reduced, provided fiscal intentions were stated clearly, sharp changes in fiscal policy eschewed, and, where the aim was to curb inflation, budget deficits avoided.[3]

Aside from these impressions, the clear lesson, to Nixon economists, was that they were heirs to a classic excess-demand inflation.

Winnowing Out Unacceptable Policies

The administration had available to it, and the Cabinet Committee on Economic Policy considered, a broad array of weapons to combat inflation, including tax policy, expenditure policy, money and credit policy, debt management policy, incomes policy (ranging from formal guidelines to presidential jawboning to some form of public review board to monitor or admonish),[4] and various policies to strengthen the competitiveness of

3. Herbert Stein expressed both views more openly than anyone else, but strong traces are to be found also in the public statements of Paul McCracken. See Stein, "Economic Policy in 1969," and "The Rehabilitation of Fiscal Policy," speech at the annual conference of the National Association of Mutual Savings Banks, Minneapolis, May 26, 1969 (Council of Economic Advisers); and Paul W. McCracken, "The Game Plan for Economic Policy," American Statistical Association, *Proceedings of the Business and Economic Statistics Section* (1969), pp. 294–98. While holding monetary policy to be very significant, McCracken felt that all too little was known about the relative importance of the money supply, bank credit, and interest rates; see statement of Paul W. McCracken in *The 1969 Economic Report of the President*, Hearings before the Joint Economic Committee, 91 Cong. 1 sess. (1969), pt. 2, p. 293. See also p. 294: "frequent adjustments of policy to correct dimly foreseen future departures from the desired path of the economy are on balance likely to be more unstabilizing than stabilizing."

4. Controls were not considered a serious option in early 1969.

labor and commodity markets. Of these available alternatives those generically termed incomes policies (broadly, wage and price setting) were the ones most readily dismissed, though it should be stressed that throughout 1969 the CEA sent memorandums to the President covering incomes policy in all its forms (including, in one option paper, controls).[5] While the arguments presented in the CCEP's discussion are not known, the positions taken by its leading members may be inferred from their public statements and writings.

President Nixon early and repeatedly stated his opposition to direct wage and price controls as being contrary to the free market principle and self-defeating in the long run. "Rationing, black markets, regimentation— that is the wrong road for America." He rejected jawboning and guidelines just as forcefully, arguing in part that if inflation were attributable chiefly to excessive federal spending it would be hypocritical and ineffective to ask business and labor leaders to urge abstinence on their constituents before the government had put an end to budget deficits and to increases in the money supply beyond the nation's physical productive capacity. Moreover, as the President made clear at his first news conference, it is unrealistic to expect labor, management, and industry to set "what is in the best interest of the nation" above "the interests of the organizations that they represent."[6]

The President's adviser on domestic affairs, Arthur F. Burns, had voiced in 1964 his considered view that guideposts for wages and prices,

5. Interviews, Herbert Stein, November 21, 1973, and Paul W. McCracken, December 29, 1973, and comments by Stein at the Conference on the Development of Wage-Price Policy in the United States, Boston University, November 1–2, 1974. There was a mutual dislike of such policies, but it was standard practice for this President to ask his advisers for a range of options, while for its part the CEA, as Stein recalls, "felt obliged . . . to give [incomes] policy as fair a run for its money as we could and not allow our own predispositions and prejudices to limit his ability to choose this kind of thing if he wanted to" (transcript of Boston Conference on Wage-Price Policy, vol. 2, p. 2-100). The options were thoroughly explored by the CEA, and the Council even commissioned a historical and comparative study of British and European experience with incomes policies. This study, carried out by Lloyd Ulman and Robert J. Flanagan, was subsequently published as *Wage Restraint: A Study of Incomes Policies in Western Europe* (University of California Press, 1971).

6. See *New York Times*, December 29, 1968, recalling a Nixon campaign statement; President's news conferences, January 27, 1960, and September 26, 1969; President's message requesting extension of the 10 percent surtax, March 26, 1969, and radio address on inflation, October 17, 1969, all in *Nixon: The First Year of His Presidency* (Congressional Quarterly, Inc., 1970), pp. 3A–4A, 27A, 43A–44A, 118A. Fear of "bureaucratic domination" was a prominent factor in the President's rejection of controls, a fear ostensibly rooted in his own experience in the Office of Price Administration during the Second World War.

if faithfully observed, would tend to "throttle the forces of competition" and the results would be little different from those in an economy where wages and prices are directly fixed by government. With a steady upward trend in productivity, a wage guidepost legitimating wage increases no greater than rises in output per man-hour would mean in practice that wages would rise every year, "regardless of the stage of the business cycle or the level of unemployment or the state of the balance of payments." In other words, macrostabilization policy would be hamstrung. Moreover, wages might increase by the average amount without regard to the circumstances of a particular employer or the condition of supply and demand for specific types of labor. On the price side, a guidepost, by fixing the ratio of prices to unit costs, would stifle an appropriate price response to different increases in demand and would impose a squeeze on profits whenever other costs rose more than unit labor costs. In short, the allocative function of the market would be weakened. Burns warned too that in practice, if observance were less than wholehearted, an administration with its prestige to maintain would have every inducement to move in the direction of outright wage and price fixing. His own preference was for "prudent control of the money supply and . . . [policies] for maintaining and enhancing the forces of competition."[7]

A similar stance was taken by Secretary of Labor George P. Shultz. Referring to the use of guideposts during the 1960s in testimony before the Joint Economic Committee, Shultz argued that (1) they had not been very effective while in force; (2) they may well have strengthened the forces of inflation in the long run by diverting attention away from the fundamental weapons of monetary and fiscal policy and manpower policy; (3) they may have contributed to more labor unrest and to higher wage settlements after their demise than would otherwise have occurred; (4) they are contrary to the spirit of competition and subvert the forces of the market; and (5) when combined with jawboning they are possibly in defiance of the nation's antitrust law.[8]

Paul McCracken shared the misgivings of Burns and Shultz about guideposts. Applied effectively, he argued, they would, through their em-

7. "Wages and Prices by Formula," Murray Lecture at the State University of Iowa, November 10, 1964, reprinted in Burns, *The Business Cycle in a Changing World*, pp. 232–53.

8. *The 1969 Economic Report of the President*, Hearings, pt. 2, pp. 457–58. For early hints of Shultz's strong preference for the unimpeded functioning of market forces, see *New York Times*, December 14 and 31, 1968.

bodiment of the cost-plus principle, stifle the forces of competition in individual markets, artificially prolonging the lives of decaying industries and slowing responses in sectors where demand was increasing. Moreover, they would tend to impart an inflationary bias since "price increases when needed may involve some abrasive moments, [and] there would [therefore] be considerable incentive to resist any price declines." On a practical level, McCracken was sensitive to the difficulties of applying an average figure in a manner appropriate to individual wage and price decisions. But most important, he felt, was that a review of domestic and foreign experience failed to yield convincing evidence that guidelines were very effective—indeed, at home they seemed to have been most effective when least needed and vice versa. In his initial testimony as chairman of the CEA before the Joint Economic Committee, McCracken argued that the government could, however, legitimately and directly concern itself with price stability where its own activities affected labor and commodity markets, international trade policy, antitrust enforcement, government procurement, the application of minimum wage laws, and the regulation of wage rates and prices. This was to become an important theme in McCracken's pronouncements as the President's economic spokesman.[9]

Not surprisingly, the new administration came out in favor of monetary and fiscal weapons to fight inflation, and also emphasized actions designed to strengthen the effectiveness of competition in commodity and labor markets. Incomes policy was rejected but not because it was judged incapable of preventing or moderating specific wage and price increases. In general, it was agreed, it would do that—for a time. It was rejected because it failed to pass two other tests. First, does it help to make markets work better? Second, does it treat causes or merely symptoms, or, as Herbert Stein put it at a later date, "Will it raise false expectations, will it be possible to terminate it without an explosion of some kind?"[10]

9. Statement of Paul W. McCracken, "Price-Cost Behavior and Employment Act Objectives," in *Twentieth Anniversary of the Employment Act of 1946: An Economic Symposium*, Hearing before the Joint Economic Committee, 89 Cong. 2 sess. (1966), pp. 67–76; statement of McCracken in *The 1969 Economic Report of the President*, Hearings, pt. 2, pp. 291–92, 310–11, 315–16; interview with *New York Times* staff members, written up by Eileen Shanahan, *New York Times*, January 24, 1969; and "A Policy for Orderly Economic Growth."

10. Interview, George P. Shultz, March 18, 1974; Herbert Stein, speech at the Business Economists' Conference, Chicago, April 26, 1971 (Council of Economic Advisers).

Gradualism

This general preference for a noninterventionist approach to controlling inflation was translated into a specific program that became known as gradualism. The gradualist game plan, as envisaged by the CEA, was to approach a noninflationary growth path from above, avoiding as far as possible a cutback in employment.[11] No one in the administration wanted to deflate aggregate demand so hard or so sharply as to produce a serious recession. Not only would this have been socially undesirable, but it assumed—falsely, in the view of the CEA—that the government could engineer the exact depth and duration of a recession. Lags were part of the problem here. They, and the experience of 1965–68, made it seem likely that a harsh dose of monetary and fiscal restraint, applied until the economy showed signs of weakening, would (because of lags) produce a more serious slowdown than intended and, in its turn, pressure for inappropriately expansive policies. As McCracken summarized the lesson:

Tight money in 1966 did not produce a 1966 recession, but it did give us a recessionette in 1967. The overly expansive fiscal and monetary policies of 1967 came to fruition in 1968. Because of lags the management of economic policy will itself induce instability if we push hard on the accelerator until we reach the desired speed—or if we keep pushing harder on the brakes until the economy actually begins to slow down.[12]

Nor did the CEA believe it was an economically or socially viable option merely to maintain the position prevailing at the end of 1968, with unemployment at its lowest (under 3.5 percent) since the Korean War and the consumer price index up by a striking 4.7 percent since December 1967. Here the problem was expectations, or built-in inflationary psychology. Both McCracken and Stein were inclined to view the Phillips trade-off as unstable. The rationale underlying this view is that, while it may be possible to reduce unemployment temporarily by increasing ag-

11. Stein, "The Transition in Economic Policy," speech delivered to the Manufacturing Chemists' Association, Washington, D.C., April 8, 1969 (Council of Economic Advisers).

12. "The New Strategy of Economic Policy," speech delivered at Heidelberg College, Tiffin, Ohio, April 28, 1969 (Council of Economic Advisers). Also, speech given at the third annual meeting of the Canadian Economics Association, York University, Toronto, June 5, 1969 (Council of Economic Advisers); and Stein, "The Transition in Economic Policy" and "Economic Policy in 1969."

gregate demand, the higher rate of inflation engendered thereby will sooner or later become anticipated; and when decisions about wage claims, saving, and spending are all made on the assumption that the current rate of inflation will continue, still more expansive monetary and fiscal policy will be necessary just to maintain unemployment at the level previously reached. In other words, the short-run Phillips curve tends to drift upward, making the long-run curve steeper than its short-run counter-part.[13] Along these lines Stein maintained early in 1969 that

to remain there, where we were at the end of 1968, was probably impossi-ble. Continuation of the rapid rate of inflation would have generated the expectation of more inflation. This would have been especially true if the government had adopted a policy of sustaining the existing rate of infla-tion. To stay where we were was not a real choice. We had either to make a serious and effective effort to get down or to accept the probability of mounting inflation.[14]

The only acceptable path, then, was to deflate, though cautiously, so as to avoid creating any more unemployment than was absolutely necessary to convince people that the government meant business and that they should accordingly revise their inflationary expectations downward. The CEA felt unable to promise *no* increase in unemployment,[15] but faced with a choice between a sharp reduction in employment for a short period and a lesser reduction stretched out over a longer time, it opted for the latter. These alternatives can be readily conceptualized in the differences between the short-run and the long-run Phillips curve, but the CEA's preference for the gradual approach was made on the more pragmatic grounds that "we ought to resist the idea of moving as far and as vigorously

13. Two clear statements of the argument are Milton Friedman, "Comments," in George P. Shultz and Robert Z. Aliber, eds., *Guidelines, Informal Controls, and the Market Place: Policy Choices in a Full Employment Economy* (University of Chicago Press, 1966), pp. 58–61, and David Laidler, "The Phillips Curve, Expecta-tions and Incomes Policy," in H. G. Johnson and A. R. Nobay, eds., *The Current Inflation* (London: Macmillan, 1971), pp. 75–98.

14. "The Transition in Economic Policy." Compare Stein, "Economic Policies of the Nixon Administration," speech given at the University of California, Berkeley, October 9, 1969 (Council of Economic Advisers); and McCracken, "A Policy for Orderly Economic Growth": "One responsibility of those managing . . . [policy] is not to keep validating private decisions which would make sense only if inflation were to continue unabated."

15. The President did promise precisely in a letter to an AFL-CIO executive meeting in Bal Harbour, Florida, late in February. McCracken, who had no previous knowledge of the President's intention, was dismayed.

as the situation at the *moment* might seem to imply, because [recent] history seemed to suggest that that almost certainly would produce oversteering of the economy."[16]

Gradualism was the unanimous choice of the President's advisers, and William McChesney Martin, Jr., chairman of the Board of Governors of the Federal Reserve, concurred with the goal of, as he put it in testimony before the Joint Economic Committee in February 1969, "trying to disinflate without deflating."

In somewhat more precise terms, the strategy was to aim for "moderate, predictable, and stable" budget surpluses in fiscal 1969 and 1970, "tight" money for at least the first half of 1969, with the possibility of asking for an extension of the tax surcharge beyond its expiry date of June 1969 left open. Complementary programs to cushion the impact of the expected slowdown were developed during the year; these included extended coverage and increased benefits for unemployment insurance, a proposal to increase the scope of manpower training programs and to ensure automatic expansion of such programs with a rise in the rate of unemployment, a restructured Office of Economic Opportunity, and a computerized job bank.[17]

Breaking the Inflationary Psychology

Once the policy of gradualism was formulated, the administration faced the further task of getting it publicly accredited. This was crucial, since inflation-mindedness was a major element in the problem. The first part of the task was to convince people that the choice of an indirect and measured approach to a noninflationary growth path reflected a serious intention to deal with inflation. To this end spokesmen for the administration naturally made much of the changes wrought in basic monetary and fiscal policy in the first half of the year: a reduction in the growth of the money supply from 6.5 percent during 1968 to 2.8 percent (annual rate) for the first five months of 1969, and achievement of a budget turn-

16. Interview, Paul W. McCracken, December 29, 1973. For an analytical presentation of the alternative policies, see Laidler, "The Phillips Curve," pp. 83–85.

17. Stein, "Beyond Inflation," speech before the Seventeenth Southern Trust Conference, Chattanooga, May 15, 1969. On the complementary programs see the President's messages on unemployment insurance, July 8, 1969, and on manpower training, August 12, 1969, and his speech on welfare reform, August 8, 1969, in *Nixon: The First Year of His Presidency*, pp. 68A–70A, 78A–79A, 81A–84A.

around from a $25 billion deficit in fiscal 1968 to a $1.3 billion surplus in 1969.[18] And as the months passed, no opportunity was lost to show and declare that this policy would be maintained for as long as was necessary. Thus Treasury Secretary Kennedy expressed concern when in mid-March the Commerce Department–Securities and Exchange Commission quarterly survey of business investment plans showed a prospective rise of 13.9 percent for commerce and industry as a whole; estimates indicated a 30 percent increase in spending for the automobile industry. The administration, Kennedy said, is "absolutely resolved" to maintain a surplus in the budget and "determined" to continue a course of monetary restraint.[19] On March 24 the President sent a letter to all government agencies urging reductions in expenditures for the year ahead. Two days later, the President reversed an election promise by requesting that the tax surcharge be extended. At the same time, he announced new budget cuts for 1970 and postponement of the scheduled reductions in the passenger car and telephone excise taxes. Together these actions were expected to produce "the strong budget surplus urgently needed to meet the inflationary threat" and to prove the "Government's serious intent to counter the upward spiral of prices and wages."[20] Proposed cuts in expenditures for 1970 were outlined more fully in a revised budget statement by the President on April 12, and in the same month he asked for repeal of the 7 percent investment tax credit.

Despite these actions and declarations, many continued to plan or act as if they expected the policies of restraint to produce only a short-lived slow-down; they were convinced that before slowdown deepened into recession the administration would surely revert to monetary and fiscal ease, as had happened in 1967. Consumers, for example, responded to the 1968 tax surcharge by reducing the ratio of their savings to disposable income during the first half of 1969 to its lowest level in five years. By mid-June the bank prime lending rate had climbed to a historic high of over 8 percent, yet demand for credit continued to be strong, with projected

18. For example, Stein, "The Transition in Economic Policy," and McCracken, "Economic Problems and Prospects," speech delivered to the Sixteenth Annual Monetary Conference of the American Bankers Association, Copenhagen, Denmark, June 18, 1969 (Council of Economic Advisers).

19. Press release, Treasury Department, K-34, March 14, 1969; New York Times, March 15, 1969.

20. New York Times, April 3, 1969; "Fiscal Policy," President's message requesting extension of the 10 percent surtax, March 26, 1969, in Weekly Compilation of Presidential Documents, vol. 5 (March 31, 1969), pp. 477–78.

increases in investment in business plant and equipment estimated by private surveys as late as mid-September at 7–9 percent for 1970 (the then-current figure for 1969 showing a 10.5 percent increase.)[21] By September, too, it was apparent that the commercial banking system had sought ways to avoid or delay the impact of the intended monetary squeeze; for instance, by borrowing heavily on the Eurodollar market, selling commercial paper through bank-affiliated holding companies, and selling assets under agreements to repurchase.[22] Finally, as late as November 21, McCracken felt it necessary to warn businessmen specially invited to a briefing in Washington that a McGraw-Hill survey showing an optimistic average expected increase in sales of 6 percent in 1970 (in *real* terms) was unrealistic: "Now this expectation will not be realized. It is simply inconsistent with this year's policies of fiscal and monetary restraint, most of whose effects on the economy . . . are yet to become visible."[23] The President assured the same meeting that "those who bet on inflation will lose their bet."[24]

The skepticism to which administration spokesmen were responding would scarcely have been sustained so long had firmness of anti-inflationary purpose been the only point at issue; though the President's early disavowal of official intervention in private pricing decisions—the "primary responsibility for controlling inflation rests with the national administration"—made the administration's task more difficult by seeming to signal that no blame would be attached to labor and management if they raised wages and prices in their own interest.[25] At least two other factors were

21. Maurice Mann, assistant director of the Bureau of the Budget, "The Road to Stable Growth," speech before the annual joint meeting of Cleveland Business Economists and Cleveland Chapter, American Statistical Association, September 23, 1969 (U.S. Bureau of the Budget); statement and testimony of David M. Kennedy, in *Investigation of Increase in Prime Interest Rate*, Hearings before the House Committee on Banking and Currency, 91 Cong. 1 sess. (1969), pp. 5–73; *New York Times*, September 21, 1969.

22. Mann, "The Road to Stable Growth." According to *The Economic Report of the President Together with the Annual Report of the Council of Economic Advisers, February 1970*, p. 37, approximately $10.2 billion was raised in these ways in the first half of 1969.

23. McCracken, "The Other Side of That Valley," remarks before a briefing for business, Washington, November 21, 1969 (Council of Economic Advisers).

24. *New York Times*, November 22, 1969. Compare the President's letter to 2,200 business and labor leaders of October 18 (*New York Times*, October 19, 1969).

25. This is made much of by Rowland Evans, Jr., and Robert D. Novak, *Nixon in the White House: The Frustration of Power* (Random House, 1971), pp. 185–86, and Leonard Silk, *Nixonomics: How the Dismal Science of Free Enterprise Became the Black Art of Controls* (Praeger, 1972), p. 57.

involved. One was associated with lags. While the prospective time-path of the economy could be traced out in general terms, considerable uncertainty necessarily surrounded the timing of the several anticipated effects of policies. The CEA and other economic advisers explained to the public regularly (1) that a six- to nine-month lag is to be expected before monetary and fiscal restraint undertaken earlier begins to show itself in the statistical indicators; (2) that after a four-year buildup of inflationary pressures the lags on this occasion would no doubt be longer than average; and (3) that events in 1969 at least were unfolding in the correct order, the restrictive policies taking effect first on real output, with the expected slackening in wage and price increases still to come. "The timing," Herbert Stein urged, "is not critical if the economy is moving generally in the desired direction."[26]

A further factor reinforcing inflationary expectations was the order in which the policies of restraint took effect. While clear signs of downturn in indicators such as housing starts, the index of consumer sentiment of the University of Michigan's Survey Research Center, and new orders for durable goods had begun to appear by September, wholesale and consumer prices and negotiated wage increases continued to rise, with the two price indexes and construction wages registering their largest gains, for the year as a whole, since 1951.[27] Pressed by businessmen to initiate

26. "Economic Policy in 1969." On the nature and relevance of lags to the interpretation of economic conditions in 1969, see Maurice Mann, "The Changing Economic Scene," speech before the annual convention of the Council of Savings and Loan Stock Companies, San Francisco, June 14, 1969 (Bureau of the Budget); McCracken, "The New Strategy of Economic Policy," and "Economic Problems and Prospects"; McCracken, "Will Washington's Economic Policy Be Successful?" speech before the Graduate School of Banking, University of Wisconsin, August 18, 1969 (Council of Economic Advisers); and Arthur Burns, testimony in The 1970 Economic Report of the President, Hearings before the Joint Economic Committee, 91 Cong. 2 sess. (1970), pt. 1, pp. 147–48. Burns was of the opinion that "a little uncertainty in the minds of the business and financial community" would have been desirable, since the wider the dispersion of views on the state of the economy, the easier it would be to break the inflationary psychology. He felt that the reiteration of the gradualist nature of the game plan by others in the administration may in itself have caused policies to take effect with a longer than usual lag. See New York Times, May 28, 1969, and Burns, testimony in The 1970 Economic Report of the President, Hearings, pt. 1, p. 161.

27. It is true that the price indexes registered lesser increases in the second half of 1969 than in the first six months of the year, but no declining trend was discernible. Administration perceptions that the policies of restraint were beginning to affect output were expressed by McCracken, "Beyond 1969," speech before the Economic Club of Detroit, September 22, 1969 (Council of Economic Advisers); Mann, "The Road to Stable Growth"; Stein, "The Transition to a Stable Economy," speech

308 NEIL DE MARCHI

some sort of action to curb wage increases, the CEA responded with two arguments to show that the situation was by no means out of hand. In the first place it must be recognized, they said, that a good deal of catch-up was reflected in the negotiated wage increases. This was largely confined to unionized sectors whose relative position had worsened in the preceding three years of inflation.[28] Second, wage increases in general could be viewed as a rational response to the "long-sustained inflationary environment." The economic atmosphere, however, would become increasingly less favorable to similar wage increases in 1970 and beyond, both because labor market tightness would loosen and because employers would be less able to pass on unit cost increases to the final consumer.[29]

It is not clear that the administration's arguments and statements had much effect on inflationary thinking, but as signs of a slowdown became more marked and widespread in the latter half of 1969, fears of a recession supplanted the earlier belief that the gradualist game plan would not work. By August, Milton Friedman, a firm supporter of gradualism, nonetheless felt that monetary "overkill" might result if the Federal Reserve pursued its restrictive policies much longer. This view was shared by two governors of the Fed, Sherman J. Maisel and George W. Mitchell. By December, Friedman was predicting a recession on the same scale as that of 1960–61, and in this prognosis he was supported by prominent business economists.[30]

Edging toward an Incomes Policy

What was not apparent in 1969, though it was to show itself during 1970, was that the strength of the inflation-mindedness and some of the

delivered to the National Association of Business Economists, September 26, 1969 (Council of Economic Advisers).

28. The ratio of median percentage changes in union/nonunion effective wage adjustments in manufacturing varied as follows during the 1960s: 1961–64, +0.7 percent; 1965–69, −0.4 percent. Compiled from data in U.S. Bureau of Labor Statistics, *Current Wage Developments*, vol. 25 (February 1973), p. 46, by Marvin Kosters, Kenneth Fedor, and Albert Eckstein, "Collective Bargaining Settlements and the Wage Structure," *Labor Law Journal*, vol. 24 (August 1973), pp. 517–25.

29. Stein, "Government Policy and the Inflationary Prospect," speech before the American Management Association, New York City, November 11, 1969 (Council of Economic Advisers); Burns, testimony in *The 1970 Economic Report of the President*, Hearings, pt. 1, pp. 139–40, 178–79; *Economic Report of the President*, 1970, pp. 49, 51.

30. *Newsweek*, August 18, 1969, p. 75, and December 22, 1969, p. 75; Sherman J. Maisel, *Managing the Dollar* (Norton, 1973), pp. 245–46.

behavior it evoked was leading several members of the administration to consider whether some supplement to monetary and fiscal policy might not be in order. Four instances may be cited.

The first evidence of this occurred at midyear, when Chairman Martin of the Federal Reserve board circulated "for comment . . . a proposal to establish a 10 per cent marginal reserve requirement for U.S. head offices" of commercial banks on net borrowings from their foreign branches. Martin was in effect asking for voluntary restraint on the part of banks that were borrowing heavily in the Eurodollar market to escape the impact of the reserve requirement on domestic funds. It was clearly implied that a regulation might be imposed.[31] To comply with the proposed requirement, the banks would have had to ration their available funds more strictly, with the probable result that business needs would be satisfied ahead of those of the municipal and mortgage markets, where interest rates were subject to statutory ceilings and where therefore the policy of monetary restraint had caused the greatest disruption and concern. Martin had already expressed his concern at a private dinner in New York on May 21, when he was host to the top bankers and urged upon them "the necessity of being bankers and not just salesmen of credit." He and Treasury Secretary Kennedy subsequently met with representatives of the largest banks. Kennedy explained that the banks chosen were "the ones that were affected most by the commercial paper problem, most by the Eurodollar problem." He and Martin denied that guidelines for credit rationing had been discussed.[32] However, it is likely that one purpose of the meeting was to reach a voluntary accord on bank actions "appropriate" to the administration's anti-inflationary stance. That some jawboning took place is strongly suggested by the attendance of Richard W. McLaren, head of the Antitrust Division of the Justice Department. McLaren not only had a continuing concern about collusive behavior, and may therefore have been brought in to advise on the implications of any gentlemen's agreement reached, but also had been involved in framing legislation designed to ensure that the bank holding company did not

---

31. The proposal was later put into effect. See "Recent Activities of Foreign Branches of U.S. Banks," *Federal Reserve Bulletin*, vol. 58 (October 1972), pp. 855–65; Maisel, *Managing the Dollar*, p. 119.

32. Letter to the author from William McChesney Martin, Jr., August 29, 1974; "Press conference of the Honorable David M. Kennedy, Secretary of Treasury, Accompanied by: Charls E. Walker, Under Secretary of the Treasury; Paul A. Volcker, Under Secretary of the Treasury for Monetary Affairs; William McChesney Martin, Chairman, Board of Governors, Federal Reserve System," transcript of proceedings, July 7, 1969 (Treasury Department).

become a vehicle for impairing competition with respect to "a scarce and essential commodity," especially in times of monetary restraint and in local markets, where "banking alternatives are few."[33] Martin and possibly Kennedy were the first in or at least close to the administration to try moral suasion.[34]

Maurice Mann, assistant director of the Bureau of the Budget, was another who was impressed by the adroitness of the banks in finding nondeposit sources of funds to cushion their operations against the Fed's tight money policy. Although Mann did not begin to express his doubts about the ability of monetary and fiscal policy to stem inflation till the spring of 1970, his close observation of the financial and banking community's behavior throughout the 1960s and especially in 1969 convinced him that these standard weapons would not necessarily be proof against the strong inflationary outlook. For the banks were merely trying to satisfy their customers' demand for credit. The basic problem was "a growth psychosis . . . combined with inflationary expectations." With such a combination "it is little wonder that consumer and business spending are difficult to check."[35]

As early as August 1969 Arthur Burns, "jolted by the excessive wage settlements in construction," began raising the possibility of jawboning or introducing some form of incomes policy in conversations with the President and in cabinet meetings. Burns was concerned that the settlements in construction would have a strong secondary effect on industrial firms, communicated in the first instance through employees with similar skills and spreading by imitation to regular industrial workers.[36] He proposed a series of related moves, including the development and imple-

33. See the President's statement on bank holding companies, March 24, 1970, in *Nixon: The First Year of His Presidency*, p. 44A, and the statement by Richard W. McLaren in *One-Bank Holding Company Legislation of 1970*, Hearings before the Senate Committee on Banking and Currency, 91 Cong. 2 sess. (1970), pt. 1, pp. 268–74, reprinted in *The 1970 Midyear Review of the State of the Economy*, Hearings before the Joint Economic Committee, 91 Cong. 2 sess. (1970), pt. 1, pp. 122–28.

34. Following oil price increases in February 1969 McCracken favored a statement expressing strong disapproval, but he could gain no support within the "troika" (the secretary of the treasury, the director of the Budget Bureau, and the chairman of the CEA) and drew staunch opposition from Burns. Interview, Paul W. McCracken, December 29, 1973.

35. "The Road to Stable Growth," p. 10. Also, "Remarks of Maurice Mann," speech before the Bank Management Conference, Mississippi Bankers' Association, Jackson, February 13, 1970 (Bureau of the Budget).

36. Interview, Arthur F. Burns, March 19, 1974. A similar message was conveyed to the CEA and other government departments at about this time by various in-

mentation of a substantial training program to increase the supply of skilled labor in the construction industry; a cutback in federal spending on construction; the outlawing of contracts calling for exclusive hiring through the trades union hall; and suspension of the Davis-Bacon Act.[37] Labor Secretary Shultz was opposed to the direct intervention implied by the latter two proposals, and Burns won approval for only certain of the items on his list.[38]

On September 4 the President ordered a 75 percent reduction in federally financed new construction projects, established a Cabinet Committee on Construction, and directed the secretaries of the Departments of Labor and Health, Education, and Welfare to develop programs "for manpower training and vocational education in order to achieve a major increase in skilled labor for the construction industry." In addition, the President called on state and local governments to cooperate by voluntarily cutting their own construction contracts, and asked private businesses to restrict their plans for nonresidential construction. This announcement was followed up on September 22 by the establishment of a tripartite Construction Industry Collective Bargaining Commission, whose task was to seek ways of upgrading the skills and the size of the construction work force, reducing the seasonality of activity and employment in the industry, and increasing the participation of national labor organizations and associations of contractors in dispute settlements. The commission was also to intercede in labor disputes when, in its judgment, the terms or application of the agreement seemed likely to be significant.[39]

---

dustrialists, some of whom formed a Construction Users' Anti-inflation Roundtable, headed by Roger M. Blough, former chairman of United States Steel. Interviews, Herbert Stein, November 21, 1973, and Marvin Kosters, February 7, 1974. The roundtable was organized in the summer of 1969 at the urging of some contractors and was made up of a number of major companies that were feeling the effects of rapid increases in construction labor costs. Letter to the author from Roger M. Blough, August 21, 1974. The roundtable's case may be found in *Economic Prospects and Policies*, Hearings before the Joint Economic Committee, 92 Cong. 1 sess. (1971), pt. 2, pp. 337–86.

37. This act requires payment of wages and fringe benefits to workers on federal government projects at rates determined by the secretary of labor to be "prevailing" in the locality in which work is being performed. For a detailed consideration of the act and its economic effects, see John P. Gould, *Davis-Bacon Act: The Economics of Prevailing Wage Laws* (American Enterprise Institute for Public Policy Research, 1971).

38. Interview, Arthur F. Burns, March 19, 1974.

39. *New York Times*, September 5, 1969; Executive Order 11482, September 22, 1969; *Economic Report of the President*, 1970, pp. 42–43. A detailed account of the

One other member of the administration was moved in the direction of a more activist stance by the events of 1969. Secretary of Housing and Urban Development George W. Romney naturally viewed with concern the lack of funds in the mortgage market and the sharp decline in housing starts (down 30 percent between January and August 1969), which was an undesired side effect of the tight money policy. While programs could be, and were, developed to subsidize interest payments and home buying by low-income families, and to support the mortgage market (through the Federal Home Loan Bank and the Federal National Mortgage Association), it was clear to all that housing would continue to suffer as long as policies of general restraint were required to combat inflation. In this sense an end to inflation was, as Romney said, "the absolutely indispensable foundation" for a sound housing sector; but if monetary policy took too long to do the job then housing could only benefit from still more rigorous attention to the expenditure side of the budget or from some form of incomes policy—specifically, some direct actions to cut construction costs.[40] Romney supported Burns's efforts in both these directions.[41]

Containing the Forces of Cost-Push

The year 1970 opened with compelling evidence that the restrictive policies of the preceding year had had their anticipated effect on output. Real growth averaged 3 percent for the year 1969, but was practically zero in the last quarter. In the CEA's view, "the sluggishness of total demand was clearly the main factor" responsible for this slowdown in real growth.[42] Prices were still rising at the end of 1969, though at a slightly reduced rate. Predictably, the policy objectives for 1970, as explained by the CEA, were "to reduce the rise of prices and to revive the growth of output." These twin goals were to be realized by a combination of

maneuvering that preceded the President's announcement of September 4 is given in Evans and Novak, *Nixon in the White House*, pp. 190–92.

40. In a speech before the annual convention of the National Association of Home Builders, Houston, Texas, January 19, 1970, Romney unveiled programs to subsidize the sale of mortgages held by the Government National Mortgage Association to the Federal National Mortgage Association, and to subsidize interest payments. On the same occasion he denounced recent wage settlements in construction as "outrageous" and warned of a "wage-cost-price spiral" affecting housing costs. As reported in *Facts on File*, vol. 30 (January 22–28, 1970), p. 35.

41. Evans and Novak, *Nixon in the White House*, pp. 192, 202–03.

42. *Economic Report of the President*, 1970, p. 29.

"modest" budget surplus and "moderate" monetary restraint, the latter being a rate somewhere between the expansion of 1967–68 and the severe restraint of the last part of 1969. Translated into a projected path for the economy, the objectives and policy position represented an expectation that growth in real output would continue close to zero till about the middle of the year, with price increases about the same in the first quarter as at the close of 1969, but diminishing thereafter. In the second half of 1970 a "moderately more rapid rise of money demand," induced by a revived growth in the money supply, the termination of the tax surcharge, and increased social security benefits, would bring about an increase in real output, though this would be consistent with a continued reduction in the rate of inflation.[43]

In its published report for 1970 the CEA was quite frank about the conditional nature of its predictions. Within the Council, however, there was considerable confidence that the path described would be realized. In large measure this confidence stemmed from the model of the unemployment-price mechanism which its own staff had been estimating. The approach was to start with an agreed "troika" forecast for gross national product and break it down in a provisional way into changes in real GNP and changes in the deflator. A set of two relations was then used to arrive at consistent estimates for real GNP, the rate of inflation, and the rate of unemployment: (1) an Okun's law equation relating unemployment to the gap between provisionally estimated real GNP and potential GNP; (2) a price equation relating changes in the GNP deflator directly to immediate past inflation and inversely to the rate of unemployment in the current quarter and the rate two quarters back.[44]

43. Ibid., pp. 57–60. It was anticipated that the GNP deflator and unemployment would behave as follows during 1970:

	Quarter			
	1	2	3	4
Percentage increase in GNP deflator (annual rate)	4.4	4.1	3.8	3.5
Percent unemployment	4.0	4.3	4.4	4.5

Council of Economic Advisers, memorandum, William H. Branson to T_2 and T_3 (second and third levels of the troika), January 21, 1970.

44. For Okun's law, see Arthur M. Okun, "Potential GNP: Its Measurement and Significance," in American Statistical Association, *Proceedings of the Business and Economic Statistics Section* (1962), pp. 98–104; reprinted in Okun, *The Political Economy of Prosperity* (Brookings Institution, 1970), appendix.

The precise form of the price equation was:

$$\Delta GNPD_t = - .00613 + .618 \Delta GNPD_{t-1} + .0321/u_t + .019/u_{t-2}.$$

See "Inflation Fighters See a Ray of Hope," *Business Week*, April 18, 1970, p. 114. My discussion of the CEA approach draws heavily on this report, and on letters to

Underlying the price equation was the view that changes in aggregate demand directly influence the level of unemployment; changes in the rate of unemployment serve as a proxy for the degree of tightness in labor markets generally, and an increase in tightness (decline in the percentage of the work force unemployed) will cause wages and, given productivity, also unit costs to increase. If these cost increases are passed on, prices will rise. Price increases, furthermore, induce workers and consumers to try to recapture lost real earnings and to hedge against inflation by increasing current spending. Hence current prices tend to change in the same direction as prices in the immediate past. Conversely, restrictive policies will tend to increase unemployment; this should moderate demand and with it wage and price increases; and as the public incorporates the expectation of lower rates of inflation into its behavior, price increases will moderate still further.[45] This was how gradualism was expected to work. The form of the CEA price equation captured two elements prominent in Council thinking throughout 1969: the importance of demand factors (reflected in the dependence of price changes on unemployment) and the importance of expectations (embodied in the dependence of current on past price changes). The Council's confidence in this approach was confirmed by the good performance of the model on 1969 data.[46]

This confidence was not shared by non-CEA staff workers at the third level of the troika (T_3) or by Murray Weidenbaum and Maurice Mann, who, with Herbert Stein, made up T_2. The Treasury economists especially were critical, on technical grounds, of the optimism built into the CEA price equation because of its stress on demand rather than cost factors. With unemployment expected to rise even slightly during 1970 as a result of the previous restrictive policies, a dramatic improvement in inflation was suggested by the equation. Even when it became necessary to revise the first-quarter increase in the GNP deflator from a December 1969 expectation of a 4 percent annual rate of increase to an actual rate of 5.2

me from William H. Branson (senior staff economist at the CEA at the time the 1970 report was prepared), June 3, 1974, and Robert L. Joss (at that time a Treasury staff economist assisting Murray Weidenbaum, assistant secretary for economic policy), May 21, 1974.

45. The CEA model was one among many variants of Phillips-curve approaches to explaining inflation. A useful general survey is Thomas M. Humphrey, "The Economics of Incomes Policies," Federal Reserve Bank of Richmond, *Monthly Review*, vol. 58 (October 1972), pp. 3–11.

46. Stein, "The Transition to a Stable Economy"; and "The View from the Valley," speech to the Downtown Economists Luncheon Group, New York City, April 1, 1970 (Council of Economic Advisers).

percent, the increase in prices for the fourth quarter of 1970 was predicted by the equation to be only 3.4 percent, up a mere 0.1 percent from the December 1969 estimate. The Treasury economists' view was that an equation which "did not learn" should not be the basis for policy.[47]

The troika had abandoned the CEA model as the basis of its forecasting by June 1970, but before this Murray Weidenbaum had sent the first of a series of internal memorandums to his Treasury colleague Paul Volcker, arguing that both price and unemployment figures for the near future were likely to be less satisfactory than the CEA's estimates suggested; that most actions that would reduce unemployment would be inflationary, while most anti-inflationary measures would exacerbate a shortage of liquidity that the business and financial community was already finding serious; that anyway the current inflation was of a cost-push variety and largely immune to fiscal and monetary restraint; hence, the administration should initiate action "in the difficult wage-price area." Weidenbaum suggested a range of possible policies including compulsory wage-price controls, a temporary voluntary freeze, wage-price guideposts promulgated by the executive branch, wage-price objectives developed by a public board of private citizens, and appeals by the President for responsible behavior. He rejected the first as "too coercive and perhaps self-defeating" and the last as "useless" and serving only to expose the administration to ridicule. As for guideposts, "they became discredited, in part because of the demand-pull inflation which we have since successfully fought." By elimination, Weidenbaum was led to embrace a temporary voluntary freeze and a set of wage-price objectives developed by a board of citizens. He did not think of this approach as a panacea, but hoped it might help alter inflationary expectations.[48] Weidenbaum communicated his dissatisfaction with current policy to Treasury Secre-

---

47. The optimistic bias was acknowledged by Frank C. Ripley, senior staff economist at CEA, the person most directly responsible for the price equation. Memorandum, Ripley and Murray Foss to Stein, "The Economic Outlook for FY 1971 and 1972," June 22, 1970: "In the judgmental [Treasury and Office of Management and Budget] approach the current level of the unemployment rate is discounted while the cost-push forces behind the inflation are given more weight." Also memorandum, Ripley to Stein, "Estimates of the Range of Uncertainty About the Price-Unemployment Outlook," November 12, 1970: "The CEA equations are explicitly based on demand forces in the economy. Consequently, they give the slowest inflation rates." Letter to the author from Robert L. Joss, May 21, 1974.

48. "A Revised Economic Policy for 1970," memorandum, Weidenbaum to Volcker, May 15, 1970. This memorandum expressed views that Weidenbaum had first set down in March of that year; interview, Murray L. Weidenbaum, March 7, 1974.

tary Kennedy, and as a third step he pursued more vigorously with a small, hand-picked task force of noncareer Treasury officials various aspects of incomes policy, with a view to developing a really workable alternative.[49]

Weidenbaum did not immediately make his criticisms or proposals public. The first open declaration that gradualism was not enough came from the new chairman of the Federal Reserve, Arthur Burns, who argued, in a speech on April 29, 1970, that "we have moved from demand-pull inflation to a transitional phase in which cost-push adjustments are prevalent." In another speech on May 18 he elaborated on the implications of this change. If the current inflation reflected factors other than the balance between aggregate demand and supply, Burns contended, making monetary and fiscal policies still more restrictive not only would be ineffective but would invite recession. On the other hand, inflationary pressures would almost certainly resurge if the monetary authorities simply expanded the supply of money and credit so as to allow businesses to pass on the unit cost increases that they had accepted or had had imposed on them. Given a determination on the part of the administration *not* to validate the effects of cost increases on prices, however, the longer the inflationary wage settlements and price increases continued, the more would actual GNP fall short of its potential. Under these special circumstances, if this loss to the nation was to be minimized and the economy was to pass as quickly as possible through the transition phase, Burns concluded, "there may be a useful—albeit a very modest—role for an incomes policy to play." Burns was very careful to stress that he did not countenance wage and price controls, that "an incomes policy applied over a long period would be completely impractical," and that cost-push inflation is necessarily self-limiting in a restrictive monetary and fiscal environment.[50] In other words, what he had in mind was a short-term,

49. Interview, Murray L. Weidenbaum, March 7, 1974. The first studies by the Treasury task force date back to the fall of 1969, when Weidenbaum was disenchanted with what he perceived as an undue reliance on monetary policy by the CEA. In this connection, see Weidenbaum, "Is Fiscal Policy Dead?" paper delivered before the annual meeting of the Allied Social Science Associations, 1969, published in *Financial Analysts Journal*, vol. 26 (March–April 1970), pp. 31–32. The task force kept its deliberations quite secret, and apparently its accumulated experience was unknown to others in the administration when a search for those who had studied the issue of incomes policy was undertaken as part of the crash program to formulate and implement a post-freeze policy of controls in the weeks after August 15, 1971.

50. "Federal Reserve Monetary Policy," speech before the seventh meeting of Governors of Central Banks of the American continent, Viña del Mar, Chile, April 29, 1970 (Federal Reserve System), p. 6; and "Inflation: The Fundamental Challenge to Stabilization Policies," pp. 11–14.

strictly supplementary device to help the economy reach more quickly and at a lower cost the price stability that it was bound to achieve anyway.

Burns made no specific proposal in the speeches just outlined. Indeed, the tone of his remarks was less that of one eager to move in the direction of incomes policy than that of one who felt he must warn those in the executive branch that the public's patience was not inexhaustible and that the prudent path might be to consider seriously some supplement to gradualism lest activist sentiment precipitate congressional action more direct and sweeping than was either wise or necessary.

A specific proposal *was* made by George Romney in a speech in New York, also on May 18, in which he urged the formation of a presidential commission to call public attention to excessive wage and price increases.[51] But this modest suggestion was overshadowed and Burns's fears confirmed by the vote of a subcommittee of the House Committee on Government Operations on May 26 approving a bill under which the CEA would be required to establish guidelines.[52]

Pressure for action of this sort had been building up for some time. Since late in the summer of 1969 the Construction Users' Anti-inflation Roundtable had been urging—admittedly as part of a much wider-ranging series of government and voluntary private measures that might be adopted to cut back the rate of wage increases in the construction industry —that the Davis-Bacon Act be suspended. By year's end, past presidential advisers Walter Heller and Arthur Okun were advocating the development of an improved form of guidelines, or "ground rules." And on Wall Street, Robert V. Roosa, former under secretary of the treasury, suggested a six-month moratorium on increases in prices, wages, and dividends.[53] At the Joint Economic Committee hearings on the President's 1970 Economic Report, Democratic Congressman Henry S. Reuss, chairman of the Subcommittee on International Exchange and Payments of the Joint Economic Committee and sponsor of the above-mentioned bill to amend the Employment Act to incorporate a wage-price guidepost, espoused a price freeze as the obvious way to cope with the cost-push after-effect of sustained inflation once monetary and fiscal policies have eliminated ex-

51. George W. Romney, address to the Second Annual Collective Bargaining Forum, New York, May 18, 1970, in *Amending the Employment Act to Provide for Price-Wage Guideposts*, Hearing before a subcommittee of the House Committee on Government Operations, 91 Cong. 2 sess. (1970).

52. A copy of the bill, introduced by Congressman Henry S. Reuss on October 22, 1969, appears in *Amending the Employment Act*, Hearing.

53. Robert D. Hershey, Jr., *New York Times*, November 11, 1969; Leonard S. Silk, ibid., January 11, 1970.

cess demand. And in March 1970 a majority of the Joint Economic Committee called for a "consciously enunciated price and incomes policy" as a standard tool of stabilization policy; at the same time Chairman Wright Patman and Congressmen Reuss and William S. Moorhead specifically proposed a temporary freeze.[54]

Ten days after Burns's May 18 speech, Under Secretary of the Treasury Charls E. Walker said he would welcome the regular publication of "what happens in the wage-price area," because of the educational value of such information.[55] Others in the administration sensed that perhaps the circumstances were appropriate for them to give vent to their dissatisfaction with the gradualist game plan. On June 2, testifying before a subcommittee of the Joint Economic Committee, Murray L. Weidenbaum volunteered the opinion that "the time has come to give some serious consideration to some form of incomes policy." Under persistent questioning, Weidenbaum outlined the range of alternatives that he had already fully developed in internal Treasury memoranda and stated his own preference for something in between direct controls and appeals to responsible behavior.[56] A few days later, Maurice Mann, in a series of speeches, rhetorically asked why prices were behind and unemployment ahead of schedule in this second stage of the game plan and in his answer suggested that the administration's economic policy was perhaps trying to do too much: "we are using only two instruments—fiscal and monetary policy—to accomplish an assortment of objectives that may not necessarily be mutually compatible in the short-run." Mann listed the major objectives as curbing prices, holding down unemployment, reducing long-term interest rates, stimulating housing starts, and reinvigorating corporate profits (and thereby stock prices). Then, alluding to what he regarded as the all-too-mechanistic approach of the CEA, he complained that accomplishing all of these objectives is in practice rather more complex than the solutions to econometric models would suggest. "If we are not successful

54. *The 1970 Economic Report of the President*, Hearings, pt. 1, pp. 26, 114; 1970 *Joint Economic Report*, H. Rept. 91-972, 91 Cong. 2 sess. (1970), pp. 21, 58.
55. NBC's *Today Show*, May 28, 1970. Walker, however, was speaking out in part to forestall any move toward direct controls (interview, Charls E. Walker, February 12, 1974). Compare his earlier assessment of the situation in "Cost-Push Inflation: What It Is and What Not To Do About It," speech before the Conference Board's Financial Conference, New York City, February 27, 1970, reprinted in *The Conference Board Record*, vol. 7 (April 1970), pp. 24–27.
56. *Changing National Priorities*, Hearings before the Subcommittee on Economy in Government of the Joint Economic Committee, 91 Cong. 2 sess. (1970), pt. 1, p. 73.

fairly soon on the price front," Mann concluded, "then we may have to add another tool to our public policy kit." Mann's own choice of a third instrument was some form of jawboning that would enlist the support of business and labor leaders in holding the line against excessive price and wage increases. Like Burns, Mann hoped this might accelerate the transition to more stable prices.[57]

The administration's official response to these various proposals was strongly negative. In his capacity as the President's economic spokesman, Paul McCracken said that the administration was "emphatically" opposed to mandatory wage and price controls—though anything less would be ineffective—and protested that the Council of Economic Advisers did not have the staff to monitor wage and price decisions on a more or less continuous basis.[58] This official reaction was unduly sharp, since no one in the administration had called for anything stronger than a public review board or voluntary guidelines; but behind it was the fear that even a hint that controls were being considered might induce some price increases as businessmen acted to avoid being caught in an unfavorable position if the controls were implemented.[59]

McCracken's personal view was close to Charls Walker's in that both men saw some potential educational value in assembling and making public the facts surrounding large wage and price increases. McCracken did not believe that this would make more than the "marginal contribution" of fielding "the few wild-ball price and wage situations that might occur."[60] What he hoped for instead was that the public would become more aware of the tendency of unit costs and (in a competitive environment) prices to rise by the excess of hourly compensation over the trend in output per man-hour, and that this awareness would have a moderating influence on the trend of wage claims and pricing decisions. More than this—for example, some "kind of voluntary agreement to divide up the national income without inflation"—could not be expected and had been

57. Notes of a speech before the District of Columbia Bankers Association annual convention, Hot Springs, Virginia, June 5, 1970, Papers of Maurice Mann.

58. Report in *Facts on File*, vol. 30 (May 21–27, 1970), p. 363; Evans and Novak, *Nixon in the White House*, p. 205.

59. This was the view that George Shultz, in particular, took of public calls for an incomes policy by those within the administration. Interview, George P. Shultz, March 18, 1974; Evans and Novak, *Nixon in the White House*, p. 205.

60. See McCracken's testimony in *The 1970 Midyear Review of the State of the Economy*, Hearings, pt. 3, pp. 425–26; and McCracken, "Price-Cost Behavior and Employment Act Objectives," p. 73.

found not to work in "large, complex, decentralized societies" like that of the United States.[61] Hence, partly to lend weight to the idea of informed self-interest as an anti-inflation device, and partly because "the come-let-us-get-together approach [characterizing jawboning and presidential appeals] can be a device that builds up a power structure in Government which circumvents the legislative process," McCracken, in collaboration with Richard McLaren, drafted a bill whereby a special trade court would be established to try cases of price or wage increases alleged to be "excessive in relation to market or economic conditions or productivity gains." Arthur Burns liked this idea but rejected it for fear it would give considerable power to those administering the scheme without proper guidelines within which they should work having been specified. Shultz opposed it as an attempt to deploy legal power in a guidelines manner.[62] This, indeed, was the intention; and by implication it acknowledged that the effect of a policy of containing inflation by restrictive monetary and fiscal policy alone might be delayed by particular groups determined to recoup relative or absolute real income losses and incorporate expectations of continued inflation into their wage claims and pricing decisions, even though this may yield only temporary gains or involve some loss of jobs within the group. However, in the face of general opposition to a coupling of guidelines with legal sanctions McCracken kept his peace and made the scheme public as a way of attacking "abuses of economic power" that contribute to inflation only after he had left the administration.[63]

Harmless Concessions to the Advocates of Incomes Policy

In the intensified discussion of economic policy that followed the public statements of Burns, Romney, Weidenbaum, Walker, and Mann in mid-1970, the views of George Shultz, newly appointed director of the Office of Management and Budget, carried considerable weight. It was widely recognized that lagging productivity was one major reason for the

---

61. Testimony, *The 1971 Midyear Review of the Economy*, Hearings before the Joint Economic Committee, 92 Cong. 1 sess. (1971), p. 36.

62. McCracken, "Price-Cost Behavior and Employment Act Objectives," p. 72; and McCracken, "Fighting Inflation After Phase Two," *Fortune*, vol. 85 (June 1972), pp. 84ff. Interviews, Arthur F. Burns, March 19, 1974, and George P. Shultz, March 18, 1974.

63. McCracken, "Fighting Inflation," p. 158.

long delay between the easing of demand pressures in 1969 and the slowing of inflation. As McCracken explained to the Joint Economic Committee in July 1970, "from the fourth quarter of 1968 to the first quarter of 1970, compensation per man-hour in the private non-farm economy rose at the annual rate of 6.4 percent, but productivity actually declined at the annual rate of 0.8 percent, with the result that labor costs per unit of output rose at an annual rate of 7.2 percent." Shultz urged that, rather than embark on a program of wage and price controls or the guidelines that everyone agreed were less objectionable but that were also likely to be less effective, the administration should simply wait for the effects of a recovery in productivity that was already showing itself and for the longer term should take steps to maintain and improve productivity and the efficiency of markets.[64] To explore ways to encourage the growth of productivity Shultz proposed the setting up of a commission modeled on the President's Advisory Committee on Labor-Management Policy, on which he had served as a consultant during the Kennedy administration and composed of able, thoughtful representatives of business, labor, the public, and government. The idea, as a way of achieving "a balance between costs and productivity that will lead to more stable prices," was given first place on a list of three measures announced by the President on June 17. In addition to a National Commission on Productivity, the President established a Regulations and Purchasing Review Board "to determine where Federal purchasing and regulations drive up costs and prices" (the scope of review to include import policy) and announced a system of periodic "inflation alerts," to be prepared by the CEA and designed to "spotlight the significant areas of wage and price increases and objectively analyze their impact on the price level."[65]

McCracken had long advocated giving close attention to import policy and government operations in the search for price stability, and this part of the President's new program reflected his thinking as much as that of Shultz.[66] But there were some, such as Charls Walker, who felt that the

---

64. *The 1970 Midyear Review of the State of the Economy*, Hearings, pt. 3, pp. 391, 401.

65. Interview, George P. Shultz, March 18, 1974; "Economic Policy and Productivity: The President's Address to the Nation, June 17, 1970," in *Weekly Compilation of Presidential Documents*, vol. 6 (June 22, 1970), p. 777. The membership of the Productivity Commission was announced on July 10, and Shultz was subsequently made chairman. On the work of the commission, see *First Annual Report of the National Commission on Productivity* (1972).

66. "Price-Cost Behavior and Employment Act Objectives," pp. 73–74.

idea of getting labor and business and private citizens and government representatives together should have been for the *immediate* purpose of working out mutually acceptable, noninflationary positions on wage and price increases, and he was distressed that, despite a promise that it would "give first priority to the problems we face now," the Productivity Commission's impact, if any, could only be long term.[67]

The program unveiled on June 17 thus gave formal expression to two ways in which Shultz and McCracken felt monetary and fiscal policy might legitimately be supplemented, but this betokened no change in the administration's position from that of January 1969. Indeed, it is probably fair to say that the concessions embodied in the President's June 17 speech were meant only as a sop to those clamoring for a more interventionist stance. The Regulations and Purchasing Review Board, for example, may have had its genesis in the lame duck Committee on Government Activities Affecting Prices and Costs which was established by President Eisenhower in January 1959. The implied authorization of this committee was to interfere with the policies of various government departments and agencies, and it succeeded only in arousing resentment.[68] This experience can scarcely have been lost on then Vice-President Nixon or on Paul McCracken, who was a member of the CEA at the time. Moreover, there was never any doubt that the province of the Productivity Commission was *long-run* trends in productivity, and even Charls Walker, who had hoped for something rather different, was motivated in part by a desire to accommodate activist elements in Congress and avoid a strong move toward mandatory intervention.[69]

So far as the inflation alerts are concerned, there was a sharp distinction drawn between turning the spotlight on significant wage or price increases and actual intervention to secure more moderate behavior in particular industries. While their tone became sharper, the basic purpose of the inflation alerts, of which there were three (August 7 and December 1, 1970, and April 13, 1971), was to inform, not to judge. Those who drafted the alerts sought for the most part to avoid dubbing such specific wage or price changes as were discussed either inflationary or noninflationary. Changes were of course assessed against various benchmarks. Was a wage settlement excessive in relation to increases in industry or national productivity? Was it out of line with the trend of settlements in the same industrial category? Would a wage increase become a target in other ne-

67. Interview, Charls E. Walker, February 12, 1974.
68. See chapter 2 above, pp. 122–23.
69. Interview, Charls E. Walker, February 12, 1974.

gotiations or a price increase have a significant impact on user industries? Would international competitiveness be impaired? Would a wage or price increase, if generalized, be compatible with the goal of long-run price and cost stability? But only in isolated instances were these bases of comparison used as grounds for indictment, since that was thought both unnecessary and inappropriate: unnecessary because, as it was expressed in the second alert, "the economic system imposes its own sanctions on costs that are clearly out of line with general trends"; inappropriate since, as CEA member Hendrik Houthakker argued in another context, "the function of prices is to equate supply and demand, and in some circumstances this may conceivably require large price changes. Few things are more harmful to a free economy than the mistaken notion that price behavior in particular markets can be judged against some average standard."[70] The only cases in which corrective action by the administration was deemed in order were those in which it seemed likely that "monopoly" power had been used to secure wage or price increases in excess of what the free operation of competitive forces would imply.

The inflation alerts were superb educational documents. They elucidated in clear and simple terms the relations between costs, productivity, and prices; they contained comprehensive reviews of recent sectoral price trends; and they concluded with useful capsule assessments of the impact of selected wage and price increases. However, it was not made clear just how a better-educated public was supposed to influence the rate of inflation. Presumably it was expected that there were enough citizens who would place national and long-run considerations above their immediate personal interests to constitute an effective restraining force. Such a group, sufficiently well informed and aided by the media, might perhaps shame individual businesses or labor unions into backing down on excessive price increases or wage claims. Or by exercising their power as consumers such citizens might perhaps quicken the disciplinary forces of the market. In releasing the first alert, McCracken would say only that if it was successful in raising the "level of visibility and understanding and awareness of these complex developments in the price-cost area," then "in the inscrutable way that these do, they can start to have some impact on public policy."[71]

---

70. "Second Inflation Alert," A Report by the Council of Economic Advisers (December 1, 1970; processed), p. 27 (compare p. 2); Hendrik S. Houthakker, "Copper: The Anatomy of a Malfunctioning Market," speech at Duke University, March 11, 1970 (Council of Economic Advisers).

71. Quoted in Silk, *Nixonomics*, p. 54.

Incomes Policy with a Market Orientation

Once the in-house revolt in favor of incomes policy had been contained, attention turned again to what the CEA recalled in its 1971 report as having been "the primary goal of anti-inflation policy in 1970"—namely, limiting the decline in output resulting from the earlier restrictive measures and ensuring that output would begin to rise again in the second half of the year.[72] In view of successively lower monthly price increases and some evidence of a decelerating rate of increase in average private compensation per man-hour (from 7.7 percent in the fourth quarter of 1969 to 7.6 percent in the second quarter of 1970), plus an expectation that, with more than 90 percent of the labor force *not* involved in major wage negotiations in 1970, settlements would respond positively to the lower inflationary trend, Paul McCracken concluded in August 1970 that "the basis for a more stable cost level in the economy is . . . beginning to take shape." While unemployment remained unexpectedly high, McCracken argued that the economy overall had suffered the mildest of all the postwar recessions except for the brief slowdown in 1967. And while the anticipated budget surplus for fiscal 1970 had turned into a deficit, when revenues were recalculated on a full employment basis to reflect the below-capacity operation of the economy, the position was again reversed.[73] By October, with signs of a recovery emerging, McCracken felt that the economy was moving into a new phase, marked by "stronger gains in output, larger increases in productivity, a slower rise in the price level and in labor costs per unit of output, and further gains against inflation . . . a phase where we more nearly have the best of both worlds."[74]

72. *Economic Report of the President Together with the Annual Report of the Council of Economic Advisers, February 1971*, p. 23.

73. In December 1969 unemployment was expected to be 4.3 percent in the second quarter of 1970 and 4.4 percent in the third quarter. The actual rates were 4.7 percent and 5.2 percent. McCracken's assessment is in "Will Washington's Economic Policy Be Successful?—One Year Later," speech before the Graduate School of Banking, University of Wisconsin, Madison, Wisconsin, August 17, 1970 (Council of Economic Advisers). The principle of balancing the budget at full employment had been publicly espoused by the President in a statement, "Congressional Action and Government Spending," issued on July 18 (*Weekly Compilation of Presidential Documents*, vol. 6, July 20, 1970), but had a long prior history and was used by the CEA in its 1970 report as the standard when discussing long-run fiscal policy. Council of Economic Advisers, memorandum, Herbert Stein to James W. Knowles, "The Full-Employment Surplus," March 2, 1970.

74. "The Management of Resumed Expansion," speech before the Economic Club of Detroit, October 19, 1970 (Council of Economic Advisers).

This sanguine prognostication was ill-fated. A three-month strike against General Motors from mid-September contributed to real output's being lower in the final quarter than in the third. Prices and wages also rebounded in the final quarter of 1970, so that by year's end the consumer price index stood 5.5 percent above its level at the end of 1969 (although it had increased 6.1 percent from January 1969 to January 1970) and the mean level of major wage and benefit packages negotiated had risen by 8.9 percent, averaged over the life of contracts (7.6 percent in 1969). Unemployment stood at 6.0 percent, 1.5 percent above the fourth-quarter level expected at the beginning of the year. As in 1969, the problem was most marked in the construction industry, where an average first-year wage and benefit increase of 19.6 percent was recorded (13.6 in 1969), with wage and benefit increases averaged over the life of agreements running at 15.6 percent. At the same time, unemployment in the industry had risen from 6.8 percent in the third quarter of 1969 to 12.3 percent in the same quarter of 1970. The combination of inflation and unemployment in the construction industry was vexatious, but more baffling was the fact that the economy as a whole seemed to be behaving in this paradoxical way. As the CEA conceded in its 1971 report:

Sophisticated econometric analysis of the relation between the behavior of prices and a large number of variables that might help to explain it—such as the level and rates of change of unemployment, the gap between actual and potential output, past prices, and the like—did not generally predict the rate of inflation experienced in 1970, given the actual conditions in 1970.[75]

The unexpected developments in late 1970 produced renewed calls for a more direct assault on excessive price, and especially wage, increases. In mid-August, Congress passed the Economic Stabilization Act of 1970 (an amendment to the Defense Production Act of 1950), granting the President authority to freeze wages, salaries, prices, and rents. The move stemmed in part from a desire of Democrats to embarrass the President.[76] Nixon promptly repeated the opposition he had often expressed to con-

75. *Economic Report of the President, 1971*, p. 60. Data on wages are from Bureau of Labor Statistics, *Current Wage Developments* (July 1971), pp. 43, 44; other data are from *Economic Report of the President*, various issues.

76. *National Journal*, vol. 3 (October 2, 1971), pp. 2018–19, reporting a comment made by Senator William Proxmire on William F. Buckley's program, *Firing Line*, September 22, 1971. For the substance and circumstances surrounding the passing of the Economic Stabilization Act of 1970 (Public Law 91-379), see Harry B. Yoshpe and others, *Stemming Inflation: The Office of Emergency Preparedness and the 90-Day Freeze* (Government Printing Office, 1972), pp. 14ff.

trols and declared that the new authority was entirely unwelcome. However, this did nothing to stem the tide of public sentiment in favor of stronger measures. The conservative Business Council in October sent a message of censure to the White House for the administration's failure to check excessive wage and price increases.[77] On November 23 the Committee for Economic Development issued a policy statement identifying the causes of the current inflationary problem as cost-push forces and long-term structural factors not amenable to control by aggregate demand policies. The CED recommended measures to improve market efficiency and productivity, but also a three-man prices and incomes board, which would promulgate "broad norms of appropriate noninflationary wage and price behavior that would give some guidance to business and labor groups which may be affected by Inflation Alerts." The statement acknowledged that academic opinion was divided on whether demand restraint alone could produce both price stability and full employment, but the CED declared that "inflation is too serious a problem to permit us the luxury of ignoring potential weapons for curbing it that are at our disposal."[78] Also on November 23 fifty-eight Democratic members of the House called on the President to work out long-term guideposts and to stand ready to wield the weapon of a freeze.

The President responded in a speech before the National Association of Manufacturers on December 4 in which he reaffirmed the administration's belief in the efficacy of its approach to price stability with full employment via monetary and fiscal policy, with supplementary attention to making sure that markets operated under the discipline of competition. In line with this sort of supplementary action, he announced a liberalization of oil imports and a decision to assume from the states the authority to restrict oil imports and gas production from federal offshore leases, as measures to keep down the cost of fuel. These actions were triggered by November increases in the posted price of crude oil and of gasoline at wholesale, at a time when petroleum inventories stood above their usual seasonal level. Government investigation revealed that in certain states allowable crude oil production was cut or kept well below capacity to prevent normal market forces from undermining the new higher prices.

77. Arnold R. Weber, *In Pursuit of Price Stability: The Wage-Price Freeze of 1971* (Brookings Institution, 1973), p. 6.
78. Research and Policy Committee of the Committee for Economic Development, *Further Weapons Against Inflation: Measures to Supplement General Fiscal and Monetary Policies* (CED, 1970), pp. 24, 14.

Further, and perhaps more significant since it was his first use of jaw-boning, the President warned that, unless labor and management in the construction industry could find ways to improve collective bargaining and to keep settlements in the industry closer to the national average, the government would intervene directly in wage negotiations on federally funded construction projects.[79]

Within the administration the only further encouragement to adopt an incomes policy came from Arthur Burns. In a famous speech at Pepperdine College on December 7, he reiterated his long-standing concern about "pressures on costs arising from excessive wage increases" and declared that in his view it would be desirable to supplement monetary and fiscal weapons with an incomes policy, "in the hope of thus shortening the period between suppression of excess demand and the restoration of reasonable relations of wages, productivity, and prices."[80] This speech could be viewed as a challenge to the President, perhaps even a veiled threat to make the monetary expansion essential to recovery conditional upon the executive's acceptance of an incomes policy. There was a certain amount of tension between the President and the chairman of the Federal Reserve at this time, the President being desirous of a more substantial growth in the monetary supply than Burns felt could safely be undertaken, and Burns convinced of the need for some special policy weapon to get at the forces of cost-push, particularly in construction. Burns had in fact raised again in prior conversations with the President the possibility of suspending the Davis-Bacon Act, and this was to have formed part of the President's speech until Shultz intervened with the persuasive objection that the action would unnecessarily antagonize the hard-hat unions.[81] In view of the potential grounds for dissension, however, what is really striking about the two speeches is their congruence. Burns made no mention of guidelines, and in recommending "a high-level Price and Wage Review Board" was careful to specify that it should have no powers of enforcement. Burns envisaged this board's adopting a case-by-case approach. Case law may be codified, but while it was conceivable that a set

79. Speech at the annual meeting of the National Association of Manufacturers, New York City, December 4, 1970, in *Weekly Compilation of Presidential Documents*, vol. 6 (December 7, 1970), pp. 1623–29; "Second Inflation Alert," pp. 32–34.

80. "The Basis for Lasting Prosperity," address in the Pepperdine College Great Issues Series, Los Angeles, December 7, 1970 (Federal Reserve System), pp. 20–21.

81. Interview, Arthur F. Burns, March 19, 1974; Evans and Novak, *Nixon in the White House*, pp. 370–71.

of guidelines would emerge from the process of handling individual cases, to lay down rigid guidelines in advance was unacceptable to Burns. Indeed, the defining characteristic of incomes policies, as he portrayed them, was that "they are market-oriented . . . their aim is to change the structure and functioning of commodity and labor markets in ways that reduce upward pressures on costs and prices." Accordingly, Burns was able to commend the President's actions to restrain fuel cost increases and his insistence that the structure of collective bargaining in the construction industry be so modified as to yield less inflationary settlements. Burns also offered a list of other possible actions, along the lines of the recommendations he had made to the President in the fall of 1969.[82] With Burns's diagnosis of the problem essentially unchanged, his Pepperdine College speech serves as a benchmark for gauging how far the President had changed *his* position.

No substantive change was discernible in early December 1970. The President reiterated his aversion to controls. What is more, his threat to intervene in the construction industry collective bargaining process could be rationalized as an attempt to equalize bargaining strength, the advantage in which clearly lay with the unions. His attitude toward guidelines, too, remained one of staunch opposition. Only on the value of exhortation was there a perceptible shift. Whereas early in 1969, when "Government was the major culprit in contributing to inflation," it would have been inappropriate to appeal for "responsible" behavior on the part of others, "now that Government has done its part in holding down the budget, in a restrictive monetary policy . . . it is time for labor and management to quit betting on inflation and to start help fighting inflation."[83]

A series of actions taken in the first three months of 1971 show that the President was prepared to be more forceful should his December appeal for restraint be ignored. These, however, fell far short of—indeed, were never intended to be—a general wage-price policy. The guiding principle remained: intervene as little as possible, and then only to strengthen competitive forces.

The administration soon found itself locked in conflict with a major

82. "The Basis for Lasting Prosperity," pp. 23, 21.
83. "The President's News Conference of December 10, 1970," in *Weekly Compilation of Presidential Documents*, vol. 6 (December 14, 1970), p. 1654; and speech at the annual meeting of the National Association of Manufacturers, December 4, 1970. This shifting of responsibility is first discernible in the President's television and radio address of June 17, 1970.

industry, steel. On January 11 Bethlehem Steel Corporation announced price increases for carbon steel plates and structural shapes averaging 12.5 percent, effective March 1. Bethlehem Chairman Stewart S. Cort had discussed the intended increases with CEA Chairman McCracken before making the decision public. Cort found McCracken unenthusiastic, but he was unprepared for receiving the following day a sharp presidential denunciation of the move, together with a message to the industry as a whole that the administration could not, either in the interests of major users such as construction or in the interests of the competitive viability of the steel industry itself, undertake to protect it indefinitely from foreign competition, to which it had steadily been losing ground. Several days later, the United States Steel Corporation announced price increases averaging only 6.8 percent on products used by the construction industry, and Bethlehem Steel rolled back its posted prices to conform more closely to the latter figure.[84]

The President's action was somewhat surprising, a spokesman for McCracken having confirmed only a day before that administration policy remained one of refraining from comment on individual price decisions. What had induced the President to intervene directly in this particular case? Some probable reasons may be adduced. In the first place, the President was undoubtedly genuinely concerned about the wage escalation in construction, but he had resisted for over a year calls to suspend the Davis-Bacon Act. Any leverage he might have had with the construction unions, and his appeals to employers to resist excessive wage claims, would have been weakened had he meekly acquiesced in a steel price increase that would have significantly augmented *nonwage* costs in construction. Second, on two counts Bethlehem's action was ill timed. The price increase was made known the same day that the administration announced a liberalization of depreciation allowances; had it gone unchallenged the administration would have been vulnerable to allegations

84. This was the message consistently purveyed by the administration to the steel industry. See "Third Inflation Alert," A Report by the Council of Economic Advisers (April 13, 1971; processed), pp. 27–30; George P. Shultz, "Prescription for Economic Policy: 'Steady As You Go,'" speech before the Economic Club of Chicago, April 22, 1971 (U.S. Office of Management and Budget). The third inflation alert and Shultz's speech both included cautionary remarks about the wage negotiations in the steel industry that were to begin later in the year. This was also a departure from previous policy, the first two alerts having been confined to *past* wage and price increases. For details of the price rollback in steel, see Silk, *Nixonomics*, pp. 43–44, and the report in *Facts on File* (January 14–20, 1971), pp. 29–30.

that industry was being exempted from the rule enunciated in the President's December 4 speech that "fighting inflation is everybody's business." Moreover, wage negotiations in the steel industry were scheduled for the summer, and the United Steelworkers could hardly be called upon to obey unilaterally the President's further injunction to "stop freezing into wage settlement and price actions any expectation that inflation will continue in the future at its peak rate of the past."[85]

In further actions, the President met with the Construction Industry Collective Bargaining Commission on January 18, and in lieu of suspending the Davis-Bacon Act or imposing a freeze on construction prices and wages, requested that it devise within thirty days a voluntary plan that would have a marked effect on the wage-price spiral in the industry.[86] On the same day the Cabinet Committee on Economic Policy directed the CEA to report to it all important cases of wage or price increases "so that remedial Federal action might be considered," and later in the month the Regulations and Purchasing Review Board intervened for the first time "in a case before a regulatory agency involving an application for a rate increase," opposing the application on the grounds that the rate increase would be inflationary.[87] When no satisfactory voluntary plan was forthcoming from the construction industry the President, on February 23, suspended the Davis-Bacon Act. The act was reinstated on March 29, after Secretary of Labor James D. Hodgson had obtained agreement from the labor unions to participate in a tripartite group, subsequently named the Construction Industry Stabilization Committee, whose task was to abate wage increases to something like the rate that had prevailed from 1961 to 1968.[88]

Summarizing these and other actions of the preceding half-year in his

85. *Weekly Compilation of Presidential Documents*, vol. 6 (December 7, 1970), p. 1627.

86. *Facts on File*, vol. 31 (January 14–20, 1971), p. 30; Harry Lenhart, Jr., "Economic Report: Construction Wage-Stabilization Efforts Provide Tests for Nixon's Phase 2," *National Journal*, vol. 3 (November 6, 1971), pp. 2209–23, especially pp. 2210, 2216–17.

87. Testimony of Paul W. McCracken in *The 1971 Economic Report of the President*, Hearings before the Joint Economic Committee, 92 Cong. 1 sess. (1971), pt. 1, pp. 8, 9.

88. It was felt by some of those involved—for example, John T. Dunlop, chairman of the Construction Industry Collective Bargaining Commission—that grounds for agreement had been found before the Davis-Bacon Act was suspended, and that this action was unnecessary and damaging to goodwill. See the discussion in Lenhart, "Economic Report," pp. 2209–23; comments by John T. Dunlop at the Boston Conference on the Development of Wage-Price Policy.

testimony before the Joint Economic Committee, McCracken acknowledged that "we now have in effect many elements of what has come
rather loosely to be called an incomes policy. We are now considering
ways to make these elements more systematic and comprehensive, and
to provide more adequately for their management." This last comment
promised more than was really intended or could be achieved. McCracken
himself went on immediately to make it quite clear that the limited resources of the CEA were already strained, that the CEA was guided by
the principle stated in the Economic Report: "What is called for is a
policy of doing what can effectively be done, whenever it can be done,
and not pretending to do more." This meant that in "the administration's
new more active program" nothing was contemplated beyond measures
to render conditions more competitive in *particular* product and labor
markets. Such efforts were merely supplementary to the basic weapons of
monetary and fiscal policy, and one could expect from them "only a
marginal contribution to the problem of reconciling reasonably full employment with reasonable price stability." That general position was sustained also by George Shultz a few days later. "My analysis of the wage
and price situation," he told the committee, "is that the problem . . . is
widely dispersed." He acknowledged that in some sectors, most notably
construction, there were "real problems," and the administration was
working on a program there that would really do something about excessive wage settlements. It had always been a concern of the administration
to see that the discipline of competition operated in individual wage and
price markets. But in many sectors, "the wage changes that are being put
into place are quite moderate," given the rate of inflation. It was most
important, after all, to "do the sorts of things that will enable output per
man-hour to grow at a rate equal to the rate of increase in wages."[89]

Intervention in the Construction Industry

The kind of intervention that would be consistent with a market orientation may be further illustrated by looking a little more closely at the
administration's program to limit wage settlements in the construction
industry, as outlined by the President in March 1971. Wages, of course,
represent only one element in construction costs, though a highly visible

89. *The 1971 Economic Report of the President,* Hearings, pt. 1, pp. 9, 62,
64–65, 76.

one. The administration had taken steps before this time, first, to reduce the cost of materials (specifically plywood and softwood lumber) by restricting its own purchases and increasing sales of timber from federal lands (March 1969) and, second, to render more efficient the use of construction manpower and increase the supply of skilled construction workers.[90] But its most direct attempt to influence the trend of wage increases in the industry was taken with the issuance of Executive Order 11588, on March 29, 1971, which established a system for stabilizing wages (and prices) in construction through the dual structure of the tripartite Construction Industry Stabilization Committee (CISC) and bipartite craft dispute boards covering the major segments of the industry.[91] All settlements negotiated after March 28 were to be approved first by a craft dispute board, then by the CISC. Two criteria were to be employed in reviewing negotiated wage and benefit increases. First, acceptable increases were those "supportable by productivity improvement and cost of living trends," with the qualification that they should not exceed "the average of the median increases in wages and benefits over the life of the contract negotiated in major construction settlements" in the industry from 1961 to 1968 (approximately 6 percent). Second, special equity adjustments higher than increases acceptable under the first criterion might be allowed if it could be shown that they were necessary "to restore traditional relationships among crafts in a single locality and within the same craft in surrounding localities." Sanctions were implicit in the power of the CISC to delay review and acceptance of an agreement and in the power of the federal government to ignore unacceptably high settlements in setting wages on federally financed projects.

The two criteria were designed to undermine the emulatory and defensive psychology that had created a wage-price spiral in construction,

90. These were objectives set by the President for the Construction Industry Collective Bargaining Commission; Executive Order 11482, September 22, 1969. On related steps, including those taken in March 1969 to stabilize the cost of building materials, see the President's speech on housing inflation, March 17, 1970, in *Nixon: The Second Year of His Presidency* (Congressional Quarterly, 1971), pp. 98A–101A. A Task Force on Softwood Lumber and Plywood of the Cabinet Committee on Economic Policy was set up after the sharp price increases of early 1969 and continued to monitor and recommend ways to alleviate acute and long-run shortages. See "Third Inflation Alert," pp. 25–27.

91. Guidelines for acceptable prices in construction contracts and acceptable compensations outside the terms of collective bargaining agreements were to be determined by a committee appointed by the secretary of HUD. See the "Statement by the President" accompanying the issuance of Executive Order 11588, March 29, 1971 (Office of the White House Secretary).

and they were negotiated between the parties, with John T. Dunlop acting as principal intermediary. A criterion of average productivity in, say, the manufacturing industry would have made no allowance for the tendency of productivity in construction to increase less than in the manufacturing industry as a whole. This is due to three peculiar features of the construction industry. First, the product is not standardized and there has always been considerable resistance by buyers to standard design and mass production. Second, the product is specific to location, which means that product market competition does not hinge on inter-area wage or productivity differences. Third, activity in the industry is highly seasonal, underemployment characterizing the construction labor force during the winter and some spring months in most parts of the country.

Nor would a criterion embodying increases in productivity alone have achieved the government's purpose. Had adjustments to restore traditional differences not been permitted, a decline in morale and productivity and an increase in the number of strikes would have been likely. Implementing this second criterion was certainly not without problems. The criterion necessitated a case-by-case approach and this made for a sizable administration problem, since in 1971 alone about 1,400 agreements expired. Moreover, it was feared by some that the goal of wage restraint was incompatible with the equity principle, a fear apparently justified by some early settlements approved by the CISC that involved a three-year wage increase of about 30 percent. The rationale for the dual criteria was that inflationary wage settlements in construction incorporated both the phenomenon of catch-up—related to distorted differentials —and a tendency to leapfrog—reflecting an assumption that inflation would continue over the life of a contract and must therefore be allowed for in advance. The equity adjustment principle was intended to eliminate little by little the distortions induced by these two responses to past inflation, while the success of the administration's anti-inflation policy would at the same time remove the justification for continuing high new settlements. Deputy Under Secretary of Labor Michael H. Moskow, one of those who devised the CISC system, expressed the administration's expectation: "We are trying to turn a race into an orderly procession. We want everyone to end up in the traditional order, and we want a slower pace to be maintained. Thus, in the middle of the procession, some units speed up and some slow down."[92]

92. "The Wage-Price Dilemma in Construction," speech delivered at the North American Conference of Labor Statisticians, San Juan, Puerto Rico, June 17, 1971

Whether this system would be effective was widely questioned at the time of its implementation, not least from within the administration by CEA members Herbert Stein and Hendrik S. Houthakker, who felt that too little attention had been given to removing construction union barriers to entry and who opposed the equity provision on the grounds that, with wage settlements in construction running at about a 15 percent increase and including a provision to restore traditional differences, every new negotiation would tend to take place in the same range.[93] What is of more immediate interest here, however, is that the system was in effect, if not in intention, an application of the case-by-case review advocated by Burns, though with legal sanctions. Effective or not, the system was at least an attempt to take into account the difficulty of applying a guidepost of average productivity to a particular industry, or segment of it, and it stayed well within the administration's own guidelines for acceptable intervention. In Moskow's words: "The Government took upon itself not to regulate, but to set up a system of self-regulation with implicit but real sanctions available should the need arise. The CISC was set up as a halfway house between purely voluntary restraint and outright controls."[94] The action was paternalistic but not inconsistent with a basic market orientation. "There are times," the President explained to the U.S. Chamber of Commerce, "when economic freedom must be protected from its own excesses."[95]

Gradualism, Phase 2

By the time the President presented his 1972 budget early in 1971, the administration had been determined for at least six months to achieve "full" employment (4–4.5 percent unemployment) by mid-1972. The

(U.S. Department of Labor). Moskow had been a senior staff economist at the CEA, working on labor economics and manpower programs with particular reference to the construction industry, and was executive director of the Construction Industry Collective Bargaining Commission. The above discussion draws heavily on his analysis of the industry and the March 29 Executive Order. The criteria are contained in section 6 of the Executive Order.

93. Interview, Herbert Stein, November 21, 1973; also Lenhart, "Economic Report," p. 2222.

94. "The Wage-Price Dilemma in Construction."

95. "The Right to Be Confident," speech to the fifty-ninth annual meeting of the U.S. Chamber of Commerce, April 26, 1971, in *Weekly Compilation of Presidential Documents*, vol. 7 (May 3, 1971), p. 689. Compare the statement accompanying the issuance of Executive Order 11588.

perverse behavior of the economy in late 1970 had probably done harm to some Republicans in the midterm elections, and with a presidential election looming in 1972 there was no desire to hold that campaign under similar circumstances.[96] Advisers who were convinced that inflation was persisting largely as a carryover from the unusually long inflationary boom that preceded it were willing to proceed quite vigorously with policies to speed the recovery and tended to play down the worst of the statistical indicators.[97]

When antirecession measures had been mooted early in 1970, Budget Director Robert P. Mayo urged the President to exercise extreme caution before considering fiscal stimulants in addition to the shift away from restraint that was already planned for the calendar year ahead. Part of Mayo's argument, resting on a review of the previous four recessions, was that there is little scope for a speedup of expenditures within a given year, and such actions, once taken, tend to be irreversible. This meant that a positive effect might be felt only after the time for it had passed, while the long-term difficulties of keeping expenditures in check would have been needlessly increased.[98]

After Shultz took over as director of the newly designated Office of Management and Budget (OMB) on July 2, there was no marked change of view about the possibility or wisdom of expanding expenditures to induce a near-term recovery. "We must keep the momentum of Federal expenditures from carrying them again, as in 1967 and 1968, beyond the revenues produced by the tax system at full employment," Shultz told the Joint Economic Committee at its midyear hearings reviewing the state of the economy.[99] However, two significant changes did occur. First, Shultz convinced the President of the desirability of adopting the full

96. The President had bitter memories of the 1960 election in which he believed the recession had been his undoing. He had indicated at a press conference in July that "full employment . . . is a goal we think we can achieve during fiscal year 1972." "The President's News Conference of July 20, 1970," in *Public Papers of the Presidents of the United States: Richard Nixon, 1970* (1971), p. 603.

97. *Economic Report of the President, 1971*, pp. 60, 62; Stein, "Prospects and Policies for the U.S. Economy," speech at the *Financial Times* and *Investors Chronicle* Conference on the Future of the United States Economy, London, England, October 28, 1970 (Council of Economic Advisers); Shultz, testimony, *The 1971 Economic Report of the President*, Hearings, pt. 1, p. 76.

98. Memorandum, Mayo to the President, "Stimulation of the Economy Through Fiscal Actions," March 24, 1970 (U.S. Bureau of the Budget).

99. *The 1970 Midyear Review of the State of the Economy*, Hearings, pt. 3, p. 403. Compare typewritten memorandum, Troika Staff to Troika 2, "GNP Forecast and Policy Actions," December 4, 1970: "In OMB's view, there is little that can be done to move purchases from FY 72 to FY 71."

employment benchmark for thinking about the relation between revenues and expenditures and what it signified. Using the full employment budget terminology minimized the risk that renewed fears of inflation would be engendered by a projected *actual* deficit for fiscal 1971. Second, Shultz was inclined to be optimistic about the potential for expansion and gave considerable prominence to the efficacy of monetary policy in bringing about a recovery. He felt strongly that the restrictive policies of 1969 had produced a recession and was the first in the administration to call publicly for an easing of monetary restraint.[100] Shultz's optimism was reflected in the publication and defense of a target for GNP in calendar year 1971 of $1,065 billion. This was a 9.1 percent increase over 1970 and 2.7 percentage points above the average annual increase for the period 1950–70. It was also considerably above the figure predicted by private forecasters. The figure was supported by an OMB version of the St. Louis monetarist model, which suggested that a 6 percent growth in the money supply would yield the desired growth in GNP without additional stimulus from fiscal policy.[101]

The CEA had reservations about the OMB model, although it acquiesced in the $1,065 billion figure as a desirable and feasible target for 1971—to be achieved, however, by additional stimulus should that prove necessary.[102]

100. Edwin L. Dale, Jr., *New York Times*, January 7, 1970; interview, George P. Shultz, March 18, 1974.

101. Interview, Herbert Stein, November 21, 1973; interview, Maurice Mann, April 7, 1974; Maisel, *Managing the Dollar*, pp. 267–68. An outline of the OMB model is incorporated in *The 1971 Economic Report of the President*, Hearings, pt. 1, pp. 279–300.

102. Interview, Herbert Stein, November 21, 1973; Stein, "Federal Fiscal Policy in 1971," speech at the annual Financial Outlook Conference, New York City, February 17, 1971 (Council of Economic Advisers); and Stein, "$1065 Billion as Goal and Forecast," speech at the National Agricultural Outlook Conference, Department of Agriculture, February 23, 1971 (Council of Economic Advisers). At least one CEA staff economist was openly critical of models of the OMB type, on the grounds that (1) they discount the effects of government expenditures at full employment more than the evidence would warrant; and (2) they make the money supply and monetary policy endogenous, rendering it difficult to establish the direction of causality between the monetary variable and GNP. The specific OMB version of the St. Louis model was further suspect on the ground that it incorporated no lag in the effect of money supply on GNP. Memorandum, William L. Silber to the Council, "Discussion Points for OMB-CEA Seminar on Forecasting Models (with particular reference to the latest OMB model by Laffer and Ranson)," February 10, 1971. Silber concluded that because a model seems to perform better than an alternative is no basis for accepting it when both are quite poor. In such a case

The need for further stimulus was suggested, though not strongly, by the performance of the economy in the first quarter of 1971. By April, despite good growth in real output in the first three months of the year, it seemed unlikely that the $1,065 billion target would be reached, and the CEA began revising its forecasts to accommodate to a lower projected figure of $1,057 billion. The CEA staff also felt pessimistic about the unemployment rate, for reasons related to the numbers of former military personnel that would be entering the civilian labor market, the increases in productivity that could be expected with recovery, and in particular the possibility that hours worked might increase as the recovery proceeded instead of new jobs being added. In its revised "optimum feasible path" for the economy the unemployment rate was set at 4.9 percent for the second quarter of 1972, higher than the 4.5 percent goal for mid-1972.[103] Nonetheless, as Stein pointed out in April, the $1,065 billion figure was no more than an intermediate target which happened to be consistent with the basic goal, namely, "to reduce the unemployment rate as fast as is consistent with a reasonably steady and durable decline in the rate of inflation." This basic goal could be approached via a number of time-paths, and policy was not so fixed that it could not or would not be changed to ensure achievement of the desired ultimate outcome. Moreover, he said, the administration had reason to be pleased with the performance of prices in the first quarter and other signs that a sound recovery was under way.[104] Essentially the same face was put on things by the OMB.[105]

As with the initial policy of gradualism, so in managing the recovery to full capacity without engendering renewed inflation, the administration's economists had to contend with a largely skeptical Congress and public. But they were not granted the two or three additional quarters they felt would justify them in the "steady as you go" advice they were inclined to

---

"policy formulations might be better off looking at neither." This argument, he reminded the members of the Council, was analogous to the earlier one with which the CEA had rejected incomes policy.

103. Memorandum, Frank Ripley to Stein, "A Revised Optimum Feasible Path," April 8, 1971 (Council of Economic Advisers). Stein, in a generally optimistic speech, acknowledged some disappointment at the sluggishness of employment and industrial output: "On the Track?" speech before the American Textile Manufacturers Institute, Hollywood, Florida, March 25, 1971 (Council of Economic Advisers).

104. Speech at the Business Economists' Conference, Chicago, April 26, 1971.

105. Shultz, "Prescription for Economic Policy."

give at the end of the first quarter. For from about this time political considerations began to assert themselves, and the timing, and presently the substance also, of economic policy were to some extent taken out of the hands of the administration's economic advisers.

The Move to Controls

What caused this change? One element was the accession of John B. Connally to the cabinet as secretary of the treasury.[106] Connally had political connections and sagacity and a penchant for bold speech and action, which the President felt badly in need of at the end of 1970.[107] The President may have intended that Connally should, among other things, quell the fears about vigorous expansion and the related stress on a need for additional policies to restrain inflation that had long emanated from the Treasury staff and that even Secretary Kennedy had begun to express toward the end of 1970.[108] Connally, however, entered upon his duties already convinced that the administration's policies were not getting results fast enough and that no one was misled into believing otherwise by optimistic pronouncements. He was eager to receive fresh thinking on a whole range of issues and possible policy initiatives, including the problem of inflation and the tactic of a price freeze. To keep the options open in the area of incomes policy he took the unexpected step of asking Congress to extend (under H.R. 4246) the authority earlier granted the President under the Economic Stabilization Act of 1970 to impose wage and price controls. And in a series of public statements during the spring he consistently refused to reject out of hand the possibility of using that authority should the circumstances arise.[109]

This is not to say that Connally was moving inexorably toward the

106. Connally was nominated on December 14, 1970, and confirmed on February 8, 1971.

107. An excellent assessment is to be found in Evans and Novak, *Nixon in the White House*, pp. 240–41, 373–75; and William Safire, *Before the Fall: An Inside View of the Pre-Watergate White House* (Doubleday, 1975), pt. 7, chap. 4.

108. Letter to the author from Robert L. Joss, May 21, 1974.

109. Interview, Charls E. Walker, February 12, 1974; statement and testimony by Connally in *To Extend Standby Powers of the President to Stabilize Wages and Prices . . .* , Hearings before the House Committee on Banking and Currency, 92 Cong. 1 sess. (1971), pp. 4–5; remarks by Connally on the NBC show *Meet the Press* (March 1971) and in an interview reported in *U.S. News and World Report*, vol. 70 (April 12, 1971), pp. 52–57.

adoption of controls, though his analysis of the economic situation corresponded closely with that of Arthur Burns, who drew from it the inference that "monetary and fiscal tools . . . are ill suited to dealing with a rising price level that stems from rising costs at a time of rising unemployment and excess capacity"; and he was receiving advice from Murray Weidenbaum and Paul Volcker that a freeze might be a useful way of jolting inflationary expectations and effecting a recovery that seemed to be inhibited by the high interest rates resulting from the earlier restrictive monetary policy.[110] These economic analyses may have been useful to Connally as rationalizations when he later opted for controls, but in the early months of 1971 he was probably concerned primarily with finding a way out of the nation's economic difficulties that would make political capital for the President. The particular policies that such a path might entail were of secondary importance.

Two further elements intruded themselves increasingly as 1971 progressed, in the shape of heightened business and congressional agitation for a frontal assault on inflationary wage and price increases. Business organizations such as the Construction Users' Anti-inflation Roundtable saw the current inflation as largely wage-induced, and those already inclined to this view had it strengthened by a March settlement in the can industry embodying wage increases averaging approximately 9 percent a year for the life of the contract (including a guaranteed minimum cost-of-living adjustment of 3 percent a year in the second and third years). The settlement was roundly criticized in the third inflation alert (April) as being "clearly in excess of any realistic assessment of long term productivity growth prospects" and, while not out of line with other recent settlements, as representing "no progress toward the declining trend of wage increases that is essential if we are to regain increased stability of prices and costs."[111] The CEA was disturbed because settlements in the can industry tend to influence those in aluminum, copper, and steel; as early as February I. W. Abel, president of the United Steelworkers union, party to the contract with the can manufacturers, had warned, by way of response to the President's successful jawboning of Bethlehem Steel, that

110. The similarity of their analyses is apparent in the prepared statements of Burns and Connally, *The 1971 Economic Report of the President*, Hearings, pt. 1, pp. 238–45, and pt. 2, pp. 585–86; interview, Paul A. Volcker, March 18, 1974. It has recently been suggested that Burns actually undertook to instruct Connally in the nation's economic problems. Dan Rather and Gary Paul Gates, *The Palace Guard* (Harper and Row, 1974), pp. 278–79.

111. "Third Inflation Alert," pp. 29–30.

interference in the forthcoming negotiations in the steel industry would be unwelcome—and, by implication, pointless—since the steelworkers were determined to win wage increases comparable to those secured by other major unions in 1970.[112]

The employers' view was forcibly expressed at the May meeting of the prestigious Business Council, where Shultz's "steady as you go" advice came under fire. One member of the council, J. Irwin Miller of Cummins Engine Company, espoused the immediate adoption of wage and price controls, and the council itself was moved to the unprecedented step of taking a straw vote on the issue, subsequently conveying to the President an expression of discontent at the administration's failure to secure smaller wage and price increases.[113]

Similar initiatives in the Capitol contained little that was new, but the calls for action became more numerous and more insistent. Potential candidates for the Democratic presidential nomination began adding their names to the list of those urging that stronger measures be taken against inflation; Speaker of the House Carl Albert in April challenged the President to convene a national conference on unemployment and inflation; and all those advocating that the President abandon his non-interventionist position could now speak in the certain knowledge that large segments of liberal educated opinion and of the public generally would be sympathetic.[114] Gallup polls and editorials in the *New York Times* captured and broadcast this sentiment. But perhaps equally significant, even if the administration was inclined to dismiss this as uninformed, it could not deny that a similar call was being sounded with embarrassing frequency by the chairman of the Federal Reserve, whose credentials were, at least in all other respects, impeccable.[115]

112. A reference to the settlements in the automobile industry, for details of which see Bureau of Labor Statistics, "Major Wage Developments, 1970," in *Current Wage Developments*, no. 282 (July 1971). Abel's statement was reported in the *New York Times*, February 8, 1971.

113. Weber, *In Pursuit of Price Stability*, p. 6; also comments by Weber at the Boston Conference on the Development of Wage-Price Policy, transcript, vol. 2, p. 2-16. See also the report in the *New York Times*, May 9, 1971; Frank V. Fowlkes, "Economic Report: Business Council Shuns Lobbying but Influences Federal Policy," *National Journal*, vol. 3 (November 20, 1971), pp. 2302–09, especially pp. 2306–07; and Lewis Beman, "The Emerging Debate about Inflation," *Fortune*, vol. 85 (March 1972), pp. 50ff., especially p. 52.

114. See *New York Times*, February 11, 1971; also April 30, June 16, 22, and 23, 1971.

115. The *New York Times* drew on Chairman Burns's testimony before the Joint

Much of this agitation that something be done could be discounted as inevitable in a preelection year. But among the numerous messages from congressmen were some from adherents of the President's own party, and these could not be so easily ignored. As the second quarter progressed, with little evidence that headway was being made against inflation and with unemployment edging up to 6.1 percent in April and 6.2 percent in May, Republican leaders began to feel increasing dissatisfaction with the second phase of the gradualist game plan. As early as May 1971 at a briefing for Republican congressmen, McCracken was made to feel the full force of this dissatisfaction.[116] In mid-June McCracken publicly acknowledged that the economy was moving too slowly to cut into the high rate of unemployment; and at the routine midyear review of the economy at Camp David on June 26, he urged that further stimulatory measures be adopted so that unemployment would not still be around 6 percent at the end of the year. He was supported by Connally though not by Shultz, and it was decided to adopt no additional measures for the time being.[117] Secretary Connally, newly designated the President's chief economic spokesman following this meeting, announced that there would be no tax cut, no extra federal spending, no wage and price review board, and

---

Economic Committee in February and July and before the Senate Committee on Banking and Currency in May and produced a long string of comment suggesting that events might be propelling the President toward an incomes policy, deploring his failure to heed Burns's recommendations, and urging that a wage-price review board be established, accompanied by a temporary freeze to give the board time to develop procedures and standards. See *New York Times*, February 28, 1971; also March 18, April 23, May 24 and 28, June 23, July 2, 15, and 25, and August 5, 1971. Gallup polls released in March and June found that economic problems ranked second only to Vietnam in matters of national concern, with more Americans apparently worried about the state of the economy than at any time since the 1958 recession. Of those questioned in the first poll 49 percent said they would support a wage-price freeze. According to a Harris survey taken in July, 73 percent of those questioned thought the President was coping poorly with the nation's economic problems (only 22 percent approved, down from 35 percent in May); while a Gallup poll released in July revealed continuing support (by one in every two of those questioned) for wage and price controls.

116. As told by Herbert Stein at the Boston Conference on the Development of Wage-Price Policy.

117. *New York Times*, June 18 and 30, 1971; also John F. Burby and Harry Lenhart, Jr., "Economic Report: Nixon's Change in Game Plan Reflects Confidence in CEA, McCracken," *National Journal*, vol. 3 (August 21, 1971), pp. 1743–53, especially p. 1751; Juan Cameron, "How the U.S. Got on the Road to a Controlled Economy," *Fortune*, vol. 85 (January 1972), p. 77; interview, Herbert Stein, November 21, 1973.

no controls, and with this Republicans began to express their discontent more openly. Republican National Chairman Robert Dole stated in mid-July that he was concerned about the possibly damaging effect of the state of the economy on the President's chances for reelection in 1972; while early in August fourteen Republican senators declared that they would sponsor legislation calling for a permanent national council on productivity. Of this group, twelve had already announced that they intended to seek congressional approval for the establishment of a wage and price review board.[118]

These last declarations, as it turned out, were superfluous. Just a few days before, the President had decided to reverse his policy and impose a temporary wage and price freeze. With the existing economic conditions, this was only one of several responses he might have made. So far as inflation was concerned, the CEA held that it was running true to the pattern they had described in the first inflation alert: "Wholesale prices begin rising first, followed by retail and service prices and wages. This process has to run through the system before a levelling off can occur." But the longer a rapid inflation has proceeded, the longer the period required to slow it down, "because it builds in growing numbers of price increases that become higher costs for others, and it rigidifies expectations of inflation." This, plus the spread of long-term wage settlements involving catch-up and a hedge against further inflation, had frustrated anticipation of an early end to the inflation, but there was some feeling in the Council that the freeze was put into effect just when the cycle of major wage increases had about run its course and signs of a slackening rate of price increases had begun to appear.[119] From the CEA's point of view the sudden move away from gradualism was explicable by political circum-

118. *New York Times*, July 16 and August 4 and 5, 1971.
119. "Inflation Alert," Report to the National Commission on Productivity by the Council of Economic Advisers (August 7, 1970; processed), pp. I-8, I-6; comments by McCracken as reported in *New York Times*, April 24, 1971; interviews, Herbert Stein, November 21, 1973, and Sidney L. Jones, February 12, 1974. See also *The Economic Report of the President Together with the Annual Report of the Council of Economic Advisers, January* 1972, p. 108. As late as July 28 McCracken was describing the idea of a freeze as illusory, on the grounds that compliance and equity may be secured only by honoring wage increases already contracted for and, given low prevailing profit margins, by allowing businessmen to pass on at least part of the resulting increases in costs. He also dismissed the current notion of a two-part package consisting of measures to stimulate the economy and controls or incomes policy, since the two parts could not be made to work in equal degree. "Galbraith and Price-Wage Controls," *Washington Post*, July 28, 1971.

stances and mounting pressure from businessmen, but nothing in the basic structure or performance of the economy made it inevitable.

This was true in a special sense of the move to a mandatory freeze. The President might have adopted general voluntary guidelines of the sort tried during the 1960s, or brought moral suasion to bear through a public review board or justification tribunal. Admittedly, he had enjoyed scant success in his jawboning of the steel industry. The United Steelworkers had made good Abel's threat, and ended a strike early in August only after securing a three-year wage increase of about 30 percent. Meanwhile, U.S. Steel managed to turn against him the President's apparent success of February in achieving a rollback of Bethlehem's prices. The corporation announced in May a price increase for rolled sheet and strip steel of 6.25 percent, without having first notified the administration of its intention, the rationale for this omission being that since Bethlehem's 6.8 percent increase in prices of structural steel in February had sparked no official protest this was presumably an acceptable guideline figure.[120] Moreover, the large wage settlement in the industry came in apparent disregard of a meeting of labor and management with the President on July 6, during which he had requested that a "constructive" settlement be reached; and it was followed by a further price increase by five major steel producers.[121] This experience, then, could scarcely have encouraged the President to depend on jawboning as a major weapon in his anti-inflation program. Indeed, at an unscheduled news conference on August 4, he more or less acknowledged that jawboning can be effective only in special circumstances. But the argument that he then turned against guidelines and moral suasion generally—that they will work only for brief periods— could equally well be applied to a freeze. Why, then, the freeze? Because the President had determined that should he ever move in that direction he would go as far as it was possible for him to go. Only thus could he outdistance his critics and deprive his political opponents of their issue.[122]

Certainly, there is no evidence that the President was converted to a

120. *New York Times*, May 6, 1971. What the White House had actually indicated in February was that it was not sanguine about even a 6.8 percent price rise, though this was preferable to the 12.5 percent increase originally announced by Bethlehem.

121. Ibid., July 7 and August 3, 1971.

122. Interview, Herbert Stein, November 21, 1973; Burby and Lenhart, "Economic Report," p. 1751. For the relevant portions of the President's news conference, see *Nixon: The Third Year of His Presidency* (Congressional Quarterly, 1972), pp. 150A–52A.

belief in permanent controls. The decision to impose a freeze was taken without much thought for what would follow it, and the form of controls eventually unveiled as Phase II of the economic stabilization program owed much of its stringency and comprehensiveness to the unexpectedly strong public support with which the move to impose a freeze was greeted. Moreover, the organization devised to administer the controls was the very antithesis of what is implied by jawboning and moral suasion, and strongly suggests that Nixon wanted to avoid being personally identified with controls. For while as President he retained formal responsibility for the whole program, he was in practice quite removed from the business of having to decide individual cases, policy guidance being supplied by the Cost of Living Council without White House intervention, and reviews of price and pay increases being undertaken by the Price Commission and the Pay Board.[123]

While the decision to impose a wage and price freeze was taken in late July or early August, no date was fixed for its implementation. At his August 4 news conference the President said that he was prepared to look afresh at proposals for a wage and price review board. He expressed doubts that a review system could be made to work without creating an unacceptable "new bureaucracy with enormous criminal powers, to fasten itself on the American economy," and added that this option "would be considered favorably" only if congressional hearings (to be held after Labor Day) convinced him that "enforcing an incomes policy could be accomplished without stifling the economy."[124] This allowed a few mem-

123. Letter to the author from Louis P. Neeb, November 20, 1974. Neeb moved from the Office of Emergency Preparedness to become executive secretary of the Price Commission. Also, comments by Arnold R. Weber and Herbert Stein at the Boston Conference on the Development of Wage-Price Policy, transcript, vol. 2, pp. 2-94–2-98, 2-109–2-113; and Cameron, "How the U.S. Got on the Road to a Controlled Economy," pp. 74, 158, 160. Gallup and Harris polls taken after the August 15 announcement showed roughly 75 percent approval of the freeze.

124. Nixon: The Third Year of His Presidency, pp. 151A, 152A. Connally, also on August 4, issued a list of questions to which such an examination might address itself, and this list was so detailed and searching that it must have betrayed an intense and recent interest in the subject within the administration. "Memo to the Press," C-108, U.S. Department of the Treasury, News, August 4, 1971. There is a triple irony in the move to a controls system. Not only was the step taken under a statute intended only to embarrass the administration, but the statute—for the very reason that it was not intended to be used—failed to specify subpoena powers or standards of due process and was devoid of substantive guidelines. In other words, it lacked all those checks to the abuse of power, the absence of which had earlier led Shultz and Burns to reject the McCracken-McLaren idea of a review process with

bers of the administration to apply themselves to the subject of controls without provoking questions about what might be afoot.[125]

The main components of the President's New Economic Policy, as it came to be called, were determined in two Monday night sessions with Shultz and Connally on August 2 and 9. A package of measures designed to ease both domestic and international economic pressures was prepared. A ninety-day freeze of wages, prices, and rents was to be combined with tax and expenditure cuts, the net effect of which, it was intended, would be stimulatory. On the international side, the President decided he would seek a realignment of currencies, and at Connally's behest a temporary 10 percent import surcharge would be imposed to give the United States some leverage in the negotiations this would involve. Coinciding with the announcement of these measures, the United States would suspend its commitment to redeem foreign-held dollars for gold.[126]

The freeze was strictly separable from the international elements in this new program and might still have been introduced had no action on the dollar been taken. Burns, indeed, argued strongly against closing the gold window, while accepting passively the other proposals.[127] But the notion of a grand, coordinated set of measures held both personal and political appeal for the President, and bearing this in mind one can find in the international aspects of the situation both a setting for and explanation of the timing of the New Economic Policy.[128]

---

legal sanctions. Finally, by about the time the controls were lifted, those in charge had adapted computer technology to the problem of multiple case review with such success that the need for a massive bureaucracy, so feared by the President, had been eliminated. Comments by Weber and Quinn Mills at the Boston Conference on the Development of Wage-Price Policy.

125. See Weber, *In Pursuit of Price Stability*, pp. 7–8.

126. Interviews, George P. Shultz, March 18, 1974; Paul W. McCracken, December 29, 1973; Paul A. Volcker, March 18, 1974; Cameron, "How the U.S. Got on the Road to a Controlled Economy," p. 77. William Safire (*Before the Fall*, p. 527) reports a comment by President Nixon after the Camp David weekend, August 13–15, that the basic elements of the New Economic Policy had been "cooked up" by him and Connally as early as mid-June.

127. Interview, Arthur F. Burns, March 19, 1974; and comments by Stein at the Boston Conference on the Development of Wage-Price Policy, transcript, vol. 2, pp. 2-123–2-124. Burns found controls too radical, and would have been satisfied with a review process combined with the jawboning of leaders in key, pace-setting industries.

128. President Nixon's closest economic advisers recall him as "a strategist, a relater of things." For perceptive analyses of his personal and presidential style, see Bruce Mazlish, *In Search of Nixon: A Psychohistorical Inquiry* (Pelican, 1973), and James

The United States had run substantial deficits in its balance of payments in almost every year since World War II. Thus the ratio of U.S. dollar liabilities to foreign governments to U.S. international reserve assets (chiefly gold) grew steadily (from 0.42 in 1958 to 1.8 at the end of 1970), as did the ratio of dollar liabilities to all other forms of international reserves. It had therefore become a matter of concern whether the United States, as the world's banker, would be able to meet the claims on its assets. Added to this fundamental cause for disquiet, the U.S. balance of trade, which had traditionally displayed a strong surplus, showed a marked decline in the late 1960s as imports rose sharply and exports, partly because of mounting domestic inflation, failed to match this growth. The crisis was triggered when the trade statistics early in the second quarter suggested a sharp plunge into deficit, and there was a large movement from dollars into (principally) deutsche marks.[129]

That the dollar was overvalued was clearly recognized by the Nixon administration from the beginning. But Burns and Volcker were fearful that the heavily patched fabric of the international monetary system might begin to come apart if the United States initiated a change in the value of its currency. Volcker hoped in 1969 that "if our inflationary experience turned out as well as it seemed it could and if other's inflationary experiences turned out as bad as it seemed they could, we could see it through." By the second quarter of 1971 this was clearly no longer a tenable position. The May flight away from the dollar was ended after repeated Treasury declarations that no change in U.S. gold or foreign exchange policies was contemplated and the German monetary authorities decided to allow the mark to float. But this did little to change the general weakness in the United States' trading position, which continued to worsen until, in mid-July, realizing that time was running out, the Treasury began to give serious thought to closing the gold window.[130]

On July 15 came the surprising announcement that the President had accepted an invitation to Peking. A few days earlier the June trade figures had revealed that the nation had run up a trade deficit for the third

David Barber, *The Presidential Character: Predicting Performance in the White House* (Prentice-Hall, 1972).

129. The background to the crisis is well described in M. June Flanders, "The International Monetary System: The 'Crises' of 1971," *Israel Quarterly of Economics*, vol. 1 (Spring 1972), pp. 5–17, on which my discussion draws, and from which the figures cited above are taken.

130. Interview, Paul A. Volcker, March 18, 1974.

month in a row. McCracken, along with Treasury officials, feared that this would unsettle the foreign exchange markets and concluded that action to close the gold window might well be required within the month. Shortly after the July 15 announcement he suggested to the President that there was a need now for something "of Peking proportions" in economic policy, explaining that this would mean cutting loose from gold, going on a flexible exchange rate, and pursuing a more expansionist policy at home. The suggestion evoked an immediate and favorable response, which is not surprising in view of this President's taste for the dramatic plus the fact that he had long been aware that the dollar was overvalued and that the domestic economic recovery was proceeding too slowly to meet the goal of 4 to 4.5 percent unemployment by mid-1972.[131] Once a coordinated set of policies to deal with these difficulties had been formulated—and presented, moreover, as a fitting complement to the new China policy—a wage and price freeze may have seemed an appropriate finishing touch. Economically, it could be explained as a desirable counterweight to expansionary moves; politically, it might regain the initiative from the Democrats, and it could be represented—as was skillfully done in the President's speech to the nation announcing the New Economic Policy on August 15—as a radical change for essentially conservative purposes: a step toward creating an economic environment in which "workers, employers, consumers . . . working together" could beat back inflation and redirect the competitive spirit to truly productive ends.[132]

On the international economic front events moved on apace while the details of the New Economic Policy were still in the drafting stage and staff work on implementing a freeze had scarcely begun. On August 6 a Joint Economic Committee report was issued, calling for an incomes policy and recommending a devaluation of the dollar as part of a general currency realignment. This, it suggested, might be accomplished through

131. Interview, Paul W. McCracken, December 29, 1973. The President may have been influenced also by the case for a more assertive international negotiating position on trade policy that Assistant for International Economic Affairs Peter G. Peterson had been presenting since April. Peterson's arguments can be found in his "The United States in the Changing World Economy," 2 vols. (Government Printing Office, 1971; processed). An account of part of the discussion at Camp David on August 13–15 and fascinating insight into the process of arriving at a formula for "selling" the package is given by Safire, *Before the Fall*, pt. 7, chap. 5.

132. Compare Mazlish, *In Search of Nixon*, p. 137. The text of the President's televised announcement of the New Economic Policy can be found in *Congressional Quarterly*, vol. 29 (August 21, 1971), pp. 1769–71.

the International Monetary Fund or, should that body refuse the responsibility, by unilaterally closing the gold window.[133] Despite Treasury disclaimers, this was read by some as the administration's way of testing reaction to such steps and produced a massive movement out of dollars and, from the Bank of England, a request that the United States guarantee the gold value of Britain's dollar holdings.[134] In this heady atmosphere it was decided that a fairly quick implementation of the New Economic Policy would be desirable, and following planning sessions with his top economic advisers at Camp David from August 13 to 15, the President announced to the nation that immediate action was to be taken, "not timidly, not halfheartedly, and not in piecemeal fashion."[135]

The Unfinished Experiment

The first Nixon administration will surely be remembered for the sequence of wage-price controls programs that followed the August 15, 1971, change of policy. It should not be forgotten that the freeze interrupted an equally important and intriguing experiment in the management of a large, decentralized economy. The experiment began as an attempt to determine whether traditional monetary and fiscal policies could return an economy to its long-term growth path, from a starting position above it, without overshooting. The underlying conception was of a stable path and an essentially self-correcting economy, the mechanism of which, however, had been prevented from functioning properly by some overzealous tinkering. This had resulted in a distorted pattern of signals and an economy that was behaving with an inflationary bias. Essentially the problem was to eliminate the excess demand that had engendered a self-fulfilling set of inflationary expectations and actions.

President Nixon's economic advisers proceeded on the assumption that this inflation-mindedness would alter as their restrictive monetary and fiscal policy created the appropriate environment. They tried to create

133. *Action Now to Strengthen the U.S. Dollar*, Report of the Subcommittee on International Exchange and Payments of the Joint Economic Committee, 92 Cong. 1 sess. (1971), especially pp. 10, 13.

134. Cameron, "How the U.S. Got on the Road to a Controlled Economy," pp. 76, 77; "Memo to the Press," C-114, Department of the Treasury, *News*, August 7, 1971.

135. "Text of President's Announcement on Economy," *Congressional Quarterly* (August 21, 1971), p. 1769.

what Paul McCracken once referred to as "the ingredients . . . of a social bargain or compact" by showing, in the first place, that the government was prepared to set its own house in order by curtailing expenditures, then simply pointing out that public and private interests are at one in the business of fighting inflation.[136]

There was no doubt from the start that, in McCracken's words, "we are . . . dealing with a process in which the passage of time is critical." This did not mean simply setting the dials and waiting for the desired effects to accrue. But for three reasons anything beyond monetary and fiscal policy was regarded as being at most supplementary. First, the capacity of the CEA to monitor the functioning of individual markets was strictly limited by its meager staff resources. As a practical matter, it was believed that any move in the direction of a systematic and comprehensive market-oriented incomes policy was constrained by this insufficiency. The guiding principle at the CEA, McCracken explained, had to be "doing what can effectively be done, whenever it can be done, and not pretending to do more."[137] Second, it was felt that too little was known about the institutional elements conceivably relevant to devising a comprehensive incomes policy or establishing the basis for a workable social compact. If, as McCracken later suggested, "therapy for inflation should . . . include some action against the various agglomerations of power that are impeding the effective operation of our economy," there was a prior need to examine whether "the freedom and openness of our markets have been seriously eroded" and whether, and to what extent, it is true that the "rough balance of power at the bargaining table . . . no longer exists."[138]

136. McCracken, "The Management of Expansion," speech before the U.S. Council of the International Chamber of Commerce, New York City, November 9, 1970 (Council of Economic Advisers); the President's speech announcing the appointment of a National Commission on Productivity, June 17, 1970, and his news conference, December 10, 1970.

137. McCracken, testimony in *The 1971 Economic Report of the President*, Hearings, pp. 8, 9. The resources constraint was in fact less binding than here described. The CEA under McCracken produced careful and perceptive analyses of a large number of specific price and wage developments (in the form of the inflation alerts) and supplied the backbone staff for detailed investigations of particular markets under the auspices of the Cabinet Committee on Economic Policy, including transportation, lumber, copper, and steel.

138. McCracken, "Fighting Inflation After Phase Two." The phrase "agglomerations of power" should not necessarily be read as a reference to industrial concentration. A Department of Justice investigation conducted for Richard McLaren by economist Leonard Weiss and covering the period 1963–69 found no significant positive correlation between degree of concentration and rates of inflation for that period as

350 NEIL DE MARCHI

There was a clear need, too, for a better understanding of the dynamics of inflationary expectations. How far, for example, was the "growth psychosis" that Maurice Mann pointed to attributable, as McCracken implied, to a shift to a more youthful work force "less cautious than their forebears, more insistent on immediate realization of the material comforts of life, reflecting a revolution of rising domestic expectations ... [demanding] income gains far beyond those the economy could validate through the relatively slow secular rise in productivity"?[139] Or again, what caused the wage distortions in the construction industry to emerge "with such a vengeance" in 1969 and 1970, and by what mechanism were those distortions perpetuated? These questions do not obviously fall under the aegis of macrostabilization policy, and in 1969–71 there was little basis for offering more than conjectural replies to them.[140] Third, the administration was convinced that the economy was basically competitive and that a market-oriented incomes policy would not add much to the anti-inflationary effort.

Though no substitute for a formal evaluation, it may not be amiss to mention in conclusion two issues with which such an evaluation should deal. In the first place, it bears repeating that the policy of gradualism, in both its phases, was very much a product of the view that checking the inflation was largely a matter of correcting past excesses in macropolicy. Complementing this view, on a micro level, was a belief that prices could be relied on to respond—without special intervention—to changes in the degree of market tightness. Even before the breakdown of the CEA's forecasts in 1970, it was acknowledged within the Council that an adequate explanation of recent and current wage trends might have to embody not just the current tightness of labor markets but also wage distortion, and a tendency to build catch-up and anticipation of continuing inflation into long-term contracts. But there have been many critics who argue that these and comparable rigidities impairing the responsiveness

---

a whole, while a negative relation seemed to hold for the years 1968–69, when prices rose rapidly. This was interpreted as evidence that concentrated industries do not constitute a serious inflationary threat, except to the extent that prices may continue to rise over a longer period in such industries once a general inflation has gotten under way. George P. Shultz openly rejected the argument of some (such as John Kenneth Galbraith) who saw concentration as a major factor in accounting for inflation. See McLaren's statement, *The 1970 Midyear Review of the State of the Economy*, Hearings, pt. 1, pp. 108–21; Shultz, "Prescription for Economic Policy."

139. McCracken, "Fighting Inflation After Phase Two."
140. Interview, Marvin Kosters, February 7, 1974. Work was in fact proceeding

of *commodity* prices to changes in market demand might have been recognized sooner and addressed more seriously had anti-inflation policy been less backward-looking and had the President's economic advisers been less predisposed to believe in the free market system.

Second (though not unrelated), while some intervention was undertaken, ostensibly to strengthen market forces, a good deal of reliance was also placed on appeals for "responsible" public behavior. The assumption on which such appeals were based was that, as the President put it in his speech of June 17, 1970, "if businessmen and workingmen are willing to raise their sights by lowering their demands, they will help themselves by helping to hold down everybody's cost of living." The problem was to ensure that all lowered their demands in unison. If this could not be guaranteed—and under prevailing institutional arrangements it could not —the inescapable conclusion, as the CEA acknowledged in its second inflation alert, was that "slowing down the inflation means that those who come later will get smaller wage or price increases than those who came earlier." Without any other compensating advantage for being late in the queue, it was not at all unreasonable (as the inflation alert also conceded) for separate economic units to try to recoup past real income losses, restore their relative positions, and guard themselves against the possible recurrence of such losses in the near future. The second inflation alert properly pointed out that if this were done generally it would prolong inflation and invite policies that would result in unemployment. But this warning carried little conviction, since the administration had already shown itself unwilling to induce a major recession and was increasingly unlikely to adopt this approach as 1972 drew nearer.[141] Insofar as the administration was serious in its appeals for restraint and serious also about avoiding recession, it was in effect asking the socially responsible to bear the burden of fighting inflation while underwriting the actions of the irresponsible. While these contradictions suggest that the administration may for too long have paid insufficient attention to the institu-

---

both inside and outside the administration (in the CEA and the CED) in an attempt to account for wage trends from 1969, *not* in terms of cost-push and the strength of demand in the labor markets at a particular time, but by looking at the degree of wage dispersion, worker response to unanticipated inflation, and the prevalence of long-term contracts. See Kosters, Fedor, and Eckstein, "Collective Bargaining Settlements and the Wage Structure"; and Arnold H. Packer and Seong H. Park, "Distortions in Relative Wages and Shifts in the Phillips Curve," *Review of Economics and Statistics*, vol. 55 (February 1973), pp. 16–22.

141. "Second Inflation Alert," pp. 6–7.

tional and political constraints within which gradualist policies had to operate, it must also be said that most of its critics were unconscionably vague about the details of incomes policies and controls systems and how they might be implemented.

This last issue was perforce resolved in the hectic days following the August 15 policy change. Unfortunately, it is still unknown whether, in an economy committed to full employment, characterized by significant pockets of "market power," and in which there has been rapid and sustained inflation, gradualist policies, granted enough time, can succeed without help from some form of incomes policy less direct and general than controls and without structural reforms.

VI

The Continuing Courtship: Wage-Price Policy through Five Administrations

ARNOLD R. WEBER

SINCE the end of World War II, the United States has carried on a continuous flirtation with wage-price policy. In the Eisenhower administration, the courtship was cool and distant. In other instances, as during the Nixon administration, a deep infatuation ended in estrangement. Despite evidence that the lady has lost her innocence, she is still alluring to both politicians and economic policymakers. Although wage-price policy lacks the respectability of other economic measures, it now constitutes a recognized policy alternative in the management of the national economy.

The Emergence of Wage-Price Policy

The emergence of government policies to influence specific wage and price movements is the result of a variety of factors. First, the intellectual triumph of Keynesian economics and its legislative expression, the Employment Act of 1946, reinforced governmental concern about inflation as a side effect of the treatment for stagnation and unemployment. Once the nation became committed to full employment as a national goal, some method had to be found to cope with the inflation that so often was the concomitant of success. Wage and price policy seemed an attractive solution. Full employment would be achieved by manipulating fiscal and monetary aggregates, while price stability would be preserved by influencing key wage and price decisions in the overall structure of the economy. Thus wage and price policy appeared to be the missing piece in the puzzle whereby full employment and price stability could be simultaneously attained.

This quest for full employment with price stability became the special responsibility of the President. As a consequence of the New Deal and the Employment Act, the President was now regarded as Chief Economist of the United States. The establishment of the Council of Economic Advisers institutionalized this role and gave it a strong executive character. It is not surprising that wage-price policy has been associated primarily with executive action rather than with legislative measures. Presidents Kennedy and Johnson, in particular, established an activist pattern that has strongly conditioned expectations about the behavior of future chief executives.

If acceptance of the goal of full employment set the framework for wage and price policies, wars gave these policies high priority, familiarity, and the aura of success. By diverting resources from civilian production, wars created strong inflationary pressures while suffusing the economy with the glow of full employment. Theoretically, these pressures on prices could be contained by aggressive fiscal policies, but the political response was usually inadequate to the economic requirements and other forms of government intervention were used. By the end of World War II, wage and price policies—direct controls—had a high degree of acceptance. Controls, strengthened by rationing, had kept wage and price increases at a tolerable level and acquired the coloration of patriotism.

With full employment the principal goal of postwar economic policy, it was inevitable that controls should be viewed as an appropriate device to deal with the inflationary perils of reconversion. When peacetime controls were blocked by Congress, President Truman converted the issue into a major political controversy that contributed to his upset victory in the 1948 presidential election. Although concern about inflation had subsided by 1948–49, wage-price policy regained high visibility with the onset of the Korean War. Again, in Truman's battles with Congress over an effective stabilization program, the President portrayed wage-price policy as a matter of national virtue.

Under President Johnson the cumulative weight of the Vietnam War made wage-price policy a centerpiece of the administration's overall economic strategy. The use of "guideposts" and "jawboning" had started under President Kennedy as part of an effort to restore economic growth and full employment. During the Johnson administration these policy instruments were transformed into defenses against inflation in an economy that was subject to increasing strains from the Vietnam War. When Johnson rejected the advice of his economists to seek a tax increase in

1966, wage-price policy was the most appealing of the few weapons left in the arsenal.

Neil de Marchi's study of the Nixon administration (chapter 5) clearly indicates the initial attempt to avoid direct intervention in wage and price decisions. Instead, the administration adopted a strategy of "gradualism" whereby monetary and fiscal restraint would slow the inflation rate without precipitating large-scale unemployment. Despite these sanguine expectations, the economic momentum generated by the Vietnam War combined with the consequences of "gradualism" to create a politically untenable situation of high unemployment and rising prices during 1970–71. For this reason and other factors noted by de Marchi, the Nixon administration executed its historic volte-face and imposed wage and price policies in their most draconian form with the freeze of August 15, 1971.

Thus wars have generated the wide oscillations in economic performance that, together with the technical difficulties of achieving full employment and price stability simultaneously, have made wage-price policy an almost irresistible policy choice. Moreover, during the Vietnam period the distinction between "wartime" and "peacetime" was blurred so that adopting wage and price policies was tacit recognition of the economic consequences of a war to which Americans were unwilling to make a national commitment as a political matter.

The growth of trade unions and collective bargaining has been a less dramatic but equally significant factor in the evolution of wage and price policies in the United States. The effective application of these policies depends on the assumption that many labor and product markets are characterized by noncompetitive conditions. If all wages and prices were promptly and fully determined by market forces, presumably government intervention would have a counterproductive effect and result in distortions that would ultimately raise wages and prices. This line of reasoning, of course, is at the heart of the free market criticism of wage-price policy. However, if there are monopoly elements in the economy, the appropriate form of "incomes policy" is the vigorous application of the antitrust laws. Wage-price policy as such then becomes only a short-term supplement to long-term structural remedies.

Resorting to the antitrust laws is usually inappropriate or infeasible in dealing with union "power." With the passage of the Wagner Act and the articulation of the concept of the "exclusive bargaining agent," union organization became a protected activity and the successful unions were granted a significant degree of monopoly power. Hence, wage policy has always had a particular appeal in the United States as a device for dealing with the problems of economic stabilization arising from the legitimate exercise of monopoly power through collective bargaining. Indeed, in the United States wage policy has been the pivot of active efforts by the government to influence wages and prices. It is significant to note that throughout the Kennedy and Johnson administrations actions to restrict price behavior in the large oligopolistic industries usually began with preliminary efforts to obtain a "responsible" wage settlement through collective bargaining.

With the acceptance of monopoly power in the labor market, wage policy has had to be fashioned and applied with a certain amount of finesse, if not deviousness. On the one hand, various actions have been taken to induce unions to exercise their power responsibly—with price restraint as the quid pro quo. On the other hand, efforts have been made to identify egregious instances of monopoly power that appear to go beyond the limits defined by the Wagner and Taft-Hartley Acts. The construction unions have been a favorite target of these efforts. Collective bargaining in the construction industry received special attention from the Johnson administration and was the subject of a separate control effort during the Nixon administration. Under Nixon the government responded to the "excessive" exercise of union power in construction by suspending the Davis-Bacon Act, under which the government itself has acted to reinforce the unions' power derived from the Wagner Act. Direct wage controls were applied in March 1971, a full five months before the comprehensive freeze was instituted.

The quest for effective wage-price policy has also been given impetus by the increased American sensitivity to the international economy. By the early 1960s economic relations between the United States and the other Western industrialized nations had changed significantly and the U.S. balance of payments came under increasing pressure. Aside from threatening the position of the dollar, this deterioration of the balance of payments implied that other Western countries were "exporting" their unemployment to the United States. Indeed, in one of the earliest representations made to President-elect Kennedy, Walt W. Rostow recommended wage and price policies as a means by which the administration could achieve leadership in international affairs and avert "stop-go" efforts to manage the balance of payments.

By 1971 continued adherence to fixed exchange rates, the devaluation of foreign currencies, and the transformation of the world economy had made the U.S. balance-of-payments problem more acute and set the stage for the dramatic exercise of wage-price policy by President Nixon. The proximate cause of the New Economic Policy unveiled on August 15, 1971, was the sharp deterioration of the balance of payments and the heavy pressure on the dollar in international money markets. Under these circumstances, it is not surprising that Secretary of the Treasury John Connally, whose range of action was not limited by the sense of tradition that had governed the actions of many of his predecessors, was instrumental in persuading President Nixon to link the institution of wage-price controls to the closing of the gold window and the devaluation of the dollar. Wage-price controls would help the United States preserve any trade advantage arising from the devaluation while crimping the possible inflationary effect of this action. In the absence of direct controls, domestic prices were expected to rise because of the higher prices of imports and the greater latitude these increases would give to domestic producers to raise the price of similar goods.

One of the striking consequences of the series of experiments with wage-price policy is the extent to which the framework for the discussion of policy has changed. For example, Scott Gordon's discussion (chapter 2) of the controversy precipitated by a mild passage in the President's Economic Report of 1957 calling for "shared responsibility" between government and business for price stability seems almost innocent compared to the discussion of wage-price policy in 1975. Where President Eisenhower's call for "discipline" in 1957 appeared heretical, it is a cliché in 1975. Where President Eisenhower ignored demands from Senator Estes Kefauver to force the steel companies to reduce their price increases in 1958, one of the first acts of President Ford was to criticize General Motors almost casually for a price increase and to express appreciation only in passing when the company acceded to his request for a token price cut.

Throughout the 1950s the debate over wage-price policy was expressed largely in ideological terms. In 1975 the discussion has focused on the pragmatic question of whether such policy will work rather than whether it constitutes a threat to the Republic. The thirty-four-month experience with direct wage and price controls during the Nixon administration has turned the public discussion of wage-price policy to tactics and design and away from burning questions of principle. In this respect, reviewing the experience of the past five administrations clearly indicates the road the country has traveled, and may provide some directional signs for its future course.

Designing Wage-Price Policy

In analyzing wage-price policy in the five postwar administrations one is confronted with a jumble of slogans, organizations, heroes, and villains. If there is any common thread to the record of the last thirty years, it is that wage-price policy is a plastic concept whose shape has been molded by economic circumstances and immediate political requirements rather than any definitive theories or system of implementation. This plasticity is most vividly revealed by the variety of objectives the various policies have been designed to serve. Aside from general strictures about the need for wage-price policy to help vanquish inflation, its goals have never been clearly defined and, in any case, have been overwhelmed by the tactical requirements of the moment.

First, wage-price policy has sometimes served a neopopulist objective by providing a forum in which the government could confront powerful economic aggregations—that is, monopolies that are allegedly unwilling to act in the public interest. This objective was expressed in the Truman administration's formulation of wage-price policy. Truman asserted that controls were necessary immediately after the war to prevent business from reaping excessive profits during the reconversion period. Although Craufurd Goodwin and Stanley Herren describe in chapter 1 how this initial objective was transformed into a broader goal of preventing inflation that might lead to economic collapse, the populist stirrings were readily revealed by political factors. Thus rhetoric easily overwhelmed any sense of economic design during the election campaign of 1948. In a flurry of speeches, Truman reminded the electorate that he had urged that price controls be retained until production caught up with demand. The Republican Congress, controlled by special interests, had been unwilling to take this step, which was so clearly in the public interest. In characteristic terms, Truman stated:

They [the Congress] have decided that the National Association of Manufacturers and the National Chamber of Commerce of the United States know all about prices and price controls.

Well now, we have price controls and rationing now, just as we have under Government controls, only those price controls are controls so that only the man who has the money is able to get the necessities of life.[1]

Wage-price policy was also used for mounting broadside attacks on "power" in the Kennedy administration. Here the most notable exercise of presidential machismo came during Kennedy's controversy with the steel industry. When United States Steel raised prices following the 1962 labor negotiations, apparently in contravention of a pledge to the President, Kennedy launched a furious verbal assault that Theodore Roosevelt would not have been ashamed of. The price hike was rescinded when Inland Steel was persuaded not to follow U.S. Steel's lead.[2] Even in the Nixon administration, wage-price policy was used to identify, if not to stigmatize, a particular set of villains. In this case, the Nixon administration turned the spotlight on the construction unions, which, in its judgment, were prime conveyers of the inflationary virus.

The use of wage-price policy for such populist objectives essentially serves a political rather than an economic purpose. In macroeconomic terms, it is misleading to believe that assaults aimed at particular villains are useful. While there is the hope that taking an individual company or union to task will set an example and restrain other businesses and unions in their wage and price decisions, in most instances the impact will be ephemeral because of the complexity and sheer magnitude of the U.S. economy. Moreover, wage and price policies that spring from populist ardor have limited staying power and are easily blunted by other political considerations. For example, William Barber's examination (chapter 3) of the Kennedy administration indicates that the victory over the steel industry in 1962 was a Pyrrhic one; the hostility in the business community was so intense after "the Battle of Blough Run"

1. "Rear Platform Remarks in . . . [Gary] Indiana," *Public Papers of the Presidents of the United States: Harry S. Truman* (1948), p. 114.
2. Although it is sometimes asserted that Inland Steel was a sympathetic accomplice in President Kennedy's efforts to roll back the price increase, the president of Inland described the incident in the following terms twelve years later: "In April, 1962 [the] major companies announced a $6 per ton across-the-board price increase to offset costs absorbed over the previous four-year period. President Kennedy accused the steel companies of 'irresponsible defiance of public interest and ruthless disregard of national obligation.' The price increases were rescinded." "The Anatomy of a Steel Shortage," speech delivered to the annual convention of the American Institute of Steel Construction by Michael Tenenbaum, president of Inland Steel Company, October 29, 1974; reprinted in "Quote," American Iron and Steel Institute, Public Relations Department (no date; processed), p. 3.

that Kennedy had no stomach for another confrontation when the industry raised its prices again the following year. The use of wage-price policy as a springboard for general attacks on power also means that the choicest targets are more likely to be business than organized labor. This creates serious problems of inequity and, in addition, skirts a major problem of wage-price policy: to the extent that unions contribute to inflationary pressures their power should be dealt with directly by government policies rather than by indirect and sporadic efforts to stiffen employers' resistance to union wage demands.

Second, wage-price policy has been used as a defensive adjunct to other expansionist policies. This objective was expressed during the Kennedy administration. As Barber indicates, wage-price policy was proposed to President Kennedy by his advisers as insurance that a tax cut and other expansionist measures would not result in inflation. Ultimately, this counsel was accepted, particularly after successful experiences in jawboning the steel and automobile industries persuaded an uneasy President that he would not run an undue economic—or political—risk in opting for growth and employment.

Similarly, during the Nixon administration wage-price policy was used to underwrite an aggressive expansionist policy. In addition to difficulties with the balance of payments, the major political problem from the administration's point of view was the failure of "gradualism" to achieve an acceptable trade-off between unemployment and price stability. Indeed, during 1970–71 the administration appeared to have the worst of both worlds, with unemployment high and prices rising rapidly. The defeats suffered by the Republicans during the election of 1970 precipitated a chorus of demands for action and the carefully orchestrated policy of gradualism was abandoned in favor of growth and employment. As in the Kennedy administration, wage-price controls were temporarily attractive because there was considerable excess capacity in the economy and it was believed possible to have controls without grossly impairing the operation of the market system. Moreover, public confidence in the administration's economic policy had plummeted, making it necessary to take dramatic steps to demonstrate that the President could be "tough" on inflation while stimulating a new surge of prosperity.

For this reason, the wage-price freeze became highly attractive and, more than the arcane details of devaluation, symbolized the administration's resolve to set things right. One consequence of the freeze, however, was to lock the administration into a more rigorous and comprehensive program of controls than was necessary or desired by Nixon's top economic advisers. This system persisted through Phase II, but almost from the moment Phase II went into effect the administration worked on a strategy of decontrol that culminated in Phases III and IV. The second freeze in 1973 was a perverse political effort to restore confidence in a system that the administration itself had undermined.

Third, wage-price policy has been used as a substitute for fiscal and monetary policies. As Barber notes, one of the important arguments made in selling wage-price policy to President Kennedy was that a distinction should be made between demand-pull and cost-push inflation. Where there was excess capacity in the economy, inflationary tendencies were symptomatic of cost-push factors that could be restrained through wage-price policy. On the other hand, demand-pull inflation required broader fiscal and monetary measures. This text was adhered to through the Kennedy administration and in the early stages of the Johnson administration. But when strong inflationary pressure developed with the enlargement of the Vietnam War, it became obvious that strong fiscal measures were necessary. For political reasons associated with conduct of the war, Johnson rejected the recommendations for a tax increase, and the administration had little recourse but to broaden the application of wage-price policy.

Fourth, if wage-price policy has sometimes been used as a substitute for fiscal and monetary measures, it has also been brandished in an effort to permit fiscal and monetary measures to work by deflecting pressure for more direct government intervention. This paradoxical, if not cunning, approach was taken by President Eisenhower. To the extent that the Eisenhower administration had any wage-price policy at all, it was vague and hortatory. When the President included sermonettes on the need for restraint in his Economic Report, they were taken as evidence of his willingness to enter the battle against inflation more strenuously. Scott Gordon's analysis, however, indicates that Eisenhower intended nothing of the kind. The only major case of direct government intervention discussed by Gordon was that during the prolonged strike in the steel industry in 1959. In this instance the main issue was not wages but work rules. The intervention was carried out by Vice-President Nixon, who was showing his wares preliminary to the 1960 presidential election campaign.

The Nixon administration also went through an extended period in which pseudo wage-price policies were formulated to divert pressure for government intervention in private decision-making. If gradualism was to have an opportunity to work, demands for action had to be accommodated, at least superficially. Such a feint was executed in the spring of 1970 when the administration initiated a series of "inflation alerts" and established the National Commission on Productivity. The inflation alerts were a series of ex post facto admonitions to business or unions that quickly sank to inaudible levels. The Commission on Productivity, on the other hand, tried to direct the attention of the nation to more fundamental factors affecting prices and wages.[3]

There is a great disposition to criticize the lack of precision in defining the objectives of wage-price policy. But this criticism is beside the point. The significant generalization is that only rarely has this policy been intended to control wage and price movements in any rigorous or comprehensive sense. Even in cases that have involved the favored targets of wage-price policy—the steel and automobile industries—it was not obvious whether the government was courting the industry or controlling it. When Nixon took the plunge during Phases I and II, there was a systematic effort to control wages and prices, but the initial exultation soon turned to a flush of embarrassment and the half-hearted programs of Phases III and IV. Thus wage-price policy has been employed primarily as a tactic in the general political maneuvering over inflation rather than as a program with explicit objectives that were sustained in their own right.

Coverage

The coverage of wage-price policies has reflected the variety and imprecision of the program objectives—indeed, its dominant features have been selectivity and uncertainty. The only time that coverage was made explicit was as a concomitant of direct wage and price controls during the Nixon administration, when the need for a clear demarcation was dictated as much by the legal requirements of the program as by the objectives and administration of it. With this exception, wage-price policy has been applied more or less on a "reserve power" basis whereby the execu-

3. A similar approach was adopted in the early stages of the Ford administration. Within the first month after he took office, President Ford forced a token rollback of prices in the automobile industry, established an agency to monitor wages and prices without attempting to clarify its authority, strongly disclaimed any desire to impose mandatory wage-price controls on the grounds that they do not work, and focused his policies on monetary and fiscal measures designed to grind down inflation over a longer haul.

tive branch selects its target to support the program objective that is appropriate at the time.

If any generalization can be made about the experience of the past thirty years, it is that the broader the ostensible coverage of the wage-price policy, the more narrowly was the policy applied. This paradox is perhaps best explained by relating coverage to the catalog of policy objectives. For instance, the neopopulist objective of wage-price policy enunciated during the Truman administration presumably included any monopoly or center of economic power capable of exacting a toll from the economy —members of the U.S. Chamber of Commerce and the National Association of Manufacturers. But it is significant how infrequently this highly activist, sometimes bellicose President attempted to translate this objective into action in specific cases. The only important case noted by Goodwin and Herren was the seizure of the steel industry in 1952, and this was not so much a direct attack on prices as a way to force the steel companies to accept a wage settlement and to avert a strike during wartime.

When the objective of wage-price policy has been to provide a protective mantle for expansionist policies, the coverage has been shaped by tactical considerations. In the Kennedy administration, wage-price policy was largely brought to bear in highly visible situations where it could be demonstrated that the policy was an effective defense against the exercise of market power. The requirements for this demonstration of muscle-flexing were twofold: that the industry be "basic" in the sense that price movements in it had reverberations throughout the economy, and that it be oligopolistic so that the policy could effectively be applied on an ad hoc basis through executive daring. The industry was even more attractive when it also involved a large union, enabling parallel interventions on wages and prices. From the outset, Rostow and other Kennedy advisers expressed the desirability of arranging "wage-price treaties" whereby the union would agree to a moderate wage settlement in return for a pledge that the companies with whom it bargained would respond with similar restraint. The concept of a "wage treaty" was to emerge thirteen years later in more grandiloquent terms as a "social compact."[4]

---

4. The term "social compact" is somewhat ambiguous in its usage. In the United Kingdom it has been used to describe a general agreement between the government and the national labor federation under which the trade unions will moderate otherwise justifiable wage demands in return for a government commitment to reduce the erosion of real earnings and to expand various social programs. In the United

For these reasons, the most frequent targets of wage-price policy were the steel and automobile industries. When the Kennedy administration appeared to enjoy some success in moderating wage and price movements in these industries, various task forces moved on to other metal industries. In these cases, the wage agreements did not quite meet the technical requirements for price stability, but they were close enough to the current guidelines to justify demands that the companies absorb the increases in wage costs without seeking relief through price adjustments. On the other hand, the Kennedy administration generally failed to induce price *decreases*, as would be consistent with the current theory of wage-price policy, in cases where productivity increases exceeded the national average.

Why the union leaders played this game is not clear. However, the implementation of such accords was most effective when the union leaders were personally swayed by presidential blandishments or saw broader social goals in such cooperation. In any case, when efforts were made to control wages independent of price decisions in the same industry, they were usually unsuccessful. In 1966 Secretary of Labor Willard Wirtz made a limited attempt to restrain union wage demands in the construction industry. The government prepared for a battle with Local 825 of the International Union of Operating Engineers and, according to James Cochrane (chapter 4), came out second best when the union achieved its demands through a series of arbitration awards and supplementary arrangements. A more important setback occurred in the case involving the International Association of Machinists (IAM) and the air transport industry. Although air fares presumably were firmly under the thumb of the Civil Aeronautics Board, the machinists' union was adamant in its demands and finally settled on a contract calling for a 4.9 percent wage increase, far in excess of the current version of the guidelines.

The only situation in which efforts to control wages independent of prices were successful involved the Construction Industry Stabilization Committee (CISC) during the Nixon presidency. For three years, the construction unions actively cooperated with a special wage stabilization

States a "social compact" has sometimes been described as a pledge of wage restraint from labor in return for tax cuts by the government to compensate for increases in the consumer price level. The essential agreement in a "treaty" or "compact" is willingness of the trade unions to limit their wage demands in return for some quid pro quo. The government may be either an arbiter or a co-signer of the arrangement.

effort. The circumstances were unique; they cannot be readily duplicated in other industries. The unions had perceived an active threat from non-union competition, and wages in the industry were spiraling. The President, all other measures to control wage increases having failed, suspended the Davis-Bacon Act in February 1971. This set the stage for the establishment of the CISC, which was readily accepted by the unions, leading to the reinstatement of the Davis-Bacon Act. The effort was engineered by John T. Dunlop of Harvard University, who called upon three decades of experience and personal relationships in the industry.

When wage-price policy has served as a substitute for fiscal and monetary measures there has been some effort to establish comprehensive coverage. After President Johnson had rejected pleas for a tax increase, various task forces were organized to develop an "early warning system" to identify and influence price movements in specific industries. This special monitoring group was established by Joseph A. Califano, Jr., and direct government representations were made in more than forty cases. Bereft of statutory power over wages and prices, the Johnson administration tried to cope with the tide of rising prices engendered by the Vietnam War by expanding its informal activities. It is noteworthy that following the IAM case minimal efforts were made to influence union wage demands directly. In fact, many of the wage agreements negotiated by the major unions during this period achieved real wages that left their members in a relatively favorable position despite the increases in the price level that took place during 1969–71.[5]

The most extensive coverage was applied during the period of direct controls from August 1971 to April 1974. This experiment, which began with a universal wage-price freeze and was pruned over three years by a series of exceptions and formal acts of decontrol, can be viewed as an aberration. Because the wage-price freeze was part of a broad economic policy change, some short-term, dramatic measures were desirable. Moreover, because statutory authority to impose direct controls had been enacted by Congress to harass the President, such a step was feasible. In view of the euphoria associated with the freeze, the President could not immediately trim the program even though the administration had severe misgivings about so comprehensive and rigorous an effort. In fact, Phase

5. Marvin Kosters, Kenneth Fedor, and Albert Eckstein, "Collective Bargaining Settlements and the Wage Structure," *Labor Law Journal*, vol. 24 (August 1973), pp. 517–25.

II represented a subtle effort to sharpen the coverage of controls, which would be rigorously enforced only for firms with more than $50 million in sales and a thousand or more employees. Once the election of 1972 was over, a major step toward de facto decontrol was taken with the initiation of Phase III in January 1973. From then on, the administrators steadily retreated to a smaller perimeter, and by April 1974 only about one-quarter of the economy was under the jurisdiction of the Cost of Living Council.

Organizational Arrangements

Although considerable attention has been given to the organizational arrangements appropriate to the maintenance of wage-price policy, this issue has really been subsidiary to the general problem of devising an effective program to control inflation. For example, as Cochrane describes the situation, a great deal of energy was expended in the last stages of the Johnson administration in developing organizational options for the implementation of wage-price policy. While these efforts were not trivial, it is apparent that they masked the growing frustration of the President's economic advisers over Johnson's reluctance to adopt the appropriate fiscal measures.

Nonetheless, some significant distinctions may be inferred from the nature of the organizational arrangements used to formulate and carry out wage-price policy. Again, these distinctions are linked to the objectives of the program and its coverage. Where wage-price policy remains at the level of exhortation, organizational arrangements are generally limited to policy-oriented groups which pull together various combinations of top officials in the executive branch. In virtually every administration since World War II there has been a chameleonlike progression of cabinet committees and special task forces concerned with price stability, economic growth, and other euphemisms designed to elevate concern about price and wage developments. The composition of these cabinet committees has varied from case to case, but usually they have included the secretary of the treasury and the secretaries of the major constituent-oriented departments such as Commerce, Labor, and Agriculture. In each case, the chairman of the Council of Economic Advisers has played a major role. In the Nixon administration, the designation of the secretary of the treasury as the primary economic spokesman for the administration somewhat reduced the influence of the CEA.

As wage-price policy became more explicit and its implementation more aggressive, supportive organizational arrangements became necessary simply to carry the administrative burden. During the late stages of the Johnson administration, the cabinet-level policy mechanisms were supplemented by the Interagency Staff Price Committee (the Nelson Committee) to identify problem areas on the price side and to coordinate the strategy for negotiating with management. The actual negotiations apparently were carried out by John Douglas, an assistant attorney general, and members of the CEA. After some months, the level of involvement was raised to include Joseph Califano, the powerful assistant to President Johnson. Where the organizational arrangements are informal and lack statutory authority, the level of executive involvement tends to escalate as the deference inspired by lower echelon officials diminishes.

Of all the experiences with peacetime wage-price policy, the only instance that was associated with a formal organizational structure was during Phases I to IV in the Nixon administration. Because the program operated from a legal base and was comprehensive at the outset, the usual array of special task forces would not suffice. The wage-price freeze was administered by the Cost of Living Council, a cabinet-level group charged with making policy, and by staff commandeered from existing agencies, particularly the Office of Emergency Preparedness and the Internal Revenue Service. These arrangements were elaborated during Phase II to include a separate all-public Price Commission and a tripartite Pay Board—independent agencies set up to ensure the "fairness" of the control system. The CLC, however, continued to direct the field structure, which was centralized in a special unit of the IRS. The Pay Board and the Price Commission were abolished at the beginning of Phase III, not only to improve coordination but also to give the administration control of the application of wage-price policy and the orderly dismantling of the program.

One additional organizational strategy should be noted. Under Eisenhower, decoy organizations were set up to demonstrate the government's concern about inflation while abjuring active involvement in wage-price decisions. An example is the Cabinet Committee on Price Stability for Economic Growth, established in 1959 to monitor and review price developments. The committee was chaired by then Vice-President Nixon and, aside from Allen Wallis, the executive vice-chairman, did not have any staff. In a steady stream of press releases and speeches by Wallis, the committee waved a red flag with great energy, reducing the demands for a more active policy.[6]

The Problem of Consensus

While the various organizational arrangements have been closely tailored to the objectives and administrative requirements of specific wage-price policies, they have skirted what is the most vexing problem of such efforts—the development of mechanisms to define a consensus acceptable to the major interest groups in the economy. In a political democracy wage-price policy cannot be effective unless it is accepted, tacitly or otherwise, by the major groups that will be affected by it. Even when the program is based on statutory authority, as in the Nixon administration, its viability must stem from acceptance rather than coercion for the simple reason that in a democracy the economy cannot be managed by throwing union leaders and businessmen in jail. When wage-price policy remains in the realm of general exhortation and few specific actions, consensus is not important. But when efforts are made to restrict the latitude of the parties and to control their decisions directly, the question of defining and preserving a consensus becomes critical.

Each of the administrations examined in this book has been ineffective in establishing a durable consensus. The usual device for attempting to define a consensus has been some variant of a labor-management committee. The members of the committee generally have been drawn from the ranks of organized labor—and big labor at that—and the top executives of large firms. These labor-management committees were formed in the early days of the Kennedy administration and again during Phase III under Nixon. Earlier, the Truman administration had adopted a parliamentary approach by convening a large-scale labor-management conference shortly after the end of the war.

In every case, these devices failed to create an acceptable framework for wage-price policy. Despite intensive cultivation by the CEA, the Kennedy Advisory Committee on Labor-Management Policy never could agree on operating principles. An equally inauspicious record was made

6. Similarly, one of the first actions of President Ford was to ask Congress to establish a Council on Wage and Price Stability. The legal authorization was probably superfluous, but it dramatized the new President's concern and, by enlisting formal congressional approval, at least temporarily muted demands for the reinstitution of direct controls.

by the Labor-Management Advisory Committee during Phases III and IV, when its major pronouncement was a resolution calling for the end of controls.

When comprehensive statutory controls were initiated during the Nixon administration, the program designers resorted to the traditional tripartite concept to deal with the question of consensus, at least on the regulation of wages. The Pay Board was formed as a tripartite body and operated on this basis for five months. It provided for representation for only a very narrow sector of the economy and for persons who represented a limited constituency, or no constituency at all, and it failed to grapple with the question of a national consensus. Rather, the board sought to mitigate the opposition of powerful groups by permitting them to participate in the decision-making process even though this participation might be to the disadvantage of other groups in society. This objective was only partially achieved, and after five months four of the five labor representatives resigned as an expression of their dissatisfaction.

The Development of Standards

The general objective of wage-price policy is, of course, to control inflation. But this lofty goal must be cast into operational terms if policy is to have any influence in specific cases. When wage-price policy is limited to broad appeals for restraint, as in the Eisenhower and Ford administrations, little effort is made to develop explicit standards. Indeed, in view of the dog-in-the-manger strategy associated with such policy, there is no need for more precise standards.

When wage-price policy moves from the level of exhortation to specific application, it becomes necessary to enunciate a more sharply defined standard for behavior. In most cases, the greatest emphasis has been placed on (labor) productivity. The seed for this standard was planted in the Truman administration, poked up out of the ground during the Eisenhower administration, and came to full flower during the Kennedy-Johnson period. It was also the benchmark for "responsible" behavior at the outset of the Nixon program of direct controls.

The heavy reliance on the productivity standard has been most influential in shaping the application of wage-price policy. The productivity criterion links changes in the price level to wage movements. Presumably, if wage increases are limited to the long-term trend in national productivity, stable prices for the economy as a whole should be attainable.

Although this approach is generally credible, it may suffer when applied to specific cases. To the extent that wage-price policy is aimed at developments in particular firms and industries and that price behavior is a function of many factors besides productivity, putting all the money on this one horse may not be the best strategy. If the ultimate purpose of wage-price policy is to thwart "excessive" price increases, administrators should be allowed to move directly against prices rather than waiting until "responsible" wage changes have paved the way for intervention. The "market power" of a firm or industry may be—and frequently is—quite independent of its wage policies. It is significant that as wage-price policy took shape during the Kennedy administration almost every intervention was precipitated by the onset of collective bargaining negotiations. The strategy was clear: persuade the union to limit its demands to the range of national productivity and then use this to force the companies to minimize their price increases.

This approach probably has had several consequences. First, it focuses on collective bargaining as a causal factor of inflation even though the real culprit may be too expansive fiscal and monetary policies. Second, it narrows the scope for analyzing "acceptable" price behavior. An equally effective procedure for dealing with prices might be to examine a broad range of economic data, including profits, rate of return on investment, costs, and excess capacity. Third, the use of productivity as the dominant criterion for determining acceptable wage and price movements sidesteps the problem of the distribution of income between labor and capital. Although policy administrators strive to be neutral, the effects of the policy may be to shift income from labor to other groups. The application of the productivity criterion means that labor must subordinate its traditional aspirations for a redistribution of income. Whether the position of organized labor is correct or incorrect is unimportant; the critical factor is the criterion's requirement that labor deny the validity of a major ideological goal. For this reason, organized labor strenuously fought for, and achieved, special exemptions from the wage standard for low-income workers during both the Korean War and Phase II of the Nixon administration's stabilization program.

The problems of using productivity as the intellectual basis for wage-price policy are rendered more acute when a specific number is applied. President Kennedy endorsed the guidepost-productivity concept and a numerical range, but he did not agree to a specific number. President Johnson's economists, however, were emboldened to measure the size of

the guidepost, determined that 3.2 percent was the defensible point estimate, and set it as a standard for responsible wage behavior. The fine print
prepared by the CEA recognized that 3.2 percent might not be applicable
in many cases. But the media projected the 3.2 standard without equivoca-
tion, and it was used as a yardstick to measure the effectiveness of the
program. If the government "succeeded" in its efforts in the steel and
automobile industries by limiting wage increases to the productivity standard, it "failed" miserably in dealing with the IAM.

Significantly, once the guidepost was shattered in the IAM dispute and
the administrators were relieved of the anxiety of measuring every case
against the 3.2 standard, the system of policy implementation seemed to
be transformed. The Nelson Committee and other ad hoc administrative
units shifted the emphasis directly to prices. On the basis of a variety of
data, decisions were reached on acceptable price behavior in negotiations
between management and government officials. Under this approach, the
tactical relation between wage and price policies was reversed. If price
increases were limited by government pressure, employer resistance to
union demands above the wage standard would be stiffened.

Quite a different process took place under Nixon. Here, the administration did not gradually immerse itself in controls, but dove in with little
preparation. Once it had decided to establish independent price and wage
regulating agencies, it had to decide whether to define a goal to guide
these agencies. The initial judgment was to reject an explicit goal or standard, because of both the complexity of factors determining wage-price
movements and short-term political considerations; if a specific goal were
established, it would be easier to identify the failures of the administration, especially in an election year. It was ultimately determined that a
goal was necessary to provide some discipline for the program.

These conflicting considerations were accommodated by establishing
a goal that, in effect, had a 50 percent variance. The Cost of Living Council ordained that the objective of Phase II was to bring the rate of price
increases down to a range of "2 to 3 percent" by the end of 1972. After a
process of bargaining within the Pay Board, this translated into a wage
standard of 5.5 percent, providing for a 3 percent increase for productivity
and a 2.5 percent price increase—which was halfway between the 2 to 3
percent goal established by the CLC. The standards established a general
framework for evaluation, but individual decisions were made on a much
wider range of factors. On the price side, the greatest emphasis was given
the concept of "allowable" costs, with the profit margin rule establishing

a secondary defense. Similarly, the 5.5 percent wage standard was subject to various modifications in the light of equity and "established bargaining relationships."

The lesson of these experiences is compelling. Although productivity may have theoretical credence as a standard for the general economy and helps to define the goals of wage-price policy over time, it has limited usefulness in the administration of these policies. The wider the range of wage-price policy and the more "serious" the efforts to carry it out, the more likely it is that productivity will be of reduced relevance. This was the experience during both the Korean War and the later phases of the Nixon program.

The Use of Sanctions

The implementation of wage-price policy requires methods of enforcement appropriate to the ends it is designed to serve. When it is restricted to global statements of restraint, the methods of enforcement are equally tentative. Unions and businessmen that act in an "excessive" manner will be subject to the scorn of their peers, a flurry of critical editorials, and other manifestations of public disfavor, but these are likely to be passing shots without lasting effect on wage and price movements. Because the definition of wage-price policy at such a general level normally serves political rather than economic purposes, the situation should not be viewed as evidence of the policy's intrinsic deficiencies. For example, President Eisenhower was scarcely concerned that his sotto voce pleas for discipline were not heeded. And the Goodwin-Herren narrative leaves one with the suspicion that President Truman was experiencing such pleasure in flagellating corporations and Congress that he would have been disappointed if, say, General Motors had seen the error of its ways and announced that it was forgoing all price increases for the next year.

The rules of the game change significantly when efforts are made to apply wage-price policy in specific cases. Here the decisive factor is whether there is some statutory authority. With the exception of Nixon's stabilization program and the Korean War, wage-price policy has been administered in an extralegal framework. It has therefore been necessary to marshal an array of ad hoc weapons that reflect the current strength of government and the vulnerability of the parties that are the focus of the policy. The choice of targets under an informal system of controls is determined almost as much by the vulnerability of the parties to government action as for rational economic reasons. Thus firms in oligopolistic industries have been the customary targets of wage-price policy, and one of the favorite weapons in bringing about compliance has been the threat of prosecution under the antitrust laws. President Kennedy pulled this card out of the deck almost as a reflex during the dramatic controversy with the steel industry in 1962.

The government, of course, can use other tactics to bring about compliance by businessmen. In the case of aluminum, Alcoa revoked a price increase after negotiating with Secretary of Defense Robert S. McNamara about the disposition of the government's stockpile of "strategic materials." Obviously, the handling of the stockpile could have a major effect on prices. Beyond this, the government has a wide range of subtle, or not so subtle, weapons, including the application of the tax laws, decisions about exports and tariffs, and changes in government purchasing policies.

A legal system of enforcement was established during the Nixon administration. The regulations of the Price Commission and the Pay Board were published in the *Federal Register* and noncompliance was subject to fines, injunctions, and criminal penalties. But despite the availability of these sanctions, any system of enforcement must be based on a selective strategy. In Phases II, III, and IV, the so-called three-tier system created degrees of probability of legal prosecution: most vulnerable were firms and unions in the first tier that had to obtain prior approval of price and wage increases; units in the second tier had periodic reporting requirements, and units in the third tier generally were left with their consciences and the possibility of a visit from an IRS agent. The system of enforcement was designed to cage what Lloyd Ulman has called the "rogue elephants" while assuming that the rest of the herd would behave decorously because of fear, self-interest, and a concern for the national welfare.[7]

Aside from assuring the integrity of the program, the greatest importance of the system of sanctions is the extent to which it helps maintain a position of even-handedness in dealing with labor and management. In fact, the effectiveness of sanctions for labor and management appears to be markedly different depending on whether an informal or a formal system of wage-price policy is involved. In an informal system, such as that of the Kennedy-Johnson period, business is more vulnerable to the application of sanctions than is organized labor. Most of both Presidents' big guns were wheeled out against business in the form of threats of

7. Lloyd Ulman and Robert J. Flanagan, *Wage Restraint: A Study of Incomes Policies in Western Europe* (University of California Press, 1971), pp. 240–43.

antitrust prosecution, stockpile disposition, and other forms of "persuasion." In addition, because business has historically been the target of criticism in American society and must continue to interact with "the public" through the market system, it has shown greater sensitivity than labor to expressions of disapproval from the President. In Cochrane's account of wage-price policies during the Johnson administration, he describes the complaint of Joseph Block, chairman of Inland Steel, about the pressures that were brought to bear when the company raised the price of galvanized sheets and coils in 1964. Block said:

Last December my company raised its price on a relatively minor steel product—galvanized sheets. We did this because the cost of the coating material—zinc—had gone up considerably and we regarded our profit as inadequate. It was in reality a minor matter, yet based on the government reaction, one would have thought we had dropped an atomic bomb. We were told that we might trigger inflation. We were told that we might induce Mr. Abel here to increase his wage demands. We were told we would lose business to foreign steel.... Now all this would seem to indicate that we must have been thought pretty dumb not to have considered such matters in advance of our action. And perhaps we were.

Government strategy toward unions in the application of informal wage-price policy has been more honeyed and less effective. Apparently the normal approach was to bring the union leaders in question (usually David McDonald of the United Steelworkers and Walter Reuther of the United Automobile Workers) to the White House, where they were offered deep drafts of presidential flattery and confidential chats on the need for responsibility. In some cases, however, such as the Operating Engineers and IAM-airlines negotiations, there appeared to be little that the government could do to make intransigent union leaders cooperate. Under informal controls it was easier to bring the president of U.S. Steel to bay than a business agent in New Jersey.

In contrast, enforcement under a formal, legally based program appears to be more effective against labor than it is against business. Especially when there is some slack in the labor market, individual managers will try to apply the wage standards faithfully. All the incentives arising from economic self-interest press in this direction. And if one employer adheres to the standard in dealing with his employees, he makes it easier for other employers by reducing competitive pressure to move wages above the standard. During Phases I to IV, George Meany, president of the AFL-CIO, complained with some credence that there were four million enforcement agents (employers) on the wage side but only a handful of IRS agents on the price side.

The effect of this asymmetry is illustrated by the fate of wage-price policy under the various administrations. For example, it was organized labor that kicked over the traces during the Johnson administration, when wage-price policy was enforced through informal means. In contrast, the demise of the Nixon stabilization program was brought about by the inability of the formal administrative machinery to contain price increases, although wages generally had been held in check.

Models of Wage-Price Policy Implementation

From this welter of experience, four models of wage-price policy can be identified. These models link together objectives, elements of coverage, organizational arrangements, the nature of the standard, and sanctions. It cannot be said that the models are "rational" in the sense that they represent some efficient combination of variables to achieve the objective of controlling inflation. They do have a retrospective logic, however, in that they describe a consistent relationship between objectives, organization, and the other elements of wage-price policy.

The Decoy Model

The first model may be characterized as the "decoy model." Wage-price policies are articulated to divert political pressure for government action rather than as part of a serious effort to influence wage and price behavior. The objective of the program is stated in the most general terms so that they apply to every economic unit while having relevance for none. There is comprehensive coverage in principle but no effective coverage in fact, except when some egregious incident takes place. The standard is formulated in the broadest possible terms and may embrace slogans such as "responsibility," "discipline," or "restraint." Normally, a cabinet committee symbolizes the administration's dedication to price stability, although in some instances special organizations are established to "monitor and review" price and wage developments. Sanctions are limited to exhortation and expressions of concern. To a large degree, the decoy model is an anti–wage-price-policy model.

The decoy model was unveiled during the Eisenhower administration, refined in the early part of the Nixon administration, and revived by President Ford. In each case, the President and his economic advisers were reluctant to go beyond expressions of concern and calls for responsibility. No specific targets for government intervention or criteria for such actions were identified. Well-publicized organizations were established, such as the Cabinet Committee on Price Stability, the National Commission on Productivity, and the Council on Wage and Price Stability. There was no hint of pressure other than presidential brow-lifting.

The Defensive Model

The second combination of elements may be called the "defensive model." Here the general objective is to provide a reserve capability to intervene in particular wage and price decisions that are highly visible or identified as engendering inflationary pressures. The defensive model is especially suited to circumstances in which wage-price policy is used to support expansionist policies. Coverage is universal in principle, but in fact the policies are applicable primarily to large economic units in basic industries. A criterion for responsible behavior is defined but left in imprecise form, allowing the executive to use discretion in determining when to intervene and when not to. In implementing the program, the President will call on the existing agencies of government whose efforts will be coordinated on an ad hoc basis by some central unit, normally the Council of Economic Advisers. The sanctions employed may encompass the full range of government influence and authority, such as threats of prosecution under the antitrust laws, stockpile disposal, and so on.

The defensive model was used during the Kennedy administration and, with a few modifications, properly characterizes Phases III and IV during the Nixon administration. The Nixon case is especially interesting because here a formal regulatory system was turned into a defensive program by executive action. Although the stabilization program was founded on statutory authority, Phase III was unveiled as an exercise in self-regulation. Firms and unions were expected to conform to the existing regulations, but the "stick in the closet" was substituted for an assertive enforcement procedure. Since there was some friction between the underlying philosophy of Phases III and IV and the statutory framework within which the program was administered, an accelerated schedule of decontrol was pursued in an effort to ease it.

The Offensive Model

The third model is the "offensive model." In this case, wage-price policy is viewed as part of a serious effort to contain inflation even though it is not part of a legally based system. Coverage is broadly defined and the policy applied to sectors with a significant impact on price levels. Special administrative units are organized to link the process of review with the exercise of influence and sanctions. An effort is made to define a standard in more precise terms so that it establishes a trip point setting off government action. In effect, the executive branch is committed to act when decisions in designated sectors of the economy exceed the standard. This approach was employed during the Johnson administration when wage-price policy became a substitute for fiscal and monetary policies.

The Regulatory Model

The most robust variety of wage-price policy is the "regulatory model," in which there is an organized effort, supported by statutory authority, to directly regulate wage and price movements. Because it is founded on law, the model does not depend on positive intervention by the government. Instead, general compliance with the published standards and regulations is expected. Coverage tends to be broad and formal adjustments may be made from time to time in response to changing economic circumstances. The program is administered by self-contained agencies that usually enjoy independent status. Conventional legal sanctions for compliance, such as fines, injunctions, and criminal penalties, are available. The regulatory model has traditionally been most closely associated with wartime.

The only peacetime use of such a model was during Phases I and II of the Nixon administration, when it dealt with the consequences of extraordinary events and policies that transformed the position of the United States in the world economy. To the extent that there was a specific objective, it was to protect a highly stimulative policy and to suppress inflationary pressures as they built up in the economy. When the true test of the system of controls came at the beginning of 1973, the administration retreated to the defensive model before many shots had been fired.

These models are not of course prescriptive. Rather, they describe the various efforts that have been made to carry out wage-price policy. The primary impression is one of improvisation, with the blending of short-term economic requirements and political pressures, and resort to jerry-built organizational arrangements. If the purpose of wage-price policy has been to regulate the flow of economic events in the economy, it has been more analogous to sandbag embankments thrown up to resist flash floods than to dams built for the systematic control of the stream of wage and price decisions.

The Limits of Wage-Price Policy

Wage-price policy in the United States has now undergone thirty years of trial and error, and it is fair to say that there has been as much of the latter as the former. Even without a systematic (if not econometric) assessment of this policy's effectiveness, several deficiencies have been cast into sharp relief by this review.

First, there has been a consistent failure to develop a national consensus on the objectives of and rules governing wage-price policy. The preferred technique has been some variant of a labor-management committee. On more venturesome occasions, broadly constituted one-time conferences have been convened, bringing together representatives of diverse interest groups. The 1974 Summit Conference on Inflation was perhaps the most sophisticated of these endeavors.[8] Unfortunately, there is no evidence that these advisory committees or pseudo-parliamentary conclaves achieved anything approaching a durable consensus. Indeed, the record indicates that they have emphasized differences in interest rather than creating a common framework within which the interests could be harmonized. Nor can there be any optimism about the likelihood of defining such a consensus in the foreseeable future. Where the economy is organized on market principles of self-interest and these principles are extended into the political process, there is little prospect of agreement on the operational goals of wage-price policy except in wartime or when there is universal concern over impending catastrophe.

Second, wage-price policy has been unable to achieve an even-handed treatment of wages and prices. The imbalance has not been deliberate but

8. The conference was held in Washington on September 27 and 28, 1974, and was attended by representatives of special interest groups, such as organized labor, agriculture, finance, and housing, and economists, all of whom had participated earlier in separate "mini conferences." No formal program was adopted.

rather a consequence of the particular administrative arrangements for the implementation of the policy. And though economic objectives may not require even-handedness, political factors make any deviation from uniformity perilous.

Wages have been most severely restrained under formal systems of control, and prices have borne the brunt of government actions under informal programs. The political consequences of this asymmetry have been magnified by the fact that wage-price policy has usually been cast in broad national terms, although no one realistically expects it to be applicable to all situations. Thus each instance of different treatment is viewed as evidence of class oppression rather than as an effort to deal with economic power or market deficiencies in particular cases. Different treatment may be accepted when it is related to "surgical" efforts to deal with problems in individual industries, but not when it is viewed as part of some national scheme for shifting power relations among economic groups.

Third, the quest for a standard that is comprehensive, equitable, and sufficiently precise for effective administration has been less than successful. The productivity concept serves a useful purpose in establishing the goals of wage-price policy, but it affords only limited guidance for their attainment and may even be mischievous in individual cases. By fastening on productivity as the dominant standard, price restraint has frequently been linked to wage restraint, although the relation between them should not be determinate. Aside from problems of measurement, the relevance of productivity as a sensible basis for wage and price decisions in the short run is diminished as one moves from the economy as a whole to untidy markets for specific goods and categories of labor. To a large extent, productivity has been an attractive operational standard because of its convenience in casual systems of administration rather than its applicability in specific cases.

Fourth, there has never been a sensible theory of coverage. Presumably, wage-price policy emerged as an attractive alternative because it could bridge the gap between the macroeconomic policies that would sustain high levels of growth and employment for the economy as a whole and wage-price decisions in particular cases. These links have never been carefully identified. Consequently, wage-price policy administrators have turned almost as a reflex to the same set of industries. If the steel industry had not existed, it probably would have been invented for the convenience of the chairman of the Council of Economic Advisers. Wage-price policy has invariably been brought to bear on steel and automobiles, although the health services industry may now have a more consequential effect on the general price level.

Last, the organizational arrangements for carrying out wage-price policy have had all the continuity of a pickup volleyball team. For the most part, wage-price policy has been administered by a cast of thousands drawn from different agencies at different times. Because the objectives, coverage, and legal authority associated with wage-price policy have never been clearly established on a continuing basis, the organizational arrangements have had a consistent quality of improvisation.

A Modest Proposal

Where does this analysis leave us and what alternatives may have promise? At the outset, the notion that wage-price policy can be global and employed to control the general level of wages and prices effectively should be rejected. Such an objective is misleading and administratively infeasible within the normal range of government activity in peacetime. Instead, wage-price policy should be viewed as an instrument that can be applied selectively in particular product and labor market situations. In effect, many of its deficiencies can and should be dealt with by trimming the program so that it is less likely to become enmeshed in social and political conflicts. In addition to realistically describing the feasibility of wage-price policy, a selective approach would also dispel the illusion that such policy, by itself, is an adequate substitute for fiscal and monetary measures.

Selective controls would have two broad functions. On the wage side, they would be aimed primarily at preventing distortions in the national wage structure rather than at attempting to control the general level of wage increases directly. If wage movements have an autonomous inflationary effect, it is usually manifested in structural distortions as one union attempts to leapfrog another in its wage demands or as nonunion employers strive to maintain "traditional" wage differences vis-à-vis the unionized sector. Major upward shifts in the general level of money wages are usually more symptomatic of inflationary pressures that already suffuse the economy than of the independent exercise or augmentation of "union power." Wage policy is not likely to be an effective barrier against broadside inflationary forces, but it can help promote the effective adjustment of intraindustry and interindustry wage structures to rapidly changing economic circumstances. A wage "target" may be established for the economy as a whole, but it should be flexible when applied in particular market and collective bargaining situations. If Phase II and the Pay Board had any salutary effect, it was to preside over the restabilization of the national wage structure in the wake of dislocations induced by unusually large settlements in the construction, transportation, and retail food industries.[9]

On the price side, administrative efforts would be concentrated on situations in which competition was limited by the organization of the market (as in health services), where a firm or industry could exploit temporary imbalances in supply and demand to reap economic rents (as in energy), and on large, oligopolistic industries. Continued attention would also be given to industries in which prices are strongly influenced by government actions and policies. Governmental price policies should not be viewed as an adequate substitute for the vigorous enforcement of the antitrust laws.

Selective controls would relieve policymakers of the necessity for fashioning the consensus, or "social compact," that is necessary to sustain a global program. If such a consensus is achieved, it is unlikely to be the product of advisory committees, summit conferences, or tripartite bodies. The task of defining a consensus is properly the obligation of Congress and the executive branch. In 1967 a procedure for developing a consensus on guideposts was proposed whereby Congress would approve the President's statement of the guideposts for any year. This device holds some promise. The political system, not some artificial assemblage of economic interest groups, must bear the responsibility for establishing a consensus, however fragile. Meanwhile, wage and price policies can be exercised selectively without a supporting national compact because they will not be viewed as part of a strategy for the redistribution of power and income in society as a whole.

The selective approach also would alleviate the sense of inequity arising from the inability to treat labor and business evenhandedly. Specific interests are bound to feel either advantaged or disadvantaged by the imposition of selective wage-price policies. But as a tactical and political matter, it is easier to deal with special interests than class interests. Ex-

9. Daniel J. B. Mitchell and Arnold R. Weber, "Wages and the Pay Board," in American Economic Association, *Papers and Proceedings of the Eighty-sixth Annual Meeting, 1973* (*American Economic Review*, vol. 64, May 1974), pp. 88–92.

perience with the development of selective wage policy in the food distribution and construction industries in 1972–73 indicate that it can be maintained without arousing hostility. And by narrowing the focus of wage-price policy to specific industries, full weight can be given to all relevant economic data rather than a single criterion.

The task of developing a framework for selective wage-price policies and implementing them in specific cases should be given to a permanent wage-price commission. In the past, the establishment of such a commission has been viewed with distaste. However, these studies of wage-price policy in five administrations indicate that such bodies will always be present in some form, as a cabinet committee, a subterranean interagency task force, or some ad hoc unit. It is best to recognize that efforts to influence wage and price decisions will be a permanent element in national economic policymaking and to establish a commission on a continuing basis, independent of the hard-pressed Council of Economic Advisers. (It is significant that four months after the Cost of Living Council was quietly laid to rest on April 30, 1974, it was disinterred as the Council on Wage and Price Stability.) Moreover, a permanent commission would have a higher degree of public accountability for its actions, an accountability that has often been blurred or ignored in past exercises of wage-price policy. And finally, to the extent that expertise counts, a permanent wage-price commission would be an institutional depository for expertise in devising and administering these programs. Without this, each crisis would precipitate a frantic search for the few tired bureaucrats who were involved "the last time around."

The wage-price commission would be established by statute. It would have the authority to review wage and price developments in individual industries, develop procedures for public hearings, and, if necessary, apply mandatory controls. It is argued that if the President had such authority the political pressure to exercise it on a broad scale would be irresistible. This would be especially likely if Congress could badger the President without any involvement in the decisions. The problem can be resolved by giving the President the right to impose selective controls subject to approval by Congress within fifteen to thirty days through the process of negative legislation; that is, if Congress did not act in the prescribed time, the authority would go into effect. Also, if the authority existed on a permanent, legal basis, it would be less likely to be used promiscuously. In too many cases wage-price policy has been applied by employing the economic equivalent of political "dirty tricks." If these arguments are not persuasive, an additional proviso might be added limiting the commission's authority to impose direct controls in any individual case to one year unless the commission demonstrated to Congress that the wage and price behavior of the units involved was a continuing threat to economic stability.

All of this is rather unheroic, even prosaic. But the experience of the past thirty years clearly indicates that the heroic concept of wage-price policy has not been realized. To some extent, our attitude toward such policies is still colored by populist notions of retribution against economic power or innocent visions of full employment and price stability. It is time wage-price policy was placed in a more modest operational framework, where its contributions might be more limited but its failures less dispiriting.

VII

A Report of the Conference

CRAUFURD D. GOODWIN

A CONFERENCE of fifty-four distinguished economists and present and former public servants was held on the campus of Boston University on November 1 and 2, 1974, to discuss drafts of six of the papers published in revised form in this book. (See pages 399–400 for the participants.)

Chairman Kermit Gordon opened the conference by observing that gathered together was "the most star-studded cast of movers and shakers in economic policy-making ever to be assembled around the same table." An obvious first question for any observer, therefore, was why such a busy and active group would devote a beautiful autumn weekend to what was essentially an exercise in history. Part of the answer was suggested immediately by the chairman when he repeated Samuel Butler's remark, "Historians are more powerful than God, for while even He cannot alter the past, historians can." This conference was an attractive and unusual opportunity for the main participants in important events to have a hand in shaping and setting straight the historical record of which they had been a part.

But clearly the enthusiastic participation in the conference had deeper roots than this. It was seen also as an attempt to gain new understanding. For many in the group the formulation and implementation of wage-price policy had been a major part of their professional careers, and yet in differing degrees they felt uneasy and dissatisfied with the results. An occasion on which they might examine the past could also serve as a time to explore the present and guide the future. One commentator even suggested that historical examination of an important segment of policy formation might have a constructive and sobering effect on future advisers by warning them that their work too might be subject to review.

Part of the conference discussion was concerned with correction and amplification of the papers that became chapters 1 to 6 in this volume. But primary attention was devoted to wider questions of what the entire period teaches and how to cope with the whole set of problems wage and price policies are designed to attack. Understandably the participants became frustrated at times because the conference dealt mainly with policy formation and only peripherally with the effectiveness of the policies themselves. It was, said one conferee, "as if you are commenting on somebody's tennis skill and you are concerned with form and position and how he moves, and you comment on that, but you never systematically relate that to who won each set." More satisfactory analysis and evaluation of past policies against the full sweep of economic history, using econometric and other techniques, was noted as a subject badly in need of further research.

A main focus of the discussion was on what elements of the situation have changed to make current problems and the search for their solution different from what they were at the end of World War II. The element mentioned most often was the role of economists and economic theory in the decision-making process. Participants recalled that as recently as 1942 notions of controlling wages and prices by any economic means at all—fiscal, monetary, or direct—were considered rank heresy in many influential quarters of government. "Old-time religion" at that time consisted of budget-balancing pure and simple. Since then not only had Keynes and his doctrines joined the establishment (both Democratic and Republican) but such devices as the Phillips curve, with its concept of a measurable trade-off between employment and inflation, had become a familiar part of public debate. No one at the conference forgot that often in the distant past "good" economics had also coincided with old beliefs, as when, for example, the instinctively set goal of balanced budgets had helped to restrain inflation; on such occasions the results of wisdom and virtue could not easily be distinguished from those of mere prejudice.

There was also the danger that trained economists, represented in both the authors of the papers and some of the conferees, could overestimate the force of the ideas generated by their profession. Herbert Stein warned: "Economists tend to think that if they demonstrate that in certain conditions a certain policy was economically logically necessary, that explains why the policy was followed; whereas, of course, it doesn't at all." Robert Solow warned of the proclivity of economic policy advisers toward mild hysteria, which seemed to result from their captivation by ideas. He said: "One of the things I learned in a couple of the years I worked for all my employers who are sitting around this room is that everybody in this business pays too much attention to the straws in the wind, and I suspect that we have collected even out of the last two or three years an exaggerated notion of the depth of inflation problems."

Discussion also focused on a second major change in the milieu for wage-price policy over the past thirty years—the liberalization of the social and political attitudes and values of the American people. These were described variously as a revolution of rising expectations, an assumption of affluence, and a breakdown of the caste system which weakened restraints on the assertiveness of minorities and other depressed social groups. All of these changes were perceived as making the job of economic stabilization more difficult and complex.

The conferees thought that one result of the changes in the social milieu was an increase in the number of goals that wage-price policy was expected to help achieve. For example, under Truman the main objectives were smooth conversion from wartime, avoidance of boom and depression, and encouragement of economic growth. Subsequent administrations added, among other goals, improvement in the balance of payments and pursuit of broad social programs during wartime. Andrew Brimmer contrasted the first half of the period under study, when wage-price policy was perceived as a problem for prosperity, with the second half, when inflation and recession appeared together.

Participants noted there had been a vast improvement in economic information within the government over the period, not only about such basic inputs to policymaking as price indexes and the components of national income, but also about the details of individual industries and regions, now easily stored and analyzed by computers. Another development in the government, and in the economics profession too, was a gradual growth in the number of veterans of different experiences with wage-price policy—persons referred to occasionally as "price fighters."

Some conferees found that this growth represented a useful accretion of knowledge and wisdom. Others, however, warned that prejudice, preconceptions, and special interests had been accumulated as well. One veteran of the Kennedy years said that in the 1961 Berlin crisis "the people in the Council were . . . a bit surprised and taken aback by all the ex-World War II and Korean price controllers who came out of the woodwork snorting fire and pawing the earth and fingering their copies of the Defense Production Act of 1950 and Trading with the Enemy Act and all that." Lloyd Ulman complained that *academic* economists in government had been an especially unsatisfactory element because often they were unfamiliar with and unwilling to learn about and take into account the workings of institutions. They "have tended to approach practitioners and private interests in the general manner of the dowager duchess sniffing sour drains." Herbert Stein pictured relations of the Nixon economists with the would-be price controllers (academic and otherwise) as follows: "We were racing across the snow in a horse-drawn sled pursued by wolves who occasionally gained on us and when they got close enough to us, we threw out a baby to divert them from the pursuit for a while . . . and so we threw out the inflation alerts . . . and then we threw out the construction business, and finally we had no more babies left to throw out, so we threw out the mother-in-law on August 15, 1971."

A final change over the thirty years that was remarked on by several observers was a gradual loss of innocence among policymakers. At least until the Kennedy years there was still the presumption that over time prices would go down about as much as up—an expectation that merely seems quaint in the Ford years. At the structural level, whereas economists from the early administrations had hoped for solutions from a return to the free price economy, one conferee from the Nixon years was heard to say, "If you can consider your home the free market . . . it is not clear that we can go home again."

The search for sharp parallels in the thirty years repeatedly returned to a comparison of the last three years of the Truman administration (1950–52) with the last four under Nixon (1971–74). In the first period, some argued, the substantial inflationary pressures of the Korean War, including skyrocketing world prices for raw materials, were effectively constrained by a combination of fiscal and monetary policy and direct controls. In contrast, a lesser challenge in the Nixon years had led to a situation that had nearly gotten out of control. Skeptics of the aptness of this parallel argued that in the first period war had generated a national consensus for firm action which was lacking in the second. They also observed that corporate profit margins were much higher in the first period than in the second, and these had acted as a cushion against an inflation generated by the prices of raw materials.

One of the most gloomy views of the lessons to be learned from the past thirty years came from Neil Jacoby, who, using one of the many colorful analogies that enlivened the conference, pictured wage-price history as dominated by a melodramatic old movie played again and again to a progressively more bored and irritated audience. The movie portrayed conflict between "expansionists" pursuing high employment and "stabilizationists" aiming for price stability. "While the stabilizationists win the rhetorical skirmishes, the expansionists usually win the legislative battles. And the people of the United States, who own the economic machine, employ alternatively the expansionists and the stabilizationists to run it, and the polls show that they are dissatisfied with the economic management of both. Now, it is not important which group wears the white hat and which the black hat. That is a matter of personal values. The basic question is how much longer this tired old movie will run."

A principal objective of the conference was to confront the former makers and practitioners of wage-price policy with the record of their activities as reconstructed mainly from the written documents. Certain differences in emphasis between the papers and the participants' memories soon became apparent. The memories tended to give more emphasis than did the papers to the pervasive force of politics over economic reason, not only in the most spectacular incidents, such as President Truman's special sessions of Congress, but also in more subtle ones, such as President Johnson's reluctance to call for stern wage-price policies that might encourage warhawks in the debate over Vietnam.

Policymakers from almost all administrations reminded the authors that very often their actions were aimed as much at inflationary forces within the federal government as outside, and especially at the "mediation and arbitration fraternity in the Labor Department," whose general philosophy had been "it didn't matter what the content of the settlement was just so long as we got the settlement." Wilson Newman spoke eloquently of the instincts of leaders in the Department of Agriculture to obtain higher prices for the products of their constituents regardless of the implication for the nation as a whole.

That politicians should respond mainly to political stimuli was by no means deplored by conferees. Rather the criticism was directed more often at the form of economic advice that ignored the political dimension of policy. In the words of Arnold Weber, "We develop systems . . . that are based on the assumption that elephants can walk on water; and then when the elephant falls in and drowns, we blame the elephant . . . when we really should blame the theory."

Closely related to the need for economists to give heed to purely political considerations was a stress on the constraints imposed by the various presidential personalities and to a lesser extent the personalities of other senior figures in government. Guideposts and persuasion, for example, were pictured much less as ideas that had found their time in the 1960s than as devices that had especially appealed to President Johnson. In the words of Walter Heller: "He gave the guideposts a bear hug. That was exactly his kind of thing, arm twisting as someone suggested. These were ideally suited to that." Otto Eckstein thought an element of Johnson's character which is equally important in explaining his wage-price policy was a belief "that there exists in this country a leadership which is able to act for segments of the society." Johnson also believed in his economists, and together they tried "to shift the Phillips curve just by mobilizing the power structure or the establishment to accomplish this national goal." President Nixon, in sharp contrast to Johnson, viewed the whole concept of intervention "with great intellectual distaste. Having gotten in," said one of his economists, "he immediately opted out . . . not like Pontius Pilate but sort of like Bowie Kuhn." Another Nixon economist argued that the vigor of that President's control policies resulted largely from his need to seize the initiative in his race for reelection. He paraphrased Nixon's comments before Phase I as follows: "Well, if I decide to do something I am going to leapfrog them all; I am not going to be in the position of having done something [where] people will say, 'Well, why don't you do this next month?' and I don't want to be in a position where there is somebody out there further than I am demanding more, and so if I ever do it, I am going to do it where nobody will be able to say there is anything left to be done."

Other memories of participants about which they felt strongly concerned the complexity of wage-price policy formation, which was much greater than can easily be reproduced in a written account; this included aspects of relations with Congress, with other parts of the government, and with the public. Quinn Mills thought he could detect in the authors a tendency to view controls rather as a "black box" that could be turned on or off instead of as the complicated set of devices they were. Robert Turner reflected on the psychological complexity of wage-price policy as follows: "Prevention of inflation involves getting people, in their producer roles at least, not to do what they want to do. It involves constraining their normal behavior, and it is in their producer roles, rather than in their consumer roles, that they are more aggressive, articulate, and well-organized." Several of the economists present stressed the importance of social and structural causes of inflation. Disturbance of single variables in the complex patterns of the economy and society led to attempts to restore old relationships with resulting "wage-wage" or "price-price" inflation.

Because the virtually unanimous judgment of the conferees was that experience with wage-price policy over the thirty-year period had been unsatisfactory, their thoughts naturally turned to the future and to whether the past could provide a guide. Some of this discussion revolved around possible new organs of government; some dealt with the principles of policy and of organization that should be observed by current and future administrations. The discussion was divided also between description of lessons that had been incontrovertibly learned and identification of problems that remained to be solved.

The unsolved problems understandably took up more time. The single challenge that worried participants most was how to obtain a national consensus in support of some type of control mechanism during peacetime. A main obstacle to consensus was perceived to be the trade unions, which understandably treasured their right to free collective bargaining and in some cases saw their role as one of garnering more of the proceeds of production for their members and thus achieving income redistribution and a shift in factor shares. Unions might in a national emergency temporarily forgo their rights and normal objectives but they could not be expected to do so in the long run. There was a good deal of disappointment with efforts stretching from Truman's November 1945 Labor-Management Conference to Ford's September 1974 conference to attain some sort of anti-inflation compact between labor, management, and government. At one extreme, Robert Solow reported that he emerged from his experience in government "convinced that the only tripartite concept that works is chocolate, vanilla, and strawberry." At the other extreme, Gardner Ackley refused to accept such a pessimistic view about the possibility of obtaining consensus "because it seems to me we haven't really tried." "There has been," he said, "a consistent failure to develop arrangements for defining a national consensus concerning the objectives and rules of the game governing wage-price policies." To achieve consensus, he called for "completely new institutional mechanisms, far more radical than labor-management advisory committees or escalating summit meetings."

Several speakers suggested that a consensus in support of wage-price policy might be gained only if a second challenge could be met, that of establishing a control mechanism governed by principles of genuine equity—the problem of "standards," as it was called by Weber. The inequity of past control systems was deplored by both the lawyers and the economists present. The lawyers complained of the inadequacy of procedures and the absence of due process under both the Johnson guideposts and the Nixon phases. Judge Leventhal lamented "the lack of standards, almost wayfulness and willfulness of the decisions, according to those who experienced them. . . . Setting up standards and limiting the nature of exceptions is important to make things move, and any approach to controls on a large accumulation of individual instances and exceptions is counter-productive . . . both in terms of equity and of what people will expect and accept." Joseph Califano reiterated the argument, saying that "equity is a critical part of any consensus, even a consensus legally imposed." David Ginsburg stated that only proper procedures and standards could give controls wide use and respectability. It was, he said, a little like introducing techniques of birth control. Some reliable new method, analogous to the Pill, that was appropriate for modern society had to be developed: "For my generation," he reported, "birth control pills will never have the respectability of the rhythm method, but still they are much more secure."

The economists who had administered some form of peacetime wage-price controls were as deeply concerned as the lawyers about the inequity involved. One of the not inconsiderable causes of inequity, they pointed out, was that under the informal systems tried so far people were often unclear as to just how they were expected to behave. In the words of Lloyd Ulman, government has the responsibility "to lay down a policy which the people to whom it is addressed can, if they are in good faith, reasonably follow." Conspicuous segments of the economy, such as big industry and big labor, were the most favored candidates for arbitrary treatment. The steel industry was repeatedly made the target for controls simply because it was so conspicuous. Arnold Weber observed that "one unifying point in all those administrations is that everybody has taken a kick at the pants of the steel industry . . . just to keep in practice." Such remarks prompted Roger Blough, former chairman of United States Steel, to conclude that the reason he had been invited to the conference was so the participants could "see what a sacrificial lamb looked like."

The economists did not fail to point out to the lawyers that regrettably equity, due process, and fair standards often seemed to conflict with "efficiency" in wage-price policy, especially in systems of less than complete controls. Unfairness and arbitrariness often were prerequisites of effective and economical action. In the words of Charles Schultze, "The more you set standards down in law, the more you have it codified, the less flexible can you be and the more difficult it is to concentrate on those industries and those situations that really make a difference." Moreover, equity was a concept that might be more clearly understood by lawyers than by economists. "Productivity guideposts" had been one attempt to solve the problem of defining equity, but even these had now come to be seen by many as a device to perpetuate the existing division of factor shares, which, although thought to be equitable by some, was perceived as distinctly unfair by others. John Dunlop was adamant about the impossibility of obtaining broad social agreement on guideposts: "You can never get a consensus of labor and management people on the notion of the number; so either you have to have your number imposed by somebody or a consensus." But even if you could get agreement on a number, "it is derogatory to the bargaining process to say you are all supposed to sit down and you are all supposed to come out at the same point."

In his concluding summary at the last session of the conference, Arnold Weber argued forcefully that "the focus on national productivity as an operational standard has probably been more harmful than useful. . . . It builds sort of an automatic self-destruct mechanism into any particular episode with wage-price policies." A main reason for this failure was the burden that productivity standards placed on trade unions. They were required to make the first sacrifice, to abandon their customary assertiveness, and to accept a principle of wage determination that even the economists had no way of showing was just in specific cases. James Duesenberry pointed out that guideposts quickly became a floor rather than a ceiling—even those who in free markets would have suffered a relative decline would not accept a lower rate of increase than that specified by the guideposts. For persons more favorably situated guideposts were especially galling: "People are not going to take kindly to a proposition which really says there shouldn't be any relative wage change when . . . their market position permits them to try to get one, even if it is only temporary."

Myron Joseph noted that guidepost theory assumed not only that some wages would rise more slowly than the average, but that for the average prices of goods to remain stable some must fall. "Now, that was not only part of the logic, but if prices didn't go down, you couldn't expect the unions to sit still for their guidepost wage increase while profits ballooned, and it was very difficult, and [even] impossible to get prices to go down." Gardner Ackley was a staunch defender of productivity guideposts as a guide to wage and price increases. He said: "A standard which says something about what that rate ought to be is something that I don't see how you can get along without."

Standards to control profits were especially hard to conceive in theory, let alone to specify in practice. Ackley declared, "The productivity principle is an entirely inadequate and unworkable standard for price inter-

vention, for price policy itself. . . . In practice wherever we intervened in
the price side it was without specific reference to the productivity standards, except in a few real instances." Looking to the future James Duesenberry said: "We may have to bite the intellectual and ideological bullets
about the profit standards. . . . We have to get some public utility attitude
in the more concentrated industries." Joseph Pechman thought that, in
fact, "some homework" would yield "the essential profit standard that
is still missing." Walter Heller advised the group to remember that in the
future productivity standards for both prices and wages would be harder
to administer because more of the product would be "in the hands of the
oil sheiks . . . exporters to the United States . . . [and] the farmers."

Finally, it had to be faced that principles of equity might be impossible
to identify so long as there was no agreement on the goals of wage-price
policy. Leon Keyserling, for example, insisted that a main objective had
to be attainment of "an appropriate distribution of incomes." Failure to
agree on what was "appropriate" in the specification of such an objective
would clearly preclude agreement on standards of equity.

Toward the end of the conference the discussion turned repeatedly to
the question raised in Arnold Weber's paper of whether a new mechanism
of government is needed to deal with the problems of wage-price policy
that remain unsolved after thirty years. Although no detailed models for
organizational arrangements were proposed, there was considerable enthusiasm for undertaking experiments with such an innovation. Weber
himself favored some new institution to administer "selective controls, a
permanent commission to provide an institutional memory . . . [with]
statutory powers so we establish some modicum of due process rather
than making it . . . the arena for sportive behavior for White House assistants and economists. It seems to me," he said, "that after five administrations and thirty years of not stop-go, but glory and disaster, it is time that
we looked at this program in more restrained and sensible terms to make it
more compatible to what the boundary conditions are and the burdens it
can bear." Weber favored a new institution with a moderate degree of
formality, in part because it would make the administrative system explicit instead of dependent on acts of intervention in wage and price decisions. A moderately formal institution would achieve a balance. While
he did not differ markedly with Weber's policy recommendations, Gardner Ackley rejected the argument used in their support out of hand. He
also pointed out "the econometric evidence is quite inconclusive on this
point." Ackley emphasized that for any organization to be successful

it must have a clear conception of what it wished to accomplish. One reason the Nixon controls had failed, he said, was because they had "no real strategy, no objective, no idea about what came after or any conception of what might be achieved by controls that couldn't be achieved in some other way." To this comment and others which implied that effective controls required enthusiastic controllers Herbert Stein replied, "I think the statement that controls didn't work because the people who were in charge didn't believe in them has no foundation in fact. . . . I think the system that was devised and managed was very well devised to do the job it was assigned to do."

James Duesenberry, like Weber, saw the problem of organization as a search for "some middle ground between just talking and formal control." He said, "There must be some place in the process where you go beyond monitoring and public hearings and actually have some measure of presidential power under some circumstances. I don't know the recipe . . . but . . . otherwise we will just go off and on between formal controls and no controls and possibly return from time to time to guerrilla warfare." John Lewis echoed the feelings of several others when he agreed with the need for a new agency but confessed to feeling "pretty bearish about its prospects." He would prefer changes in the character of the economy that would make such an organ unnecessary, "except I don't think many of us think it is going to happen." Often the question of a new organ was dealt with indirectly in terms of what it might do. Above all, most discussants agreed, it might give permanence, or at least continuity through changing administrations, to planning in this important field. One veteran of past frenzied efforts to formulate policies and establish structures for carrying them out with no advance warning compared the results to "pickup volleyball teams." Another described "the heady excitement of throwing a program in place overnight and waiting for the phones to be installed" and concluded "but that is not really the way to do it."

Gardner Ackley made the most specific recommendation for a new institution; he proposed "some kind of a wage-price commission established by statute with certain limited mandatory authority: certainly to require advance notice of price and wage increases, or to suspend a pending [increase, to] study, to compel testimony, and perhaps . . . some very carefully circumscribed last resort authority to impose temporary, highly selective mandatory ceilings perhaps only under and with the specific approval of the President." Duesenberry added to this list several additional tasks which included "stockpile policy" to reduce bottlenecks during periods of growth. Ackley recommended that the new institution be placed "as far away as possible from the White House, very much farther away than the Council of Economic Advisers or the Cost of Living Council or even the Council on Wage and Price Stability."

Joseph Califano agreed with Ackley on the need for a new institution but reminded the group that, like it or not, it would be viewed as an instrument of social policy and of redistribution. He argued that, to be effective, it therefore "must sit above the peers of Commerce, Labor, Treasury.... It has got to be a first among equals and that means close to the White House, or close to the Council, if not close to the President." David Ginsburg disagreed with Califano on this issue of location. "I think," he said, "that is a great mistake. I think it corrupts the White House. The frenetic activity . . . during the Johnson Administration indicates that it can't be done there."

John Dunlop saw one advantage of some form of permanent organ to be the training of experts who would know more about problem sectors of the economy—steel, cement, or fertilizer—than the "24-hour or 24-day specialists" who have been pressed into service in the past.

Another obvious responsibility of a new wage-price institution would be public education about the nature of the inflationary problem, to be undertaken in good times as well as in bad. Arthur Okun compared the task of education about inflation during years of stable prices to "lecturing a nine-year-old daughter on virginity, not really relevant at the time, but hopeful that it would be a habitual thing that would carry over when it became more relevant." Assumption of the public education function by a new organization, several veterans pointed out, would relieve the Council of Economic Advisers of a heavy burden it had often borne grudgingly.

A new wage-price organization remote from the White House would have the advantage of preserving the presidential reservoir of goodwill for use in more important situations. Otto Eckstein remarked of the Johnson period: "When you think of all the problems that the world had at that time, including . . . civil rights and the beginning of the Vietnam War . . . that all of this good talent and presidential leadership was being applied to chop two or three tenths off the index may well have been a misallocation of resources." John Lewis compared direct presidential intervention anywhere in the economy or society to a cake of soap: "It is an asset that wastes very rapidly."

The Weber-Duesenberry "middle ground" for wage-price policy was attacked from two directions. On one side, some said it did not go far enough. Walt Rostow argued that it did "not meet the scale of the problem or the mood of the country." He called instead for the draconian measure of "fixed money wages with prices falling with productivity." Such a program would require "a sense of presidential conviction . . . support by Congress . . . and in the present context . . . related programs in the fields of energy, agriculture, raw materials, and perhaps other areas." John Kenneth Galbraith objected to the notion of selective controls over "an embarrassingly large number of prices" implicit in the "middle ground," and recalling the success of full wartime controls, he suggested that the country "move generally and act selectively on the exceptions." Galbraith denied the validity of the widespread belief that wartime conditions alone were appropriate for full controls. "I don't think that anything much happens in war that doesn't happen in peace except there is more of it." Lloyd Ulman observed that one important feature which made wartime different from peacetime was that people expected conditions to be temporary and were thus willing to put up with various forms of restriction.

On the other side, skeptics of a different kind said that the "middle ground" presented insuperable problems of timing and a tendency to grow into full controls. Myron Joseph asked, "How do you keep your selective control mechanism from spreading rapidly, from taking on most of the economy?" Charles Schultze saw as a fundamental problem the existing human inability to understand the intricacies of the pricing process; it is extraordinarily difficult to control effectively what you do not fully comprehend. In addition, Schultze saw inflation less as a secular problem than as an episodic one. Toward the end of the conference he put forth the provocative, but essentially optimistic, proposition that "the American economy doesn't generate much inflation. . . . Its major problem is that when it does generate inflation, it can't get out of it." Herbert Stein likened any middle ground to the mythical nonfattening hot fudge sundae and said that people would deceive themselves that this "gave you everything you wanted in the way of prices without interfering with the economy in any adverse way."

An especially eloquent critique of the "middle ground" came from Otto Eckstein. He said, "I think that wage-price control or indeed activist wage-price policies bring out what is most wrong with our political system as represented by the Federal Government, to the extent that it is controlled by outside interests, to the extent that the Congress is not a strong leader, to the extent that the Presidents have very short-sighted goals, to the extent that they do pick up staffs overnight; and in many other regards, all of that is highlighted by the process of attempting to have controls." The only desirable policy Eckstein could see for the long run was "a massive program of structural reform . . . to make the economy operate a little better." Without this program he was not at all certain that "the capitalist system can survive."

The conference ended as it began, on a note of hesitation. The participants remained unhappy with the past and uncertain about the present. Historians looking back on the event thirty years from now, however, may find this mood a hopeful sign for the future.

Conference Participants

Gardner Ackley *University of Michigan*
William J. Barber *Wesleyan University*
James H. Blackman *National Science Foundation*
Roger M. Blough *White and Case*
Roy Blough *S. Sloan Colt Professor Emeritus, Columbia University*
Andrew F. Brimmer *Harvard University*
Joseph A. Califano, Jr. *Williams, Connolly and Califano*
Benjamin Caplan *Washington, D.C.*
James L. Cochrane *University of South Carolina*
Neil de Marchi *Duke University*
Michael V. DiSalle *Chapman, Duff and Lenzini*
James S. Duesenberry *Harvard University*
John T. Dunlop *Harvard University*
Otto Eckstein *Harvard University*
George M. Elsey *American Red Cross*
Dan H. Fenn, Jr. *John F. Kennedy Library*
John Kenneth Galbraith *Harvard University*
David Ginsburg *Ginsburg, Feldman and Bress*
Arthur J. Goldberg *Caplin and Drysdale*
Craufurd D. Goodwin *Duke University*
H. Scott Gordon *Indiana and Queen's Universities*
Kermit Gordon *Brookings Institution*
Lawrence J. Hackman *John F. Kennedy Library*
Walter W. Heller *University of Minnesota*
R. Stanley Herren *Vanderbilt University*
Neil H. Jacoby *University of California at Los Angeles*
Myron L. Joseph *Carnegie-Mellon University*

Leon H. Keyserling *Washington, D.C.*

Marvin H. Kosters *American Enterprise Institute for Public Policy Research*

Robert F. Lanzillotti *University of Florida*

Harold Leventhal *U.S. Court of Appeals*

John P. Lewis *Princeton University*

Harry J. Middleton *Lyndon Baines Johnson Library*

Daniel Quinn Mills *Massachusetts Institute of Technology*

Charles S. Murphy *Morison, Murphy, Abrams and Haddock*

Louis P. Neeb *Steak and Ale Restaurants of America*

J. Wilson Newman *Dun and Bradstreet*

Arthur M. Okun *Brookings Institution*

Don Paarlberg *U.S. Department of Agriculture*

Joseph A. Pechman *Brookings Institution*

Daniel J. Reed *National Archives and Records Service*

James B. Rhoads *National Archives and Records Service*

Walt W. Rostow *University of Texas*

Walter S. Salant *Brookings Institution*

Charles L. Schultze *Brookings Institution*

Rocco C. Siciliano *The TI Corporation*

David C. Smith *Queen's University*

Robert M. Solow *Massachusetts Institute of Technology*

Herbert Stein *University of Virginia*

James Tobin *Yale University*

Robert C. Turner *University of Indiana*

Lloyd Ulman *University of California at Berkeley*

Arnold R. Weber *Carnegie-Mellon University*

John E. Wickman *Dwight D. Eisenhower Library*

Bibliography

Abernathy, John Hugh, Jr. "Wage-Price Guidelines and Free Collective Bargaining." Ph.D. dissertation, Louisiana State University, 1969.

Ackley, Gardner. "The Contribution of Economists to Policy Formation," *Journal of Finance*, vol. 21 (May 1966).

———. "Selected Problems of Price Control Strategy, 1950–1952." Washington: Defense History Program, 1953. Processed. Copies are in the White House Office Library and at the National Archives (Record Group 295; microfilm).

Alexander, Arthur J. "Prices and the Guideposts: The Effects of Government Persuasion on Individual Prices," *Review of Economics and Statistics*, vol. 53 (February 1971).

The American Assembly. *Wages, Prices, Profits and Productivity*. New York: American Assembly, Columbia University, 1959.

Auerback, Carl A. "Presidential Administration of Prices and Wages," *George Washington Law Review*, vol. 35 (December 1966).

Bach, G. L. *Inflation: A Study in Economics, Ethics, and Politics*. Providence: Brown University Press, 1958.

———. *Making Monetary and Fiscal Policy*. Washington: Brookings Institution, 1971.

Backman, Jules. *Wage Determination: An Analysis of Wage Criteria*. Princeton: Van Nostrand, 1959.

Bailey, Stephen K. *Congress Makes a Law: The Story Behind the Employment Act of 1946*. New York: Columbia University Press, 1950.

Bernstein, Barton J. "The Truman Administration and Its Re-Conversion Wage Policy," *Labor History*, vol. 6 (Fall 1965).

Blough, Roy. "The Role of the Economist in Federal Policy Making," in *Edmund J. James Lectures on Government*, Sixth Series. Urbana: University of Illinois Press, 1954.

Bowen, William G. *Wage Behavior in the Postwar Period: An Empirical Analysis*. Princeton: Industrial Relations Section, Department of Economics, Princeton University, 1960.

Bronfenbrenner, Martin. *Income Distribution Theory*. Chicago: Aldine, 1971. Chapter 17, "Guidelines, Guideposts, and Incomes Policies."

———. "Postwar Political Economy: The President's Reports," *Journal of Political Economy*, vol. 56 (October 1948).

———, and Franklyn D. Holzman. "Survey of Inflation Theory," *American Economic Review*, vol. 53 (September 1963).

Burns, Arthur F. *The Management of Prosperity.* New York: Columbia
University Press, 1965.
————. *Prosperity Without Inflation.* New York: Fordham University Press
for Carnegie Institute of Technology, 1957.
————, and Paul A. Samuelson. *Full Employment, Guideposts, and Eco-
nomic Stability.* Washington: American Enterprise Institute for Public
Policy Research, 1967.
Cagan, Phillip, and others. *A New Look at Inflation: Economic Policy in the
Early 1970s.* Washington: American Enterprise Institute for Public Policy
Research, 1973.
Carmichael, William D. "Problems in Price Control: An Examination of
the Effectiveness of Governmental Control over Prices in Combatting
Inflation." Ph.D. dissertation, Princeton University, 1960.
Christian, James W. "Bargaining Functions and the Effectiveness of the
Wage-Price Guideposts," *Southern Economic Journal,* vol. 37 (July
1970).
Clark, John M. *The Wage-Price Problem.* New York: Committee for Eco-
nomic Growth without Inflation, American Bankers Association, 1960.
Colm, Gerhard, ed. *The Employment Act: Past and Future.* Washington:
National Planning Association, 1956.
Committee for Economic Development. *Defense Against Inflation: Policies
for Price Stability in a Growing Economy.* New York: CED, 1958.
————. *Further Weapons against Inflation: Measures to Supplement Gen-
eral Fiscal and Monetary Policies.* New York: CED, 1970.
Cox, Archibald. "Wages, Prices, Government and Lawyers," *Harvard Law
School Bulletin,* vol. 13 (June 1962).
Crispo, John H., ed. *Wages, Prices, Profits and Economic Policy.* Proceed-
ings of a Conference. Toronto: University of Toronto Press, 1968.
Denison, Edward F. *Guideposts for Wages and Prices: Criteria and Con-
sistency.* Ann Arbor: University of Michigan, Institute of Public Policy
Studies and Department of Economics, 1968.
Dunlop, John T. "The Decontrol of Wages and Prices," in Colston E.
Warne and others, eds., *Labor in Postwar America.* Brooklyn: Remsen
Press, 1949.
Eckstein, Otto. "Money Wage Determination Revisited," *Review of Eco-
nomic Studies,* vol. 35 (April 1968).
————, and Roger Brinner. *The Inflation Process in the United States.* A
Study Prepared for the Use of the Joint Economic Committee. 92 Cong.
2 sess. Washington: Government Printing Office, 1972.
————, and Gary Fromm. *Steel and the Postwar Inflation.* Prepared in Con-
nection with the Study of Employment, Growth, and Price Levels for the
Joint Economic Committee. 86 Cong. 1 sess. Washington: Government
Printing Office, 1959.
Edelman, Murray, and R. W. Fleming. *The Politics of Wage-Price Decisions: A Four-Country Analysis.* Urbana: University of Illinois Press, 1965.
Estey, Marten. *Wages, Wage Policy and Inflation, 1962–1971.* Special

Analysis 19. Washington: American Enterprise Institute for Public Policy Research, 1971.

Fellner, William, and others. *The Problem of Rising Prices*. Paris: Organisation for European Economic Co-operation, 1961.

Flash, Edward S., Jr. *Economic Advice and Presidential Leadership: The Council of Economic Advisers*. New York: Columbia University Press, 1965 edition.

Galenson, Walter, ed. *Incomes Policy: What Can We Learn from Europe?* Ithaca: New York State School of Industrial and Labor Relations, Cornell University, 1972.

Gitlow, Abraham L. *The National Wage Policy: Antecedents and Application*. A Research Study. New York: New York University, Schools of Business, 1964.

Hansen, Alvin H. *Economic Issues of the 1960s*. New York: McGraw-Hill, 1960.

Harris, Seymour E. "The Economics of Eisenhower: A Symposium," *Review of Economics and Statistics*, vol. 38 (November 1956).

Heller, Walter W. *New Dimensions of Political Economy*. Cambridge: Harvard University Press, 1966.

Holmans, A. E. "The Eisenhower Administration and the Recession, 1953–5," *Oxford Economic Papers*, n.s., vol. 10 (February 1958).

———. *United States Fiscal Policy, 1945–1959: Its Contribution to Economic Stability*. London: Oxford University Press, 1961.

Hoopes, Roy. *The Steel Crisis*. New York: John Day, 1963.

Jacoby, Neil H. *Can Prosperity Be Sustained? Policies for Full Employment and Full Production without Price Inflation in a Free Economy*. New York: Holt, 1956.

Johnson, H. G., and A. R. Nobay, eds. *The Current Inflation*. Proceedings of a Conference Held at the London School of Economics. London: Macmillan Press, 1971.

Joseph, Myron L. "Wage-Price Guideposts in the U.S.A.," *British Journal of Industrial Relations*, vol. 5 (November 1967).

Levine, Marvin J. "The Economic Guidelines," *Labor Law Journal*, vol. 18 (August 1967).

Levy, Michael E., ed. *Containing Inflation in the Environment of the 1970's*. A Report from The Conference Board. New York: The Conference Board, Inc., 1971.

Lewis, Ben W. "Economics by Admonition," *American Economic Review*, vol. 49 (May 1959).

Lewis, John P. "The Lull That Came to Stay," *Journal of Political Economy*, vol. 63 (February 1955).

Lewis, Wilfred, Jr. *Federal Fiscal Policy in the Postwar Recessions*. Washington: Brookings Institution, 1962.

Lipsett, Charles H. *Price and Wage Controls*. New York: Atlas Publishing, 1970.

Lundberg, Erik, and others. *On Incomes Policy*. Papers and Proceedings

from a Conference in Honour of Erik Lundberg. Stockholm: The Industrial Council for Social and Economic Studies, 1969.

McManus, George J. *The Inside Story of Steel Wages and Prices, 1959–
1967*. Philadelphia: Chilton, 1967.

Meany, George, Roger M. Blough, and Neil H. Jacoby. *Government Wage-
Price Guideposts in the American Economy*. The Moskowitz Lectures.
New York: New York University Press, 1967.

Moore, Thomas G. *U.S. Incomes Policy, Its Rationale and Development*.
Special Analysis 18. Washington: American Enterprise Institute for Public
Policy Research, 1971.

Nourse, Edwin G. *Economics in the Public Service: Administrative Aspects
of the Employment Act*. New York: Harcourt, Brace, 1953.

Okun, Arthur M. *The Political Economy of Prosperity*. Washington: Brookings Institution, 1970.

————. "Statement," in *The President's New Economic Program*, part 2.
Hearings before the Joint Economic Committee. 92 Cong. 1 sess. Washington: Government Printing Office, 1971. Brookings Reprint 212.

————, and others. *Inflation: The Problems It Creates and the Policies It
Requires*. New York: New York University Press, 1970.

Organisation for Economic Co-operation and Development. *Inflation: The
Present Problem*. Report by the Secretary General. Paris: OECD, 1970.

Paish, F. W., and Jossleyn Hennessy. *Policy for Incomes?* Hobart Paper 29.
Second edition. London: Institute of Economic Affairs, 1966.

Parkin, Michael, and Michael T. Sumner, eds. *Incomes Policy and Inflation*.
Manchester, England: Manchester University Press, 1972.

Perry, George L. *Unemployment, Money Wage Rates, and Inflation*. Cambridge: M.I.T. Press, 1966.

————. "Wages and the Guideposts," *American Economic Review*, vol. 57
(September 1967). See also comments by Paul S. Anderson, Michael L.
Wachter, Adrian W. Throop, with a reply by Perry, in ibid., vol. 59 (June
1969).

Phillips, A. W. "The Relation Between Unemployment and the Rate of
Change of Money Wage Rates in the United Kingdom, 1861–1957,"
Economica, n.s., vol. 25 (November 1958).

Phillips, Almarin, and Oliver E. Williamson, eds. *Prices: Issues in Theory,
Practice, and Public Policy*. Philadelphia: University of Pennsylvania
Press, 1967.

Rees, Albert. "An Incomes Policy for the United States?" *Journal of Business*, vol. 38 (October 1965).

————. "Postwar Wage Determination in the Basic Steel Industry," *American Economic Review*, vol. 41 (June 1951). See also comment on this
by Lloyd Ulman, "The Union and Wages in Basic Steel," and Rees'
reply in ibid., vol. 48 (June 1958).

————. *Wage-Price Policy*. Morristown, N.J.: General Learning Corporation,
1971.

Roberts, Benjamin C. *National Wages Policy in War and Peace.* London: George Allen and Unwin, 1958.

Robertson, D. J. "Guideposts and Norms: Contrasts in U.S. and U.K. Wage Policy," *Three Banks Review,* no. 72 (Edinburgh: Royal Bank of Scotland, December 1966).

Rockwood, Charles E. *National Incomes Policy for Inflation Control.* Tallahassee: Florida State University Press, 1969.

Rostow, W. W. *The Diffusion of Power: An Essay in Recent History.* New York: Macmillan, 1972.

Rowley, C. K. *Steel and Public Policy.* New York: McGraw-Hill, 1971.

Salant, Walter S. "Some Intellectual Contributions of the Truman Council of Economic Advisers to Policy-Making," *History of Political Economy,* vol. 5 (Spring 1973).

Samuelson, Paul A., and Robert M. Solow. "Analytical Aspects of Anti-Inflation Policy," *American Economic Review,* vol. 50 (May 1960).

Saulnier, Raymond J. "Anti-inflation Policies in President Eisenhower's Second Term." Paper delivered before the American Historical Association, San Francisco, December 30, 1973. Processed.

———. *The Strategy of Economic Policy.* New York: Fordham University Press, 1963.

Schultze, Charles L. "Statement," in *The President's New Economic Program,* part 1. Hearings before the Joint Economic Committee. 92 Cong. 1 sess. Washington: Government Printing Office, 1971. Brookings Reprint 212.

Sheahan, John. "Incomes Policies," *Journal of Economic Issues,* vol. 6 (December 1972).

———. *The Wage-Price Guideposts.* Washington: Brookings Institution, 1967.

Shultz, George P., and Robert Z. Aliber, eds. *Guidelines, Informal Controls, and the Market Place: Policy Choices in a Full Employment Economy.* Chicago: University of Chicago Press, 1966.

Slichter, Sumner H. "How Bad Is Inflation?" *Harper's Magazine,* vol. 205 (August 1952).

Smith, David C. *Incomes Policies: Some Foreign Experiences and Their Relevance for Canada.* Economic Council of Canada, Special Study 4. Ottawa: Queen's Printer, 1966.

Stein, Herbert. *The Fiscal Revolution in America.* Chicago: University of Chicago Press, 1969.

———, and others. "How Political Must the Council of Economic Advisers Be?" *Challenge,* vol. 17 (March–April 1974).

Stieber, Jack. "The President's Committee on Labor-Management Policy," *Industrial Relations,* vol. 5 (February 1966).

Tobin, James. *The Intellectual Revolution in U.S. Economic Policy-Making.* Noel Buxton Lecture. London: Longmans, Green for the University of Essex, 1966.

Turner, H. A., and H. Zoeteweij. *Prices, Wages, and Incomes Policies in*

Industrialised Market Economies. Studies and Reports, n.s., no. 70. Geneva: International Labour Organisation, 1966.

Ulman, Lloyd, and Robert J. Flanagan. *Wage Restraint: A Study of Incomes Policies in Western Europe*. Berkeley: University of California Press, 1971.

U.S. Congress. House. Subcommittee of the Committee on Government Operations. *Congressional Review of Price-Wage Guideposts*. Hearing on H.R. 11916. 89 Cong. 2 sess. Washington: Government Printing Office, 1966.

————. *Price-Wage Guideposts*. Hearings on H.R. 13278. 91 Cong. 1 sess. Washington: Government Printing Office, 1969.

U.S. Congress. Joint Economic Committee. *Twentieth Anniversary of the Employment Act of 1946: An Economic Symposium*. 89 Cong. 2 sess. Washington: Government Printing Office, 1966.

Walka, Joseph J. "The Origins of the Wage-Price Guideposts: An Exercise in Presidential Staff Initiative," *Public Policy*, vol. 16 (1967).

Wallich, Henry C. "The American Council of Economic Advisers and the German *Sachverstaendigenrat*: A Study in the Economics of Advice," *Quarterly Journal of Economics*, vol. 82 (August 1968).

Weber, Arnold R. *In Pursuit of Price Stability: The Wage-Price Freeze of 1971*. Washington: Brookings Institution, 1973.

White, Lawrence J. *The Automobile Industry since 1945*. Cambridge: Harvard University Press, 1971.

Yoshpe, Harry B., and others. *Stemming Inflation: The Office of Emergency Preparedness and the 90-Day Freeze*. Washington: Government Printing Office, 1972.

Appendix: Statistical Tables

THIS APPENDIX gives the major economic statistics of the United States for the period covered in this book. Many of the statements in the text are based on the figures in these tables.

Table A-1. *Gross National Product, 1947–74*

Billions of current dollars; seasonally adjusted at annual rates

Year	First quarter	Second quarter	Third quarter	Fourth quarter
1947	223.6	227.6	231.8	242.1
1948	248.0	255.6	262.5	263.9
1949	258.5	255.2	257.1	255.0
1950	266.0	275.4	293.1	304.5
1951	318.0	325.8	332.8	336.9
1952	339.5	339.1	345.6	357.7
1953	364.2	367.5	365.8	360.8
1954	360.7	360.4	364.7	373.4
1955	386.2	394.4	402.5	408.8
1956	410.6	416.2	420.6	429.5
1957	436.9	439.9	446.3	441.5
1958	434.7	438.3	451.4	464.4
1959	474.0	486.9	484.0	490.5
1960	503.0	504.7	504.2	503.3
1961	503.6	514.9	524.2	537.7
1962	547.8	557.2	564.4	572.0
1963	577.4	584.2	594.7	605.8
1964	617.7	628.0	638.9	645.1
1965	662.8	675.7	691.1	710.0
1966	729.5	743.3	755.9	770.7
1967	774.4	784.5	800.9	815.9
1968	834.0	857.4	875.2	890.2
1969	907.0	923.5	941.7	948.9
1970	958.5	970.6	987.4	991.8
1971	1,027.8	1,047.3	1,061.3	1,083.2
1972	1,115.0	1,143.0	1,169.3	1,204.7
1973	1,248.9	1,277.9	1,308.9	1,344.0
1974	1,358.8	1,383.8	1,416.3	1,430.9

Source: Official data of U.S. Department of Commerce, published in *Survey of Current Business.*

Table A-2. *Gross National Product in 1958 Dollars, 1947–74*

Billions of 1958 dollars; seasonally adjusted at annual rates

Year	First quarter	Second quarter	Third quarter	Fourth quarter
1947	306.4	309.0	309.6	314.5
1948	317.1	322.9	325.8	328.7
1949	324.5	322.5	326.1	323.3
1950	339.6	348.5	362.8	370.1
1951	374.8	381.5	388.7	388.7
1952	391.4	389.6	393.9	405.3
1953	412.1	416.4	413.7	408.8
1954	402.9	402.1	407.2	415.7
1955	428.0	435.4	442.1	446.4
1956	443.6	445.6	444.5	450.3
1957	453.4	453.2	455.2	448.2
1958	437.5	439.5	450.7	461.6
1959	468.6	479.9	475.0	480.4
1960	490.2	489.7	487.3	483.7
1961	482.6	492.8	501.5	511.7
1962	519.5	527.7	533.4	538.3
1963	541.2	546.0	554.7	562.1
1964	571.1	578.6	585.8	588.5
1965	601.6	610.4	622.5	636.6
1966	649.1	655.0	660.2	668.1
1967	666.6	671.6	678.9	683.6
1968	692.6	705.3	712.3	716.5
1969	722.4	725.8	729.2	725.1
1970	721.2	722.1	727.2	719.3
1971	736.9	742.1	747.2	759.1
1972	770.9	786.6	798.1	814.2
1973	832.8	837.4	840.8	845.7
1974	830.5	827.1	823.1	804.0

Source: Same as table A-1.

Table A-3. *Net Exports of Goods and Services, 1947–74*

Billions of current dollars; seasonally adjusted at annual rates

Year	First quarter	Second quarter	Third quarter	Fourth quarter
1947	11.5	12.0	12.5	10.1
1948	8.2	6.2	5.9	5.5
1949	7.4	7.2	6.1	3.8
1950	3.1	2.6	0.5	1.0
1951	1.1	3.1	5.0	5.5
1952	4.8	3.0	1.1	0.0
1953	0.5	0.1	0.3	0.6
1954	1.1	1.7	1.9	2.7

Table A-3. *Continued*

Year	First quarter	Second quarter	Third quarter	Fourth quarter
1955	2.8	1.6	2.0	1.6
1956	2.3	3.8	4.1	5.6
1957	6.6	6.3	5.5	4.5
1958	2.6	2.4	2.4	1.4
1959	0.2	—0.8	0.4	0.7
1960	2.4	3.5	4.3	6.0
1961	6.6	5.6	4.9	5.3
1962	4.6	5.7	5.3	4.9
1963	4.6	6.2	5.6	7.1
1964	8.9	7.8	8.7	8.5
1965	6.2	8.1	7.3	6.0
1966	6.2	5.6	4.4	4.9
1967	5.5	5.8	5.6	4.0
1968	1.9	3.4	3.4	1.3
1969	1.2	1.1	2.6	2.7
1970	3.6	3.9	4.2	2.8
1971	2.9	—0.2	0.1	—3.4
1972	—7.1	—6.9	—4.8	—5.3
1973	—0.8	0.5	6.7	9.3
1974	11.3	—1.5	—3.1	—1.9

Source: Same as table A-1.

Table A-4. *Implicit Price Deflator for Gross National Product, 1947–74*

1958 = 100

Year	First quarter	Second quarter	Third quarter	Fourth quarter
1947	73.0	73.7	74.9	77.0
1948	78.2	79.2	80.6	80.3
1949	79.7	79.1	78.8	78.9
1950	78.3	79.0	80.8	82.3
1951	84.8	85.4	85.6	86.7
1952	86.7	87.1	87.7	88.3
1953	88.4	88.3	88.4	88.4
1954	89.5	89.6	89.5	89.8
1955	90.2	90.6	91.0	91.6
1956	92.6	93.4	94.6	95.4
1957	96.4	97.1	98.0	98.5
1958	99.3	99.7	100.1	100.6
1959	101.1	101.5	101.9	102.1
1960	102.6	103.1	103.5	104.0
1961	104.3	104.5	104.5	105.1
1962	105.5	105.6	105.8	106.3
1963	106.7	107.0	107.2	107.8
1964	108.2	108.5	109.1	109.6

Table A-4. *Continued*

Year	First quarter	Second quarter	Third quarter	Fourth quarter
1965	110.2	110.7	111.0	111.5
1966	112.4	113.5	114.5	115.4
1967	116.2	116.8	118.0	119.4
1968	120.4	121.6	122.9	124.3
1969	125.6	127.2	129.1	130.9
1970	132.9	134.4	135.8	137.9
1971	139.5	141.1	142.0	142.7
1972	144.6	145.3	146.5	148.0
1973	150.0	152.6	155.7	158.9
1974	163.6	167.3	172.1	178.0

Source: Same as table A-1.

Table A-5. *Implicit Price Deflator for Personal Consumption Expenditures, 1947–74*

1958 = 100

Year	First quarter	Second quarter	Third quarter	Fourth quarter
1947	76.2	76.8	78.3	80.3
1948	81.1	82.0	83.3	83.0
1949	82.3	81.8	81.3	81.4
1950	81.3	81.7	83.5	84.9
1951	87.9	88.2	88.5	89.7
1952	90.0	90.1	90.6	91.2
1953	91.3	91.5	92.0	92.0
1954	92.6	92.6	92.4	92.3
1955	92.6	92.6	92.9	93.0
1956	93.6	94.3	95.3	95.8
1957	96.7	97.3	98.1	98.5
1958	99.6	100.0	100.1	100.3
1959	100.6	100.9	101.6	102.0
1960	102.3	102.7	103.0	103.6
1961	103.8	103.7	104.0	104.2
1962	104.5	104.7	105.0	105.3
1963	105.6	106.0	106.2	106.7
1964	106.9	107.3	107.4	107.8
1965	108.2	108.8	109.0	109.3
1966	110.2	111.3	111.9	112.8
1967	113.3	113.8	114.8	115.7
1968	116.8	118.0	118.8	120.1
1969	121.2	122.7	124.3	125.9
1970	127.5	128.6	129.7	131.6
1971	132.7	134.1	135.0	135.6

Table a-5. Continued

Year	First quarter	Second quarter	Third quarter	Fourth quarter
1972	136.8	137.7	138.7	139.7
1973	141.4	144.3	147.0	150.8
1974	155.8	160.2	164.7	169.6

Source: Same as table a-1.

Table a-6. Industrial Production Index, 1954–74[a]

1967 = 100

Year	First quarter	Second quarter	Third quarter	Fourth quarter
1954	51.4	51.2	51.5	52.9
1955	55.8	58.2	59.1	60.5
1956	60.7	60.5	60.1	62.4
1957	62.9	62.1	62.3	59.7
1958	56.4	55.4	58.3	60.9
1959	63.6	66.7	64.0	64.3
1960	68.2	66.7	65.6	64.0
1961	63.0	65.6	67.6	70.0
1962	71.1	71.7	72.5	73.1
1963	74.3	76.2	76.8	78.1
1964	79.2	81.1	82.4	83.6
1965	86.3	88.0	89.9	91.8
1966	94.8	97.2	98.9	99.8
1967	98.8	98.8	99.9	101.6
1968	103.5	105.2	106.2	107.2
1969	109.5	110.4	111.6	110.6
1970	108.0	107.8	107.1	103.8
1971	105.8	107.1	106.5	107.4
1972	110.1	113.8	116.3	120.2
1973	123.1	124.9	126.7	127.0
1974	124.9	125.5	125.4	121.3

Source: Board of Governors of the Federal Reserve System, Federal Reserve Bulletin, various issues.

a. Quarterly average of monthly series.

Table a-7. Consumer Price Index for All Items, 1948–74[a]

Seasonally adjusted; 1967 = 100

Year	First quarter	Second quarter	Third quarter	Fourth quarter
1948	70.7	71.9	73.1	72.4
1949	71.7	71.6	71.0	70.9
1950	70.7	71.2	72.5	74.0
1951	77.0	77.7	77.7	78.8
1952	79.1	79.4	79.9	79.9

Table A-7. *Continued*

Year	First quarter	Second quarter	Third quarter	Fourth quarter
1953	79.7	80.0	80.4	80.6
1954	80.7	80.6	80.5	80.1
1955	80.2	80.2	80.2	80.4
1956	80.5	81.0	81.8	82.5
1957	83.2	83.9	84.7	85.1
1958	86.1	86.7	86.6	86.7
1959	86.8	87.0	87.4	88.0
1960	88.1	88.6	88.6	89.2
1961	89.4	89.4	89.7	89.8
1962	90.2	90.5	90.8	91.0
1963	91.3	91.5	92.0	92.3
1964	92.7	92.8	93.0	93.4
1965	93.7	94.3	94.6	95.1
1966	96.0	96.9	97.7	98.5
1967	98.9	99.4	100.4	101.3
1968	102.5	103.5	104.7	106.0
1969	107.4	109.1	110.6	112.2
1970	114.0	115.7	116.9	118.6
1971	119.6	120.8	121.9	122.7
1972	123.8	124.6	125.7	126.9
1973	128.8	131.5	134.4	137.5
1974	141.6	145.4	149.7	154.2

Source: Calculated from official data of U.S. Bureau of Labor Statistics, currently published in the Bureau's monthly report "The Consumer Price Index."
a. Quarterly average of monthly series.

Table A-8. *Consumer Price Index for Food, 1947–74*[a]

Seasonally adjusted; 1967 = 100

Year	First quarter	Second quarter	Third quarter	Fourth quarter
1947	68.1	68.9	71.1	74.1
1948	75.6	77.0	77.8	75.6
1949	74.3	74.2	73.1	72.6
1950	72.0	73.0	75.5	77.3
1951	82.6	82.7	81.9	84.1
1952	84.2	84.2	84.6	84.3
1953	83.1	82.8	83.0	82.9
1954	83.5	83.2	82.9	81.9
1955	82.0	81.8	81.4	81.1
1956	80.7	81.8	82.9	83.3
1957	83.8	84.3	85.8	85.6
1958	88.2	89.4	88.3	87.9
1959	87.4	86.7	86.9	87.0

Table A-8. *Continued*

Year	First quarter	Second quarter	Third quarter	Fourth quarter
1960	86.8	88.1	88.0	89.3
1961	89.4	89.0	88.9	88.9
1962	89.6	89.8	89.9	90.4
1963	91.1	90.8	91.4	91.5
1964	92.0	92.1	92.4	93.0
1965	92.7	94.3	95.1	95.7
1966	98.1	99.0	99.4	100.1
1967	99.4	99.3	100.3	100.8
1968	102.1	103.1	103.9	105.2
1969	106.1	107.7	109.8	111.9
1970	114.0	114.9	115.2	115.8
1971	116.2	118.3	119.1	120.0
1972	121.7	122.5	124.0	126.1
1973	131.4	138.0	145.6	150.7
1974	156.7	159.4	162.1	168.7

Source: Same as table A-7.
a. Quarterly average of monthly series.

Table A-9. *Wholesale Price Index for All Commodities, 1948–74*[a]

Seasonally adjusted; 1967 = 100

Year	First quarter	Second quarter	Third quarter	Fourth quarter
1948	81.8	83.0	83.9	82.7
1949	80.5	79.0	77.8	77.4
1950	77.8	79.3	83.2	86.9
1951	92.0	92.3	90.1	90.1
1952	89.3	88.8	88.6	87.7
1953	87.1	87.1	87.8	87.5
1954	87.7	87.9	87.4	87.2
1955	87.4	87.5	88.0	88.5
1956	89.1	90.5	91.0	92.2
1957	92.7	92.9	93.8	93.9
1958	94.5	94.6	94.6	94.7
1959	94.7	95.1	94.8	94.5
1960	94.7	95.0	94.8	95.0
1961	95.0	94.3	94.3	94.5
1962	94.8	94.5	94.9	94.8
1963	94.3	94.3	94.6	94.8
1964	94.7	94.4	94.6	95.0
1965	95.2	96.4	97.0	97.8
1966	98.9	99.5	100.5	100.1
1967	99.7	99.6	100.1	100.6
1968	101.5	102.2	102.7	103.6
1969	104.6	106.1	107.0	108.4

Table A-9. *Continued*

Year	First quarter	Second quarter	Third quarter	Fourth quarter
1970	109.4	109.8	110.3	111.6
1971	112.3	113.5	114.4	115.5
1972	116.7	117.9	119.6	122.1
1973	126.8	132.9	138.3	141.0
1974	148.8	154.1	164.8	172.6

Source: Official data of the Bureau of Labor Statistics, currently published in the Bureau's monthly report "Wholesale Prices and Price Indexes."
a. Quarterly average of monthly series.

Table A-10. *Wholesale Price Index for Farm Products, Processed Foods, and Feeds, 1948–74*[a]

Seasonally adjusted; 1967 = 100

Year	First quarter	Second quarter	Third quarter	Fourth quarter
1948	102.3	103.2	103.0	97.4
1949	92.1	90.4	88.5	87.8
1950	88.6	90.5	96.9	99.5
1951	108.6	108.5	104.1	106.4
1952	104.2	103.0	103.1	100.3
1953	97.4	95.4	95.8	95.4
1954	97.1	96.5	95.1	94.1
1955	93.4	92.5	90.4	88.4
1956	88.1	90.8	91.3	92.4
1957	92.2	92.5	94.5	95.5
1958	98.7	99.4	97.8	96.7
1959	94.9	94.3	93.0	91.7
1960	92.4	93.9	93.4	95.1
1961	95.1	92.7	93.3	93.8
1962	94.9	93.4	95.2	95.3
1963	93.4	93.7	94.0	94.1
1964	93.5	92.7	93.2	93.3
1965	93.5	96.7	98.0	100.1
1966	103.5	102.7	105.0	102.8
1967	100.3	99.7	100.2	99.8
1968	100.9	102.0	102.7	103.6
1969	103.9	107.0	108.3	110.1
1970	112.2	111.3	111.8	111.4
1971	111.7	114.1	113.6	115.8
1972	117.7	119.8	123.5	128.9
1973	114.3	155.4	170.8	169.0
1974	176.0	166.4	177.5	190.0

Source: Same as table A-9.
a. Quarterly average of monthly series.

Table A-11. *Unemployment Rates for the Civilian Labor Force,*
1948–74[a]

Percent; seasonally adjusted

Year	First quarter	Second quarter	Third quarter	Fourth quarter
1948	3.7	3.7	3.8	3.8
1949	4.6	5.9	6.7	7.0
1950	6.4	5.6	4.6	4.2
1951	3.5	3.1	3.2	3.4
1952	3.1	3.0	3.2	2.8
1953	2.7	2.6	2.7	3.7
1954	5.2	5.8	6.0	5.4
1955	4.7	4.4	4.1	4.2
1956	4.0	4.2	4.1	4.1
1957	4.0	4.1	4.2	4.9
1958	6.3	7.4	7.3	6.4
1959	5.8	5.1	5.3	5.6
1960	5.2	5.2	5.6	6.3
1961	6.8	7.0	6.8	6.2
1962	5.6	5.5	5.6	5.5
1963	5.8	5.7	5.5	5.6
1964	5.5	5.2	5.0	5.0
1965	4.9	4.7	4.4	4.1
1966	3.9	3.8	3.8	3.7
1967	3.8	3.8	3.8	3.9
1968	3.7	3.5	3.5	3.4
1969	3.4	3.4	3.6	3.6
1970	4.3	4.7	5.2	5.8
1971	5.9	5.9	6.0	6.0
1972	5.8	5.7	5.6	5.3
1973	5.0	4.9	4.8	4.7
1974	5.1	5.1	5.5	6.6

Source: Official data of the Bureau of Labor Statistics, currently published in *Employment and Earnings.*

a. Quarterly average of monthly series.

Table A-12. *Civilian Nonagricultural Employment, 1948–74*[a]

Millions of people; seasonally adjusted

Year	First quarter	Second quarter	Third quarter	Fourth quarter
1948	50.3	50.9	51.0	50.8
1949	50.2	49.6	49.8	50.5
1950	50.6	51.5	52.3	52.5
1951	53.1	53.2	53.3	53.3
1952	53.4	53.6	53.7	54.2
1953	55.3	55.1	54.9	54.4
1954	53.9	53.8	53.7	54.2

Table A-12. *Continued*

Year	First quarter	Second quarter	Third quarter	Fourth quarter
1955	54.7	55.3	56.1	56.6
1956	57.1	57.4	57.6	57.9
1957	58.1	58.1	58.2	58.0
1958	57.3	57.2	57.4	57.9
1959	58.4	59.0	59.4	59.5
1960	59.9	60.6	60.4	60.3
1961	60.3	60.5	60.5	60.9
1962	61.2	61.6	62.0	62.2
1963	62.4	63.0	63.3	63.6
1964	64.1	64.9	64.9	65.3
1965	65.9	66.4	67.0	67.6
1966	68.1	68.6	69.2	69.7
1967	69.8	70.3	70.8	71.2
1968	71.2	72.1	72.3	72.8
1969	73.5	73.9	74.6	75.1
1970	75.3	75.1	75.1	75.2
1971	75.2	75.3	75.9	76.6
1972	77.4	78.0	78.5	78.9
1973	79.8	80.7	81.3	82.0
1974	82.1	82.5	82.9	82.3

Source: Same as table A-11.
a. Quarterly average of monthly series.

Table A-13. *Average Hourly Earnings Index for Manufacturing, 1948–74*[a]
Seasonally adjusted; 1967 = 100

Year	First quarter	Second quarter	Third quarter	Fourth quarter
1948	46.4	47.3	48.9	49.6
1949	49.9	50.3	50.3	50.4
1950	50.8	51.3	51.8	53.5
1951	54.7	55.6	56.4	57.0
1952	57.7	58.5	59.2	60.0
1953	61.0	61.6	62.6	63.1
1954	63.6	64.0	64.2	64.6
1955	64.9	65.5	66.5	67.2
1956	68.0	69.2	70.1	71.1
1957	71.9	72.7	73.6	74.4
1958	75.2	75.9	76.6	77.1
1959	77.9	78.5	78.9	79.4
1960	80.3	80.9	81.6	82.0
1961	82.7	83.3	83.7	84.5
1962	85.0	85.4	85.9	86.5
1963	87.0	87.5	88.1	88.8
1964	89.5	90.0	90.6	90.8

Table A-13. *Continued*

Year	First quarter	Second quarter	Third quarter	Fourth quarter
1965	91.5	92.2	92.9	93.7
1966	94.2	95.2	96.1	97.3
1967	98.3	99.5	100.6	102.0
1968	103.8	105.4	106.8	108.6
1969	110.0	111.5	113.5	115.2
1970	116.6	118.6	120.9	122.2
1971	124.8	126.7	128.6	129.9
1972	132.6	134.4	136.1	138.1
1973	139.9	141.9	144.5	147.1
1974	149.6	153.6	158.1	162.5

Source: Same as table A-11.

a. Quarterly average of monthly series; index adjusted for overtime and interindustry employment shifts.

Table A-14. *Average Weekly Hours in Manufacturing, 1948–74*[a]

Millions of hours; seasonally adjusted

Year	First quarter	Second quarter	Third quarter	Fourth quarter
1948	40.3	40.2	40.0	39.7
1949	39.2	38.8	39.2	39.3
1950	39.7	40.3	40.9	41.0
1951	40.9	40.9	40.4	40.4
1952	40.6	40.3	40.6	41.1
1953	41.0	40.9	40.3	39.8
1954	39.5	39.5	39.6	39.9
1955	40.5	40.7	40.6	40.9
1956	40.6	40.3	40.3	40.5
1957	40.4	40.0	39.8	39.1
1958	38.7	38.8	39.4	39.7
1959	40.2	40.5	40.2	40.0
1960	40.2	39.9	39.6	39.1
1961	39.3	39.7	39.9	40.4
1962	40.3	40.5	40.5	40.3
1963	40.4	40.4	40.5	40.6
1964	40.4	40.8	40.7	40.9
1965	41.3	41.1	41.0	41.3
1966	41.5	41.5	41.3	41.1
1967	40.6	40.4	40.7	40.7
1968	40.6	40.6	40.9	40.8
1969	40.6	40.7	40.7	40.6
1970	40.2	39.9	39.8	39.6
1971	39.8	39.9	39.8	40.1
1972	40.3	40.6	40.7	40.7

Table A-14. *Continued*

Year	First quarter	Second quarter	Third quarter	Fourth quarter
1973	40.8	40.7	40.7	40.6
1974	40.4	39.9	40.1	39.7

Source: Same as table A-11.
a. Quarterly average of monthly series.

Table A-15. *Privately Owned Housing Units Started, 1959–74*[a]

Millions; seasonally adjusted at annual rates

Year	First quarter	Second quarter	Third quarter	Fourth quarter
1959	1.6	1.5	1.5	1.4
1960	1.4	1.3	1.2	1.2
1961	1.3	1.3	1.4	1.4
1962	1.4	1.5	1.4	1.5
1963	1.4	1.6	1.7	1.7
1964	1.7	1.5	1.5	1.5
1965	1.4	1.5	1.5	1.5
1966	1.4	1.3	1.1	0.9
1967	1.1	1.2	1.4	1.5
1968	1.4	1.4	1.5	1.6
1969	1.7	1.5	1.4	1.3
1970	1.2	1.3	1.5	1.7
1971	1.8	2.0	2.1	2.2
1972	2.4	2.2	2.4	2.4
1973	2.4	2.2	2.0	1.6
1974	1.6	1.5	1.2	1.0

Sources: U.S. Bureau of the Census, *Construction Reports*, Series C20 Supplement, *Housing Starts, 1959 to 1971* (1972), and subsequent C20 monthly reports.
a. Quarterly average of monthly series.

Table A-16. *Total Value of Private New Construction, 1948–74*[a]

Billions of dollars; seasonally adjusted at annual rates

Year	First quarter	Second quarter	Third quarter	Fourth quarter
1948	20.3	21.8	22.1	21.0
1949	20.1	19.7	20.2	21.7
1950	23.7	26.0	28.3	28.0
1951	28.1	26.5	25.6	25.4
1952	25.6	25.7	25.9	26.9
1953	27.7	28.2	27.9	27.8
1954	27.8	28.9	30.1	31.4
1955	33.9	35.0	35.3	34.7
1956	34.4	35.1	35.0	34.9
1957	35.0	35.1	35.1	35.0

Table A-16. *Continued*

Year	First quarter	Second quarter	Third quarter	Fourth quarter
1958	34.0	33.4	34.3	36.6
1959	38.6	39.8	39.7	38.9
1960	40.1	38.2	37.2	37.6
1961	37.6	37.7	38.4	39.1
1962	39.8	41.5	42.5	42.1
1963	41.4	44.1	44.2	46.0
1964	45.7	45.7	45.8	46.1
1965	48.3	49.5	50.3	52.4
1966	53.5	52.0	51.4	48.2
1967	48.2	47.9	51.6	53.8
1968	56.1	57.6	56.4	59.1
1969	64.3	65.5	66.7	64.9
1970	65.0	64.4	65.7	69.2
1971	72.8	77.9	81.5	84.1
1972	90.8	92.4	93.6	97.4
1973	103.3	101.9	105.0	102.0
1974	98.4	97.9	96.3	92.1

Sources: Bureau of the Census, *Construction Reports*, Series C30-61 Supplement, *Value of New Construction Put in Place, 1946–1963 Revised* (1964); Series C30-70S, *Value of New Construction Put in Place, 1958–1970* (1971); and subsequent C30 monthly reports.
  a. Quarterly average of monthly series.

Table A-17. *Money Stock, 1947–74*[a]

Billions of dollars; seasonally adjusted

Year	First quarter	Second quarter	Third quarter	Fourth quarter
1947	109.8	111.6	112.6	113.1
1948	113.1	112.1	112.2	111.8
1949	111.2	111.4	111.0	111.0
1950	112.0	113.7	114.9	115.9
1951	117.1	118.2	119.7	121.9
1952	123.5	124.5	125.8	127.0
1953	127.6	128.4	128.6	128.7
1954	129.1	129.4	130.6	132.0
1955	133.5	134.3	134.9	135.1
1956	135.6	135.9	136.0	136.6
1957	136.9	136.9	137.0	136.2
1958	136.1	137.6	139.0	140.7
1959	142.6	143.8	144.5	143.6
1960	143.0	142.8	143.9	144.2
1961	144.8	146.0	146.9	148.3
1962	149.2	149.8	149.5	150.4
1963	151.8	153.3	154.8	156.4
1964	157.3	158.8	161.4	163.4

Table A-17. *Continued*

Year	First quarter	Second quarter	Third quarter	Fourth quarter
1965	164.5	165.8	167.7	170.5
1966	173.2	175.3	175.0	175.2
1967	177.0	179.6	183.6	186.3
1968	188.7	192.2	196.2	200.2
1969	203.9	206.1	207.3	208.5
1970	210.8	214.1	217.4	220.6
1971	224.1	230.0	233.7	235.1
1972	238.2	242.9	247.9	253.3
1973	257.6	262.3	265.9	269.2
1974	273.1	278.1	280.8	283.4

Source: Same as table A-6.
a. Quarterly average of monthly series.

Table A-18. *Three-Month Treasury Bill Rate, Market Yield, 1948–74*[a]
Percent

Year	First quarter	Second quarter	Third quarter	Fourth quarter
1948	1.0	1.0	1.0	1.1
1949	1.2	1.2	1.0	1.1
1950	1.1	1.2	1.2	1.3
1951	1.4	1.5	1.6	1.6
1952	1.6	1.6	1.8	1.9
1953	2.0	2.2	2.0	1.5
1954	1.1	0.8	0.9	1.0
1955	1.2	1.5	1.9	2.3
1956	2.3	2.6	2.6	3.0
1957	3.1	3.1	3.4	3.3
1958	1.8	1.0	1.7	2.7
1959	2.8	3.0	3.5	4.2
1960	3.9	3.0	2.4	2.3
1961	2.4	2.3	2.3	2.5
1962	2.7	2.7	2.8	2.8
1963	2.9	2.9	3.3	3.5
1964	3.5	3.5	3.5	3.7
1965	3.9	3.9	3.9	4.2
1966	4.6	4.6	5.0	5.2
1967	4.5	3.7	4.3	4.7
1968	5.0	5.5	5.2	5.6
1969	6.1	6.2	7.0	7.3
1970	7.2	6.7	6.3	5.4
1971	3.8	4.2	5.0	4.2
1972	3.4	3.8	4.2	4.9
1973	5.7	6.6	8.3	7.5
1974	7.6	8.2	8.2	7.4

Source: Same as table A-6.
a. Quarterly average of monthly series.

Index

knowledge, 387; consensus, 388, 391; episodic inflation, 397; equity, 391–92; force of politics, 389, 390; free market, 388; labor-management accord, 391; multiple goals, 387, 397; new selective controls institution, 394; price fighters, 387; productivity guideposts, 392–93; profit standards, 394; role of producer, 390; role of theory, 386

Wage-push inflation, 106–08, 177, 188, 351n. *See also* Inflation

Wage Stabilization Board, 71, 89; soft coal industry and, 109; steel industry actions, 84; wage freeze by, 78, 79n, 83

Wagner Act, 355

Wagner, Robert F., Sr., 37

Wagnon, William O., Jr., 63n, 66n

Walker, Charls E., 318, 319, 321–22

Wallace, Donald, 65n

Wallace, Henry A., 16n, 19n

Wallich, Henry C., 68n, 102n

Wallis, Allen, 123–25, 367

War Labor Board Protective Association, 254

War Mobilization and Reconversion, Office of, 12, 30

Warne, Colston E., 14n

War Production Board, 15

Warren, Robert, 42n

Watkins, Ralph, 54n

Waugh, Fred, 42n

Webb, James E., 46, 54n

Weber, Arnold R., 326n, 340n, 345n, 381n, 389, 392, 393, 394

Weber, Peter, 258

Weeks, Sinclair, 110

Weidenbaum, Murray L., 314, 315, 316, 318, 339

Weinberg, Nat, 204n

Weiss, Leonard, 349n

Westinghouse Electric, 82

Wheeling Steel Corporation, price increases by, 182

White, Lawrence J., 250n, 276n

Wholesale prices: in 1949, 63–64; in 1950, 75; in 1951, 82; in 1965, 222; rate of increase, 49

Wickens, A. J., 121n

Williams, Kenneth B., 10n

Willis, Charles F., Jr., 110n, 112n

Wilson, Charles E., 79, 85, 110

Wilson, Don, 95n

Wilson, Henry, 234

Wilson, Thomas A., 107n

Winch, Donald N., 10n

Wirtz, Willard, 180, 204, 205, 206–07, 209, 213, 225, 242, 244, 258–59, 260, 263–64, 278, 288, 364

Woodcock, Leonard, 213

Wood, Harleston R., 119n

Woods, Tighe, 88

Yoshpe, Harry B., 325n

Zwick, Charles, 280